Communications in Computer and Information Science   **658**

Commenced Publication in 2007
Founding and Former Series Editors:
Alfredo Cuzzocrea, Dominik Ślęzak, and Xiaokang Yang

More information about this series at http://www.springer.com/series/7899

Rafael Valencia-García · Katty Lagos-Ortiz
Gema Alcaraz-Mármol · Javier del Cioppo
Nestor Vera-Lucio (Eds.)

Technologies and Innovation

Second International Conference, CITI 2016
Guayaquil, Ecuador, November 23–25, 2016
Proceedings

Springer

Editors
Rafael Valencia-García
Universidad de Murcia
Murcia
Spain

Katty Lagos-Ortiz
Universidad Agraria del Ecuador
Guayaquil
Ecuador

Gema Alcaraz-Mármol
Universidad de Castilla-La Mancha
Toledo
Spain

Javier del Cioppo
Universidad Agraria del Ecuador
Guayaquil
Ecuador

Nestor Vera-Lucio
Universidad Agraria del Ecuador
Guayaquil
Ecuador

ISSN 1865-0929   ISSN 1865-0937 (electronic)
Communications in Computer and Information Science
ISBN 978-3-319-48023-7   ISBN 978-3-319-48024-4 (eBook)
DOI 10.1007/978-3-319-48024-4

Library of Congress Control Number: 2016954941

Printed on acid-free paper

This Springer imprint is published by Springer Nature
The registered company is Springer International Publishing AG
The registered company address is: Gewerbestrasse 11, 6330 Cham, Switzerland

Preface

The Second International Conference on Technologies and Innovation (CITI 2016) was held during November 23–25 2016, in Guayaquil, Ecuador. The CITI series of conferences aims to provide an international framework and meeting point for professionals who are mainly devoted to research, development, innovation, and university teaching in the field of computer science and technology applied to any important field of innovation. CITI 2016 was organized as a knowledge-exchange conference consisting of several contributions about current innovative technology. These proposals deal with the most important aspects and future prospects from an academic, innovative, and scientific perspective. The goal of the conference was the feasibility of investigating advanced and innovative methods and techniques and their application in different domains in the field of computer science and information systems that represent innovation in current society.

We would like to express our gratitude to all the authors who submitted papers to CITI 2016, and our congratulations to those whose papers were accepted. There were 65 submissions this year. Each submission was reviewed by at least three Program Committee (PC) members. Only the papers with an average score of ≥ 1.0 were considered for final inclusion, and almost all accepted papers had positive reviews or at least one review with a score of 2 (accept) or higher. Finally, the PC decided to accept 21 full papers.

We would also like to thank the PC members, who agreed to review the manuscripts in a timely manner and provided valuable feedback to the authors.

November 2016

Rafael Valencia-García
Katty Lagos-Ortiz
Gema Alcaraz-Mármol
Javier del Cioppo
Nestor Vera-Lucio

Organization

Honorary Committee

Martha Bucaram Leverone	Universidad Agraria del Ecuador, Ecuador
Javier del Cioppo, Msc	Universidad Agraria del Ecuador, Ecuador
Nestor Vera Lucio, Msc	Universidad Agraria del Ecuador, Ecuador
Mitchell Vásquez Bermúdez	Universidad Agraria del Ecuador, Ecuador

Organizing Committee

Rafael Valencia-García	Universidad de Murcia, Spain
Katty Lagos-Ortiz	Universidad Agraria del Ecuador, Ecuador
Gema Alcaraz-Mármol	Universidad de Castilla-La Mancha, Spain
Javier del Cioppo	Universidad Agraria del Ecuador, Ecuador
Nestor Vera Lucio	Universidad Agraria del Ecuador, Ecuador

Program Committee

Claudia Victoria Isaza Narvaez	Universidad de Antioquia, Colombia
Alejandro Rodríguez-González	Universidad Politécnica de Madrid, Spain
Carlos Cruz-Corona	Universidad de Granada, Spain
Dagoberto Catellanos-Nieves	Universidad de la Laguna, Spain
Juan Miguel Gómez-Berbís	Universidad Carlos III de Madrid, Spain
Jesualdo Tomás Fernández-Breis	Universidad de Murcia, Spain
Francisco García-Sánchez	Universidad de Murcia, Spain
Antonio Ruiz-Martínez	Universidad de Murcia, Spain
Maria Pilar Salas-Zárate	Universidad de Murcia, Spain
Mario Andrés Paredes-Valverde	Universidad de Murcia, Spain
Luis Omar Colombo-Mendoza	Universidad de Murcia, Spain
Alejandro Rodríguez-González	Universidad Politécnica de Madrid, Spain
Katty Lagos-Ortiz	Universidad Agraria del Ecuador, Ecuador
José Medina-Moreira	Universidad de Guayaquil, Ecuador
Mitchel Vasquez	Universidad Agraria del Ecuador, Ecuador
Jorge Hidalgo	Universidad Agraria del Ecuador, Ecuador

Vanessa Vergara	Universidad Agraria del Ecuador, Ecuador
Rocio Cuiña	Universidad Agraria del Ecuador, Ecuador
Ileana Herrera	Universidad Agraria del Ecuador, Ecuador
Muhammad Fahim	Istanbul Sabahattin Zaim University, Turkey
José María Álvarez-Rodríguez	Universidad Carlos III de Madrid, Spain
Pavel Novoa-Hernández	Universidad Técnica Estatal de Quevedo, Ecuador
Thomas Moser	St. Pölten University of Applied Sciences, Austria
Lisbeth Rodriguez Mazahua	Instituto Tecnologico de Orizaba, Mexico
Raquel Vasquez Ramirez	Instituto Tecnologico de Orizaba, Mexico
Jose Luis Sanchez Cervantes	Instituto Tecnologico de Orizaba, Mexico
Cristian Aaron Rodriguez Enriquez	Instituto Tecnologico de Orizaba, Mexico
Viviana Yarel Rosales Morales	Instituto Tecnologico de Orizaba, Mexico
Humberto Marin Vega	Instituto Tecnologico de Orizaba, Mexico
Silvana Vanesa Aciar	National University of San Juan, Argentina
María Teresa Martín-Valdivia	Universidad de Jaén, Spain
Miguel A. García-Cumbreras	Universidad de Jaén, Spain
Begoña Moros	Universidad de Murcia, Spain
Salud M. Jiménez Zafra	Universidad de Jaén, Spain
Arturo Montejo-Raez	Universidad de Jaén, Spain
José Javier Samper-Zapater	Universidad de Valencia, Spain
A.M. Abirami	Thiagarajar College of Engineering, Madurai, India
Elena Lloret	Universidad de Alicante, Spain
Anatoly Gladun	V.M. Glushkov of National Academy Science, Ukraine
Yoan Gutiérrez	Universidad de Alicante, Spain
Miguel A. Mayer	Universidad Pompeu Fabra, Spain
Gandhi Hernandez	Universidad Tecnológica Metropolitana, Mexico
Manuel Sánchez-Rubio	Universidad Internacional de la Rioja, Spain
Mario Barcelo-Valenzuela	Universidad de Sonora, Mexico
Alonso Perez-Soltero	Universidad de Sonora, Mexico
Gerardo Sanchez-Schmitz	Universidad de Sonora, Mexico
Mahmoud Al-Ayyoub	Jordan University of Science and Technology, Jordan
Francisco García-Peñalvo	Universidad de Salamanca, Spain
Rubén González	Universidad Internacional de la Rioja, Spain
José Luis Hernández-Hernández	Universidad Autónoma de Guerrero, Mexico
Marca Bayas San Pedro	Vinnitsa National Technical University, Ukraine
Ronald Rovira Jurado	Vinnitsa National Technical University, Ukraine
Martin Lukac	Nazarbayev University, Kazakhstan
Manuel Campos	Universidad de Murcia, Spain
Jose M. Juarez	Universidad de Murcia, Spain

Mario Hernández   Universidad Autónoma de Guerrero, Mexico
  Hernández
Guido Sciavicco   University of Ferrara, Italy

Local Organizing Committee

Andrea Sinche Guzmán   Universidad Agraria del Ecuador, Ecuador
Maritza Aguirre Munizaga   Universidad Agraria del Ecuador, Ecuador
Carlota Delgado Vera   Universidad Agraria del Ecuador, Ecuador
Evelyn Solís Avilés   Universidad Agraria del Ecuador, Ecuador
Laura Ponce Ortega   Universidad Agraria del Ecuador, Ecuador
William Bazán Vera   Universidad Agraria del Ecuador, Ecuador
Ana María Herrera Espinoza   Universidad Agraria del Ecuador, Ecuador
Vanessa Vergara Lozano   Universidad Agraria del Ecuador, Ecuador
Karina Real Avilés   Universidad Agraria del Ecuador, Ecuador
Raquel Gómez   Universidad Agraria del Ecuador, Ecuador
Elke Yerovi Ricaurte   Universidad Agraria del Ecuador, Ecuador
Mariuxi Tejada Castro   Universidad Agraria del Ecuador, Ecuador
Wilson Molina Oleas   Universidad Agraria del Ecuador, Ecuador
María del Pilar Avilés   Universidad Agraria del Ecuador, Ecuador
Jorge Hidalgo Larrea   Universidad Agraria del Ecuador, Ecuador
José Salavarria   Universidad Agraria del Ecuador, Ecuador

Sponsoring Institutions

http://www.uagraria.edu.ec/

http://www.springer.com/series/7899

Contents

Knowledge Representation and Natural Language Processing

A Knowledge-Based Platform for the Development of Critical
Thinking Abilities 3
   Carlota Delgado-Vera, Maritza Aguirre-Munizaga, Evelyn Solis-Avíles,
   Andrea Sinche, and Néstor Vera-Lucio

Knowledge-Based Model for Curricular Design in Ecuadorian Universities. . . . 14
   Vanessa Vergara, Katty Lagos-Ortiz, Maritza Aguirre-Munizaga,
   Maria Aviles, José Medina-Moreira, Jorge Hidalgo,
   and Ana Muñoz-García

IXHEALTH: A Multilingual Platform for Advanced Speech Recognition
in Healthcare 26
   Pedro José Vivancos-Vicente, Juan Salvador Castejón-Garrido,
   Mario Andrés Paredes-Valverde, María del Pilar Salas-Zárate,
   and Rafael Valencia-García

The Extended Hierarchical Linguistic Model in Fuzzy Cognitive Maps 39
   Maikel Leyva-Vázquez, Eduardo Santos-Baquerizo,
   Miriam Peña-González, Lorenzo Cevallos-Torres,
   and Alfonso Guijarro-Rodríguez

Ontological Model of Knowledge Management for Research and
Innovation 51
   Ana Muñoz-García, Katty Lagos-Ortiz, Vanessa Vergara-Lozano,
   José Salavarria-Melo, Karina Real-Aviles, and Néstor Vera-Lucio

Sentiment Analysis and Trend Detection in Twitter 63
   María del Pilar Salas-Zárate, José Medina-Moreira,
   Paul Javier Álvarez-Sagubay, Katty Lagos-Ortiz,
   Mario Andrés Paredes-Valverde, and Rafael Valencia-García

Cloud and Mobile Computing

Usage of Diabetes Self-management Mobile Technology: Options
for Ecuador 79
   Jose Medina-Moreira, Katty Lagos-Ortiz, Harry Luna-Aveiga,
   Ruth Paredes, and Rafael Valencia-García

A Cloud Computing Based Framework for Storage and Processing
of Meteorological Data   90
   Maritza Aguirre-Munizaga, Raquel Gomez, María Aviles,
   Mitchell Vasquez, and G. Cristina Recalde-Coronel

An M-Learning Open-Source Tool Comparation for Easy Creation
of Educational Apps   102
   Antonio Ortega-García, Antonio Ruiz-Martínez,
   and Rafael Valencia-García

Study of Use, Privacy and Dependence on Social Networks by Students
in the Ecuadorian Universities   114
   Marcos Antonio Espinoza-Mina and Patricia Leonor Suárez-Riofrío

Software Engineering

Analysis of Risk Factors of ERP (Enterprise Resource Planning) Systems
Information Technologies.   131
   William Bazán, Teresa Samaniego, Abel Alarcón, and Ana Rodríguez

Analyzing HTML5-Based Frameworks for Developing Educational
and Serious Games   143
   Humberto Marín-Vega, Giner Alor-Hernandez,
   Ramón Zatarain-Cabada, and M. Lucía Barrón-Estrada

A Dynamic Recognition Approach of Emotional States for Car Drivers   155
   Jose Aguilar, Danilo Chavez, and Jorge Cordero

Towards Supporting International Standard-Based Software Engineering
Approaches Using Semantic Web Technologies: A Systematic
Literature Review   169
   Ricardo Colomo-Palacios, Luis Omar Colombo-Mendoza,
   and Rafael Valencia-García

Expert Systems and Soft Computing

Autonomous Cycle of Data Analysis Tasks for Learning Processes   187
   Jose Aguilar, Omar Buendia, Karla Moreno, and Diego Mosquera

The Present World of the Expert System and its Competitive Contribution
in Medicine   203
   William Bazán, Valeria Bazán, Abel Alarcón, Teresa Samaniego,
   Oscar Bermeo, and Ana Rodríguez

A General Framework for Learning Analytic in a Smart Classroom.   214
   Jose Aguilar, Priscila Valdiviezo, Jorge Cordero, Guido Riofrio,
   and Eduardo Encalada

Platform for Project Evaluation Based on Soft-Computing Techniques   226
  Gilberto Fernando Castro, Iliana Pérez, Pedro Piñero, Surayne Torres,
  Mitchell Vásquez, Jorge Hidalgo, and Néstor Vera-Lucio

MiSCi: Autonomic Reflective Middleware for Smart Cities   241
  Jose Aguilar, Marxjhony Jerez, Maribel Mendonca,
  and Manuel Sánchez

Designing Assistive Technologies for Children with Disabilities:
A Case Study of a Family Living with a Daughter
with Intellectual Disability   254
  Janio Jadán-Guerrero, Ileana Altamirano, Hugo Arias,
  and Johann Jadán

ADL-MOOC: Adaptive Learning Through Big Data Analytics
and Data Mining Algorithms for MOOCs   269
  Juan Miguel Gómez-Berbís and Ángel Lagares-Lemos

Author Index   281

Knowledge Representation and Natural Language Processing

A Knowledge-Based Platform
for the Development of Critical
Thinking Abilities

Carlota Delgado-Vera[✉], Maritza Aguirre-Munizaga,
Evelyn Solis-Avíles, Andrea Sinche, and Néstor Vera-Lucio

Faculty of Agricultural Sciences, Computer Science Department,
Agrarian University of Ecuador, Av. 25 de Julio y Pio Jaramillo,
P.O. BOX 09-04-100, Guayaquil, Ecuador
{cdelgado,maguirre,esolis,asinche,
nvera}@uagraria.edu.ec

Abstract. Critical thinking is closely related to the main objectives in current educational reforms worldwide. It permits to develop cognitive skills of interpretation, analysis, evaluation, inference, explanation, and auto-regulation, which are essential in today's job market. Critical thinking is being implemented in different e-learning platforms with outstanding results. This paper presents an ontology-based platform for the development of critical thinking in universities. The platform is divided into three main modules: user management, course management and learning resources repository. A case study in the Agrarian University of Ecuador is presented and the results obtained by the use of the developed platform are promising.

Keywords: Critical thinking · Knowledge-based systems · Learning resources · Ontologies

1 Introduction

The development of critical thinking [1] is gaining momentum in e-learning systems, because it is closely related to some of the main objectives of the current educational reforms, such as the creation of civic and ethical skills. Besides, professionals are required to have new skills related to the permanent learning and the development of the scientific thought.

Some studies reveals the importance of critical thinking and investigation skills in higher education students that permit them to analyse, interpret and evaluate how theory can be applied to practice [2].

In fact, critical thinking is being implemented in different e-learning environments [3] with very satisfactory results.

Formation of critical thinking is linked to the creation of capacities for lifelong learning, research, innovation and creativity [4]. It generates active and scientific minds, training students in reasoning, the logical thinking, the detection of fallacies, the intellectual curiosity, and problem solving. There are studies focused on the analysis of

© Springer International Publishing AG 2016
R. Valencia-García et al. (Eds.): CITI 2016, CCIS 658, pp. 3–13, 2016.
DOI: 10.1007/978-3-319-48024-4_1

the efficiency of stimulating the critical thinking in academic subjects such as the work presented in [5].

On the other hand, knowledge-based technologies provide a consistent and reliable basis to face the challenges for organization, manipulation and visualization of the data and knowledge, playing a crucial role as the technological basis of the development of a large number of information systems [6]. In this context, an ontology defines a set of representational primitives allowing to model a domain of knowledge or discourse [7]. Nowadays, the use of ontologies in knowledge-based systems has significantly grown, becoming an important component in enhancing the Web intelligence and in supporting data representation. Indeed, ontologies are being applied to different domains such as Biomedicine [8], Finance [9], Innovation Management [10], Cloud computing [11, 12] and recommendation [13, 14], among others.

This paper is structured as follows: Sect. 2 describes some related work. Section 3 introduces the platform presented in this paper, where the architecture design, modules and interrelationships of the proposed approach are described. The evaluation of the platform is explained with a case study in Sect. 4. Finally, conclusions and future work are presented in Sect. 5.

2 Related Work

Critical thinking is an intellectual process that, in a decisively, deliberately and self-regulated way seeks to reach a reasonable judgment, a process that is characterized by an honest effort of interpretation, analysis, evaluation. Besides, the judgment can be explained or justified based on evidence, contextual considerations and criteria.

Thinking critically mainly requires a set of intellectual and personal skills that can be applied to different domains such as software development [15]. Other works, such as the one presented in [16], focus on the use of critical thinking for the development of cognitive abilities through an interactive methodology.

For the purpose of this research the Delphi method [17] was taken as a reference. This method exposes that critical thinking develops cognitive skills of interpretation, analysis, evaluation, inference, explanation, and auto-regulation. These skills are characterized when an intellectual process of high level is manifested.

The fundamental skills of critical thinking in education are absolutely necessary to obtain the capacity for analysis, evaluation and the reflexive formulation of arguments.

Educators must be aware of the necessity to promote the critic thinking in students to face effectively the new social and technological changes of the modern world. As it has been done in previous research [18], it is necessary to design and implement proposals or cognitive intervention software programs to develop the critical thinking into different education levels. In Fig. 1 the critical thinking skills are shown and explained.

- Verbal reasoning and argument analysis skills: They allow to identify and evaluate the quality of ideas, coherent conclusions of an argument.
- Hypothesis testing: Hypotheses are tentative ideas that represent possible solutions or explanatory reasons for a fact, situation or problem. They can explain, predict

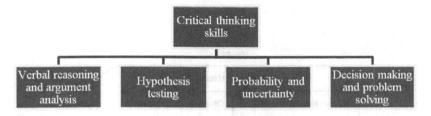

Fig. 1. Critical thinking skills

and control events of daily life. Hypothesis approaches promote new arguments that facilitate the construction of learning either by checking or contrasting processes.

- Probability and uncertainty skills: They determine quantitatively the possibility that a given event may occur, in addition to analyzing and evaluating different alternatives that are necessary for decision making in a given situation, according to the advantages and disadvantages of this event.
- Decision making and problem solving skills: They allow to exercise reasoning abilities in the recognition and definition of a problem from certain data, in the selection of relevant information. Besides, they permit to contrast different alternative solutions and their results.

3   The Knowledge Based Platform

In this section the knowledge-based methodology and platform developed in this research is explained. This system is a web-based platform that was developed through a planned process and according to the curriculum defined by the National Secretary of Higher Education, Science, Technology and Innovation (SENESCYT[1]) entity, which deals with basic processes of thought, understanding, reading, communication, and verbal reasoning allowing a better development.

Three different roles exist in the platform: the administrator, the teacher and student role. Different modules were developed for each role. For example the main functionality of the administrator is related to the courses and users (teachers and students) management. Teachers can develop different processes and teaching resources, such as units, video tutorials and exercises to encourage critical thinking in the students. Finally, students can access to the learning resources and assessment. These resources consist of the design of a website, or the presentation of activities, games and videos, which enables users to develop skills interacting with the platform.

The development of the web application was based on the philosophical tendency called constructivism and meaningful learning [19] where the student learns by doing and building. The platform architecture is shown in Fig. 2.

The platform is basically composed of three modules: user management, course management and learning resources repository. The user management module permits

---

[1] http://www.educacionsuperior.gob.ec/.

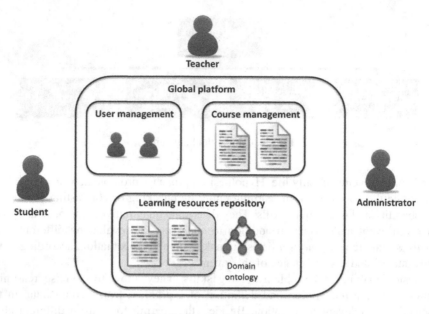

Fig. 2. System architecture

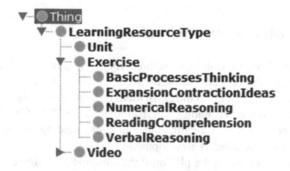

Fig. 3. Excerpt of the domain ontology

to manage users that will access to the system. The course management module permits to introduce different learning contents and learning resources for a specific course. Finally, the learning resource repository stores the learning resources published by teachers and they can be shared among different courses. More concretely, this repository is a large repository of exercises that can help in the development of critical thinking. There are different kinds of exercises: exercises for expanding and contraction of ideas, basic thinking processes, reading comprehension, verbal reasoning, and numerical reasoning. This classification is based on the work proposed in [16].

The learning resources repository uses an ontology to semantically represent each learning resource. This ontology contains information about the different kinds of resources and some terminology about the content of the resource. Figure 3 shows an excerpt of the domain ontology and some details of this ontology are shown in Table 1.

Table 1. Details of the ontology

	Ontology
Classes	210
Datatype properties	4
Object properties	16
Subclass_of relationships	234
Max. Depth of Class Tree	5
Min. Depth of Class Tree	2
Avg. Depth of Class Tree	3
Max. Branching Factor of Class Tree	9
Min. Branching Factor of Class Tree	1
Avg. Branching Factor of Class Tree	4

Students can access and interact with the system, by doing the activities and finding results of the evaluations, including the number of questions answered, and the number and percentage of hits. In addition, the student can access to a series of videos that are related to the development of critical thinking skills. In Figs. 4 and 5 two screenshots of the user interface are shown.

This whole process will help students strengthen their knowledge, abilities, associated attitudes to the styles of convergent and divergent thinking, and logical, critical and creative reasoning, which are required for acting as critical and responsible learning managers through continuous personal growth.

Fig. 4. Screenshot of the web application

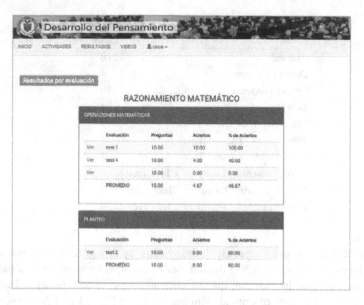

Fig. 5. Screenshot of the web application

4 Case Study

To evaluate the proposed methodology a teaching experience was performed in the introductory course of the Computer Science degree of the Agrarian University of Ecuador. Thus, different learning resources, such as video tutorials, logical exercises, reasoning activities and other tests were developed. These resources were related to introductory concepts in computer science such as binary code, algebra and algorithms. The course was taught by 4 professors and they suggested different activities to encourage the students' critical thinking development.

At the end of the teaching experiment students were asked to answer an opinion poll in order to show their perceptions, and whether the different practical works had allowed them to improve their critical thinking. This poll is based on the work presented in [20], and up to 100 students participated during 2015-2016. The opinion poll consisted of different questions (see Table 2) related to the experience. Our students evaluated each question by choosing a value between 1 and 5, where 1 means strongly disagree, 2 disagree, 3 neutral, 4 agree and 5 strongly agree. The students' evaluation is shown in Table 3 and Fig. 6.

As it can be seen in Table 3 the average of all questions is over 4, which means that students agreed with all the issues asked. In particular, the best results were obtained for questions 4 and 8 with an average of 4.54. On the other hand the worst results were obtained for questions Q6, Q7, Q12 and 16 with an average of 4.06, 4.04, 4.08 and 4.08, respectively. Finally, it is worth noting that the last three questions (Q18, Q19 and Q20) - more related to the experiment - obtained a very good mark, showing that students agree with the usefulness of the proposed framework.

Table 2. Questions of opinion poll

N	Question
Q1	Do you think that critical thinking contributes to understanding, giving opinion, deducing or judging any situation in a correct way?
Q2	Do you think that the development of critical thinking helps in the teaching and learning process?
Q3	Do you think that critical thinking helps to improve the students' learning process and academic performance?
Q4	Do you think that the development of critical thinking abilities is very important at every educational level?
Q5	Do you think that the use of ICTs allows to generate, disseminate and socialize knowledge?
Q6	Do you think that ICTs assure the students' understanding?
Q7	Do you agree that ICTs facilitate the complex instructions explanation?
Q8	Do you agree that ICTs permit the development of interactive classes?
Q9	Do you think that ICTs estimulates the students' motivation for learning?
Q10	Do you agree that ICTs contributes to universal information, communication and learning access?
Q11	Do you think that ICTs improve people's quality of life?
Q12	Do you think that ICTs allows the use of images for education?
Q13	Do you think that the use of ICTs improves the students' memory?
Q14	Do you think that ICTs facilitate learning and contribute to the development of critical thinking abilities?
Q15	Do you think that it is better to do practical exercises using ICT than manually?
Q16	Do you think that the use of multimedia tools contributes to critical thinking development?
Q17	Do you think that critical thinking abilities can be obtained through logical excercises?
Q18	Do you think that the proposed activities in the system improve the students' critical thinking?
Q19	Do you think that video tutorials contribute to critical thinking development?
Q20	Do you think that the proposed system contributes to the development of critical thinking abilities?

The mode is also shown in Table 3. All the questions obtained a mode of 4 or 5, suggesting that the majority of students who answered the survey marked 4 or 5 in each question, so that they agree and strongly agree, respectively, with the proposed questions.

Other conclusions of the survey are that 94 % of students think that critical thinking development contributes to improving the responsibility in students. In addition, 88 % answered that the use of ICTs improves people's quality of life through the generation, dissemination and socialization of knowledge. Besides, having universal access to the information, communication and education increases motivation, and contributes to the development of critical thinking skills. In fact, 84 % believe that these ICTs tools ensure the understanding of academic content, as well as the explanation of complex instructions.

Table 3. Opinion poll results

Question	5	4	3	2	1	Average	Mode
1	48	48	4	0	0	4.44	5
2	48	48	4	0	0	4.44	5
3	48	46	6	0	0	4.42	5
4	58	38	4	0	0	4.54	5
5	52	36	12	0	0	4.4	5
6	22	62	16	0	0	4.06	4
7	20	64	16	0	0	4.04	4
8	58	38	4	0	0	4.54	5
9	52	36	12	0	0	4.4	5
10	40	48	12	0	0	4.28	4
11	40	48	12	0	0	4.28	4
12	26	56	18	0	0	4.08	4
13	46	48	6	0	0	4.4	4
14	40	48	12	0	0	4.28	4
15	48	50	2	0	0	4.46	4
16	24	60	16	0	0	4.08	4
17	36	62	2	0	0	4.34	4
18	48	50	2	0	0	4.46	4
19	48	44	8	0	0	4.4	5
20	48	46	6	0	0	4.42	5

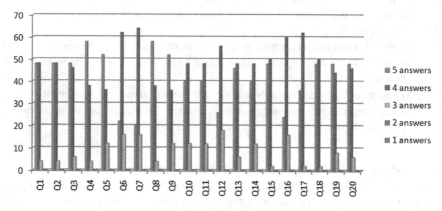

Fig. 6. Results

On the other hand, many students prefer to develop reasoning exercises by using ICTs because the use of images and multimedia features contributes to the development of critical thinking. Furthermore, video tutorials and logical reasoning exercises favorably improve the intellectual and academic performance of students improving these skills themselves.

5 Conclusion and Future Work

The development of critical thinking skills is gaining momentum in e-learning environments and experts believe that these skills have to be developed in all the educational levels. This paper presents a knowledge-based methodology to promote critical thinking skills development in all courses in order to educate future critical professionals that are capable to solve problems taking into account the current social changes. This methodology was implemented on a web-based platform and an evaluation of the platform was done in the introductory course of the computer science degree of the Agrarian University of Ecuador. The platform allows students to improve their level of critical thinking, by encouraging them to build their own knowledge based on different exercises posed in the system.

The case study presented in this work reveal that students believe that systems for promoting critical thinking in university courses are useful and should be implemented in other universities and courses. For that, a survey of 10 question was answered by 100 students of the computer science degree of the Agrarian University of Ecuador. The results show that almost all the students agreed the questions proposed by this case study.

The platform will allow teachers to propose different activities to improve the students' cognitive skills. However, the platform only permits to develop closed questions. As future work, it is planned to introduce some intelligent methodologies to automatically evaluate open questions like the work presented in [21]. In this work, semantic web and natural language processing technologies are applied for the automatic evaluation of open questions.

Finally, it is also planned to extend the case study to different courses in the same degree in order to evaluate the platform with different students at different levels. A statistical evaluation of the effectiveness of the platform will be also performed. We will follow the study proposed in [22]. In this paper, a case study of a university-level course delivered by computer conferencing examined student participation and critical thinking is presented. It was guided by two purposes: (a) to determine whether the students were actively participating, building on each other's contributions, and thinking critically about the discussion topics; and (b) to determine what factors affected student participation and critical thinking. The results suggest that the emergence of a dynamic and interactive educational process that facilitates critical thinking is contingent on several factors: appropriate course design, instructor interventions, content, and students' characteristics.

Acknowledgements. We would like to thank to the Agrarian University of Ecuador that supported this project.

References

1. Gunstone, R. (ed.): Critical Thinking. In: Encyclopedia of Science Education, p. 238. Springer Netherlands, Dordrecht (2015)
2. Solbrekke, T.D., Englund, T., Karseth, B., Beck, E.E.: Educating for professional responsibility: from critical thinking to deliberative communication, or why critical thinking is not enough. In: Trede, F., McEwen, C. (eds.) Educating the Deliberate Professional: Preparing for future practices, pp. 29–44. Springer International Publishing, Cham (2016)
3. Saadé, R.G., Morin, D., Thomas, J.D.: Critical thinking in e-learning environments. Comput. Hum. Behav. **28**(5), 1608–1617 (2012)
4. Tejada Fernández, J.: Professionalisation of teaching in universities: implications from a training perspective. RUSC. Rev. Univ. Soc. del Conoc. **10**, 345–358 (2013)
5. Tiruneh, D.T., Weldeslassie, A.G., Kassa, A., Tefera, Z., de Cock, M., Elen, J.: Systematic design of a learning environment for domain-specific and domain-general critical thinking skills. Educ. Technol. Res. Dev. **64**, 1–25 (2015)
6. Valencia-García, R., Alor-Hernández, G.: Special issue on knowledge-based software engineering. Sci. Comput. Program. **121**, 1–2 (2016)
7. Gruber, T.: Ontology. In: Liu, L., Özsu, M.T. (eds.) Encyclopedia of Database Systems, vol. 5, p. 3748. Springer, New York (2003)
8. Ruiz-Martínez, J.M., Valencia-García, R., Martínez-Béjar, R., Hoffmann, A.: BioOntoVerb: a top level ontology based framework to populate biomedical ontologies from texts. Knowl. Based Syst. **36**, 68–80 (2012)
9. Lupiani-Ruiz, E., García-Manotas, I., Valencia-García, R., García-Sánchez, F., Castellanos-Nieves, D., Fernández-Breis, J.T., Camón-Herrero, J.B.: Financial news semantic search engine. Expert Syst. Appl. **38**(12), 15565–15572 (2011)
10. Hernández-González, Y., García-Moreno, C., Rodríguez-García, M.Á., Valencia-García, R., García-Sánchez, F.: A semantic-based platform for R&D project funding management. Comput. Ind. **65**(5), 850–861 (2014)
11. Rodríguez-García, M.Á., Valencia-García, R., García-Sánchez, F., Samper-Zapater, J.J.: Ontology-based annotation and retrieval of services in the cloud. Knowl. Based Syst. **56**, 15–25 (2014)
12. Rodríguez-García, M.Á., Valencia-García, R., García-Sánchez, F., Samper-Zapater, J.J.: Creating a semantically-enhanced cloud services environment through ontology evolution. Future Gener. Comput. Syst. **32**, 295–306 (2014)
13. Carrer-Neto, W., Hernández-Alcaraz, M.L., Valencia-García, R., García-Sánchez, F.: Social knowledge-based recommender system. Application to the movies domain. Expert Syst. Appl. **39**(12), 10990–11000 (2012)
14. Colombo-Mendoza, L.O., Valencia-García, R., Rodríguez-González, A., Alor-Hernández, G., Samper-Zapater, J.J.: RecomMetz: a context-aware knowledge-based mobile recommender system for movie showtimes. Expert Syst. Appl. **42**(3), 1202–1222 (2015)
15. Chouseinoglou, O., Bilgen, S.: Introducing critical thinking to software engineering education. In: Lee, R. (ed.) Software Engineering Research, Management and Applications, pp. 183–195. Springer International Publishing, Heidelberg (2014)
16. Dwyer, C.P., Hogan, M.J., Harney, O.M., O'Reilly, J.: Using interactive management to facilitate a student-centred conceptualisation of critical thinking: a case study. Educ. Technol. Res. Dev. **62**, 687–709 (2014)
17. Facione, P.A.: Critical Thinking: A Statement of Expert Consensus for Purposes of Educational Assessment and Instruction. Research Findings and Recommendations (1990)

18. Noor, H.M.: Visual thinking courseware (VTC): enhancing critical thinking skills among spatial learners. In: Luaran, E.J., Sardi, J., Aziz, A., Alias, A.N. (eds.) Envisioning the Future of Online Learning: Selected Papers from the International Conference on e-Learning 2015, pp. 291–304. Springer Singapore, Singapore (2016)
19. Bretz, S.L.: Novak's theory of education: human constructivism and meaningful learning. J. Chem. Educ. **78**(8), 1107 (2001)
20. Pereniguez-Garcia, F., Ruiz-Martínez, A., Muñoz, F.R., Marín-López, R., Ruiz-Martínez, P. M.: Experimenting with different virtualization tools for the practical learning of computer networks. In: EDULEARN12 Proceedings, pp. 714–721 (2012)
21. Castellanos-Nieves, D., Fernández-Breis, J.T., Valencia-García, R., Martínez-Béjar, R., Iniesta-Moreno, M.: Semantic web technologies for supporting learning assessment. Inform. Sci. **181**(9), 1517–1537 (2011)
22. Bullen, M.: Participation and critical thinking in online university distance education. Int. J. E-Learn. Distance Educ. **13**(2), 1–32 (2007)

Knowledge-Based Model for Curricular Design in Ecuadorian Universities

Vanessa Vergara[1]([⊠]), Katty Lagos-Ortiz[1], Maritza Aguirre-Munizaga[1], Maria Aviles[1], José Medina-Moreira[1], Jorge Hidalgo[1], and Ana Muñoz-García[2]

[1] Faculty of Agricultural Sciences, Computer Science Department, Agrarian of Ecuador University, Av. 25 de Julio y Pio Jaramillo, P.O. BOX 09-04-100 Guayaquil, Ecuador
{vvergara,klagos,maguirre,maviles,jmedina,
jhidalgo}@uagraria.edu.ec
[2] Universidad de Los Andes, Mérida, Venezuela
anamunoz@ula.ve

Abstract. The contemporary generation of students needs to acquire competences that help them to exercise judgment and solve problems aiming to face current economic and technological challenges. On the basis of this understanding, competence-based education with its teaching and learning approaches has received a good deal of attention and support in recent years. In this sense, the correct design of curriculums represents one of the main means for the gradual and systematic formation of these competences. Despite this fact, in Ecuador there is not a knowledge management model for competence-based curricular design at university education level. Hence, in this work, we propose a knowledge-based model for the design of competence-based curriculums that allow professionals to use teaching and learning strategies that facilitate the development and demonstration of competence, thus contributing to the academic formation of high-level professionals in Ecuadorian universities. All aforementioned will be possible thanks to the implementation of a Cloud-based platform that combines current technologies such as social networks, data mining, and ontologies in order to provide Ecuadorian professionals with the means for the design of competence-based curriculums.

Keywords: Knowledge management · Ontologies · Curricular design · Education · Competences

1 Introduction

The contemporary generation of students needs to acquire competences that help them to exercise judgment and solve problems aiming to face current economic and technological challenges. A competence refers to those characteristics – knowledge, skills, mindsets, thought patterns, and the like – that when used whether singularly or in various combinations, result in successful performance [1]. Competence-based education with its teaching and learning approaches has received a good deal of attention and support in recent years [2]. In this sense, higher education institutions have focused on the

© Springer International Publishing AG 2016
R. Valencia-García et al. (Eds.): CITI 2016, CCIS 658, pp. 14–25, 2016.
DOI: 10.1007/978-3-319-48024-4_2

development of individual competences through the understanding of how people learn and how teachers can facilitate learning, and more importantly, how to apply that knowledge to the learning environment. In summary, competence-based education requires that teachers as experts define the necessary competences to become a fully qualified professional. With this in mind, correct curriculum design represents one of the main means for the gradual and systematic formation of these competences. Also, it is necessary to highlight that both the curriculum, as well as the knowledge generated from the curricular design process, should be disseminated among universities.

Nowadays, the Council of Accreditation, Assessment and Quality Assurance in Higher Education (CEAACES) is the responsible for evaluating the academic quality of higher education institutions in Ecuador. This council has awarded the highest category to universities that feature competence-based curriculum designs for each of the degrees that they offer. Despite this fact, at university education level there is no knowledge management model for competence-based curricular design. Hence, in this work, we propose a knowledge-based model for the design of competence-based curriculums that allows professionals to use teaching and learning strategies that facilitate the development and demonstration of competence [3], thus contributing to the academic formation of high-level professionals in Ecuadorian universities.

Our approach takes into account two main knowledge streams, the competence-based curricular design and the research lines acting as a transverse axis. On the one hand, our approach is focused on competences due to the fact that they are part of the integral education [4], and thereby it will be covering the fourth objective (Strengthen the capacities and potentialities of citizenship) of the National Plan for Good Living [5]. In addition, the research lines will allow the articulation of the curricular content, because all courses will be interrelated, which in turn allows the establishment of a permanent, purposive and proactive dialogue between teachers of the different courses [6]. All aforementioned will be possible thanks to the implementation of a Cloud-based platform that combines current technologies such as social networks, data mining, and ontologies in order to provide Ecuadorian professionals with the means for the design of competence-based curriculums.

In summary, the model proposed aims to facilitate the management of knowledge derived from the competence-based curriculum design process, thus allowing professionals to decide what the most appropriate content for a specific degree is, as well as to explain, evaluate, and share such content in order to plan future content.

The remainder of this paper is structured as follows. Section 2 presents a review of the literature concerning curricular design. Section 3 describes both the methodology followed for designing the model for curricular design and the model as such. The technological architecture that supports the knowledge-based model for curricular design, its components and interrelationships are described in Sect. 4. Finally, conclusions and future work are presented.

2 Related Works

In the last years there have emerged several approaches that aim to improve the competences of university students. A clear example of these efforts is presented in [7], where the authors extensively report on the present-day curricular scope and sequence, genre-based pedagogies, and associated assessment practices that were developed and implemented in a four-year undergraduate German program. The authors emphasized the decisions that were made while also demonstrating the outcomes of these decisions in the form of practicable educational efforts and products. Another example is found in [8]. Here the authors presented a methodological guide for design and application of curricular strategies in Medical sciences. The researchers performed a review of curricular, methodological and normative documents of different degrees. Also, they conducted analysis and discussion sessions with groups of experts (curricular design consultants, methodological consultants, and teachers). In [9] the authors presented a framework focused on the alignment of interdisciplinary learning objectives. This framework will be useful for both curricular designers and education researchers to understand how integrated science curricula can be designed to support interdisciplinary learning objectives. Alternatively, in [10] the authors present an analysis of the methods to include competences in the professional profile. Furthermore, the authors concluded that it is very important to assume the competence based approach as well as the training of designers and the executors of the process. In [11] a project spine for software engineering curricular design is presented. This project addresses the technologically challenging, rapidly evolving discipline that represents the software engineering education, where engineers not only design but also construct the technology. Therefore, this project focuses on vertical integration of project experiences in undergraduate software engineering degree programs or course consequences. In [12] the authors discuss about a three-year experience implementing an evolving curricular design, which is focused on exploring how students valued different instructional methods. As conclusions, the authors establish that educational change is best viewed through a longer term lens, acknowledging the necessity for teachers to grow experience in implementing new methods in the context of their institution. Finally, in [13] the researchers present an engineering program whose main goal is to expand the engineering educational alternatives in the Maine Mid-Coast region, while at the same time implementing advances in engineering pedagogy with the aim of achieving a high level of curriculum integration. Furthermore, the authors expect that these measures enhance the learning experience.

The above-presented works have made a significant contribution to improving the competences of university students through the establishment of approaches focused on curriculum design and generation at different areas such as medicine and software engineering. Despite their contributions, these works do not address all issues that our approach aims to solve. More specifically, our approach puts the intellectual capital as the center stage of the model proposed. This decision is based on a detailed analysis of current state of the Ecuadorian university environment which is described in Sect. 3. Furthermore, our approach puts special attention on creating an environment that allows teachers, coordinators, and curricular design experts, among other professionals, to share knowledge and experiences that allow them to design the correct curriculum based on the competences and needs of the students of the different degrees offered by the Ecuadorian universities. This environment will be based on an architecture that integrates current technologies such as social networks, data mining, and ontologies. This architecture is described in Sect. 4.

3   Knowledge-Based Model for Curricular Design

The design of the knowledge-based model for competence-based curricular design was performed following the model proposed in [14]. This model is composed by four phases:

1. Diagnosis. Aiming to develop a successful strategy, it was necessary to know what the current state of the organization is. Therefore, an analysis based on the strategic position of the organization was performed. This analysis aimed to determine the corporative resources that express the organization's knowledge and its use in the proposal of projects oriented to the organization's knowledge representation, its exploitation, as well as its use in the qualitative improvement of the organization.
2. Design. The main goal of this phase is the establishment of a logic and technique base on which the different projects will be developed. They are oriented to the knowledge management. Among the activities performed in this phase we find: the development of a knowledge strategy that allows the organization to change from its current state to the desired state; in order to carry out the aforementioned task, the Nonaka Takeuchi [15] model was used. This model enables managing the dynamic aspects of organizational knowledge. The central theme of this model is that organizational knowledge is created through a continuous dialogue between tacit and explicit knowledge.
3. Implementation. This phase aims to perform the implementation of the project as well as to establish the basic guidelines. This phase includes activities such as the implementation of the developed plans, and a periodic review of the strategies through the goals and plans associated with them.
4. Evaluation. The goal of this phase consists of the evaluation of the project implementation results, validating the knowledge strategy and providing feedback of the diagnosis process in order to generate a new knowledge management cycle.

As a result of this phase, we identified, selected and measured the tangible and intangible assets within universities' degrees. The accomplishment of this task was based on the Intelect model [16], which aims to provide relevant information that supports the decision-making process, as well as to provide information concerning the value of the company. This model groups intangible assets according to their nature: human capital, structural capital and relational capital. Each asset must be measured and managed through a dimension that integrates future and present as a dynamic and evolving perspective of the concept [17]. Additionally, it provides a general view of the organizational capacity for the generation of sustainable results, continuous improvement, and long-term growth. The Intelect model obtained for this work is shown in Table 1.

Table 1. Intelect model for the establishment of a knowledge-based model for curricular design

Present	Future
Human capital	
Staff: teachers, coordinators, secretaries, curricular design experts, researchers. *Human competences*: own degree, Information and communications technology (ICT), pedagogy, research, educational quality, teamwork. *Leadership*: degree coordinator, planning coordinator. *Teamwork*: Interdisciplinary working groups.	*Improved skills*: Updating of knowledge associated with the curriculum design process, updating of communication tools, new ways of knowledge acquisition
Structural capital	
Organizational culture: Regulations and internal and external policies of higher education institutions. *Business philosophy*: Vision and mission of the degree. *Organizational structure*: Organization chart of higher education institutions. *Design processes*: training processes, curricular organization, learning planning. *Knowledge capture processes*: Information management. *Dissemination and communication mechanisms*: Organizational communication, Collaborative Social Network. *Information Technology*. Technological architecture that supports the model.	*Innovation processes*: Educational innovation of the curricular design.
Relational capital	
Strategic alliances: University networks, Inter-Institutional Agreements	*Capacity improvement*: Providing the bases for higher education institutions, teacher's training on pedagogical innovation, adaptive curriculum.

As we can see in Table 1, human capital assets refer to the different knowledge and skills that university staff has. These assets represent the basis for the generation of intellectual capital. Also, they will allow the development of a model for competence-based curricular design. Concerning structural capital assets, we have identified the knowledge that the organization, in this case the university, is able to systematize and internalize and that at the beginning can be latent in the staff. It is worth noting that a solid structural capital improves the knowledge flow across organization thus improving its effectiveness. Finally, relational capital refers to the value perceived by the university concerning the relations that it has with different social agents. These assets are directly linked to the university's ability to integrate into its socioeconomic environment and develop collaborative networks.

Once the current state of the universities has been analyzed, in addition to establishing a general view of its capacity for the generation of sustainable results, continuous improvement, and long-term growth, we establish the knowledge-based model for competence-based curricular design. For this purpose, we took into account the curricular-design process proposed by Tobón [4], as well as the Tuning project [18]. According to the Tobón's process, the competences are complex performance processes that allow addressing problems through suitability and ethical commitment. This fact demands curricular transformation processes as well as a learning plan based on problem-solving activities and workshops. With regards to the Tuning project, it is an independent project, promoted and coordinated by universities in many different countries in both Latin America and Europe. This project puts the competences at the central stage in the process of curriculum reform and modernization. It is worth noting that competences established by the Tuning project are taken into account by the CEAACES in order to evaluate the different degrees offered by higher education institutions in Ecuador. Therefore, the present model focuses on the courses of action of the Tuning project. Figure 1 presents a general view of the proposed model for competence-based curricular design.

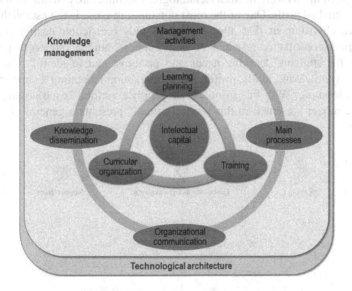

Fig. 1. Model for competence-based curricular design.

As we can see in Fig. 1, our approach puts the intellectual capital at the central stage of the model proposed. The intellectual capital refers to the collective knowledge (whether or not documented) of the individuals in an organization, in this case, of the different kind of people involved in the curricular design process such as teachers, coordinators, secretaries, curricular design experts, researchers. At first instance, structural capital assets such as processes of learning planning, training, and curricular organization, work around the intellectual capital. These assets will allow identifying and planning learning activities that help students achieve the course goals and objectives of each degree's curriculum. Furthermore, they will allow selecting curriculum elements from the subject, the current social life and the student's experience, then designing the selected curriculum elements appropriately so that they can form the curriculum structure and type. At second instance, the intellectual capital is surrounded by knowledge management processes such as management activities, knowledge dissemination and organizational communication. These processes will allow communicating results to potential users as well as to gauge their effectiveness on outcomes such as knowledge acquisition, changes in attitudes and changes in practice [19]. Finally, the model described above will be supported by an architecture that combines current technologies such as social networks, data mining, cloud computing and ontologies in order to provide professionals with the means for generating competence-based curriculums. This architecture is described in the next section.

4   Technological Architecture

As it was mentioned in the previous section, the knowledge-based model for curricular design presented in this work needs a technological architecture that allows it to accomplish the established goals. One of the most outstanding goals is the establishment of a collaborative environment that allows professionals (curricular design consultants, methodological consultants, researchers, and teachers, among others) to pay special attention to the students' learning needs and patterns, and to identify the expected competences (knowledge, skills, professional's behaviors), creating a supportive environment for learning. With this in mind, we propose a cloud-based architecture that supports the model presented in this work. Figure 2 presents a general view of such architecture.

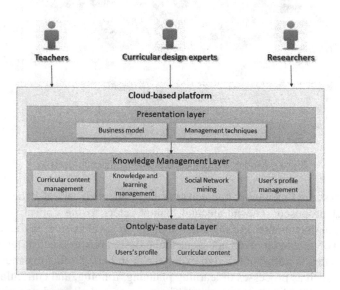

Fig. 2. Technological architecture that supports the model for curricular design

The architecture proposed in this work is based on a cloud computing approach which offers advantages such as simplified software installation and maintenance and centralized control over versioning. Moreover, end-users can access the service "anytime, anywhere", share data and collaborate more easily, keeping the data safely in the infrastructure [20]. Also, this approach has been successfully applied in works such as [21, 22, 23]. As we can see in Fig. 2, the architecture is composed of three layers namely: presentation layer, knowledge management layer and data layer. These layers are described in detail in the next sections.

4.1 Presentation Layer

This layer is composed of the business model and management techniques modules. On the one hand, the business model module refers to the activities related to knowledge generation, curricular design and content searching. Therefore, these processes aim to follow the plan implemented by our model to generate knowledge concerning curricular design, and make profit from the knowledge generated i.e., designing the correct curriculum based on the competences that the students must have according to their degree. On the other hand, the management techniques module deals with internal communication processes as well as shared online services. The main goal of this module is to deliver an internal communication framework that supports the internal communication plans, as well as to ensure the correct communication among all professionals, thus allowing them to manage and share knowledge that promote competence-based learning in higher education.

4.2 Knowledge Management Layer

This platform focuses on the management of knowledge in curricular design along with examples of a curriculum plan and sample modules. It is necessary to have clear evidence of the curricular design process in order to demonstrate the correct performance of the model. Therefore, the present module aims to consciously and comprehensively gather, organize, share, and analyze the knowledge generated in terms of resources, documents, and people skills. In this sense, this layer is composed of four modules: curricular content management, knowledge and learning management, social network mining, and user profiles management. These modules are described below.

Curricular Content Management. Curricular content represents a main level of education quality. Therefore, this module deals with the management of all information that describes the activities concerning the knowledge, skills, and attitudes imparted in learning subjects, cross-cutting approaches, and extracurricular activities. The correct management of this knowledge plays a key role on the general performance of the model proposed due to the role of every professional involved in the curricular design process. These professionals will be able to see what is intended and required in terms of curriculum provisions and learning results.

Knowledge and Learning Management. This module deals with the fact that just as human beings are unable to draw on the full potential of their brains, organizations are generally not able to fully utilize the knowledge that they possess [24]. Therefore, this module aims to allow professionals to acquire and create potentially useful knowledge and make it available to all users of the platform, thus allowing to achieve the maximum effective usage in order to positively influence the design of competence-based curriculums.

Social Network Mining. There is a constant increase in the number of people who consider the Internet as a powerful means of communication. In this sense, the social media mining approach has emerged as the process of representing, analyzing, and extracting actionable patterns from social media data [25]. Nowadays, there are lots of tools that allow to obtain and combine information from multiple sources such as social networks [26, 27]. On the basis of this understanding, this module will allow professionals to obtain information from academic groups established on social networks such as Facebook. These groups will be analyzed by means of data mining techniques in order to identify and obtain the information concerning competence-based learning in higher education.

User's Profile Management. As mentioned throughout this document, the competence-based curricular design demands the support of a multi-disciplinary team of professionals such as teachers, a curriculum design committee, and curriculum design experts, among others. Therefore, this architecture provides a module focused on the management of the profiles of all kind of users involved in the curricular design process. Hence, this module is directed, at a first instance, to teachers who are now teaching or who have not had experience in competence-based teaching and learning strategies; learners which must be engaged and active in all aspects of acquiring the knowledge, skills and professional behaviors needed to demonstrate practice in a specific discipline; as well as to a curriculum design committee composed of representatives of various university stakeholders responsible for the design process, thus providing experience to the other professionals involved.

4.3 Ontology-Based Data Layer

The amount of information available on the Web, intranets or databases has been steadily increased. This fact is present in this work because the curricular design process generates a lot of information from internal sources as well as social networks. Most of this information contained in this kind of sources is designed to be read by humans, and not to be meaningfully manipulated by machines. In this sense, the semantic Web has emerged as an extension of the current web, where information has well-defined meaning which is understandable not only by humans, but also by computers [28]. One of the most important components of the Semantic Web are the ontologies which are viewed as a formal and explicit specification of a shared conceptualization [29]. Also, it should be mentioned that ontology-based knowledge bases has significantly grown and are being applied to different domains such as information retrieval [30] and opinion mining [31]. On the basis of this understanding, we find the present uses of the ontology proposed in [32] in order to represent the concepts, relationships and instances of the presentation and knowledge management layer. This layer will allow integrating semantic mechanisms that support the decision-making process performed by professionals during the selection of educational content and the design of the appropriate curriculum according to the needs of the Ecuadorian university students. In summary, the ontology model used in this layer will guide the integration and dissemination of all knowledge generated from the model for curricular design proposed in this work.

5   Conclusions and Future Research

Nowadays, the Ecuadorian higher education institutions are being evaluated by an academic and government organization known as CEAACES. This council has awarded the highest category to universities that feature competence-based curriculum designs for each of the degrees that they offer. Therefore, in this work, we presented our research effort to provide a model for curricular design that allows professionals from different universities to select the content needed for students to acquire the knowledge, skills and professional behavior so that they can demonstrate practice in a specific discipline. Also, this model is based on the learning through competences approach, on the seventeen competences of the Tuning project oriented to measure the learning results, as well as on the ones stipulated by the CEAACES in its guide for the creation and accreditation of professional degrees.

As future work, we plan to implement the model for curricular design as well as the architecture presented in this work at the Agrarian University of Ecuador. Furthermore, we need to define measures for impact, and determine how this model fits with the established pattern for curricular design in engineering programs of Ecuadorian universities. Therefore, we plan to use quantitative and qualitative data. On the one hand, quantitative data refer to program size, institution type, college and student background. On the other hand, qualitative data can be collected through surveys and interviews of all professionals involved in the curricular design process. All aforementioned information can be collected via the technological architecture proposed in this work.

Concerning the implementation process, it must be emphasized that teaching and learning processes in whatever type of curriculum require common goals, shared responsibility and accountability between teachers and students, and supportive environments to maximize success. Therefore, the success of this work will require the provision of a sense of shared purpose and concrete support of change in addition to the development of policies that support the use of this model among the Ecuadorian higher education institutions.

References

1. Dubois, D., Shadden, M., Kaufman, R., Brethower, D.: The competence casebook: twelve studies in competence-based performance improvement. Perform. Improv. **39**(1), 37–40 (2000). doi:10.1002/pfi.4140390113
2. Albanese, M.A., Mejicano, G., Mullan, P., Kokotailo, P., Gruppen, L.: Defining characteristics of educational competences. Med. Educ. **42**(3), 248–255 (2008). doi:10.1111/j.1365-2923.2007.02996.x
3. Fullerton, J.T., Ghérissi, A., Johnson, P.G., Thompson, J.B.: Competence and competence: core concepts for international midwifery practice. Int. J. Childbirth **1**(1), 4–12 (2011). doi:10.1891/215652811795481140
4. Tobón, S.: La formación basada en competencias en la educación superior: el enfoque complejo, México Univ. Autónoma Guadalaj (2008)
5. Objetivo 4. Fortalecer las capacidades y potencialidades de la ciudadanía - Plan Nacional 2013–2017. http://www.buenvivir.gob.ec/objetivo-4.-fortalecer-las-capacidades-y-potencialidades-de-la-ciudadania. Accessed 17 Jul 2016
6. Ramírez, U.F.: La investigación, eje transversal en la formación en trabajo social en Colombia. Espac. Reg. Rev. Estud. Soc. **1**(9), 13–27 (2012)
7. Byrnes, H., Maxim, H.H., Norris, J.M.: Realizing advanced foreign language writing development in collegiate education: curricular design, pedagogy, Assessment. Mod. Lang. J. **94**, i-235 (2010)
8. Sierra Figueredo, S., Pernas Gómez, M., Sacasas, F., Cobelo, J.A.D, Manuel, J., Miralles Aguilera, E., Torre Castro, G., González García, N., Cardona Monteagudo, M., Acosta Hernández, Z.: Modelo metodológico para el diseño y aplicación de las estrategias curriculares en Ciencias Médicas. Educ. Médica Super. **24**(1), 33–41 (2010)
9. Gouvea, J.S., Sawtelle, V., Geller, B.D., Turpen, C.: A Framework for analyzing interdisciplinary tasks: implications for student learning and curricular design. CBE-Life Sci. Educ. **12**(2), 187–205 (2013). doi:10.1187/cbe.12-08-0135
10. Ortiz García, M., Cires Reyes, E.: Diseño curricular por competencias. Aplicación al macrocurrículo. EDUMECENTRO **4**(1), 10–17 (2012)
11. Gary, K., Lindquist, T., Bansal, S., Ghazarian, A.: A project spine for software engineering curricular design. In: 2013 26th International Conference on Software Engineering Education and Training (CSEE T), pp. 299–303 (2013). doi:10.1109/CSEET.2013.6595265
12. Davidson, L.K.: A 3-year experience implementing blended TBL: active instructional methods can shift student attitudes to learning. Med. Teach. **33**(9), 750–753 (2011). doi:10.3109/0142159X.2011.558948
13. Friess, W.A.: WIP; From General to Integrated; an Evolutionary Engineering Curriculum Design Approach. World Engineering Education Forum, Cartagena (2013)
14. Soto Balbón M.A., Barrios Fernández, N.M.: Gestión del conocimiento. Parte II. Modelo de gestión por procesos, Revista Cubana de los Profesionales de la Información y de la Comunicación en Salud (2006). http://eprints.rclis.org/9217/. Accessed 17 Jul 2016
15. Nonaka, I.: A dynamic theory of organizational knowledge creation. Organ. Sci. **5**(1), 14–37 (1994). doi:10.1287/orsc.5.1.14
16. Bueno, E., Azúa, S.: Medición del capital intelectual: modelo Intelect, Madr. Inst. Univ. Euroforum Escorial (1998)
17. Lovera D., Dávila, D.F.L. Aplicación del modelo de gestión del conocimiento intelect a las actividades de investigacion del IIGEOUNMSM. Rev. Inst. Investig. Fac. Ing. Geológica Minera Metal. Geográfica, **9**(17), 129–134 (2012)
18. Tuning Project. http://www.tuningal.org/en. Accessed 16 Jul 2016

19. Lafrenière, D., Menuz, V., Hurlimann, T., Godard, B.: Knowledge dissemination interventions. SAGE Open **3**(3), 2158244013498242 (2013). doi:10.1177/2158244013498242
20. Armbrust, M., Fox, A., Griffith, R., Joseph, R.D., Katz, R.H., Konwinski, A., Lee, G. Patterson, D.A., Rabkin, A., Stoica, I. et al.: Above the clouds: A berkeley view of cloud computing (2009)
21. Colombo-Mendoza, L.O., Alor-Hernández, G., Rodríguez-González, A., Valencia-García, R.: MobiCloUP!: a PaaS for cloud services-based mobile applications. Autom. Softw. Eng. **21**(3), 391–437 (2014). doi:10.1007/s10515-014-0143-5
22. Xu, L., Huang, D., Tsai, W.T.: V-lab: a cloud-based virtual laboratory platform for hands-on networking courses. In: Proceedings of the 17th ACM Annual Conference on Innovation and Technology in Computer Science Education, New York, NY, USA, pp. 256–261 (2012). doi: 10.1145/2325296.2325357
23. Xu, L., Huang, D., Tsai, W.T.: Cloud-based virtual laboratory for network security education. IEEE Trans. Educ. **57**(3), 145–150 (2014). doi:10.1109/TE.2013.2282285
24. King, W.R (ed.): Knowledge Management and Organizational Learning, pp. 3–13. Springer, New York (2009). doi:10.1007/978-1-4419-0011-1_1
25. Buettner, R.: Predicting user behavior in electronic markets based on personality-mining in large online social networks. Electron. Mark., pp. 1–19, July 2016. doi:10.1007/s125 25-016-0228-z
26. Paredes-Valverde, M.A., Alor-Hernández, G., Rodríguez-González, A., Valencia-García, R., Jiménez-Domingo, E.: A systematic review of tools, languages, and methodologies for mashup development. Softw. Pract. Exp. **45**(3), 365–397 (2015). doi:10.1002/spe.2233
27. Russell, M.A.: Mining the Social Web: Data Mining Facebook, Twitter, LinkedIn, Google +, GitHub, and More. O'Reilly Media Inc, Sebastopol (2013)
28. Berners-Lee, T., Hendler, J., Lassila, O., et al.: The semantic web. Sci. Am. **284**(5), 28–37 (2001)
29. Gruber, T.R.: Toward principles for the design of ontologies used for knowledge sharing? Int. J. Hum.-Comput. Stud. **43**(5–6), 907–928 (1995). doi:10.1006/ijhc.1995.1081
30. Paredes-Valverde, M.A., Rodríguez-García, M.A., Ruiz-Martínez, A., Valencia-García, R., Alor-Hernández, G.: ONLI: an ontology-based system for querying DBpedia using natural language paradigm. Expert Syst. Appl. **42**(12), 5163–5176 (2015). doi:10.1016/j.eswa. 2015.02.034
31. Salas-Zárate, M.P., Valencia-García, R., Ruiz-Martíne, A., Colomo-Palacios, R.: Feature-based opinion mining in financial news: an ontology-driven approach, J. Inf. Sci., p. 165551516645528, May 2016. doi:10.1177/0165551516645528
32. Muñoz, A., Lopez, V., Lagos, K., Vásquez, M., Hidalgo, J., Vera, N.: Knowledge management for virtual education through ontologies. In: Ciuciu, I., et al. (eds.) OTM 2015 Workshops. LNCS, vol. 9416, pp. 339–348. Springer, Heidelberg (2015). doi:10.10 07/978-3-319-26138-6_37

IXHEALTH: A Multilingual Platform for Advanced Speech Recognition in Healthcare

Pedro José Vivancos-Vicente[1], Juan Salvador Castejón-Garrido[1],
Mario Andrés Paredes-Valverde[2], María del Pilar Salas-Zárate[2],
and Rafael Valencia-García[2(✉)]

[1] VOCALI Sistemas Inteligentes S.L., Parque Científico de Murcia,
Ctra. de Madrid km. 388, Complejo de Espinardo, 30100 Murcia, Spain
{pedro.vivancos,juans.castejon}@vocali.net
[2] Department of Informatics and Systems, Universidad de Murcia, Murcia, Spain
{marioandres.paredes,mariapilar.salas,valencia}@um.es

Abstract. Nowadays, there are many healthcare systems focused on the optimization and improvement of processes such as the generation of medical records and medical test reports. The interaction with this kind of systems is mainly done through user interfaces that demand the use of a keyboard or a mouse, which reduces the productivity of healthcare professionals. For example, pathological anatomy professionals use both sight and hands to analyse a sample by means of a microscope; therefore, the use of information systems through traditional interfaces (keyboard and mouse) involves a considerable waste of time and effort. In this sense, this work presents IXHEALTH, a multilingual platform for advanced speech recognition that allows healthcare professionals to perform transcription and dictation activities, as well as the definition and management of voice commands to interact with healthcare information systems. From this perspective, IXHEALTH was evaluated in terms of its ability to allow users to perform dictation activities and to interact with healthcare information systems by means of speech recognition and natural language technologies. The evaluation results seem promising and have proved that IXHEALTH platform is highly useful to healthcare professionals.

Keywords: Speech recognition · Speaker recognition · Text-to-Speech · Natural language processing · Semantic annotation

1 Introduction

In the last years, there have arisen many healthcare systems whose main goal is to optimize and improve processes such as the generation of medical records, medical test reports, clinical trials, and the filling out of electronic forms, among others. The interaction with most of these systems is mainly done through user interfaces that require the use of a keyboard, a mouse or a touch screen. The use of these interfaces often reduces the productivity of healthcare professionals. For example, in the context of pathological anatomy, professionals use both sight and hands to analyse a sample by means of a microscope; therefore, the use of information systems through traditional interfaces

R. Valencia-García et al. (Eds.): CITI 2016, CCIS 658, pp. 26–38, 2016.
DOI: 10.1007/978-3-319-48024-4_3

(keyboard and mouse) involves a considerable waste of time and effort. More recently, speech transcription mechanisms have been successfully applied in healthcare areas such as radiology [1]. These speech transcription systems provide commands to work with written texts or to perform tasks in the corresponding dictation application. However, these mechanisms have several drawbacks such as lack of commands to perform complex tasks, as well as high coupling, i.e. the high degree of interdependence between software modules, a fact that limits the development of new functionalities.

The wide set of healthcare information systems with diverse interaction patterns makes the healthcare domain a challenging environment for the design and implementation of intuitive and easy-to-use applications for the end-users. In this sense, the speech recognition technology offers the potential of endless opportunities for new applications and services in the healthcare domain that enable users to interact with healthcare information systems, in order to carry out daily work activities in a faster, easier and intuitive way.

In this work, we present a multilingual speech recognition platform known as IXHEALTH, which enables healthcare professionals to perform transcription and dictation activities, as well as the definition and management of voice commands to interact with healthcare information systems. The IXHEALTH platform deals with three main issues: (1) the need for friendly, intuitive and easy-to-use mechanisms to interact with healthcare information systems; (2) security; and (3) support for multiple languages. The platform here presented addresses the first aforementioned issue through two main modules, a speech recognition module and a Text-to-Speech (TTS) based module. On the one hand, the speech recognition module allows users to interact with information systems through natural language (NL) voice commands. The NL paradigms generally deem to be very intuitive from a user point of view [2]. Furthermore, the NLP paradigm has been successfully applied in domains such as linked data [3, 4] and opinion mining [5–7]. On the other hand, the TTS-based module enables this platform to provide users, in a spoken way, with information contained in the information systems they work with; in this way, healthcare professionals can perform other activities without paying attention to the main interface, thus saving time and effort. Concerning security, a real-time speaker verification module is implemented aiming to authenticate that someone is who they claim to be [8], thus avoiding the use of healthcare information systems by non-allowed users. Finally, with regards to multilingual support, IXHEALTH implements a module for the management of commands and linguistic resources in multiple languages such as Spanish and Portuguese. It should be noted that these resources are used by the other modules to perform their corresponding functions.

The remainder of this paper is structured as follows. Section 2 presents a review of the literature about speech recognition at the healthcare domain. The architecture design of the IXHEALTH platform, its components and interrelationships are described in Sect. 3. Section 4 presents the evaluation results concerning the effectiveness of the platform to allow users to perform dictation activities. Finally, conclusions and future work are presented.

2   Related Works

Research efforts focusing on the generation of speech recognition-based solutions to increase the usability of healthcare information systems have experienced substantial growth over the last years. For example, in [9] the authors propose a Cloud-based framework that allows patients to seek for medical assistance by means of speech commands. This framework implements an IDP-based (Interlaced Derivative Pattern) speech recognition system which has proven to work reasonably well even when the speech is transmitted via smartphones. Another research effort is the one presented in [10], where the authors report their experience using Powerscribe for Radiology, which provides a speech recognition engine for radiology reporting. This system eliminated the delays associated with report transcription and reduced report turnaround times. On the other hand, in [11] the authors evaluated the efficacy of a commercial voice-recognition software system with pathology vocabulary in generating pathology reports. The authors concluded that computer-based continuous speech-recognition systems in pathology can be successfully used in practice. In [12] the authors present a study concerning the use of speech recognition and information extraction to generate drafts of Australian nursing handover documents. As conclusions, authors mentioned that the use of the aforementioned technologies avoids information loss, delays, and misinterpretations. Moreover, in [13] a report concerning volume and use of the send-to-editor function and the use of voice recognition shortcuts was performed. This evaluation was applied to voice recognition dictation systems installed in a six-hospital system. The results show that radiologists who used the send-to-editor function generated significantly more reports than radiologists who did not. In the context of semantic annotation, there are well-known tools focused on automatic mapping and identification of medical concepts. Among them we can find MetaMap [14] and Apache cTakes [15]. MetaMap is a configurable program to map biomedical text to the UMLS (Unified Medical Language System) Metathesaurus or, equivalently, to discover concepts referred to in text. Apache cTakes is a natural language processing system for extraction of information from electronic medical record clinical free-text. The aforementioned tools have been successfully applied in works such as [16,17]. In the first work, the authors use NLP techniques to extract diagnostic criteria from MedlinePlus articles about infectious diseases. In the second work, a combination of MetaMap and Apache cTakes is implemented to perform the named entity recognition and normalization of disorders.

The works previously presented have made a significant contribution to improving the performance of healthcare processes through speech recognition technologies. Despite their contributions, these works do not address all issues that the IXHEALTH platform aims to solve. More specifically, the issues addressed are: (1) the definition and management of voice commands that allows users to interact with several healthcare information systems including the operating system upon which they run, (2) the system's ability to read any text contained in the information system and convert it into speech, thus allowing that healthcare professionals perform other activities without paying attention to a graphical interface, (3) security, and (4) support for multiple languages. The way in which these issues are addressed by our approach will be discussed in detail along the platform's architecture description which is presented in the following sections.

3 IXHEALTH Platform

IXHEALTH is a multilingual platform for advanced speech recognition focused at optimizing process-oriented information systems in healthcare. On the one hand, IXHEALTH allows professionals to perform transcription and dictation activities in order to edit clinical documents and to fill out electronic forms. On the other hand, this platform allows the definition and management of voice commands to interact with several healthcare information systems including the operating system upon which they run.

As we can see in Fig. 1, the IXHEALTH platform is composed of five main modules: (1) the speech recognition module, (2) the speaker verification module, (3) the TTS (Text-to-Speech) module, (4) the module of management of multilingual commands and linguistic resources, and (5) the semantic annotation module. The first module allows users to interact with information systems through natural language voice commands, as well as to perform transcription and dictation activities such as the edition of clinical documents. The second module performs a real-time speaker verification to avoid the use of healthcare information systems by non-allowed users. The TTS module enables the IXHEALTH platform to read any text contained in the information systems and convert it into speech, thus allowing healthcare professionals to perform other activities without paying attention to the main interface. The fourth module allows the management of commands and linguistic resources, used by other modules, for languages such as Portuguese and Spanish. Finally, the semantic annotation module obtains a semantic interpretation of the information involved in the voice recognition process such as medical records, medical test reports, and clinical trials, among others. The aforementioned modules are explained in detail in the next sections.

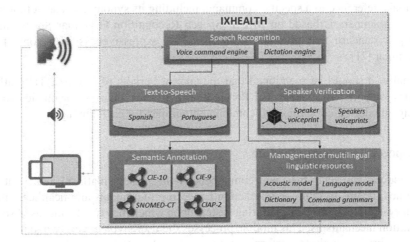

Fig. 1. IXHEALTH platform's functional architecture.

3.1 Management of Multilingual Commands and Linguistic Resources

The speech recognition module needs linguistic resources such as acoustic models, language model, dictionaries and command grammars in order to perform its respective processes, i.e. the voice command recognition and the dictation process. The present module allows the management of the aforementioned resources in such way that their edition does not affect the general performance of the system. What is more, this approach facilitates the addition of resources in different languages, thus providing multilingual support to the platform. Next, the aforementioned resources are briefly explained.

- Acoustic model. This model provides a statistical representation of the relationships between an audio signal and the phonemes or other linguistic units that make up speech. This model is based on the HMM (Hidden Markov Model) approach [18]. The acoustic models also include pronunciation models that describe how a set of linguistic units are used to represent larger speech units such as words or phrases. Furthermore, these models allow recalculating the feature vectors and pronunciation models to improve the system performance with respect to the speaker.
- Language model. The goal of this model is to determine the joint probability function of sequences of words in a language [19]. This model is based on text corpora which are used to calculate the probability that a certain word appears before or after another word.
- Dictionaries. These dictionaries contain domain-specific terms including their respective pronunciation, which is based on its phonemes. These resources represent an important component of the present module because, in the healthcare domain, each medical specialty has a specific vocabulary whose detection improves the general performance of the system.
- Command grammars. The IXHEALTH platform allows users to add new voice commands that allow them to perform more tasks in the information systems with which they work. In this sense, the command grammars represent all possible ways to make reference to a specific command, including its synonyms. The definition of these grammars is based on SRGS (Speech Recognition Grammar Specification) [20], a standard that provides a high-level of expressiveness of a context-free grammar [21].

Finally, it should be mentioned that the current version of IXHEALTH platform provides support for Spanish and Portuguese, therefore, there are acoustic models, language models, dictionaries and command grammars for each language.

3.2 Speech Recognition Module

This module represents the main component of the present platform and, as it was mentioned, it aims to improve interaction between professionals and healthcare information systems including the operating system upon which they run, by means of speech recognition mechanisms. This module processes the user's voice with two main goals: (1) allow professionals to perform transcription and dictation activities such as the edition of clinical documents, and (2) detect the specific command to be executed by the information system or operating system. With regard to the second goal, this module implements a set of intra-and inter-applications voice commands in order to allow switching between applications and performing specific operations of the application that has the focus.

This module integrates a voice command engine and a dictation engine that share the same speech recognizer, thus allowing both engines to work in parallel. Therefore, when the speech recognizer receives a voice signal, both engines analyse the signal in order to determine if the user has provided a predefined voice command or he/she requires performing dictation activities. When a predefined voice command is detected, it is prioritized and the system performs the corresponding action. Next, the command and dictation engines are described in detail.

- Dictation engine. It is composed of three main elements. Firstly, a feature extraction module which identifies critical features contained in the voice signal in order to simplify the voice recognition process; secondly, a voice recognition module which combines information from feature extraction module, the acoustic model, dictionaries, and the language model aiming to determine the best word sequence; finally, an adaptation module which, based on the output of the voice recognition module, adapts the acoustic model in order to improve the system performance.
- Voice command engine. The operation of this module is similar to the first one. Nevertheless, this module defines a commands grammar instead of using a language model, and its output is a predefined voice command instead of a sequence of words. Hence, this module consists of two modules, the feature extraction module, which identifies critical features contained in the voice signal, and the speech recognition module, which combines information from the feature extraction module, commands grammar, the dictionary, and the acoustic model in order to identify the voice command provided by the user. The voice command engine recognizes two types of command:
  - Simple command. It consists of a sequence of fixed invocations. An example of this kind of command is "start dictation".
  - Two-part command. It contains a sequence of fixed invocations and a parameter consisting of one or more words. An example of this kind of command is "select introduction", where "select" represents the command, and "introduction" represents the parameter, in this case, the section to be selected.

3.3 Speaker Verification

Several healthcare processes demand high-security level in order to avoid the edition of information contained in healthcare information systems by outside users or intruders. On the basis of this understanding, this module implements a real-time speaker verification mechanism that allows authenticating that a person is who she or he claims to be. This process is performed each time that speech recognition module receives human speech from a user.

Aiming to perform the speaker verification process, it is necessary to have a speaker voiceprint (a model of the speaker's voice) of each system user. Therefore, this module carries out a voiceprint generation from the desktop application by means of a voice profile training process which requires the user participation. This process decomposes the speech signal received from the speaker into its frequency components i.e., this module extracts a set of features that must meet the following criterion [22]: low variability for the same speaker and high variability among different speakers, robust against noise and distortion, and difficult to imitate. The first phase of this process is the noise reduction by means of a Wiener filter [23]. After that, a VAD (Voice Activity Detection) phase is performed in order to delete the audio fragments that do not contain voice. Then, the MFCC (Mel-Frequency Cepstral Coefficients) technique [24] is used to extract the speaker features from the audio fragments that contain voice. The main goal of this technique is to obtain a statistical model of the speaker's voice with a high precision level. Finally, this module uses a GMM-based (Gaussian Mixture Model) technique based on a Universal Background Model (UBM) in order to adapt the speaker voiceprint [25]. This technique allows addressing the lack of data that occurs during the speaker voiceprint generation.

Once the speaker verification module has the speaker voiceprint of at least one system user, it can perform the speaker verification process. In this sense, this module receives a human speech from the user that claims identity. This input speech is converted into a voiceprint and compared to the voiceprint of the user that has logged in previously. The results of the comparison are quantified and compared to an acceptance/rejection threshold to determine whether the two voiceprints are similar enough for the system to accept the identity claim. This decision is based on an LLR (log-likelihood ratio) punctuation.

3.4 Text-to-Speech Module

This module enables the platform to read any text contained in the information systems and convert it into speech. In this way it is possible for healthcare professionals to perform other activities without paying attention to the interface provided by the information system, thus saving time and effort.

As was previously mentioned, the goal of this module is to convert a text file into speech through a grapheme-to-phoneme transcription of the sentences to utter [26]. Aiming to accomplish this goal, the TTS module performs next process.

1. It organizes the input sentences into a manageable list of words. Then, it identifies numbers, abbreviations, and acronyms and transforms them into the full text when needed.
2. It performs an LTS (Letter-To-Sound) process aiming to determine the phonetic transcription of the incoming text. The LTS process uses a dictionary-based solution which consists of storing a maximum of phonological knowledge into a lexicon. This approach has been successfully applied in works such as [27, 28]. In addition to the dictionaries aforementioned, this process uses the dictionaries

described in Sect. 3.1, which contain domain-specific terms including their respective pronunciation.

3. A prosody generation process is performed. It identifies properties of the speech signal related to audible changes in pitch, loudness, and syllable length aiming to generate a syntactic-prosodic structure. Once the syntactic-prosodic structure of the input text has been derived, it is used to obtain the precise duration of each phoneme (and of silences), as well as the intonation to apply on them.

4. In order for the output signal to match the input text, the TTS module must take into account articulatory constraints such as the control of the articulatory muscles and the vibratory frequency of the vocal folds. In this sense, this module uses a concatenative synthesizer approach which produces a concatenation block of speech segments. These segments are examples of phonetic transitions and co-articulations, used as ultimate acoustic units, which are stored in a speech segment database. These databases can store speech segments in multiple languages and voices (male and female) thus providing a multilingual support to the platform.

5. Once the concatenation block has been generated, the TTS module generates a single compact signal containing all segments in a coherent way. This signal is stored as an mp3 file so that any device can reproduce it.

3.5 Semantic Annotation Module

Semantic technologies provide a consistent and reliable basis that can be used to confront the challenges related to the organization, manipulation and visualization of data and knowledge. Therefore, this module performs the semantic annotation of the resources involved in healthcare processes such as medical records, medical test reports, and clinical trials, among others, in order to obtain a semantic interpretation of them. This module is based on previous works of our research group [29, 30] and it was developed by using the GATE [31] framework, and it consists of two main phases:

1. Text pre-processing. In this phase, the tokenization, sentence splitting and stemming process are performed. The first process divides the input text into a sequence of tokens, which roughly correspond to words. The sentence splitting process divides the input text into its component sentences. Finally, a stemming process is performed in order to determine the stem of each word in the input text. A stem represents the part of the word that is common to all its inflected variants. This process is based on the Snowball [32] approach.

2. Detection of medical concepts. This phase is responsible for the detection and annotation of medical concepts contained in the input text. These concepts are identified by using a combination of JAPE rules and lists of Gazetteers. On the one hand, JAPE is a rich and flexible regular expression-based rule mechanism offered by GATE framework which allows recognising regular expressions in annotations on documents. On the other hand, a gazetteer consists of a set of lists containing names of entities such as diagnoses, procedures, allergies, alerts, among others. Aiming to provide semantic interoperability these gazetteers are based on the following standard terminologies:

(a) SNOMED-CT. It is the most comprehensive, multilingual clinical healthcare terminology in the world. It contains comprehensive and scientifically validated clinical content which enables consistent representation of clinical content in electronic health records. Nowadays, SNOMED-CT is only available in English, Spanish, Danish and Swedish. Hence, we have implemented a partial translation of it into Portuguese which has been verified by medical experts.

(b) CIE-9. The International Classification of Diseases, ninth edition, classifies diseases, conditions, and external causes of disease and injury (mortality and morbidity).

(c) CIE-10. It represents the tenth revision of the International Classification of Diseases presented above.

(d) CIAP-2. The Classification of Primary Care is a taxonomy of terms and expressions commonly used in general medicine. It compiles the reasons for consultation, health problems, and care processes.

4   Evaluation and Results

Despite the fact that the IXHEALTH platform is composed of several modules and services, the evaluation was focused on measuring its effectiveness to complete radiology reports by means of speech recognition methods. The evaluation was performed in a single hospital system by a representative group of ten radiologists, whose specialties are: neuroradiology, cardiac radiology, chest radiology, diagnostic radiology, and pediatric radiology. All ten radiologists are native Spanish and Portuguese speakers (one per each specialty). Also, all of them had extensive experience generating radiology reports. The experiments were performed during a period of four months divided into two phases. During the first phase, corresponding to the first two months, the users performed the generation of reports by means of traditional interfaces (mouse and keyboard). Along the second phase, the participants carried out their corresponding activities by means of the IXHEALTH platform. The procedure of the evaluation performed during the second phase is described below.

Firstly, voice recognition training and instruction on creating and modifying radiology reports by using the platform were provided to the participants. Secondly, each radiologist carried out the report generation by using a headset microphone and a personal computer with Windows OS and the IXHEALTH software installed. It should be mentioned that all participants spent a portion of their clinical time at generating reports by means of the IXHEALTH platform. Therefore, the data reported in this work do not represent the total productivity of the radiologists during this period of time. Finally, system accuracy was assessed by measuring its word recognition rate [33]. For the purpose of accuracy determination, punctuation marks and formating commands (e.g. new paragraph) were considered words. On the one hand, a word was considered correctly recognized only if it was transcribed exactly as intended. On the other hand, errors caused by mispronunciations, homonyms, and out-of-domain words were considered incorrect. The evaluation results are shown in Table 1.

Table 1. Word recognition rate of the IXHEALTH platform for ten radiologists.

User	Subspecialty	Generated reports		Words spoken (avg)	Word recognition rate (%)
		Before	After		
1ES	Neuroradiology	60	75	379	94.1
2PT	Neuroradiology	49	63	378	98.1
3ES	Cardiac radiology	64	81	424	96.5
4PT	Cardiac radiology	70	82	339	98.7
5ES	Chest radiology	58	63	402	95.7
6PT	Chest radiology	56	71	380	94.9
7ES	Diagnostic radiology	61	79	403	96.3
8PT	Diagnostic radiology	84	95	435	97.4
9ES	Pediatric radiology	91	102	389	96.8
10PT	Pediatric radiology	79	96	412	95.2
Total		672	807	394.1	96.37

As we can see in Table 1, the number of reports generated in the first phase was 672, whereas during the second phase the number of reports generated was 807. We found a marked improvement in report generation after the implementation of the IXHEALTH platform. Specifically, the number of generated reports increased 20,08 %. Moreover, there was no significant difference in report volumes for each specialty. During dictation tasks, the word recognition rate of IXHEALTH for the ten radiologists varied from 94,1 % to 98,7 %, with a mean accuracy of 96,37 %. The mean accuracy of word recognition rate for Spanish was 95,88 %. Meanwhile, the mean accuracy of word recognition rate for Portuguese was 96,86. The word recognition errors in both languages resided in the homonyms (words with similar pronunciations but different spellings). A lower percentage of these errors was due to out-of-domain words. Finally, it should be mentioned that, although the 96,37 % word recognition rate of IXHEALTH may seem high, all ten radiologists thought that this value needs to be improved in order to reduce the editing times (correcting errors) and avoid errors that can change the meaning of a report.

5   Conclusion and Future Research

In this work we present the IXHEALTH platform, which aims to provide intuitive and easy-to-use mechanisms to interact with healthcare information systems, thus allowing healthcare professionals to save time and effort, as well as to focus on the relevant issues. The evaluation results indicate that the use of the IXHEALTH platform increased the report generation volume. Although the IXHEALTH platform holds great promise for improving productivity among radiologists, its current version does not represent a ready-to-sell product given that it requires further evolution, with a need for increased accuracy and improved grammatical sense. This fact is really important, especially considering that in the healthcare domain, a word recognition error can change the complete meaning of a report, creating health problems of the patients, thus increasing the healthcare costs.

Despite IXHEALTH was evaluated in terms of their ability to generate radiology reports by speech, achieving promising results and proving to be useful to radiologists, this platform has several limitations that could be improved in future research. We have envisioned the following future research directions: (1) IXHEALTH does not consider the filling-out of structured reports as such, therefore, this platform can and should be improved by incorporating voice command functionalities that allow filling out reports with a structured content, coded concepts, references to images, or other composite objects. This issue will also demand the establishment of a wide set of TTS functionalities focused on the improvement for the interaction between the user and the structured report forms, e.g., the system will ask the user for specific information through speech, thus reducing the use of keyboard and mouse; (2) in order to increase speech recognition accuracy, we plan to put special attention in the improvement of the language model (for both Spanish and Portuguese) based on the evaluation results presented in this work. Furthermore, we plan to perform continuous testing of the platform along incremental phases. Each phase will involve the participation of healthcare professionals from different specialties. At the end of each phase, the word recognition rate will be obtained, and the results will be analysed aiming to detect the main reasons of word recognition errors, as well as to measure the performance of our system in different specialties; (3) the current version of IXHEALTH provides support for two languages, Spanish and Portuguese, however, we plan to apply our approach to different languages such as English. This task will demand great effort as we need to adapt all linguistic resources used by the platform such as the acoustic model, language model, dictionary and command grammars. Additionally, taking into account that SNOMED-CT is only available for some languages (English, Spanish, Danish and Swedish), its use will demand the translation of it in order to use our approach to languages such as German or French. Despite the aforementioned facts, we are sure the effort necessary to perform these activities will not be so long due to the fact that all IXHEALTH modules are highly language independent;(4) finally, in order to take advantage of the semantic annotation module, which is part of the IXHEALTH platform, we also plan to implement the semantic integration of data for clinical trials and provide several services such as semantic searches for clinical trials and patient data, finding trials for a patient, and finding patients for a trial.

Acknowledgments. This work has been supported by the Murcian Government (Instituto de Fomento de la Región de Murcia) and the European Commission (FEDER/ERDF) through project IXHEALTH (2015.08.ID + I.0011).

References

1. Akhtar, W., Ali, A., Mirza, K.: Impact of a voice recognition system on radiology report turnaround time: experience from a non-English-Speaking South Asian Country. Am. J. Roentgenol. **196**(4), W485–W485 (2011). doi:10.2214/AJR.10.5426

2. Cimiano, P., Haase, P., Heizmann, J., Mantel, M., Studer, R.: Towards portable natural language interfaces to knowledge bases – The case of the ORAKEL system. Data Knowl. Eng. **65**(2), 325–354 (2008). doi:10.1016/j.datak.2007.10.007

3. Paredes-Valverde, M.A., Rodríguez-García, M.A., Ruiz-Martínez, A., Valencia-García, R., Alor-Hernández, G.: ONLI: an ontology-based system for querying DBpedia using natural language paradigm. Expert Syst. App. **42**(12), 5163–5176 (2015). doi:10.1016/j.eswa. 2015.02.034

4. Paredes-Valverde, M.A., Valencia-García, R., Rodríguez-García, M.A., Colomo-Palacios, R., Alor-Hernández, G.: A semantic-based approach for querying linked data using natural language. J. Inf. Sci. (2015). doi:10.1177/0165551515616311

5. Salas-Zárate, M.P., López-López, E., Valencia-García, R., Aussenac-Gilles, N., Almela, A., Alor-Hernández, G.: A study on LIWC categories for opinion mining in Spanish reviews. J. Inf. Sci. (2014). doi:10.1177/0165551514547842

6. Peñalver-Martinez, I., Garcia-Sanchez, F., Valencia-Garcia, R., Rodríguez-García, M.A., Moreno, V., Fraga, A., Sánchez-Cervantes, J.L.: Feature-based opinion mining through ontologies. Expert Syst. Appl. **41**(13), 5995–6008 (2014). doi:10.1016/j.eswa.2014.03.022

7. Salas-Zárate, M.P., Valencia-García, R., Ruiz-Martínez, A., Colomo-Palacios, R.: Feature-based opinion mining in financial news: an ontology-driven approach. J. Inf. Sci. (2016). doi: 10.1177/0165551516645528

8. Markowitz, J.A.: Voice biometrics. Commun. ACM **43**(9), 66–73 (2000). doi:10.1145/ 348941.348995

9. Muhammad, G.: Automatic speech recognition using interlaced derivative pattern for cloud based healthcare system. Clust. Comput. **18**(2), 795–802 (2015). doi:10.1007/ s10586-015-0439-7

10. Hart, J.L., Mcbride, A., Blunt, D., Gishen, P., Strickland, N.: Immediate and sustained benefits of a "total" implementation of speech recognition reporting. Br. J. Radiol. **83**(989), 424–427 (2010). doi:10.1259/bjr/58137761

11. Al-Aynati, M.M., Chorneyko, K.A.: Comparison of voice-automated transcription and human transcription in generating pathology reports. Arch. Pathol. Lab. Med. **127**(6), 721–725 (2003). doi:10.1043/1543-2165(2003)127<721:COVTAH>2.0.CO;2

12. Suominen, H., Johnson, M., Zhou, L., Sanchez, P., Sirel, R., Basilakis, J., Hanlen, L., Estival, D., Dawson, L., Kelly, B.: Capturing patient information at nursing shift changes: methodological evaluation of speech recognition and information extraction. J. Am. Med. Inform. Assoc. **22**(e1), e48–e66 (2015). doi:10.1136/amiajnl-2014-002868

13. Williams, D.R., Kori, S.K., Williams, B., Sackrison, S.J., Kowalski, H.M., McLaughlin, M.G., Kuszyk, B.S.: Journal club: voice recognition dictation: analysis of report volume and use of the send-to-editor function. Am. J. Roentgenol. **201**(5), 1069–1074 (2013). doi: 10.2214/AJR.10.6335

14. Aronson, A.R., Lang, F.M.: An overview of MetaMap: historical perspective and recent advances. J. Am. Med. Inform. Assoc. **17**(3), 229–236 (2010). doi:10.1136/jamia. 2009.002733

15. Savova, G.K., Masanz, J.J., Ogren, P.V., Zheng, J., Sohn, S., Kipper-Schuler, K.C., Chute, C.G.: Mayo clinical Text Analysis and Knowledge Extraction System (cTAKES): architecture, component evaluation and applications. J. Am. Med. Inform. Assoc. **17**(5), 507–513 (2010). doi:10.1136/jamia.2009.001560

16. Rodríguez-González, A., Martínez-Romero, M., Costumero, R., Wilkinson, M.D., Menasalvas-Ruiz, E.: Diagnostic knowledge extraction from medlineplus: an application for infectious diseases. In: Overbeek, R., Rocha, M.P., Fdez-Riverola, F., Paz, J.F.D. (eds.) 9th International Conference on Practical Applications of Computational Biology and Bioinformatics. AISC, vol. 375, pp. 79–87. Springer International Publishing, Switzerland (2015)

17. Xia, Y., Zhong, X., Liu, P., Tan, C., Na, S., Hu, Q., Huang, Y.: Combining MetaMap and cTAKES in Disorder Recognition: THCIB at CLEF eHealth Lab 2013 Task 1, in CLEF (Working Notes) (2013)

18. Huang, X.D., Ariki, Y., Jack, M.A.: Hidden Markov Models for Speech Recognition, vol. 2004. Edinburgh University Press, Edinburgh (1990)

19. Bengio, Y., Ducharme, R., Vincent, P., Jauvin, C.: A neural probabilistic language model. J. Mach. Learn. Res. 3, 1137–1155 (2003)

20. Hunt, A., McGlashan, S.: Speech recognition grammar specification version 1.0, W3C Recomm, March 2004

21. Bundy, A., Wallen, L.: Context-free grammar. In: Bundy, A., Wallen, L. (eds.) Catalogue of Artificial Intelligence Tools, pp. 22–23. Springer, New York (1984)

22. Rose, P.: Forensic Speaker Identification. CRC Press, New York (2003)

23. Chen, J., Benesty, J., Huang, Y., Doclo, S.: New insights into the noise reduction Wiener filter. IEEE Trans. Audio Speech Lang. Process. 14(4), 1218–1234 (2006). doi:10.1109/TSA.2005.860851

24. Davis, S., Mermelstein, P.: Comparison of parametric representations for monosyllabic word recognition in continuously spoken sentences. IEEE Trans. Acoust. Speech Signal Process. 28(4), 357–366 (1980). doi:10.1109/TASSP.1980.1163420

25. Reynolds, D.A., Quatieri, T.F., Dunn, R.B.: Speaker verification using adapted gaussian mixture models. Digit. Signal Process. 10(1), 19–41 (2000). doi:10.1006/dspr.1999.0361

26. Thierry, D.: A Short Introduction to Text-to-Speech Synthesis, TTS Res. Team TCTS Lab (1999)

27. Levinson, S.E., Olive, J.P., Tschirgi, J.S.: Speech synthesis in telecommunications. IEEE Commun. Mag. 31(11), 46–53 (1993). doi:10.1109/35.256873

28. Coker, C.H.: A dictionary-intensive letter-to-sound program. J. Acoust. Soc. Am. 78(S1), S7–S7 (1985). doi:10.1121/1.2023005

29. Rodríguez-García, M.A., Valencia-García, R., García-Sánchez, F., Samper-Zapater, J.J.: Creating a semantically-enhanced cloud services environment through ontology evolution. Future Gener. Comput. Syst. 32, 295–306 (2014). doi:10.1016/j.future.2013.08.003

30. Rodríguez-García, M.A., Valencia-García, R., García-Sánchez, F., Samper-Zapater, J.J.: Ontology-based annotation and retrieval of services in the cloud. Know-Based Syst. 56, 15–25 (2014). doi:10.1016/j.knosys.2013.10.006

31. Cunningham, H., Tablan, V., Roberts, A., Bontcheva, K.: Getting more out of biomedical documents with GATE's full lifecycle open source text analytics. PLoS Comput. Biol. 9(2), e1002854 (2013). doi:10.1371/journal.pcbi.1002854

32. Porter, M.F.: Snowball: A language for stemming algorithms (2001)

33. Makhoul, J., Schwartz, R.: State of the art in continuous speech recognition. Proc. Natl. Acad. Sci. 92(22), 9956–9963 (1995)

The Extended Hierarchical Linguistic Model in Fuzzy Cognitive Maps

Maikel Leyva-Vázquez[✉], Eduardo Santos-Baquerizo, Miriam Peña-González, Lorenzo Cevallos-Torres, and Alfonso Guijarro-Rodríguez

Facultad de Ciencias Matemáticas y Físicas, Universidad de Guayaquil,
Guayaquil, Guayas, Ecuador
{maikel.leyvav,eduardo.santosb,miriam.penag,
lorenzo.cevallost,alfonso.guijarror}@ug.edu.ec

Abstract. Fuzzy cognitive maps allow multi-expert causality modelling using linguistic 2-tuples values to improve the accuracy of the computing with words processes regarding classical symbolic approaches. Experts provide causal relations according to their knowledge, because they can have different educational backgrounds, or experiences. It seems logical that they might use different scales to express their mental models. In this work, we propose a new method for extending fuzzy cognitive maps, using the computing with words paradigm and the extended hierarchical linguistic model making it possible to model causal relation by means of linguistic information, where experts would use different linguistic scales to express causal relations. An illustrative example is shown to demonstrate the applicability of the proposed method in the modelling of interdependencies among nonfunctional requirements.

Keywords: Fuzzy Cognitive Maps · CWW · ELH · Non-functional requirement

1 Introduction

Recently Fuzzy Cognitive Maps (FCM) have been extended to use linguistic 2-tuples values [1, 2]. The use of the linguistic representation model based on linguistic 2-tuple in FCM allows to perform the Computing with Words(CWW) processes without losing information, improving accuracy regarding classical symbolic approaches [3].

Mental models are cognitive structures which are useful for causal knowledge elicitation and analysis that can be represented by means of FCM [1]. Humans have limitations for representing the world; therefore, mental models are uncompleted representations of reality making it necessary the development of collective mental models.

Modelling causality by means of linguistic information in a multi-expert environment can involve problems defined in multiple linguistic scale contexts. The extended hierarchical linguistic model (ELH) [4] allows different experts to have different uncertainty degrees about causal relations making use of several linguistic term sets with a different granularity of uncertainty.

The aim of this article is to deal with causality modelling problems defined in multi-granular linguistic frameworks using fuzzy cognitive maps. Our proposal consists of a

© Springer International Publishing AG 2016
R. Valencia-García et al. (Eds.): CITI 2016, CCIS 658, pp. 39–50, 2016.
DOI: 10.1007/978-3-319-48024-4_4

new approach for dealing with multiple linguistic scales FCM, which is able to handle any linguistic term set in a symbolic way and without losing information using ELH.

This paper is structured as follows: Sect. 2 reviews some important concepts about FCM. Section 3 provides a description of the linguistic representation model based in 2-tuples and ELH model. In Sect. 4, we present a method for modeling fuzzy cognitive maps using ELH. Section 5 shows illustrative examples of the proposed model applied to non-functional software requirements modelling. The paper ends with conclusions and further work recommendations in Sect. 6.

2   Fuzzy Cognitive Maps

Cognitive maps, introduced by Axelrod [5] nodes represent concepts or variables in a domain. Arcs indicate positive or negative causal relations. Cognitive mapping lacks representation of uncertain important factors in complex systems modeling [6].

Fuzzy cognitive maps (FCM) [7] (Fig. 1) are fuzzy graph structures for representing causal knowledge. Fuzzy cognitive maps (FCM) [7] extend cognitive maps with fuzzy values in [−1, 1] to indicate the strength of causal relations, frequently elicited from multiple experts [8, 9]. For k experts, aggregated adjacency matrix (E) can be obtained as follows:

$$E = \frac{(E_1 + E_2 + \ldots + E_k)}{k} \tag{1}$$

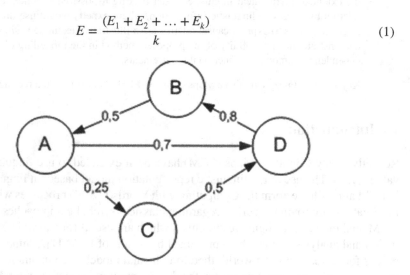

Fig. 1. Example of FCM graphical representation [10].

Fuzzy logic allows expressing the degree of causality between concepts by means of fuzzy values using linguistic expressions as "very high", "negatively weak" "positively weak", etc. In these cases, linguistic information models the knowledge from experts in a flexible way, and involves processes of computing with words (CWW).

FCM have been applied to diverse areas specially decision support and complex system analysis [11]. Further extensions have been developed such as interval fuzzy cognitive maps [12], fuzzy grey cognitive maps [13], intuitionistic fuzzy cognitive maps [14] and linguistic2-tuple fuzzy cognitive map [1].

The matrix representation of FCM allows to make causal inferences. In 2-tuple fuzzy cognitive maps [1] there are three possible types of causal relations between nodes represented in the matrix:

- $W_{ij} < s_{g/2}$, which indicates negative causality between nodes C_i and C_j. The increase (decrease) in the value of C_i leads to the decrease (increase) in the value of C_j (negative causality).

- $W_{ij} > s_{g/2}$, which indicates positive causality between nodes C_i and C_j. The increase (decrease) in the value of C_i leads to the increase (decrease) in the value of C_j (negative causality).

- $W_{ij} = s_{g/2}$, which indicates no relationship between nodes C_i and C_j (zero causality).

FCM aggregation makes the development of group causal modelseasier [15]. Experts have different experience or knowledge, so it seems logical that they might use different evaluation scales to express their opinions about causal relations in a FCM.

3 Extended Hierarchical Linguistic Model

The linguistic representation model based on 2-tuples defines a set of transformation functions for linguistic 2-tuple in order to carry out CWW process without loss of information [16]. This model has many advantages for working with linguistic information making it easy the elicitation of preferences and knowledge from experts [17].

Definition 1. [18] Being $\beta \in [0, g]$ a value that represents the result of a symbolic operation in the interval of granularity of the linguistic term terms set $s = \{s_0, \ldots, s_g\}$. The symbolic translation is a numerical value assessed in $[-0.5, 0.5)$ that supports the difference of information between a counting of information β assessed in the interval of granularity $[0, g]$ of the term set S and the closest value in $\{0, \ldots, g\}$ which indicates the index of the closest linguistic term in S.

The 2-tuple linguistic representation model defines a set of transformation functions between numeric values to facilitate linguistic computational processes.

Definition 2. [18] The 2-tuple that expresses the equivalent information to β is obtained with the function $\Delta : [0, g] \rightarrow S \times [-0.5, 0.5)$ given by,

$$\Delta(\beta) = (s_i, \alpha), \text{ with} \begin{cases} s_i, i = \text{round}(\beta) \\ \alpha = \beta - i, \end{cases} \tag{2}$$

where round is the usual rounding operation, i is index of the closed label, s_i, to β, and α is the value of the symbolic translation.

We note that Δ function is bijective [18] and $\Delta^{-1} : [0, g] \rightarrow S \times [-0.5, 0.5)$ is defined by:

$$\Delta^{-1}(s_i, \propto) = i + \propto \tag{3}$$

Then the 2-tuples of $S \times [-0.5, 0.5)$ will be identified with numerical values in the interval $[0, g]$.

In the proposal of 2-tuple fuzzy cognitive maps [1] the transformation of the 2-tuple value to the numerical equivalent value in the $[-1,1]$ interval is developed as follows:

$$\gamma:[0, g] \rightarrow [-1, 1]$$

$$\gamma(\beta): = \frac{2\beta}{g-1} - 1 \tag{4}$$

where g is the granularity of the linguistic term setS. This function makes it possible to develop the traditional inference process on FCM.

The ELH framework proposes a new way of building linguistic hierarchies (Fig. 2) and a novel unification process. To deal with any scale in the multigranular linguistic framework, extended hierarchical rules were proposed [19]:

- **Rule 1**: to construct an ELH, it should include a finite number of the levels, l(t, n(t)), with t = 1,..., m that defines the multigranular linguistic framework required by the experts to express their knowledge. It is not necessary to keep the former modal points among each other, it might be one.
- **Rule 2**: to obtain an ELH, a new level $l(t^*, n(t^*))$ with $t^* = m + 1$ should be added to keep all the former modal points of all the previous levels l(t, n(t)), t = 1,..., m within this new level.

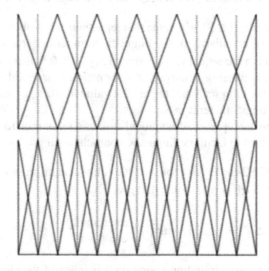

Fig. 2. A linguistic hierarchy of 7 and 13 labels [4].

An ELH is a union of the m levels required by experts and the new $l(t^*, n(t^*))$ that keeps all the previous modal points providing accuracy in the process of CWW.

$$ELH = \bigcup_{t=1}^{t=m+1} l(t, n(t)) \tag{5}$$

Values in level t can be expressed in any linguistic term set in t' level of the ELH by using the correspondent transformation function [19]:

$$TF_{t'}^{t}\left(s_i^{n(t)}, \alpha^{n(t)}\right) = \Delta^{-1}\left(\frac{\Delta\left(s_i^{n(t)}, \alpha^{n(t)}\right) \cdot \left(n(t') - 1\right)}{n(t) - 1}\right) \tag{6}$$

The transformations between levels of a linguistic hierarchy are carried out without loss of information.

4   Using the Extended Hierarchical Linguistic in Fuzzy Cognitive Maps

Our aim is to develop a framework for modeling causality based on the extended hierarchical linguistic model and fuzzy cognitive maps. The model consists of the following phases (graphically, Fig. 3).

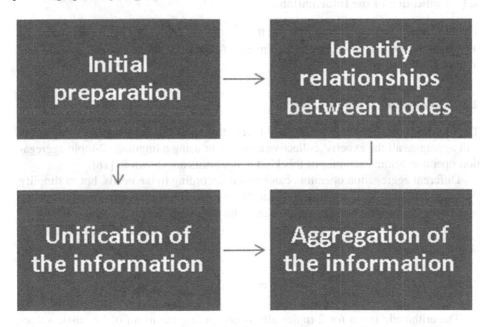

Fig. 3. A framework for using the extended hierarchical linguistic in fuzzy cognitive maps.

4.1 Initial Preparation

First, experts representing different points of view in the system to mode are selected allowing multi-expert causality modelling using linguistic 2-tuples values. Then, linguistic hierarchy (LH) is constructed. The multigranular linguistic frameworks offered by LH must satisfy several rules shown in [17]. Additionally, the limits of the system to be modelled are set and the nodes are selected.

4.2 Identify Individual Relationships Between NFR

For each expert his/her mental model is elicited using the linguistic term set previously chosen for expressing causality. The weight of the relation from node N_i to node N_j given by expert k is elicited by means of the 2-tuple linguistic model as follows:

$$w_{ij}^k = (s_u, \alpha)_{ij}^k \tag{7}$$

Experts use different linguistic scales to express causal relations according to their knowledge.

4.3 Unification of the Information

The unification process is based on the transformation function $TF_{t'}^t$ (4). By means of this function, we can develop a transformation function between any pair of term sets in the ELH.

4.4 Aggregation of the Information

The final aim is to obtain a collective FCM according to all experts. To do so, this process will aggregate all the experts' collective assessment using a linguistic 2-tuple aggregation operator. Some examples of this kind of operators are shown in [18].

Different aggregation operators can be used according to the needs, but to simplify the computation process we consider that all the experts have the same importance, so we use the-tuples arithmetic means to aggregate the FCM.

Let $x = \{(s_1, \alpha_1), \dots (s_n, \alpha_n)\}$ be a set of 2-tuples, the 2-tuples arithmetic means $\bar{x}^e$ is computed as [3]:

$$\bar{x}^e = \Delta\left(\sum_{i=1}^n \frac{1}{n}\Delta^{-1}(s_i, \alpha_i)\right) = \Delta\left(\frac{1}{n}\sum_{i=1}^n \beta_i\right) \tag{8}$$

The arithmetic mean for 2-tuples allows computing the mean of linguistic values without loss of information.

5   Illustrative Example

Software engineers are involved in complex decisions that require multiple points of view. One frequent reason that causes low quality software is associated to problems related to identifying and analyzing requirements [20]. Nonfunctional requirements (NFR) also known as nonfunctional-concerns [20] refer to global properties and usually to quality of functional requirements. It is generally recognized that NFR are an important and difficult part of the requirement engineering process; that they play a key role in software quality, and that is considered a critical problem [21].

Nonfunctional requirements are difficult to evaluate particularly because they are subjective, relative and interdependent [22]. In order to analyze NFR, uncertainty arises, making it desirable to compute with qualitative information. In software development projects analysts must identify and specify relationships between NFR. Current approaches differentiate three types of relationships: negative (−), positive (+) or null (no contribution). The opportunity to evaluate NFR depends on the type of these relationships. When two NFR which contribute positively or negatively to each other are composed, then one NFR will influence positively or negatively the correct working of the other [23].

Softgoal Interdependency Graphs is a technique used for modeling non-functional requirements and interdependencies between them but the types of contributions are only modeled using a limited scale [24]. Bendjenna [23] proposed the use of fuzzy cognitive maps (FCM) relationships between NFCs and the weight of these relationships expressed with fuzzy weights in the range 0 to 1. This model lacks additional techniques for analyzing the resulting FCM.

Interrelations among NFR are difficult to be assessed in a quantitative form. In that case, a better approach may be the use of linguistic assessments instead of numerical values. In this work we proposed a to model interdependencies in NFR using FCM, computing with words (CWW) and the extended hierarchical linguistic model (ELH) based on the proposal developed in this paper.

The granularity for each linguistic term set of the LH was defined based on linguistic hierarchy basic rules [25]. The first scale of linguistic term sets with cardinality 5 is used to provide causal relations (Table 1).

Table 1. Linguistic term set (S^5)

No	Label	Triangular fuzzy numbers
s_0	Negatively high (NVH)	$(-1, -1, -0.5)$
s_1	Negatively (N)	$(-1, -0.5, 0)$
s_2	Zero (Z)	$(-0.5, 0, 0.5)$
s_3	Positively (P)	$(0, 0.5, 1)$
s_4	Positively high (PVH)	$(0.5, 1, 1)$

Additionally a linguistic term sets with cardinality 7 is used to provide causal relations in the second scale (Table 2).

Table 2. Linguistic term set (s^7)

No	Label	Triangular fuzzy numbers
s_0	Negatively very high (NVVH)	$(-1, -1, -0.66)$
s_1	Negatively moderate (NH)	$(-1, -0.667, -0.333)$
s_2	Negatively light (NM)	$(-0.667, -0.333, 0.0)$
s_3	Zero (Z)	$(-0.333, 0, 0.333)$
s_4	Positively slight (PL)	$(0.0, 0.333, 0.667)$
s_5	Positively moderate (PH)	$(0.333, 0.667, 1)$
s_6	Positively very high (PVVH)	$(0.667, 1, 1)$

l(1,5), l(2,7) and a third level (Fig. 3) l(3,n(3)) l(3) = LCM(4,6) + 1 = 13 is defined, where LCM is the least common multiple [19] (Fig. 4). LCM was used in order to make the use and construction of an ELH simple rand minimize the granularity of the third level.

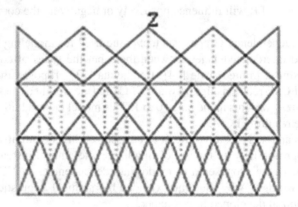

Fig. 4. An ELH of 5, 7, 13 labels.

The five non-functional concerns $R = (r_1, \ldots, r_5)$ are shown in Table 3.

Table 3. Non-functional requirements

Node	Description
NFR_1	Quality
NFR_2	Reliability
NFR_3	Functionality
NFR_4	Competitiveness
NFR_5	Cost

The experts provide the following linguistic causal relations:

$$W^1 = \begin{pmatrix} s^5_{\frac{5}{2}} & s^5_{\frac{5}{2}} & s^5_{\frac{5}{2}} & s^5_4 & s^5_{\frac{5}{2}} \\ s^5_4 & s^5_{\frac{5}{2}} & s^5_{\frac{5}{2}} & s^5_{\frac{5}{2}} & s^5_{\frac{5}{2}} \\ s^5_4 & s^5_{\frac{5}{2}} & s^5_{\frac{5}{2}} & s^5_{\frac{5}{2}} & s^5_{\frac{5}{2}} \\ s^5_{\frac{5}{2}} & s^5_{\frac{5}{2}} & s^5_{\frac{5}{2}} & s^5_{\frac{5}{2}} & s^5_{\frac{5}{2}} \\ s^5_{\frac{5}{2}} & s^5_{\frac{5}{2}} & s^5_{\frac{5}{2}} & s^5_1 & s^5_{\frac{5}{2}} \end{pmatrix}$$

$$W^2 = \begin{pmatrix} s^7_{\frac{5}{3}} & s^7_{\frac{5}{3}} & s^7_{\frac{5}{3}} & s^7_5 & s^7_{\frac{5}{3}} \\ s^7_6 & s^7_{\frac{5}{3}} & s^7_{\frac{5}{3}} & s^7_{\frac{5}{3}} & s^7_{\frac{5}{3}} \\ s^7_6 & s^7_{\frac{5}{3}} & s^7_{\frac{5}{3}} & s^7_{\frac{5}{3}} & s^7_{\frac{5}{3}} \\ s^7_{\frac{5}{3}} & s^7_{\frac{5}{3}} & s^7_{\frac{5}{3}} & s^7_{\frac{5}{3}} & s^7_{\frac{5}{3}} \\ s^7_{\frac{5}{3}} & s^7_{\frac{5}{3}} & s^7_{\frac{5}{3}} & s^7_1 & s^7_{\frac{5}{3}} \end{pmatrix}$$

$$W^3 = \begin{pmatrix} s^7_{\frac{5}{2}} & s^7_{\frac{5}{2}} & s^7_{\frac{5}{2}} & s^7_{\frac{5}{2}} & s^7_{\frac{5}{2}} \\ s^7_6 & s^7_{\frac{5}{2}} & s^7_{\frac{5}{2}} & s^7_6 & s^7_{\frac{5}{2}} \\ s^7_5 & s^7_{\frac{5}{2}} & s^7_{\frac{5}{2}} & s^7_{\frac{5}{2}} & s^7_{\frac{5}{2}} \\ s^7_{\frac{5}{2}} & s^7_{\frac{5}{2}} & s^7_{\frac{5}{2}} & s^7_{\frac{5}{2}} & s^7_{\frac{5}{2}} \\ s^7_{\frac{5}{2}} & s^7_{\frac{5}{2}} & s^7_{\frac{5}{2}} & s^7_0 & s^7_{\frac{5}{2}} \end{pmatrix}$$

The experts' information is transformed into linguistic 2-tuples in the level $t = 3$ by means of the transformation functions, TF^1_3 and TF^2_3. The results of this transformation are shown:

$$W^1 = \begin{pmatrix} s^{13}_6 & s^{13}_6 & s^{13}_6 & s^{13}_{12} & s^{13}_6 \\ s^{13}_{12} & s^{13}_6 & s^{13}_6 & s^{13}_6 & s^{13}_6 \\ s^{13}_{12} & s^{13}_6 & s^{13}_6 & s^{13}_6 & s^{13}_6 \\ s^{13}_6 & s^{13}_6 & s^{13}_6 & s^{13}_6 & s^{13}_6 \\ s^{13}_6 & s^{13}_6 & s^{13}_6 & s^{13}_3 & s^{13}_6 \end{pmatrix}$$

$$W^2 = \begin{pmatrix} s^{13}_6 & s^{13}_6 & s^{13}_6 & s^{13}_{10} & s^{13}_6 \\ s^{13}_{12} & s^{13}_6 & s^{13}_6 & s^{13}_6 & s^{13}_6 \\ s^{13}_{12} & s^{13}_6 & s^{13}_6 & s^{13}_6 & s^{13}_6 \\ s^{13}_{12} & s^{13}_6 & s^{13}_6 & s^{13}_6 & s^{13}_6 \\ s^{13}_6 & s^{13}_6 & s^{13}_6 & s^{13}_2 & s^{13}_6 \end{pmatrix}$$

$$W^3 = \begin{pmatrix} s^{13}_6 & s^{13}_6 & s^{13}_6 & s^{13}_{10} & s^{13}_6 \\ s^{13}_{12} & s^{13}_6 & s^{13}_6 & s^{13}_6 & s^{13}_6 \\ s^{13}_{10} & s^{13}_6 & s^{13}_6 & s^{13}_6 & s^{13}_6 \\ s^{13}_6 & s^{13}_6 & s^{13}_6 & s^{13}_6 & s^{13}_6 \\ s^{13}_6 & s^{13}_6 & s^{13}_6 & s^{13}_0 & s^{13}_6 \end{pmatrix}$$

The information is aggregated applying the linguistic 2-tuple arithmetic mean operator (6) [18].

$$W^{13} = \begin{pmatrix} (s_6^{13},0) & (s_6^{13},0) & (s_6^{13},0) & (s_{11}^{13},-0.333) & (s_6^{13},0) \\ (s_{12}^{13},0) & (s_6^{13},0) & (s_6^{13},0) & (s_6^{13},0) & (s_6^{13},0) \\ (s_{11}^{13},-0.333) & (s_6^{13},0) & (s_6^{13},0) & (s_6^{13},0) & (s_6^{13},0) \\ (s_6^{13},0) & (s_6^{13},0) & (s_6^{13},0) & (s_6^{13},0) & (s_6^{13},0) \\ (s_6^{13},0) & (s_6^{13},0) & (s_6^{13},0) & (s_2^{13},-0.333) & (s_6^{13},0) \end{pmatrix}$$

The collective FCM in s^5 is shown.

$$W^5 = \begin{pmatrix} (s_2^5,0) & (s_2^5,0) & (s_2^5,0) & (s_4^5,-0.444) & (s_2^5,0) \\ (s_4^5,0) & (s_2^5,0) & (s_2^5,0) & (s_2^5,0) & (s_2^5,0) \\ (s_4^5,-0.444) & (s_2^5,0) & (s_2^5,0) & (s_2^5,0) & (s_2^5,0) \\ (s_2^5,0) & (s_2^5,0) & (s_2^5,0) & (s_2^5,0) & (s_2^5,0) \\ (s_2^5,0) & (s_2^5,0) & (s_2^5,0) & (s_1^5,-0.444) & (s_2^5,0) \end{pmatrix}$$

Figure 5 shows the collective FCM in s^7.

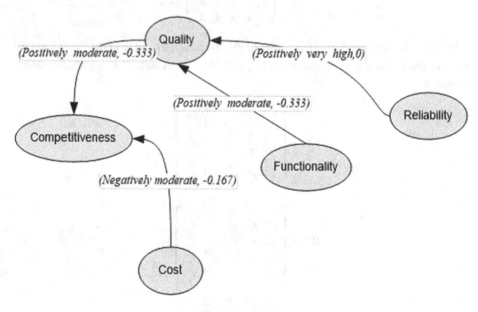

Fig. 5. Final FCM in s^7.

The experts found that FCM in conjunction with ELH offers great flexibility for representing causality. The interpretability of the 2-tuple linguistic representation model is another strength. Additionally, the resulting collective mental model can be useful for future decision support and knowledge management in software engineering. Software developer can use this FCM to increase the competitiveness and to improve the product quality through scenario and static analysis with high degree of interpretability.

The proposed model provides the flexibility for dealing with mental models elicitation with FCM defined in multiple linguistic scale contexts. Additionally, the computations of the proposed approach n are quick and simple.

6 Conclusions

FCM are useful for eliciting causal relations for multiple experts, this can involve problems defined in multiple linguistic scales contexts. This paper proposes a new framework for modelling FCM, using CWW and the ELH. The linguistic 2-tuples representation model is used to develop CWW process.

The inclusion of ELH in this model makes it possible to represent causal relation by means of linguistic information where experts use different linguistic scales to express causal relations. Building a 2-tuple fuzzy cognitive map using ELH follows amore similar approach to human mental models representation. An illustrative example applied to NFR modelling was presented showing the applicability of the proposal.

Further work will concentrate on three objectives:

- Developing a consensus model using ELH including automatic search mechanisms for conflict areas and recommendations generation to the experts to bring their mental models closer.
- Developing an expert system based on 2-tuple fuzzy cognitive maps for reasoning about interrelations among NFR.
- Developing new forms of inference 2-tuple fuzzy cognitive maps based on 2-tuple aggregation operators.

References

1. Pérez-Teruel, K., Leyva-Vázquez, M., Estrada-Sentí, V.: Mental models consensus process using fuzzy cognitive maps and computing with words. Ing. Univ. **19**(1), 173–188 (2015)
2. Obiedat, M., Samarasinghe, S.: A novel semi-quantitative fuzzy cognitive map model for complex systems for addressing challenging participatory real life problems. Appl. Soft Comput. **48**, 91 (2016)
3. Herrera, F., Martínez, L.: A 2-tuple fuzzy linguistic representation model for computing with words. IEEE Trans. Fuzzy Syst. **8**(6), 746–752 (2000)
4. Espinilla, M., Liu, J., Martínez, L.: An extended hierarchical linguistic model for decision-making problems. Comput. Intell. **27**(3), 489–512 (2011)
5. Axelrod, R.: Structure of Decision: The Cognitive Maps of Political Elites. Princeton University Press, New Jersey (2015)
6. Puente Águeda, C., Olivas Varela, J.A., Sobrino Cerdeiriña, A.: Estudio de las relaciones causales. Anales de mecánica y electricidad **87**, 54–59 (2010)
7. Kosko, B.: Fuzzy cognitive maps. Int. J. Man Mach. Stud. **24**(1), 65–75 (1986)
8. Papageorgiou, E.I., Salmeron, J.L.: A Review of fuzzy cognitive maps research during the last decade. IEEE Trans. Fuzzy Syst. **21**, 67 (2012)
9. Ping, C.W.: A Methodology for Constructing Causal Knowledge Model from Fuzzy Cognitive Map to Bayesian Belief Network, in Department of Computer Science. Chonnam National University. Doctoral Thesis (2009)

10. Leyva-Vázquez, M., et al.: Técnicas para la representación del conocimiento causal: un estudio de caso en Informática Médica. Revista Cubana de información en ciencias de la salud **24**(1), 73–83 (2013)
11. Leyva-Vázquez, M., et al.: Modelo para el análisis de escenarios basados en mapas cognitivos difusos: estudio de caso en software biomédico. Ing. Univ. **17**(2), 375–390 (2013)
12. Papageorgiou, E.I., Stylios, C.D., Groumpos, P.P.: Introducing interval analysis in fuzzy cognitive map framework. In: Antoniou, G., Potamias, G., Spyropoulos, C., Plexousakis, D. (eds.) SETN 2006. LNCS (LNAI), vol. 3955, pp. 571–575. Springer, Heidelberg (2006)
13. Salmeron, J.L.: Modelling grey uncertainty with fuzzy grey cognitive maps. Expert Syst. Appl. **37**(12), 7581–7588 (2010)
14. Iakovidis, D.K., Papageorgiou, E.: Intuitionistic fuzzy cognitive maps for medical decision making. IEEE Trans. Inf Technol. Biomed. **15**(1), 100–107 (2011)
15. Khan, M.S., Quaddus, M.: Group decision support using fuzzy cognitive maps for causal reasoning. Group Decis. Negot. **13**(5), 463–480 (2004)
16. Herrera, F., et al.: Computing with words in decision making: foundations, trends and prospects. Fuzzy Optim. Decis. Making **8**(4), 337–364 (2009)
17. Pérez-Teruel, K., Leyva-Vázquez, M., Espinilla-Estevez, M.: A linguistic software requirement prioritization model with heterogeneous information. In: 4th International Workshop on Knowledge Discovery, Knowledge Management and Decision Support (EUREKA 2013), Mazatlán, México (2013)
18. Herrera, F., Martínez, L.: A 2-tuple fuzzy linguistic representation model for computing with words. IEEE Trans. Fuzzy Syst. **8**(6), 746–752 (2000)
19. Espinilla, M., Liu, J., Martínez, L.: An extended hierarchical linguistic model for decision making problems. Comput. Intell. **27**(3), 489–512 (2011)
20. Ejnioui, A., Otero, C.E., Qureshi, A.A.: Software requirement prioritization using fuzzy multi-attribute decision making. In: 2012 IEEE Conference on Open Systems (ICOS). IEEE (2012)
21. Sena-Montoya, É.: Estado actual de la investigación en requisitos no funcionales. Ing. Univ. **16**(1), 225–246 (2012)
22. Chng, L., et al.: Non-functional Requirements in Software Engineering, vol. 5. Springer Science and Business Media, Berlin (2012)
23. Bendjenna, H., Charrel, P.-J., Zarour, N.E.: Identifying and modeling non-functional concerns relationships. J. Softw. Eng. Appl. **3**(08), 820 (2010)
24. Chung, L., et al.: Softgoal interdependency graphs. In: Chung, L., Nixon, B.A., Yu, E., Mylopoulos, J. (eds.) Non-Functional Requirements in Software Engineering. International Series in Software Engineering, vol. 5, pp. 47–88. Springer, Heidelberg (2000)
25. Martínez, L., Rodriguez, R.M., Herrera, F.: Decision making in heterogeneous context: 2-tuple linguistic based approaches. In: Martínez, L., Rodriguez, R.M., Herrera, F. (eds.) The 2-Tuple Linguistic Model, pp. 51–82. Springer, Heidelberg (2015)

Ontological Model of Knowledge Management for Research and Innovation

Ana Muñoz-García[1,2]($\boxtimes$), Katty Lagos-Ortiz[3], Vanessa Vergara-Lozano[3],
José Salavarria-Melo[3], Karina Real-Aviles[3], and Néstor Vera-Lucio[3]

[1] CEMISID Universidad de Los Andes, Mérida, Venezuela
anamunoz@ula.ve
[2] Grupo GIC Universidad Politécnica Territorial de Mérida Kleber Ramírez, Mérida, Venezuela
[3] Escuela de Computación Universidad Agraria del Ecuador, Guayaquil, Ecuador
{klagos,vvergara,jsalavarria,kreal,nvera}@uagraria.edu.ec

Abstract. Organizations should focus on effective knowledge management in order to improve their competitiveness in the current Knowledge Age. Given this need, ontologies have emerged as a new approach for the development and implementation of knowledge management systems. Ontologies allow applying modeling methods in order to design the structure of the organizational knowledge.In this work we present an ontology-based model for the knowledge management in research and innovation. The knowledge-based model proposed allows describing aspects such as the business model processes, the organizational intellectual capital, and the dynamic behavior of the processes of a research and innovation organization.

Keywords: Business model · Business process · Ontology · Knowledge management · Research and innovation

1 Introduction

Research and innovation are a mixture of different skills and activities. Throughout history, research and innovation as a way of knowledge generation have taken routes through which disciplinary knowledge has transited. These routes became less clear taking into account the current world, where the amount of information available in the Web and internal organizations have been steadily increased. Therefore, there is a need for new mechanisms that allow performing knowledge management activities in an efficient way. Knowledge management within university research institutions must be identified with the organizational culture, the dynamism of knowledge generation, and a multidisciplinary approach. This fact requires to consider the intellectual capital through its three areas, human capital, structural capital and relational capital, as well as the organizational learning. The present work is based on the business model processes and is focused on the research and innovation processes. Applying our approach to the aforementioned process will allow measuring and assessing the generation and dissemination of knowledge, as well as providing the users with this knowledge, avoiding withholding knowledge at the organization.

© Springer International Publishing AG 2016
R. Valencia-García et al. (Eds.): CITI 2016, CCIS 658, pp. 51–62, 2016.
DOI: 10.1007/978-3-319-48024-4_5

An ontology is a formal and explicit specification of a shared conceptualization [1]. It provides a formal representation of knowledge structures in a reusable and sharable way. Ontologies provide common vocabulary with different levels of formality for a domain. Also, they define the semantics of the terms and the relationships between them. Knowledge management processes require determining the structure of the knowledge in order to promote problem solving. As was previously mentioned, the ontology allows the representation and sharing of the knowledge. Therefore, we used an ontology-based approach in order to represent the knowledge generated from research and innovation processes.

In this work, we propose an ontological model for the knowledge management at a Research and Innovation center. This model describes the research and innovation processes and the technologies that support such activities. This work is structured as follows. Section 2 presents the state of the art concerning knowledge management. Section 3 discusses the justification of our model. Section 4 presents the theoretical basis of this model. The methodology followed as well as the model itself are presented in Sect. 5 and 6 respectively. Finally, conclusions and future work are presented.

2 State of the Art

Nowadays, there are research efforts that adopt an ontology-based approach for knowledge management. In [2] the authors present an integrated enterprise-knowledge management architecture, focusing on how to support multiple ontologies and manage ontology evolution. Another research effort is the presented in [3], where the authors present a generic ontology-based user modeling architecture, known as OntobUM, which is applied in the context of a knowledge management system. The proposed user modeling system relies on a user ontology, using Semantic Web technologies, based on the IMS LIP specifications, and it is integrated in an ontology-based KMS called Onto-logging. In [4] the authors present IkeWiki, a semantic wiki focused on collaborative knowledge engineering. This wiki provides support for different levels of formalization ranging from internal texts, to formal ontologies, and its sophisticated, interactive user interface.

Bueno [5] defines the intellectual capital as knowledge accumulation that generates value or cognitive richness in an organization. It consists of a set of intangible assets (intellectual) or knowledge-based resources and capabilities, which when put into action by a determined strategy in combination with tangible capital, is able to create value and core competencies in the market. The author recognizes the intellectual capital as an entrepreneurship and innovation generation system. Also, he emphasizes the role of the components or capital that integrate the model: human capital (Capital related to the people's knowledge), structural capital (Organizational and technological capital which refers to the knowledge related to the intangible assets created by the organization and its technological development), relational capital (Business and social capital linked to the intangible assets developed by the organization and the individuals who belong to it. Also, the development of this capital is based on the relationships established with the market agents and the society in general). On the other hand, the Intellectus Model [6] seeks the evolution capacity of the intellectual capital from a new component or entrepreneurship and innovation capital as a set of accelerators identified in the elements and variables of the aforementioned components, which act with a multiplier effect of intangible assets in the organization. Osterwalder [7] defines the business model as an abstract representation of the business logic of an organization through an ontology model. This model consists of three large blocks. The first block represents the resources, activities and third-parties that help to produce and maintain the offered value. The second group reflect the value of incomes and costs of the first block. Finally, the third block represents the customer-related activities.

The works cited in this section represent significant research contributions to the knowledge management area. However, they are not focused on the research and innovation domain, which is the focus of this work. Furthermore, this model is based on the Intellectus Model, the business model proposed by Osterwalder, and the process model for knowledge management proposed by Nonaka and Takeuchi [8]. Our approach aims to provide a model, supported by a technological architecture, for knowledge management at university research and innovation centers.

3 Justification

In 1998, higher education systems received a call from UNESCO to increase their ability to live in the middle of uncertainty, in order to meet social needs, change and bring about change under precepts of solidarity and equality, to preserve and implement rigor and originality, making scientific research a requirement to achieve and maintain an essential quality education level [9].Over the following decade, UNESCO ratified this call emphasizing the need for universities to become a dynamic factor of social development by means of its processes and resources. Among the recommendations made by this organization are [9]:

- Quality assurance requires qualified, talented, and committed teachers and researchers.
- Universities must pay special attention on the establishment of interinstitutional relations, aiming to encourage the generation and strengthening of the capacities of the countries, thus ensuring diverse sources of good academic staff in the fields of research and knowledge generation, at a regional and global scale.
- Research systems at higher educational institutions must have flexible organization in order to promote science and interdisciplinary at the service of society, establish an appropriate balance between basic and applied research, as well as to maintain effective links between global knowledge and local problems.

The impact of knowledge management on Research and Innovation at higher education is given by the changes produced in this new vision of the universities, which establishes that there must be interdependence between scientific disciplines. Therefore, from a point of view of Research and Innovation, knowledge management is imperative. Knowledge management supports research processes and its production activities, as well as the register of good practices.

The ontological model presented in this work provides the Research and Innovation center of the Agrarian University of Ecuador with a guide to managing the experiences and results of research activities, as well as a scheme for the creation of memory, experience, and knowledge of research and innovation. The proposed model focuses on four fundamental axes that support continuous knowledge interchange: (1) the register of researchers' experiences through their products, (2) the dissemination of such knowledge among research centers, universities, sponsors, and society, (3) the preservation of that knowledge, and (4) the availability and accessibility of that knowledge as needed. With this understanding, this model will allow continuous learning improvement and the generation, access, and application of that knowledge, thus providing competitive advantages such as talent, effective leadership, learning, and collaborative work.

4   Theoretical Bases

Ontologies have been applied to different domains such as biomedical [10], neuroscience [11], information management [12], finance [13], management [14] and cloud computing [15]. Osterwalder [7] adopts the ontology-based approach to represent the business logic of an organization. This ontological model describes the business model through nine blocks focused on the value of a business proposal oriented to the customers.

On the one hand, the basic components of knowledge management are the creation, preservation and transfer of knowledge [16–18]. Knowledge creation depends on the internal and external learning [19]. Preservation and transfer of knowledge enable the organization to have an organizational memory, thus making it possible the access to knowledge as needed [20]. On the other hand, the knowledge creation model proposed by Nonaka [8] distinguishes between tacit and explicit knowledge. This model is based on the relationship between tacit and explicit knowledge through socialization, externalization and combination processes.

Nowadays, the ontology-based approach represents the basis of current knowledge technologies. This approach requires an information and communication infrastructure that allows sharing knowledge. This infrastructure must include elements such as knowledge repository, directory of knowledge sources, directory of learning sources and groupware tools, among others [21].

In this paper, we propose an ontology-based model for knowledge management in Research and Innovation which is based on three main works, the CANVAS model [7], the Intellectus model [5], and the Nonaka and Takeuchi model [8]. The next section describes the methodology followed for the design of the aforementioned model.

5   Methodology

The methodology used to develop the model proposed in this work was adapted from the one presented in [22]. Figure 1 shows the structure of this model which is composed of three layers: business model and processes, knowledge management, and knowledge management technologies. These layers are represented by means of ontological models, this fact allows to represent all knowledge generated from research and innovation processes. In addition, the researcher can visualize the knowledge from the same perspective.

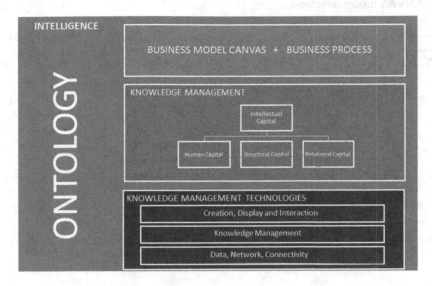

Fig. 1. Methodological structure for the development of Ontological Model for knowledge management in research and innovation.

The business model layer describes the logic of a research and innovation center, from the business model to its organization. The knowledge management layer describes the intellectual capital through the knowledge generated by business processes. The above-mentioned layers are supported by a technological architecture that allows the establishment of a collaborative environment.

The first phase of the design process consists of the identification of the business model and the business processes. Then, the intellectual capital is established based on the business processes and taking into account the knowledge management processes. These phases are supported by knowledge management technologies. Finally, all collected knowledge is represented by ontological models. The ontology development phase was performed by using the Ontological Engineering, specifically Methontology [23] and the Protégé OWL. The next section describes the ontological model proposed in this work.

6 Ontological Model for Knowledge Management in a Research and Innovation Center

As was previously mentioned, the first phase of the model design process was the development of the CANVAS model which describes the logic processes of a research and innovation center. This model is composed of nine blocks: key partners, hey activities, value proposition, customer relationship, customer segment, key resource, distribution channel, cost structure and revenue stream. Each block is decomposed into constituent parts defined at different levels of granularity that meet the specific needs. Figure 2 shows the CANVAS model developed.

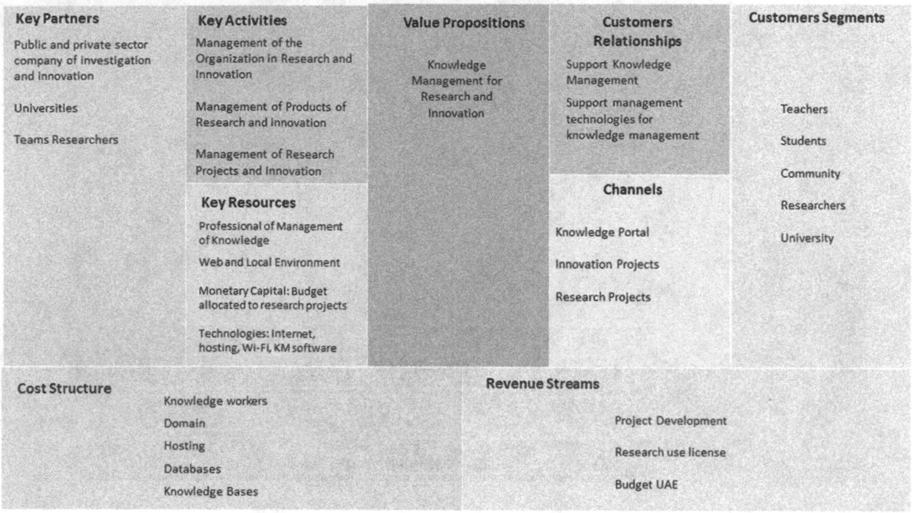

Fig. 2. Ontology business model CANVAS for research and innovation

This model is focused on researchers, teachers, students and universities. The value proposition of the business model is the effective performance of knowledge management in research and innovation centers. Figure 2 shows the key business activities which make up the CANVAS model, they are: organizational management, product management and the management of innovation projects sponsored by public institutions and other universities and researchers, and the resources such as laboratories and technological infrastructure. These activities are supported by the revenue sources managed from an established budget.

The activities described above are immersed in the intellectual capital parameters as follows: Human capital describes who does what in the organization and describes the roles, thus providing support to the organizational management. Product and project management are modeled by means of the structural and relational capital. These kinds of capital are presented in Fig. 3.

The organizational capital allows managing the following activities:

- The management of users and research groups. This activity takes into account the environmental conditions, which refer to the elements that guide the activities of the organization, including organizational culture, scientific and technological surveillance and external relations.
- The organizational culture is the set of values, principles, habits, rules and regulations governing the activities between researchers and research groups. These activities are composed of economic and university policies and internal and external

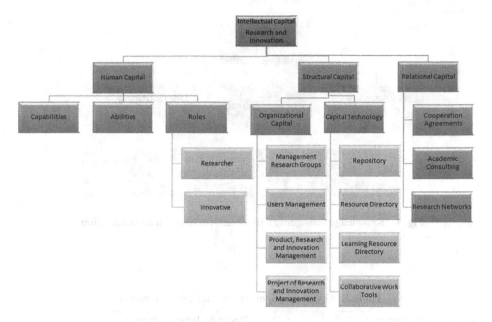

Fig. 3. Intellectual capital for research and innovation.

regulations that serve as a reference for the organization, structuring, and implementation of the research and innovation center.
- Product management. It consists of activities such as scientific and technological surveillance which aim to monitor the guidelines, progress and scientific and technological advances, by means of external variables that affect the domain to be monitored, thus allowing the generation of research and innovation products.
- Project management. It refers to activities focused on the planning, development and monitoring of research and innovation projects.

The technological capital contains the management processes related to the human, structural and relational capital. Relational capital manages both internal and external relations and research centers. These relations are generated through requirements, agreements, consulting and research networks. The processes of human, structural and relational capital and its sub-processes are complemented by the organizational activities such as those shown in Fig. 3. For example, the research group management is performed by the researchers who must have certain skills and abilities. These activities are supported by technologies. Furthermore, they have relationships with other researchers through cooperation agreement.

Figure 4 shows the knowledge management processes which are related to the development of the environmental conditions and the intellectual capital of research. These processes describe how the human capital must interact by using technological products and knowledge products that make up the intellectual capital of the model. These processes are represented using the model of Nonaka and Takeuchi [8] which allows representing the dynamisms of the model.

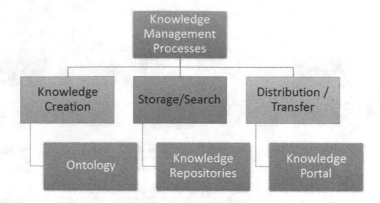

Fig. 4. Knowledge management processes for research and innovation.

Table 1. Ontology axioms of research and innovation

Natural language sentence	First order logic predicate
The Business Model of Knowledge Management of Research and Innovations have Customer Segments, have Customer Relationships, have Key Resources, have Revenue Streams, have Channels, have Cost Structure, have Key Activities, have Key Partners and have Value Propositions	V x BusinessModelR&I(x) => have (x, CustomerSegments) ∧ have (x, CustomerRelationships) ∧ have (x, RevenueStreams) ∧ have (x, Key Resources) ∧ have (x, Channels) ∧ have (x, CostStructure) ∧ have (x, KeyActivities) ∧ have (x, KeyPartners) ∧ have (x, ValuePropositions)
The Research and Innovation Knowledge Management have Intellectual Capital	V x R&IKM (x) => have (x, IntellectualCapital)
The Intellectual Capital have Human Capital, have Structural Capital and Relational Capital	V x IntellectualCapital (x) => have (x, HumanCapital) ∧ have (x, StructuralCapital) ∧ have (x, RelationalCapital)
The Human Capital have Role, have Abilities, and have Capabilities	V x HumanCapital (x) => have (x, Roles) ∧ have (x, Abilities) ∧ have (x, Capabilities)
The Role is a Novel Research, or is a Senior Research, or is a Novel Innovative, or is a Senior Innovative, or is a Group Coordinator	V x Role (x) => isA (x, NovelResearcher) V isA (x, SeniorResearcher) V isA (x, NovelInnovative) V isA (x, SeniorInnovative) V isA (x, GroupCoordinator)
The Structural Capital have Organizational Capital and have Technological Capital	V x StructuralCapital (x) => have (x, OrganizationalCapital) ∧ have (x, TechnologicalCapital)
The Relational Capital have Cooperations Agreements, have Academic Consulting and have Research Networks	V x RelationalCapital (x) => have (x, CooperationsAgreements) ∧ have (x, AcademicConsulting) ∧ have (x, ResearchNetworks)
The Knowledge Process have Knowledge Creation, have Knowledge Storage, have Knowledge Search, Knowledge Distribution, Knowledge Transfer	V x KnowledgeProcess (x) => have (x, KnowledgeCreation) ∧ have (x, KnowledgeCreation) ∧ have (x, KnowledgeDistribution) ∧ have (x, KnowledgeTransfer)

The knowledge creation process refers to the conversion of tacit knowledge possessed by researchers, students, and innovators, and also to explicit knowledge, for example by creating research and innovation products. The Storage/Search process is the set of actions that allow saving and searching the collected knowledge, e.g., the type of knowledge searching that occurs in technological and scientific monitoring. The Distribution/Transfer process refers to the information exchange that enables knowledge dissemination among internal and external individuals. This task is supported by knowledge management technologies such as ontologies. This ontology is obtained from the business model, the intellectual capital and the knowledge management processes for research and innovation centers. Table 1 shows the first-order axioms that describe and define the knowledge model.

The knowledge model is expressed through the first-order logic predicates shown in Table 1. These statements are translated through concepts, properties and axioms. Figure 5 shows the ontological model for research and innovation. It should be mentioned that this ontological model is based on the model proposed in [24]. The first version of this ontology is composed by more than sixty classes and three inferred classes. On the one hand, the orange ellipses represent the inferred classes, which are obtained through axioms. On the other hand, the yellow ellipses represent the asserted classes.

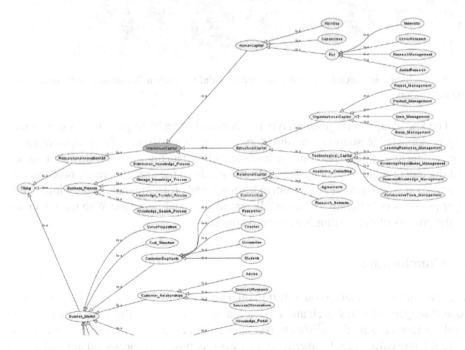

Fig. 5. An excerpt of the ontology of knowledge management for research and innovation. (Color figure online)

The technological architecture that will provide support to the model here proposed is based on the architecture presented in [25]. Figure 6 shows the architecture proposed in this work, which is focused on the research and innovation process.

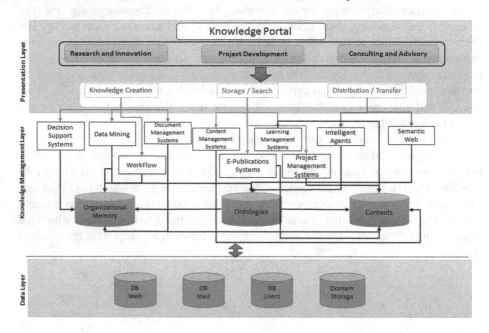

Fig. 6. Technological architecture of ontological model for knowledge management in research and innovation

The knowledge management layer is composed of technologies that support directory of knowledge sources, the directory of learning sources and groupware tools. Concerning knowledge creation, this layer considers data mining, workflow, ontologies and document management systems. With regards to the storage/search process, this layer provides a tool for content, system learning, and project management. Finally, this layer provides collaborative tools, intelligent agents, and Semantic Web tools focused on the process of distribution/transfer of knowledge.

7 Conclusions

The present work presented our effort to offer an ontology-based model for the knowledge management in research and innovation centers. This model aims to address the need for mechanisms that allows universities to improve their competitiveness in the current Knowledge Age. Furthermore, this work is based on successful applied works such as the Intellectus Model, the business model proposed by Oster-walder, and the process model for knowledge management proposed by Nonaka and Takeuchi.

In addition to the model proposed in this work, we also suggest a technological architecture that aims to provide support to the ontological model for research and innovation. This architecture will allow users to generate, integrate, and share the knowledge generated from research and innovation processes. The interaction among the layers that compose the architecture will be guided by the ontological model. It should be mentioned that, as future work, we plan to assess the ontology from a point of view of a particular criterion of application [26], in order to determine the effectiveness of its application in a research and innovation domain.

References

1. Gruber, T.R.: Toward principles for the design of ontologies used for knowledge sharing? Int. J. Hum.-Comput. Stud. **43**(5–6), 907–928 (1995). doi:10.1006/ijhc.1995.1081
2. Maedche, A., Motik, B., Stojanovic, L., Studer, R., Volz, R.: Ontologies for enterprise knowledge management. IEEE Intell. Syst. **18**(2), 26–33 (2003)
3. Razmerita, L., Angehrn, A., Maedche, A.: Ontology-based user modeling for knowledge management systems, in user modeling. In: Brusilovsky, P., Corbett, A.T., de Rosis, F. (eds.) UM 2003. LNCS, vol. 2702. Springer, Heidelberg (2003). doi:10.1007/3-540-44963-9_29
4. Schaffert, S.: IkeWiki: a semantic wiki for collaborative knowledge management. In: 15th IEEE International Workshops on Enabling Technologies: Infrastructure for Collaborative Enterprises (WETICE 2006), pp. 388–396 (2006). doi:10.1109/WETICE.2006.46
5. Campos, E.B.El: capital intelectual como sistema generador de emprendimiento e innovación. Econ. Ind. **388**, 15–22 (2013)
6. Bueno, E., Murcia, C., Longo, M., Merino, C., Real, H., Fernández, P., Salmador, M.: Modelo Intellectus: Medición y Gestión del Capital Intelectual, ResearchGate, November 2011
7. Osterwalder, A., Pigneur, Y.: Business Model Generation: A Handbook For Visionaries, Game Changers, And Challengers. Wiley, Hoboken (2010). ISBN 978-0-470-87641-1
8. Nonaka, I.: The Knowledge-Creating Company. Harvard Business Review Press, New York (2008). ISBN 978-1-63369-137-7
9. Bernheim, C.T.: Las conferencias regionales y mundiales sobre educación superior de la UNESCO y su impacto en la educación superior de América Latina, Universidades (2010). http://www.redalyc.org/articulo.oa?id=37318570005. Accessed 22 Jul 2016
10. Ruiz-Martínez, J.M., Valencia-García, R., Martínez-Béjar, R., Hoffmann, A.: BioOntoVerb: a top level ontology based framework to populate biomedical ontologies from texts. Knowl. Based Syst. **36**, 68–80 (2012). doi:10.1016/j.knosys.2012.06.002
11. Prieto-González, L., Stantchev, V., Colomo-Palacios, R.: Applications of ontologies in knowledge representation of human perception. Int. J. Metadata Semant. Ontol. **9**(1), 74–80 (2014). doi:10.1504/IJMSO.2014.059128
12. Colomo-Palacios, R., García-Crespo, A., Soto-Acosta, P., Ruano-Mayoral, M., Jiménez-López, D.: A case analysis of semantic technologies for R&D intermediation information management. Int. J. Inf. Manag. **30**(5), 465–469 (2010). doi:10.1016/j.ijinfomgt.2010.05.012
13. Lupiani-Ruiz, E., García-Manotas, I., Valencia-García, R., García-Sánchez, F., Castellanos-Nieves, D., Fernández-Breis, J.T., Camón-Herrero, J.B.: Financial news semantic search engine. Expert Syst. Appl. **38**(12), 15565–15572 (2011). doi:10.1016/j.eswa.2011.06.003
14. Hernández-González, Y., García-Moreno, C., Rodríguez-García, M.A., Valencia-García, R., García-Sánchez, F.: A semantic-based platform for R&D project funding management. Comput. Ind. **65**(5), 850–861 (2014). doi:10.1016/j.compind.2013.11.007
15. Rodríguez-García, M.A., Valencia-García, R., García-Sánchez, F., Samper-Zapater, J.J.: Creating a semantically-enhanced cloud services environment through ontology evolution. Fut. Gener. Comput. Syst. **32**, 295–306 (2014). doi:10.1016/j.future.2013.08.003

16. Grant, R.M.: Toward a knowledge-based theory of the firm. Strateg. Manag. J. **17**(S2), 109–122 (1996). doi:10.1002/smj.4250171110

17. Spicer, D.P., Sadler-Smith, E.: Organizational learning in smaller manufacturing firms. Int. Small Bus. J. **24**(2), 133–158 (2006). doi:10.1177/0266242606061836

18. Zhang, Z., Lee, M.K.O., Huang, P., Zhang, L., Huang, X.: A framework of ERP systems implementation success in china: an empirical study. Int. J. Prod. Econ. **98**(1), 56–80 (2005). doi:10.1016/j.ijpe.2004.09.004

19. Bierly, P., Chakrabarti, A.: Generic knowledge strategies in the US pharmaceutical industry. Strat. Manag. J. **17**(S2), 123–135 (1996). Wiley (2014). http://onlinelibrary.wiley.com/doi/10.1002/smj.4250171111/abstract. Accessed 22 Jul 2016

20. Cegarra-Navarro, J.G., Sánchez-Polo, M.T.: Influence of the open-mindedness culture on organizational memory: an empirical investigation of Spanish SMEs. Int. J. Hum. Resour. Manag. **22**(1), 1–18 (2011). doi:10.1080/09585192.2011.538963

21. Fernández-Breis, B.T., Martínez-Béjar, R.: A cooperative framework for integrating ontologies. Int. J. Hum.-Comput. Stud. **56**(6), 665–720 (2002). doi:10.1006/ijhc.2002.1010

22. Muñoz, A., Sandia, B., Páez, G.: Un modelo ontológico para el aprendizaje colaborativo en la educación interactiva a distancia. I Congreso Iberoamericano de Enseñanza de la Ingeniería, Margarita Venezuela, Noviembre 2009

23. Fernández-López, M., Gómez-Pérez, A., Juristo, N.: METHONTOLOGY: from ontological art towards ontological engineering. In: Proceedings of the Ontological Engineering AAAI 1997 Spring Symposium Series. Stanford University, EEUU (1997)

24. Munoz, A., Lamolle, M., Le Duc, C.: Un modèle ontologique pour l'apprentissage collaboratif en formation interactive à distance. 1er Congrès Natl. Rech. En IUT Tours Fr. (2012)

25. Muñoz, A., Lopez, V., Lagos, K., Vásquez, M., Hidalgo, J., Vera, N.: Knowledge management for virtual education through ontologies. In: Ciuciu, I., et al. (eds.) OTM 2015 Workshops. LNCS, vol. 9416, pp. 339–348. Springer, Heidelberg (2015). doi: 10.1007/978-3-319-26138-6_37

26. Brank, J., Grobelnik, M., Mladenic, D.: A survey of ontology evaluation techniques. In: Proceedings of the Conference on Data Mining and Data Warehouses (SiKDD 2005), pp. 166–170 (2005)

Sentiment Analysis and Trend Detection in Twitter

María del Pilar Salas-Zárate[1]([✉]), José Medina-Moreira[2,3], Paul Javier Álvarez-Sagubay[3],
Katty Lagos-Ortiz[2,3], Mario Andrés Paredes-Valverde[1], and Rafael Valencia-García[1]

[1] Departamento de Informática y Sistemas, Universidad de Murcia, 30100 Murcia, Spain
{mariapilar.salas,marioandres.paredes,valencia}@um.es
[2] Universidad Agraria del Ecuador, Avenida 25 de Julio, Guayaquil, Ecuador
{jmedina,klagos}@uagraria.edu.ec
[3] Universidad de Guayaquil Cdla. Universitaria Salvador Allende, Guayaquil, Ecuador
{paul.alvarezs,jose.medinamo,katty.lagoso}@ug.edu.ec

Abstract. Social networks such as Twitter are considered a rich resource of information about actual world actions of all types. Several efforts have been dedicated to trend detection on Twitter i.e., the current popular topics of conversation among its users. However, despite these efforts, sentiment analysis is not taken into account. Sentiment analysis is the field of study that analyzes people's opinions and moods. Therefore, applying sentiment analysis to tweets related to a trending topic also enables to know if people are talking positively or negatively about it, thus providing important information for real-time decision making in various domains. On the basis of this understanding, we propose SentiTrend, a system for trend detection on twitter and its corresponding sentiment analysis. In this paper, we present the SentiTrend's architecture and functionality. Also, the evaluation results concerning the effectiveness of our approach to trend detection and sentiment analysis are presented. Our proposal obtained encouraging results with an average F-measure of 80.7 % for sentiment classification, and an average F-measure 80.0 % and 75.5 % for trend detection.

Keywords: Twitter · Social media analysis · Sentiment analysis · Trend detection

1 Introduction

The messages posted in social networks provide a solid background about the ideas and opinions not only about the users of the social networks but also about the environment where they live. This information can be used and consumed by a wide range of institutions and organisms for strategic decision making.

Nowadays, Twitter is one of the most popular online social networking and microblogging services that enables its users to send and read text-based posts of up to 140 characters, known as tweets. Millions of users use Twitter to keep in touch with friends, meet new people and discuss about everything [1]. Companies are increasingly using Twitter to advertise and recommend products, brands, and services; to build and maintain reputations; to analyze users' sentiment regarding their products or those of their competitors; to respond to customers' complaints; and to improve decision making and business intelligence [2].

© Springer International Publishing AG 2016
R. Valencia-García et al. (Eds.): CITI 2016, CCIS 658, pp. 63–76, 2016.
DOI: 10.1007/978-3-319-48024-4_6

Several pieces of research have been conducted in recent years in order to automatically process the information on social networks [3–6]. An outstanding issue which provides research opportunities is trending topic detection. In the context of Twitter, trending topics represent the popular "topics of conversation", among its users [7]. Monitoring and analyzing this rich and continuous flow of user-generated content can yield valuable information. However, most works about trend detection fail to take sentiment into consideration. Sentiment analysis gives an effective and efficient means to expose public opinion timely which gives vital information for decision making in various domains.

In this work, we propose an approach, known as SentiTrend, to trending topic detection on Twitter and its subsequent polarity detection. SentiTrend collects messages from Twitter and processes them in order to determine their trending topic based on the TF-IDF (Term Frequency–Inverse Document Frequency) model. Then, an estimated positive, negative or neutral sentiment value is assigned to each tweet related to the trending topic detected. The task of assigning a sentiment value to a tweet is done using a free software from Stanford University, known as Stanford Classifier. The Stanford Classifier is a Java-based implementation of a maximum entropy classifier, which takes data and applies probabilistic classification [8].

On the other hand, it is worth mentioning that studies exclusively deal with the English language, perhaps owing to the lack of resources in other languages. Considering that the Spanish language has a much more complex syntax than many other languages, and that it is the third most widely spoken language in the world, we firmly believe that the computerization of Internet domains in this language is of utmost importance. For this reason, this work is mainly motivated in the Spanish language.

This paper is structured as follows: Sect. 2 presents the state of the art on sentiment analysis and trend detection on social networks. Section 3 presents the architecture and functionality of our proposal. Section 4 shows a set of experiments carried out to validate the proposed approach concerning the effectiveness of our approach to trend detection and sentiment analysis. Finally, Sect. 5 describes our conclusions and future work.

2 Related Work

2.1 Sentiment Analysis

In recent years, several researchers have introduced methods for sentiment classification. Most of these efforts are based on two approaches: the semantic orientation approach and the machine learning approach. Both approaches have their advantages and drawbacks. The semantic orientation approach is based on opinion words, namely, words that are commonly used in expressing positive or negative sentiment. Opinion words are typically contained in a dictionary called opinion lexicon.

For example, Ghosh & Animesh [9] presented a rule-based method that can be used to identify the sentiment polarity of opinion sentences. They use SentiWordNet to calculate the overall sentiment score of each sentence. The results obtained in this work indicate that SentiWordNet could be used as an important resource for sentiment classification tasks. Peñalver-Martínez et al. [10], meanwhile, propose an innovative opinion mining methodology that takes advantage of new semantic Web-guided solutions to enhance the results obtained with traditional natural language processing techniques, sentiment analysis processes and Semantic Web technologies. Their proposal is specifically based on three different stages: (1) an ontology-based mechanism for feature identification, (2) a SentiWordNet-based technique to assign a polarity to each feature, and (3) a new approach for opinion mining based on vector analysis. Montejo-Ráez et al. [11] presented an unsupervised approach for polarity classification in Twitter. They integrated SentiWordNet to compute the final value of polarity. The synsets values are weighted with the PageRank scores obtained in the random walk process over WordNet.

However, tweets are not considered "normal" pieces of text, since the 140-character threshold imposes limitations in the length. A further peculiarity of the tweets is the extensive usage of jargon expressions, abbreviations, and emoticons. A disadvantage is the fact that jargon expressions are often domain dependent. These factors lead to a low recall when the lexicon-based method is applied on informal corpora of text, like posts from micro-blogs [3].

An alternative approach is the application of machine learning techniques. This approach is based on using a collection of data to train classifiers. The drawback of the machine learning-based methods is mainly focused on the manual labeling required over massive sets of tweets. However, several pieces of research showed that the machine learning approach outperforms the semantic orientation approach [12].

For example, Mohammad et al. [13] propose a basic automatic system to classify tweets and determine who is feeling certain emotion, and towards whom. They trained a Support Vector Machine (SVM) classifier for that. Sidorov et al. [14], meanwhile, examine how classifiers work while carrying out opinion mining of Spanish Twitter data. They explore how different settings (n-gram size, corpus size, the number of sentiment classes, balanced vs. unbalanced corpus, various domains) affect the precision of the machine learning algorithms and experiment with Naïve Bayes, Decision Tree, and Support Vector Machines. Some other works [15, 16] combine NLP (Natural Language Processing) and machine learning techniques in order to increase the effectiveness of their method. Salas-Zárate et al. [15] present a method that uses a hybrid feature extraction method based on POS (part-of-speech) pattern and dependency parsing. The features obtained are enriched semantically through common sense knowledge bases. Then, a feature selection method is applied to eliminate the noisy and irrelevant features. Finally, a set of classifiers is trained in order to classify unknown data. Habernal et al. [16] present in-depth research on supervised machine learning methods for sentiment analysis of Czech social media. They explore different pre-processing techniques and employ various features and classifiers. The authors also experiment with five different feature selection algorithms and investigate the influence of named entity recognition and preprocessing on sentiment classification performance.

Finally, some other more recent proposals are based on psycholinguistic tools for sentiment analysis such as LIWC [17, 18].

2.2 Trend Detection

There are several studies that have addressed trend detection on social networks. For example, [19] present a trend prediction method for news event or news topics on Twitter.

Experimental results show that the method is simple and effective. The authors also propose and analyze several possible reasons for the trend rising and falling of news topics on Twitter. Kaleel & Abhari [6] propose a system for event detection and trending from tweet clusters which are discovered using LSH (Locality Sensitive Hashing) technique. Specifically, the key issues addressed by the authors are: (1) construction of a dictionary using incremental term TF–IDF in high dimensional data to create tweet feature vector, (2) leveraging LSH to find truly interesting events, (3) trending the behavior of events based on time, geo-locations and cluster size, and (4) speed-up the cluster discovery process while retaining the cluster quality. Ding et al. [20], meanwhile, focus on automated personalization of tweets for popular trending topics. The main objective is to classify the tweets information as "Like" or "Dislike" on a particular topic based on personal preferences. Martinez-Romo & Araujo [1] present a methodology based on two main aspects: the detection of spam tweets in isolation and without previous information of the user; and the application of a statistical analysis of language to detect spam in trending topics. Mathioudakis & Koudas [21] present TwitterMonitor, a system that performs trend detection over the Twitter stream. The system identifies emerging topics on Twitter in real time and provides meaningful analytics that synthesize an accurate description of each topic. Users interact with the system by ordering the identified trends using different criteria and submitting their own description for each trend.

We should state that our work differs from the existing works for two reasons: (1) Our approach is based on the Spanish language in comparison to most studies that exclusively deal with the English language, and (2) Our approach obtains an estimated positive, negative or neutral sentiment value for each tweet related to the trending topic detected.

3   SentiTrend Architecture

SentiTrend consists of a Back-End and a Front-End layer (see Fig. 1). On the one hand, The Back-End is divided into five main components: (1) Retrieve module, (2) Data extraction and verification module, (3) Pre-processing module, (4) Trend detection module, and (5) Sentiment analysis module. On the other hand, the Front-End consists

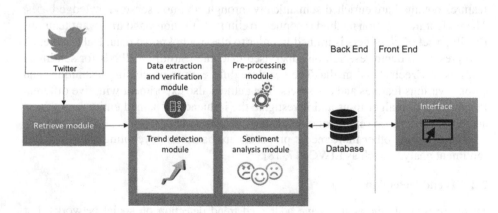

Fig. 1. SentiTrend's architecture.

of a web application developed in Java that allows users to view the trending topics detected, and the tweets corresponding to the selected trending topic including the percentage of positive, negative or neutral tweets.

3.1 Back-End Layer

As was previously mentioned, the Back-End layer is divided into five main components:

1. Retrieve module. This module is responsible for establishing, maintaining a connection with Twitter and retrieving tweets.
2. Data extraction and verification module. It avoids storing repetitive tweets and extracts valuable information from the tweets such as user, text, followers, etc.
3. Pre-processing module: This module carries out the data cleansing of each tweet by means of NLP techniques. In other words, it removes from the tweets information such as hyperlinks, emoticons, among others.
4. Trend detection module. It performs the trend detection based on a TF-IDF model.
5. Sentiment Analysis module. This module classifies tweets as positive, negative, or neutral.

A detailed description of the modules contained in the architecture shown above is provided in the following sections.

Retrieve module. This module handles establishing and maintaining the connection with Twitter servers to retrieve tweets. We use Twitter4J, a Java library that gives access to the Twitter API and assists in integrating the Twitter service into any Java application. In order to obtain useful results, we have established two search filters: (1) Track, and (2) Locations. The first filter consists of a comma-separated list of phrases which will be used to determine which tweets will be delivered on the stream. The second filter consists of a comma-separated list of longitude, latitude pairs specifying a set of bounding boxes to filter Tweets. Each bounding box should be specified as a pair of longitude and latitude pairs, with the southwest corner of the bounding box coming first. For example, to obtain the tweets from Spain, we need the following coordinates:

```
upper right point:
Latitude:43.834527
Length:1.423828
lower left point:
Latitude:36.119713
Length: -9.47461
```

Data extraction and verification module. In this module, information about each tweet is extracted. Also, a verification process is carried out. Next, a detailed description of the process performed is presented.

1. It obtains a tweet of the tail of tweets.
2. This module retrieves the tweet information namely, id, date, number of retweets, text, language, the user who wrote it, number of the user's followers and hashtags and users that appear in the tweet.

3. It verifies if a tweet is original or a retweet
    (a) If a tweet is original, it verifies if it exists in the database with its id
        (i) If the tweet is not in the database, a sentiment classification is carried out ("sentiment analysis module"), and all information is stored in the database.
        (ii) Otherwise, data such as number of followers, number of retweets are updated in the database.
    (b) If a tweet is a retweet, the original tweet is obtained, as well as its id, date, number of retweets, text, language, the user who wrote it, the user'sfollowers, the user name, hashtags, and users named in the tweet.
        (i) If the original tweet is not in the database, a sentiment classification is carried out ("sentiment analysis module"), and all information is stored in the database.
        (ii) Otherwise, data such as number of followers and number of retweets are updated in the database.

Pre-processing module. The pre-processing module carries out the data cleansing of each tweet by means of NLP techniques [22, 23].

The system carries out the following steps before extracting features from the text of the tweet.

- Slang words translation: Tweets often contain slang words. Slang word translation means converting the slang words like lol, omg, among others, into their standard form.
- Tokenization: The sentences are divided into words or tokens by removing white spaces and other symbols or special characters.
- Case Normalization: The process is to turn the entire tweet into lowercase.
- Stemming: It is the process of reducing all the remaining words to their respective stems. It is worth remarking that stemming finds the stem, and not the root of the words.
- The removal of Stop Words: A stop word is defined as a word that contains no meaning or relevance in and of itself. All words that appeared as the most frequent in at least 80 % were classified as stop words. If a word was identified as a stop word, it was removed.
- Identify presence of URL using a regular expression ("https?://\\S+\\s") and remove all the URLs from the tweet.
- Remove all the private usernames identified by @user and the symbol # of hashtags.

Trend detection module. This module performs trend detection through two main phases. Firstly, a set of simple and composite features are extracted. This process is performed by using n-grams (like unigrams, bigrams and trigrams) [24]. For example, the features obtained from the sentence "big bang theory" are the following:

```
unigrams: "big", "bang", "theory".
bigrams: "big bang", "bang theory".
trigrams: "big bang theory".
```

Secondly, in order to calculate the weight of the words, a TF.IDF model is used. TF-IDF is a statistical measure that is used to estimate the importance of a word in a document or in a collection of documents [6, 25]. Having said that, term frequency can be defined as:

$$tf_{ij} = \frac{n_{ij}}{N} \tag{1}$$

where n_{ij} is the number of times word i occurs in document j and N is the total number of words in document j.

$$N = \sum_{k} n_{kj} \tag{2}$$

The second definition is often referred to as the normalized term frequency. Inverse document frequency is defined as

$$idf_i = \log\left(\frac{D}{d_i}\right) \tag{3}$$

where d_i is the number of documents that contain word i and D is the total number of documents.

Therefore, the TF-IDF score for a word w in a document d is calculated by:

$$tf - idf = tf_{ij} * idf_i \tag{4}$$

Sentiment analysis module. The last module provides the negative, positive or neutral polarity of the tweets. Aiming to perform such a task, this module needed the previous development of a Machine Leaning-based module able to determine the polarity of a tweet, i.e. to determine if a tweet is positive, negative or neutral concerning a topic. The development of this module involved two main phases. Firstly, a corpus consisting of 1000 positive tweets, 1000 negative tweets, and 1000 neutral tweets was obtained. We used the Twitter API to collect the tweets. After downloading the tweets, each tweet was individually processed as described in a "pre-processing module" section. Also, we performed a manual review of the filtered tweets in order to make sure that the obtained tweets are relevant to our study. Finally, each tweet was classified by hand in order to ensure the quality of the corpus. This time-consuming task was performed in a period of 12 months by a group of five people with a great experience in the sentiment classification domain. We do not share this dataset the Twitter policy does not all us to share tweets contents.

Secondly, the corpus mentioned above was used to training a classifier, more specifically, we use the Stanford classifier, a Java-based implementation of a maximum entropy classifier, which takes data and applies probabilistic classification. We applied a Machine Learning (ML) approach as it has been applied in several works, achieving great results for sentiment classification. The Machine learning methods often rely on supervised classification approaches. This approach is based on using a collection of data to train the classifiers. Among the machine learning techniques commonly used in sentiment polarity classification we find Support Vector Machine (SVM) [26, 27], Naive Bayes (NB) [28, 29], and Maximum Entropy (MaxEnt) [30].

3.2   Front-End Web Application

SentiTrend provides a web interface where users can carry out the following tasks: (1) view the recent trends in real-time, (2) view tweets about a selected trend, as well as, the percentage and total of positive, negative, and neutral tweets.

Next, Fig. 2 shows the SentiTrend Web application.

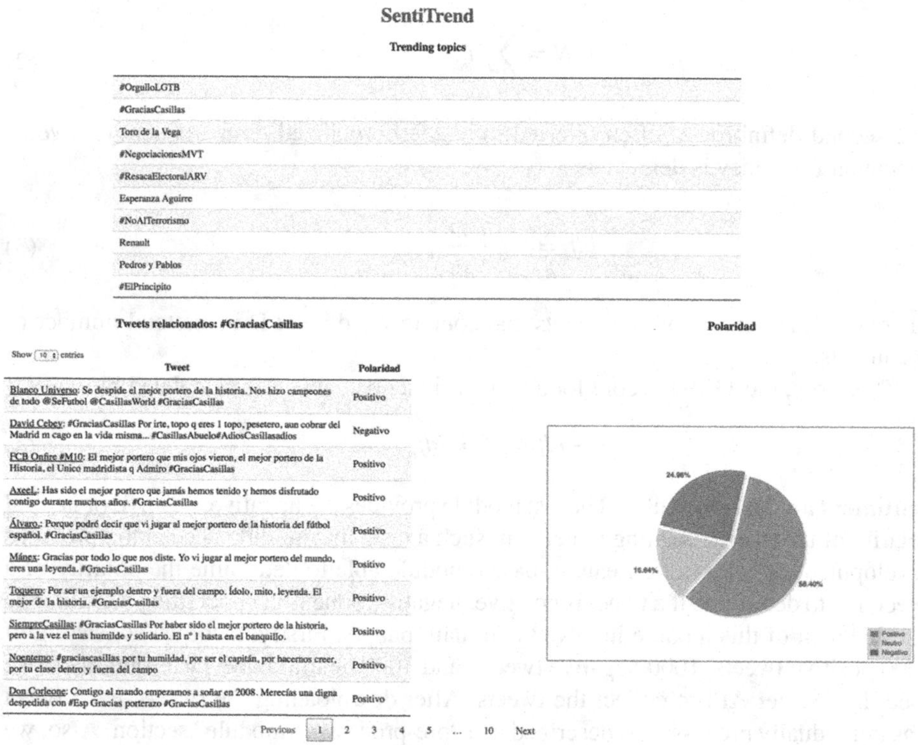

Fig. 2.   SentiTrend Web application.

4   Evaluation and Results

In order to evaluate the effectiveness of the system for sentiment classification and trend detection, we have used three evaluation measurements: precision, recall and F-measure. Recall (5) is the proportion of factual positive cases that were correctly predicted as such. On the other hand, precision (6) represents the proportion of predicted positive cases that are actually positive. Finally, F-measure (7) is the harmonic mean of precision and recall [31].

$$Recall = \frac{TP}{TP + FN} \tag{5}$$

where TP is the number of true positives and FN is the number of false negatives.

$$Precision = \frac{TP}{TP + FP} \tag{6}$$

where TP is the number of true positives and FP is the number of false positives.

$$F1 = 2 * \frac{Precision*Recall}{Precision + Recall} \tag{7}$$

The experiments carried out in this study are described in detail below.

4.1 Trend Detection

In order to evaluate the effectiveness of the system for trend detection, several experiments were carried out. The experiments involve obtaining results for different time intervals with our system (SentiTrend), Twitter API, and Trends24, and then, carry out

Table 1. Trend detection results obtained by SentiTrend.

Test	SentiTrend-Twitter			SentiTrend-Trends24		
	P	R	F	P	R	F
1	0.7	0.7	0.7	0.7	0.7	0.7
2	0.8	0.8	0.8	0.8	0.8	0.8
3	0.8	0.8	0.8	0.6	0.6	0.6
4	0.7	0.7	0.7	0.7	0.7	0.7
5	0.9	0.9	0.9	0.9	0.9	0.9
6	0.6	0.6	0.6	0.6	0.6	0.6
7	0.8	0.8	0.8	0.7	0.7	0.7
8	0.9	0.9	0.9	0.8	0.8	0.8
9	0.8	0.8	0.8	0.8	0.8	0.8
10	0.9	0.9	0.9	0.9	0.9	0.9
11	0.7	0.7	0.7	0.7	0.7	0.7
12	0.9	0.9	0.9	0.7	0.7	0.7
13	0.9	0.9	0.9	0.7	0.7	0.7
14	0.8	0.8	0.8	0.8	0.8	0.8
15	0.9	0.9	0.9	0.9	0.9	0.9
16	0.9	0.9	0.9	0.9	0.9	0.9
17	0.8	0.8	0.8	0.8	0.8	0.8
18	0.8	0.8	0.8	0.8	0.8	0.8
19	0.7	0.7	0.7	0.6	0.6	0.6
20	0.7	0.7	0.7	0.7	0.7	0.7
AVG	**0.8**	**0.8**	**0.8**	**0.755**	**0.755**	**0.755**

a comparison between the results obtained by the aforementioned tools. The experiments were evaluated using precision, recall, and F-measure metric. Aiming to calculate the corresponding scores, the following facts are considered.

- True positives: the items that were identified as trending topic by SentiTrend, Twitter API and Trends24.
- False positives: the items identified as trending topic by SentiTrend that were not identified as trending topic by Twitter API and Trends24.
- False negatives: the items identified as trending topics by Twitter API and Trends24 that were not identified as trending topics by SentiTrend.

Table 1 shows precision (P), recall (R), and F-measure (F) results obtained by Senti-Trend and Twitter API tools and SentiTrend and Trends24 tools for different time intervals.

As can be seen in Table 1, SentiTrend obtains good results for trend detection with an average precision, recall, and F-measure of 80.0 % with regards to Twitter API, and 75.5 % with respect to Trends24. In fact, the best result (precision, recall, and F-measure of 90 %) was obtained by several tests for both SentiTrend-Twitter and SentiTrend-Trends24. Also, the results show that SentiTrend obtains more matches of trending topics with Twitter than with Trends24.

Table 2. Sentiment classification results

	Precision	Recall	F-measure
1	0.800	0.800	0.799
2	0.800	0.800	0.799
3	0.817	0.817	0.817
4	0.813	0.814	0.813
5	0.810	0.810	0.810
6	0.801	0.800	0.800
7	0.807	0.807	0.806
8	0.830	0.830	0.830
9	0.774	0.773	0.773
10	0.789	0.780	0.782
11	0.832	0.803	0.813
12	0.817	0.817	0.817
13	0.807	0.807	0.807
14	0.816	0.817	0.816
15	0.794	0.777	0.780
16	0.846	0.843	0.844
17	0.800	0.800	0.800
18	0.844	0.843	0.843
19	0.766	0.763	0.764
20	0.833	0.830	0.830
AVG	**0.810**	**0.807**	**0.807**

4.2 Sentiment Classification

The experiments of sentiment analysis were carried out on a set of tweets related to a trending topic. For this purpose, the trending topic with the highest score obtained by SentiTrend for each of the twenty case studies presented in the previous section (see Sect. 4.1) was selected. Then, 300 tweets related to the trending topic were collected. Each of them was classified as positive, negative, or neutral by both, an expert group on sentiment analysis and the SentiTrend system.

Finally, a comparison of the results obtained by the aforementioned methods was carried out through precision, recall, and F-measure metrics. The evaluation results are shown in Table 2.

As can be seen in Table 2, the system provides encouraging results for sentiment classification of tweets in the Spanish language, with average Precision, Recall and F-measure values of 81 %, 80.7 %, and 80.7 %, respectively.

4.3 Discussion

General results show that the system successfully performs trend detection in Twitter and polarity detection.

With respect to trend detection, experiments show that the method is effective. However, much remains to be done about this topic. For example, we believe that analyzing fake content on twitter would be an interesting factor.

Regarding sentiment analysis, the system provides encouraging results. As mentioned above, we have used the Stanford Classifier to perform MaxEnt (Maximum Entropy) classification. The results obtained for the MaxEnt are very good. These results can be justified by the analysis presented in [32], where the authors mention that MaxEnt has been successfully employed for natural language processing tasks since the main advantages of MaxEnt are its robustness and statistic efficiency. However, it would be interesting to carry out several experiments with other classifiers such as SVM, BayesNet by using some machine learning tools, such as Weka [33] and RapidMiner [34], aiming to compare the results provided by several algorithms.

5 Conclusions and Future Work

In this work, we have proposed SentiTrend, a system for trend detection and sentiment analysis. We have also presented the experiments whose objective was to evaluate the proposed approach concerning trend detection and sentiment analysis. Our proposal yielded encouraging results, with an average F-measure of 80.7 % for sentiment analysis, and an average F-measure of 80 % and 75.5 % for trend detection with regards to Twitter API and Trends24, respectively.

In spite of all the advantages and possibilities of the proposed approach, it has several limitations that could be improved in future work. First, our approach is only able to deal with tweets expressed in Spanish, which is a disadvantage owing to the vast amount of information available in other languages. We shall therefore attempt to apply this approach to the English language. Second, our approach is not able to detect irony, sarcasm, and satire. These aspects can play the role of a polarity reverse, with respect to the words used in the tweet. This is one of the most interesting aspects to check in social media for sentiment analysis. We plan to integrate a module to detect irony, sarcasm, and satire. Third, in order to train and validate the sentiment analysis method, we collected a corpus, which was manually labeled by an expert group. However, we plan to use a standard/benchmark corpus in order to evaluate the effectiveness of our method and compare our results with other proposed works. Finally, another disadvantage of our proposal is that it is not able to identify spam users as well as spam tweets. Trending topics are a very effective method for tricking users into visiting malicious or spam websites. Accordingly, the attackers collect information regarding the most popular trending topics and include them in tweets pointing to spam websites. Therefore, we are interested in carry out a study regarding spam propagation through Twitter such as that presented in [35].

Acknowledgments. María del Pilar Salas-Zárate and Mario Andrés Paredes-Valverde are supported by the National Council of Science and Technology (CONACYT), the Public Education Secretary (SEP) and the Mexican government.

References

1. Martinez-Romo, J., Araujo, L.: Detecting malicious tweets in trending topics using a statistical analysis of language. Expert Syst. Appl. **40**(8), 2992–3000 (2013)
2. Atefeh, F., Khreich, W.: A survey of techniques for event detection in Twitter. Comput Intell. **31**(1), 132–164 (2015)
3. Kontopoulos, E., Berberidis, C., Dergiades, T., Bassiliades, N.: Ontology-based sentiment analysis of Twitter posts. Expert Syst. Appl. **40**(10), 4065–4074 (2013)
4. González-Ibáñez, R., Muresan, S., Wacholder, N.: Identifying sarcasm in Twitter: a closer look. In: Proceedings of the 49th Annual Meeting of the Association for Computational Linguistics: Human Language Technologies, vol. 2, pp. 581–586, Stroudsburg, PA, USA (2011)
5. Paltoglou, G., Thelwall, M.: Twitter, MySpace, Digg: unsupervised sentiment analysis in social media. ACM Trans Intell Syst Technol. **3**(4), 66 (2012)
6. Kaleel, S.B., Abhari, A.: Cluster-discovery of Twitter messages for event detection and trending. J. Comput. Sci. **6**, 47–57 (2015)
7. Benhardus, J., Kalita, J.: Streaming trend detection in Twitter. Int. J. Web Based Communities **9**(1), 122–139 (2013)
8. MacCartney, B.: Stanford Classifer, The Stanford Natural Language Processing Group (2015). http://nlp.stanford.edu/software/classifier.shtml. Accessed 18 May 2015
9. Ghosh, M., Animesh, K.: Unsupervised linguistic approach for sentiment classification from online reviews using SentiWordNet 3.0. Int. J. Eng. Res. Technol. **2**(9), 55–60 (2013)
10. Peñalver-Martinez, I., Garcia-Sanchez, F., Valencia-Garcia, R., Rodríguez-García, M.A., Moreno, V., Fraga, A., Sánchez-Cervantes, J.L.: Feature-based opinion mining through ontologies. Expert Syst. Appl. **41**(13), 5995–6008 (2014)
11. Montejo-Ráez, A., Martínez-Cámara, E., Martín-Valdivia, M.T., Ureña-López, L.A.: A knowledge-based approach for polarity classification in Twitter. J. Assoc. Inf. Sci. Technol. **65**(2), 414–425 (2014)

12. Ye, Q., Zhang, Z., Law, R.: Sentiment classification of online reviews to travel destinations by supervised machine learning approaches. Expert Syst. Appl. **36**(3), 6527–6535 (2009)
13. Mohammad, S.M., Zhu, X., Kiritchenko, S., Martin, J.: Sentiment, emotion, purpose, and style in electoral tweets. Inf. Process. Manag. **51**(4), 480–499 (2015)
14. Sidorov, G., et al.: Empirical study of machine learning based approach for opinion mining in tweets. In: Batyrshin, I., González Mendoza, M. (eds.) MICAI 2012, Part I. LNCS, vol. 7629, pp. 1–14. Springer, Heidelberg (2013)
15. Salas-Zárate, M.P., Paredes-Valverde, M.A., Limon-Romero, J., Tlapa, D., Baez-Lopez, Y.: Sentiment classification of Spanish reviews: an approach based on feature selection and machine learning methods. J. UCS **22**(5), 691–708 (2016)
16. Habernal, I., Ptáček, T., Steinberger, J.: Supervised sentiment analysis in Czech social media. Inf. Process. Manag. **50**(5), 693–707 (2014)
17. Balage Filho, P.P., Pardo, T.A., Alusio, S.M.: An evaluation of the Brazilian Portuguese LIWC dictionary for sentiment analysis. In: Proceedings of the 9th Brazilian Symposium in Information and Human Language Technology, Fortaleza, Ceara, pp. 215–219 (2013)
18. Salas-Zárate, M.P., López-López, E., Valencia-García, R., Aussenac-Gilles, N., Almela, Á., Alor-Hernández, G.: A study on LIWC categories for opinion mining in Spanish reviews. J. Inf. Sci. **40**(6), 749–760 (2014)
19. Lu, R., Yang, Q.: Trend analysis of news topics on Twitter. Int. J. Mach. Learn. Comput. **2**(3), 327 (2012)
20. Ding, L., Pang, C., Kew, L.M., Jain, L.C., Howlett, R.J., Weilin, L., Hoon, G.K.: Personalization of trending tweets using like-dislike category model. Procedia Comput. Sci. **60**, 236–245 (2015)
21. Mathioudakis, M., Koudas, N.: TwitterMonitor: trend detection over the TwitterStream. In: Proceedings of the 2010 ACM SIGMOD International Conference on Management of Data, pp. 1155–1158. ACM, New York (2010)
22. Paredes-Valverde, M.A., Valencia-García, R., Rodríguez-García, M.A., Colomo-Palacios, R., Alor-Hernández, G.: A semantic-based approach for querying linked data using natural language. J. Inf. Sci. (2015) doi:10.1177/0165551515616311
23. Paredes-Valverde, M.A., Rodríguez-García, M.Á., Ruiz-Martínez, A., Valencia-García, R., Alor-Hernández, G.: ONLI: an ontology-based system for querying DBpedia using natural language paradigm. Expert Syst. Appl. **42**(12), 5163–5176 (2015)
24. Agarwal, B., Mittal, N.: Prominent feature extraction for review analysis: an empirical study. J. Exp. Theoret. Artif. Intell. **28**(3), 485–498 (2016)
25. Elshater, Y., Elgazzar, K., Martin, P.: goDiscovery: web service discovery made efficient. In: 2015 IEEE International Conference on Web Services (ICWS), pp. 711–716 (2015)
26. Rushdi Saleh, M., Martín-Valdivia, M.T., Montejo-Ráez, A., Ureña-López, L.A.: Experiments with SVM to classify opinions in different domains. Expert Syst. Appl. **38**(12), 14799–14804 (2011)
27. Moraes, R., Valiati, J.F., Gavião Neto, W.P.: Document-level sentiment classification: an empirical comparison between SVM and ANN. Expert Syst. Appl. **40**(2), 621–633 (2013)
28. Xia, R., Zong, C., Li, S.: Ensemble of feature sets and classification algorithms for sentiment classification. Inf. Sci. **181**(6), 1138–1152 (2011)
29. Montejo-Ráez, A., Martínez-Cámara, E., Martín-Valdivia, M.T., Ureña-López, L.A.: Ranked WordNet graph for sentiment polarity classification in Twitter. Comput. Speech Lang. **28**(1), 93–107 (2014)
30. He, Y., Zhou, D.: Self-training from labeled features for sentiment analysis. Inf. Process. Manag. **47**(4), 606–616 (2011)

31. Salas-Zárate, M.P., Valencia-García, R., Ruiz-Martínez, A., Colomo-Palacios, R.: Feature-based opinion mining in financial news: Aan ontology-driven approach. J. Inf. Sci. (2016). doi:10.1177/0165551516645528
32. Shah, H., Bhandari, P., Mistry, K., Thakor, S., Patel, M., Ahir, K.: Study of named entity recognition for indian languages. Int. J. Inf. **6**(1), 11–25 (2016)
33. Bouckaert, R.R., Frank, E., Hall, M.A., Holmes, G., Pfahringer, B., Reutemann, P., Witten, I.H.: WEKA – experiences with a Java open-source project. J. Mach. Learn. Res. **11**, 2533–2541 (2010)
34. Hofmann, M., Klinkenberg, R.: RapidMiner: Data Mining Use Cases and Business Analytics Applications. CRC Press, Boca Raton (2013)
35. Antonakaki, D., Polakis, I., Athanasopoulos, E., Ioannidis, S., Fragopoulou, P.: Exploiting abused trending topics to identify spam campaigns in Twitter. Soc. Netw. Anal. Min. **6**(1), 1–11 (2016)

Cloud and Mobile Computing

Usage of Diabetes Self-management Mobile Technology: Options for Ecuador

Jose Medina-Moreira[1,2(✉)], Katty Lagos-Ortiz[1,2],
Harry Luna-Aveiga[1], Ruth Paredes[1], and Rafael Valencia-García[3]

[1] Universidad de Guayaquil, Cdla, Universitaria Salvador Allende,
Guayaquil, Ecuador
{jose.medinamo, katty.lagoso, Harry.lunaa}@ug.edu.ec
[2] Universidad Agraria del Ecuador, Avenida 25 de julio, Guayaquil, Ecuador
jmedina@uagraria.edu.ec
[3] Facultad de Informática, Universidad de Murcia,
Campus de Espinardo, 30100 Murcia, Spain
valencia@um.es

Abstract. Even though human kind has not even started to explore the vast expectrum of technology, it is doing its best to reach conclusions. Technology has indulged itself in many aspects that have favored the Human Race. Mobile Technology has met the accessibility, practicum, participation, feasibility and even the economic cost standards, which allows it to be the leader when it comes to select an ally that controls and treats chronic illnesses [1]. Having the discipline to follow a program of alimentation and indeed a new lifestyle is not that easy especially when the disorder is called diabetes. This investigation aims to spotlight the devices and apps currently used as an aid to control and adequately treat diabetes using m-Health focusing especially on the reality of Ecuador.

1 Introduction

Diabetes has become a social problem all over the world putting on alert to the public health systems in all the countries because of the expensiveness of its treatment. It has become one of the most dangerous, killing and steadily increasing illnesses. Ecuador is not the exception. It has considerably increased in the last ten years. By 2013, it was estimated that it occupied the first death cause reported by the official statistics of the Government of Ecuador[1]. According to INEC (Spanish acronyms for Institute of statistics and Censuses) 63.104 deaths were recorded in 2013 corresponding 4965 to Diabetes mellitus. By 2016 the situation has some variation as shown in Table 1.

These data do not consider people under the age of 30, which would considerably increase the total of cases mentioned in the table. According to the World Health Organization, a demographic change is being registered which affects the humanity worldwide. It is a fact that by the year 2020 the number of births will be less than the one of elderly people. The statistics show that nowadays there are 1,141,444 elderly

---

[1] http://www.ecuadorencifras.gob.ec/?s=diabeTes (Accessed June 8th, 2016).

© Springer International Publishing AG 2016
R. Valencia-García et al. (Eds.): CITI 2016, CCIS 658, pp. 79–89, 2016.
DOI: 10.1007/978-3-319-48024-4_7

Table 1. Number of death attributable to hyperglycemia

Age	Men	Women	Total
30–69 years	1010	1000	2010
70 years or more	1350	2360	3710
Total	2360	3360	**5720**

people in Ecuador. In 4 years it is estimated that this number will increase to 1,310,397[2]. That means that the demand of health services will be higher leading to the increment of public spending.

Indeed, Ecuadorian Society of Endocrinology expected that the number of cases existing today would not appear until 2025, however, the number of cases expected in ten years is now a reality. The sad reality is that a diabetic dies every two hours in Ecuador[3]. The other diabetes types are not mentioned but mellitus in these statistics. Undoubtedly, no matter what type of diabetes a person has, it is mandatory to have a correct management of the illness. As a matter of fact, diabetics must follow three clear "lines of action": (1) a nutritional plan, (2) a new healthy lifestyle including the practice of sports, and (3) taking appropriate medication along with the frequent medical control [2].

Nevertheless, how to promote a correct behavior among patients who do not seem to be conscious of their serious situation? This has become a problem for endocrinologists who have been looking for external support in the self-management of this chronic illness.

Technology devices like cell phones or tablets appear to be helpful enough to patients dealing with it. This goes beyond the way it has been working up to now. Traditional methods of control (talks, feeding schedules stuck on the refrigerator door, splitted containers to put pills, etc.) require an urgent updating that involve the patient in the process [3].

The new technological trend for these requirements is called mHealth. It consists on the use of ICTs to keep engaged and well communicated to the diabetic patient. In Ecuador is not common as expected and needed, therefore, it still has to be spread over the population in order to contribute significantly to the treatment and control of diabetes. International studies report that given the potential of the real-time communication provided by the app, both patients and care providers are able to be aware of its evolvement, promoting communication, sharing it or making decisions [4].

The research questions of this research are the following: how effective might the mHealth apps currently available in the play stores or app stores be? Is there a device besides the mobile phones offering a similar or better service to patients using it? Is Ecuador a good broth to develop the mHealth culture? If so, which ones must be recommended to diabetic patients and why?

---

[2] http://www.ecuadorencifras.gob.ec/proyecciones-poblacionales/ (Accessed June 8th, 2016).

[3] http://lahora.com.ec/index.php/noticias/fotoReportaje/1101748295#.V1m0N_nhDIU (Accessed June 8th, 2016).

2 App Classification

This study classifies several apps in different categories that are explained next.

2.1 Medical Management of Diabetes

In this category we can find the apps that have been verified by medical organizations to be useful for medical management of diabetes. In this category, WellDoc Diabetes Manager ("Bluestar") is the only app that has obtained FDA approval for use in the medical management of type 2 diabetes in adults [10]. The WellDoc system allows patients to track and record your blood sugar levels, and identifies trends of glucose patterns, offering a real-time response and clinical basis, serving as 'teacher' to people living with diabetes. In addition, this app can share data directly with the diabetes healthcare team. Bluestar can be obtained only by prescription from your doctor [17].

2.2 Tracking Apps that Display Information About Health

These apps allow the user to keep track of blood glucose, insulin doses, carbohydrate, weight and physical activity and review their data in different ways, such as raw numbers, graphs or summary values, as averages. A 33 % of the existing apps related to diabetes are of this category. Most monitoring apps require the user to manually enter health data in the app. Only a few apps can directly upload the data on glucose levels to a mobile phone, such as Glooko system, the blood glucose meter or glucometer IBTStarTelcare. MySugr is an app for daily use. Monitoring takes advantage from a playful style to keep users engaged and motivated. All these apps have been approved by the FDA.

2.3 Apps for Teaching and/or Form

Having access to information which allows patients to know everything related to their illness is an important factor to be aware of their treatment. Approximately 22 % of apps focused on teaching and/or training. For example, some apps teach the principles of carbohydrate counting using graphics and interactive games. Other apps are calculator's insulin dose suggesting dose of this hormone based on a target blood glucose value, the correction factor, the proportion of carbohydrates, the present level of blood sugar and calculating carbohydrates before a particular food. Tracking apps also offer training to users about the administration of medication, such as glucagon or aid in the use of devices [17].

2.4 Databases Food References

Since the diabetic patient's nutrition habits are one of the determined aspects in the control of the disease, then it is of the utmost importance to have available a data base relating the nutrition facts designed by doctor and dietitians. Approximately 8 % of the apps are references databases food carbohydrate counting. Another 5 % contained recipes for users with diabetes. Some apps combine guides for counting carbohydrates tracking tools [17].

2.5 Social Forums/Blogs

This category allows diabetic people to socialize among themselves. Approximately 5 % of apps are social networks, social forums or blogs that aim to connect people with diabetes so they can share information and experiences [17].

2.6 Apps for Physicians

In this category, the applications that can provide relevant information (reports, statistics) to the doctor are found in order to follow up and monitor diabetic patients. While most apps have been developed for people with diabetes, about 8 % are designed for the healthcare provider as a tool to give medical information. Other apps have been designed for diabetes magazines, and offer electronic access to articles [17].

3 App Analysis

The purpose of this study is threefold: (1) Screen the most popular apps available on the virtual stores and determine their effectiveness according to how they support each of the most patients' needs; (2) describe briefly the way each one works and provide a qualification that will determine how recommendable it is to the users; (3) suggest some improvements to the existing apps; (4) create and promote an mHealth culture in Ecuador through the information provided in this article considering the possibility of the intervention of the public authorities.

3.1 Methods

In order to guarantee the accuracy of the apps to be studied it was required to research on previous similar studies [5–8]. The aim was to find and analyze all the existing applications for diabetes in official stores for Android and IOS accessible to patients or users using the following terms: diabetes, glucose, sugar and insulin. On June 12th, 2016 the app store (IOS) was searched. As a result, 230 applications appeared after typing the expressions previously mentioned. From the 230, 6 applications were not considered in this research due to the lack of fulfillment of the functions proposed. Indeed, they got poor ratings and negative comments from users who had already downloaded them before. The same process was performed before in the Play Store (Android).

On June 9th, 2016 and after searching under the same key words, 224 applications were searched. It was found that 8 applications did not meet their specified function and also had negative comments from users. From both Apps Store and Play Store, a total of 440 applications that have features on diabetes such as monitoring and control of blood glucose; diaries entries to control diabetes; plans and recipes to maintain both sugar in normal levels and energy as well; magazines and information about the disease; weight control; exercise routines; glucose meter; cookbooks, etc. were screened.

3.2 Results and Findings

After the screen process, it was found that 102 applications were paid. IOS Apps might be purchased at prices from $0.99 to $49.99; while Android ones can be bought at prices between $0.97 to $41.58. In fact, 338 were freeout of the 440 applications screened, which considerably determined their popularity among users.

In addition, 53 diabetes-oriented Android applications were found according to the following parameters: Free Applications with the rating (star rating) of 4.0 to 5.0 that have been updated in 2016. On the other side, we can find 33 IOS applications following the parameters: free applications, with an evaluation of 12+ and 17+ (which means the age required to be a user) and having been updated this year were considered as the 10 ones chosen per operative system (see Fig. 1).

At the end, 20 apps were chosen as the ones proposed for Ecuadorian diabetic's users: 10 for Androids and 10 for IOS considering: accessibility to certain types of smartphones and popularity, as well as their functionality, usability, price and number of downloads as it is was done in the work presented in [9].

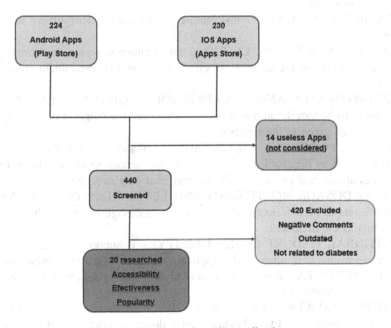

Fig. 1. Diagram of mobile applications.

Charts 2 and 3 show the 10 most selected applications for Android and IOS respectively. It's easily demonstrated that the most downloaded Android applications have been "MEDISAFE MEDICATION REMINDER" which has a million downloads while the other apps do not go beyond the one hundred thousand downloads. In other cases, the application with the most ratings has been "DIABETES:M" with a score of 4.7. All the Android applications that have been selected have a score of 4.2 downloads. On the contrary, the IOS apps do not provide such a detailed information.

Next, different functionalities related to the Diabetes domain were studied in each of the selected apps showed in Tables 2 and 3. The selected functionalities were the following:

1. GLUCOSE LEVEL REGISTRY. - this feature allows a daily registry of the glucose levels in blood.
2. SEND A REPORT TO THE DOCTOR AND/OR RELATIVES. - the moment the application collects the desired data, it emits a full report to the doctor or the relatives that are pending to such treatment.
3. STATISTICS/GRAPHIC ANALYSIS. - the applications represent the daily or weekly control throughout graphics or a statistic or resumed analysis.
4. MEDICATION INTAKE REMINDER. - this feature allows the mobile gadget to send a reminder of the medication that needs to be taken by the patient according to the doctor's prescription.
5. BODY WEIGHT REGISTRY. - this feature registers the patient's body weight daily.
6. PHYSICAL ACTIVITY AND/OR LEISURE ACTIVITY REGISTRY. - This feature provides a daily register of the physical activity done and the time taken to complete those activities.
7. SYNCHRONIZING DATA. - this feature allows data synchronizing with other gadgets.
8. STORING DATA IN THE CLOUD. - this feature allows data storage to be uploaded directly by the users to the cloud so it could be used again at any place and time.
9. CARBOHYDRATES AND CHOLESTEROL REGISTRY. - this allows for cholesterol to be monitored and it also registers the consumption of carbohydrates from the diets given to the patients.
10. SOCIAL NETWORKING. - this function establishes a connection with social networks such as Facebook or Twitter with the purpose to invite friends or send messages about their progress with the treatment they're receiving.
11. INSULIN DOSAGE MONITORING AND LEVEL REGISTRY. - it allows for insulin levels to be monitored or to calculate the dosage of insulin that is needed according to the treatment.
12. ADDITIONAL GADGET COMPATIBILITY. - it supports a wide variety of inter-connections with other health applications and medical compatible gadgets.
13. FOOD BASE DATA. - it incorporates a food data base to register the consumption of daily carbohydrates.
14. ALARMED TREATMENT CONTROL. - this function allows to receive reminders so the patient could take his/her insulin doses or other type of medications.

Table 2. Selected Android apps.

N°	Apps	Evaluation			
		Accessibility		Popularity	
		Type of mobile device	Cost	Downloads	Rating
1	DIABETES:M	ANDROID 4.0.3 (SUPERIOR)	FREE	100.000	4.7
2	BEAT0 DIABETES MANAGEMENT	ANDROID 4.0.3 (SUPERIOR)	FREE	10.000	4.6
3	DIABETES CONNECT	ANDROID 4.0 (SUPERIOR)	FREE	100.000	4.5
4	CON LA DIABETES	ANDROID 4.0 (SUPERIOR)	FREE	5.000	4.5
5	DIABETES APP - MYDIABETICALERT	ANDROID 4.0 (SUPERIOR)	FREE	10.000	4.5
6	MEDISAFE MEDICINA RECORDATORIO	ACCORDING TO THE DEVICE	FREE	1.000.000	4.5
7	GLUCOSIO	ANDROID 4.1 (SUPERIOR)	FREE	1.000	4.3
8	DIABETES & DIET TRACKER	ANDROID 4.0 (SUPERIOR)	$9,99	1.000	4.4
9	GLOOKO	VARIES ACCORDING TO THE DEVICE	FREE	10.000	4.2
10	SOCIAL DIABETES	ANDROID 2.3.3 (SUPERIOR)	FREE	50.000	4.3

15. HEALTH ADVISE. - it gives advice about preventive health for each of the patients, nutritional controls and general information for the treated illness.
16. MEDICATION RECOMENDATION. - they have a medication data base of with the manufacturers information, dosage consumption and advantages or disadvantages for each one.
17. ARTERY PRESSURE INFORMATION REGISTRY. - it allows the constant monitoring of artery pressure levels.

In Tables 4 and 5, the analysis features for both Android and IOS apps are shown. As it's shown according to the application categories, some have major functions than others. The "Diabetes:M" application has the highest number of downloads, but the "Social Diabetes" application does not feature the recommendation options about health or medication. On the other hand, others have the following applications: "Glucosio" and "Diabetes Connect" don't include a food data base nor treatment control alarm, which is why it can be concluded that many applications in such category are efficient in diabetes control but are not effective in a disease general treatment.

In the case of the IOS operative system applications, it has been determined that "Social diabetes" has the most completed range of characteristics, however, it lacks

Table 3. Selected IOS apps.

N°	Apps	Evaluation			
		Accessibility		Popularity	
		Type of mobile device	Cost	Downloads	Rating
1	SUGAR SENSE-DIABETES APP, BLOOD SUGAR CONTROL, AND CARB COUNTER	IOS 8.0	FREE	N/A	N/A
2	DIABETES PHARMA	IOS 8.0	$1.99	N/A	N/A
3	TACTIO SALUD: MI DIARIO DE SALUD CONECTADA	IOS 8.0	FREE	N/A	N/A
4	HYPERTENSION & DIABETES	IOS 7.1	FREE	N/A	N/A
5	IHEALTH GLUCO-SMART	IOS 7.0	FREE	N/A	N/A
6	SOCIAL DIABETES	IOS 7.1	FREE	N/A	N/A
7	GLUCOSE BUDDY-DIABETES LOGBOOK MANAGER	IOS 4.0	FREE	N/A	N/A
8	DIABETES IN CHECK: COACH, BLOOD GLUCOSE & CARB TRACKER.	IOS 7.1.	FREE	N/A	N/A
9	GLOOKO	IOS 8.0	FREE	N/A	N/A
10	EXERCISE DIABETES	IOS 9.2	FREE	N/A	N/A

Table 4. Features analysis of selected Android apps.

	ANDROID APP	Features																
		1	2	3	4	5	6	7	8	9	10	11	12	13	14	15	16	17
1	DIABETES: M	✓	✓	✓		✓				✓		✓	✓					✓
2	BEAT0 DIABETES MANAGEMENT	✓				✓				✓				✓				
3	DIABETES CONNECT	✓	✓	✓		✓				✓	✓							✓
4	CON LA DIABETES	✓					✓	✓										
5	DIABETES APP - MYDIABETICALERT	✓	✓		✓	✓	✓						✓	✓	✓			✓
6	GLUCOSIO	✓		✓		✓	✓			✓		✓				✓		✓
7	MEDISAFE MEDICINA RECORDATORIO		✓	✓	✓				✓				✓			✓		
8	DIABETES & DIET TRACKER			✓		✓			✓	✓		✓		✓				
9	GLOOKO	✓	✓				✓	✓		✓			✓	✓				
10	SOCIAL DIABETES	✓	✓		✓	✓	✓	✓	✓	✓	✓	✓	✓	✓	✓			
10	EXERCISE DIABETES	✓			✓		✓	✓		✓		✓			✓			✓

Table 5. Features analysis of IOS apps.

IOS APP		Features																
		1	2	3	4	5	6	7	8	9	10	11	12	13	14	15	16	17
1	SUGAR SENSE-	✓	✓	✓		✓	✓											
2	DIABETES PHARMA	✓				✓	✓					✓	✓					
3	TACTIO SALUD	✓	✓			✓	✓						✓			✓	✓	
4	HYPERTENSION & DIABETES	✓				✓										✓	✓	
5	IHEALTH GLUCO-SMART	✓	✓	✓		✓	✓	✓	✓	✓						✓		
6	SOCIAL DIABETES	✓	✓		✓		✓	✓	✓	✓	✓	✓	✓	✓				
7	GLUCOSE BUDDY-DIABETES LOGBOOK MANAGER	✓					✓			✓				✓				
8	DIABETES IN CHECK: COACH, BLOOD GLUCOSE & CARB TRACKER.	✓			✓					✓				✓		✓		
9	GLOOKO	✓			✓	✓		✓			✓			✓	✓	✓		

other important functions relating to the control and treatment of the disease like health recommendation and medication.

4 Conclusions and Future Work

Although Ecuador is a developing country, it has significant telecommunication infrastructures that will allow it to move forward and adopt new cloud services in the short and medium term, and to increase the coverage to provide more mobile devices, as well as Internet services. Indeed, the percentage of Ecuadorian population having a smartphone corresponds to 8.4 %, which means about 563,000 people, according to the latest data recorded by the INEC in 2011.

According to the Agency for Regulation and Control of Telecommunications (ARCOTEL) subscribers to Advanced Mobile Service (SMA) exceed 14 million until April 2016. According to the National Institute of Statistics and Census (INEC) 2015, 89.5 % of households had at least one cell phone, representing about 40 points more than that recorded in 2010. In terms of age, it is revealed that people between 35 and 44 years are those who have more cell activated with 83.4 %, followed by those 25 to 34 years, with 83.1 %[4]. Furthermore, according to the World Factbook by the CIA, Ecuador has 100 cell phones per 100 citizens[5]. These facts reveal an increasing tendency of having inhabitants who seem to be technology-friendly.

On the other hand there is a high demand for public health services according to the number of patients at different levels of hospital attention. It has grown rapidly according to report Ministry of public health in 2006, which mentions that 16.199.151 patients were treated while in 2014 figures increased up to 39,208,319.

---

[4] http://www.telecomunicaciones.gob.ec/telefonia-ecuador-tiene-mas-de-14-millones-de-abonados-al-servicio-movil-avanzado/ (Accessed June 8th, 2016).

[5] https://www.cia.gov/library/publications/the-world-factbook/geos/ec.html (Accessed June 8th, 2016).

This growth forces government to seek new forms of service to improve the activities of health care, without saturating public health institutions. The use of health technologies e-health and m-health may have an important role for this purpose. A strategy should be definitely created which aims at generating new regulatory policies and appropriate methodologies in use of health technologies for caring patients with potential chronic diseases such as diabetes. It is also necessary to establish an agency of evaluation in health technology and give proper promotion of services that allow educating the Ecuadorian population in adopting new services for health care.

It is important for health professionals and authorities to accept alliances with the private sector and higher education system in incorporating research and development R&D. It would be profitable to take advantage of state investment in health according to reports from the Ministry of Finance it has been increased from 535 million in 2006 to 1,774,000 in 2012.

All this is aimed at achieving a better life quality for Ecuadorian people. It will lead to reduce the number of people who acquire this chronic disease every year, causing a positive impact on each individual, family and the Ecuadorian state as well.

The results of this investigation show the reliability and efficiency of the cellular applications for the control and treatment of diabetes, just like the necessity that people have of its usage. However, application improvements need to be done in order to determine an integral solution for this problem. Thus, new models of orientation must be defined for the management of such knowledge to guarantee higher effectiveness and efficacy in the treatment of this illness.

In this investigation, 10 applications were selected for each of the operating mobile systems: Android and IOS. After studying 17 characteristics of these applications, none of them applies with the required function.

To conclude, it is noted that in the updated applications there is a lack of intelligent technology usage that can be based on knowledge to allow better monitoring, recommendation and management for the alarms.

As a future task, it is recommended to propose an application connected to the Cloud service covering all the characteristics based on intelligent technology like the tasks presented on [12, 13].

References

1. Årsand, E., Frøisland, D.H., Skrøvseth, S.O., Chomutare, T., Tatara, N., Hartvigsen, G., Tufano, J.T.: Mobile health applications to assist patients with diabetes: lessons learned and design implications. J. Diabetes Sci. Technol. 6(5), 1197–1206 (2012)
2. Gomez-Galvez, P., Mejías, C.S., Fernandez-Luque, L.: Social media for empowering people with diabetes: current status and future trends. In: 2015 37th Annual International Conference of the IEEE Engineering in Medicine and Biology Society (EMBC), pp. 2135–2138. IEEE, August 2015
3. Coleman, M.T., Newton, K.S.: Supporting self-management in patients with chronic illness. Am. Fam. Physician 72(8), 1503–1510 (2005)
4. Goyal, S., Cafazzo, J.A.: Mobile phone health apps for diabetes management: current evidence and future developments. QJM, hct203 (2013)

5. Tran, J., Tran, R., White, J.R.: Smartphone-based glucose monitors and applications in the management of diabetes: an overview of 10 salient "apps" and a novel smartphone-connected blood glucose monitor. Clin. Diabetes **30**(4), 173–178 (2012)
6. San Mauro Martín, I., González Fernández, M., Collado Yurrita, L.: Aplicaciones móviles en nutrición, dietética y hábitos saludables: análisis y consecuencia de una tendencia a la alza. NutriciónHospitalaria **30**(1), 15–24 (2014)
7. Rosser, B.A., Eccleston, C.: Smartphone applications for pain management. J. Telemed. Telecare **17**(6), 308–312 (2011)
8. Huckvale, K., Car, M., Morrison, C., Car, J.: Apps for asthma self-management: a systematic assessment of content and tools. BMC Med. **10**(1), 1 (2012)
9. Demidowich, A.P., Lu, K., Tamler, R., Bloomgarden, Z.: An evaluation of diabetes self-management applications for Android smartphones. J. Telemed. Telecare **18**(4), 235–238 (2012)
10. Dolan, B.: FDA clears WellDoc for diabetes management (2010). http://mobihealthnews.com/8539/fda-clears-welldoc-for-diabetes-management. Accessed 8 June 2016
11. Lee, J.: Hype or hope for diabetes mobile health applications? Diabetes Res. Clin. Pract. **106**(2), 390–392 (2014)
12. Mantwill, S., Fiordelli, M., Ludolph, R., Schulz, P.J.: EMPOWER-support of patient empowerment by an intelligent self-management pathway for patients: study protocol. BMC Med. Inf. Dec. Mak. **15**(1), 1 (2015)
13. Darabi, Z., Zarandi, M.F., Solgi, S.S., Turksen, I.B.: An intelligent multi-agent system architecture for enhancing self-management of type 2 diabetic patients. In: 2015 IEEE Conference on Computational Intelligence in Bioinformatics and Computational Biology (CIBCB), pp. 1–8. IEEE, August 2015

A Cloud Computing Based Framework for Storage and Processing of Meteorological Data

Maritza Aguirre-Munizaga[1(✉)], Raquel Gomez[1], María Aviles[1],
Mitchell Vasquez[1], and G. Cristina Recalde-Coronel[2,3]

[1] Facultad de Ciencias Agrarias, Escuela de Ingeniería en Computación e Informática,
Universidad Agraria del Ecuador, Av. 25 de Julio y Pio Jaramillo,
P.O. BOX 09-04-100 Guayaquil, Ecuador
`{maguirre,rgomez,maviles,mvasquez}@uagraria.edu.ec`
[2] Department of Earth and Planetary Sciences, Johns Hopkins University,
Baltimore, MD 21218, USA
`grecald1@jhu.edu`
[3] Facultad de Ingeniería Marítima, Ciencias Biológicas, Oceánicas y Recursos Naturales,
Escuela Superior Politécnica del Litoral, Campus Gustavo Galindo km 30.5 Vía Perimetral,
P.O. Box 09-01-5863 Guayaquil, Ecuador

Abstract. This document shows an analysis of emerging technology for the recovery of meteorological data and its cost-benefit using GPRS (General Packet Radio Service) data transfer in automatic meteorological stations to improve the monitoring and the prediction of the atmosphere and inland water behavior in Ecuador. In different areas of study comparisons between data or generated registers coming from Automatic Weather Station (AWS) and Conventional Weather Station (CWS) have been made. Therefore, here the authors mainly underline the importance of storing meteorological information using cloud computing. Among the benefits of cloud computing there are high data availability access and high efficiency in technical/scientific studies at lower cost due to the decrease of local investment in technological infrastructure, upgrades, maintenance of equipment and applications.

Keywords: Cloud computing · GPRS · Meteorology · Weather Station

1 Introduction

In the last few years decision makers and general public have recognized the importance to have a meteorological station network in-situ that provides accurate information to be used for both surveillance and forecast of weather, hydrological surveillance, agro-meteorological prediction or to reduce climate risk [1]. In this way the WMO –World Meteorological Organization –established the creation of the Global Framework for Climate Services (GFCS), to promote the best access and use of the climate information for the users [2]. Moreover regional efforts have been done, for example the "Latin American Observatory for Climate Events" [3] which through a database (http://dato-teca.ole2.org/) gives access to different resources for hydro-meteorological data as well as climate forecast that could be directly query by the users in an interactive manner. In

© Springer International Publishing AG 2016
R. Valencia-García et al. (Eds.): CITI 2016, CCIS 658, pp. 90–101, 2016.
DOI: 10.1007/978-3-319-48024-4_8

the same line, the CIFEN (Centro Internacional para la Investigación del Fenómeno de El Niño) participates in The International Climate Assessment & Dataset (ICA&D), which integrates meteorological, hydrological and climate information for the Andean region and supports decision makers. There is also a running regional program called PRASDES [4], which recovers and keeps meteorological, hydrological and climate information to have access to accurate and up-to-date information.

The National Institute of Meteorology and Hydrology (INAMHI) is the Ecuadorian meteorological and hydrological national service which is the responsible for delivering information related to the weather, climate and hydrological resources. INAMHI has been a key factor in the development of new projects related to weather services for the whole country, among which we can find those related to public health (for example [5, 6]) as well as agriculture. These projects have been made possible due to the automatic and conventional INAMHI weather station infrastructure, which provides the necessary data to carry out climate studies and to create new products for climate-related activities [7].

In the present study the technology that is currently used to process and keep data is analyzed in order to propose a model for the management of meteorological information through cloud computing. For example, [8] underlines the importance of the cloud for storage and information processing. Additionally, studies were done for this service application under different perspectives. Cloud storage gives the opportunity to have high availability over the historical and updated real time meteorological data to help to scientific and technical communities to access to information so that different studies can be carried out. Research also mentions [9] that in Ecuador there exists some inconvenient to data acquisition due to the fact that this job is still done manually. Consequently, in the first place we will show a short description of the model that is currently used for the manual register of data in the Conventional Weather Stations (CWS); in the second place, we talk about the transfer model through Automatic Weather Stations (AWS); and finally, we show the proposed model which consists of using cloud computing to manage meteorological data, and of which main goal is to offer access to storage data in real time using actual technologies.

2   Station Types Used in Ecuador

According to research done by different institutions dedicated to meteorological data observation in Ecuador [10], there is 2 main station types: conventional and automatic meteorological stations.

2.1   Conventional Weather Station (CWS)

A CWS is a mechanic equipment that is used to collect values of meteorological variables based on the instruments located on site to do these measures. According to related literature[10] there are three types of stations: the main station, which does five daily observations with a minimum of nine variables; the secondary station doing three daily observations with a minimum of three variables; and the precipitation measure, which does one observation per day. For this article it is considered a secondary station as reference for future comparison.

The secondary weather station does three daily observations of three variables minimum [10]; among the meteorological instrumentation we consider the following:

- Meteorological shelter: it is a box designed to protect the instruments that measure the temperature; it is usually white painted.
- Thermal hygrograph: it is an instrument used to measure temperature and relative humidity.
- Heliograph: it is used to register sunlight intensity.
- Rain gauge: it is used to measure the amount of precipitation that occurred in a specific period of time, with the help of a test tube. It is installed with WMO specifications.
- Weather-vane: it helps to generate wind data.
- Anemometer: it helps to register wind speed observations.
- Barometer: it helps the user to register atmospheric pressure.

2.1.1 Manual Data Transmission for the CWS

According to the web page of Ecuador meteorological service data from conventional station exist from 1990 in Ecuador [11].

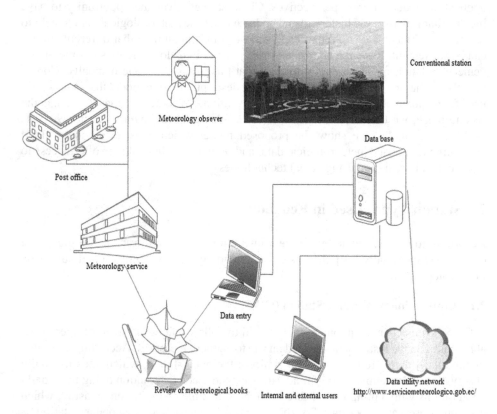

Fig. 1. Representation of how information is sent from conventional stations to the meteorological service.

Figure 1 shows the manual data transmission for CWS. As can be seen, the weather data is collected for a technical officer called Observer, who registers the weather observations in meteorological notebooks; once it is completed, the observer brings the information to the closest local office. It is important to mention that these documents frequently get lost due to some inconvenient in the transport or postal service.

Once the data is saved in the database, technicians make a data quality control of the data, following the normalized standards suggested by the WMO to accomplish with the worldwide required standards.

2.2 Automatic Meteorological Station

For this study we have developed a functioning analysis for a basic automatic meteorological station that measures speed and direction of the wind, humidity, temperature, sunlight intensity and atmospheric pressure. The station has two ways to collect information. Figure 2 shows that meteorological observation registered by the sensors initially is stored in the internal memory of a datalogger to be transmitted by GPRS to a specific storage site. There is another option to download data from the datalogger directly to a computer through software called Lizard [12]. Daily data from the Data logger could be downloaded through RS 232 [12] and RS485 [12] serial protocols for further analysis.

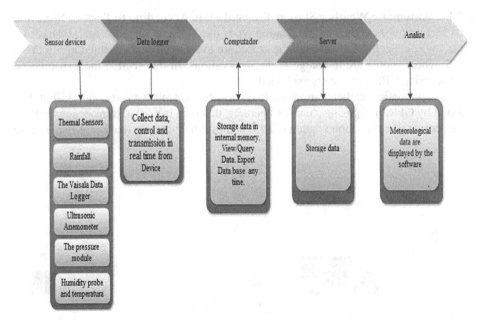

Fig. 2. The Treasure Data Cloud Computing depicts transmission flow for data based in the analysis done in this article; the information after collection is kept in a server so it must be extracted for further analysis.

In order to detail the sensors, Table 1 shows a description of the devices that are part of an automatic meteorological station. These sensors must be calibrated with special instruments at least every two years to confirm if the observations are done correctly. For this type of stations there is also installation standards based on WMO recommendations. The stations are generally installed in a place separated from buildings or tree shadow in a 6 * 6 m^2 room.

Table 1. Sensor description and automatic meteorological specifications analyzed in this article

Devices	Descriptions
Thermal sensors	It is a solar radiation sensor that is applied in most common solar radiation observations
Rainfall	It is a freestanding receptacle for measuring precipitation
Data logger QML201C	It incorporates Vaisala's proven sensor technology
Ultrasonic Anemometer	It is a wind tunnel fully tested and calibrated to provide reliable and accurate wind measurement
The pressure module BAROCAP	It has excellent accuracy, repeatability and long term stability in a wide range of operating temperatures
Humidity probe and temperature	It provides reliable measurement of humidity and temperature

2.2.1   Automatic Weather Station Transmission, According to Present Situation

This section refers to the communication types used to send meteorological data from each AWS; in Sect. 2.1.1 we detail the procedure to send the data collected in situ in the CWS, where people are in charge to do observations. In this section the transmission scheme using GPRS service is explained.

The automatic weather station has two ways to transmit data, see Fig. 3; first data are sent by GPRS [13] using a mobile operator; this path is used to transfer information from remote site; the second option is a 1.6 MB internal memory that keeps data in case

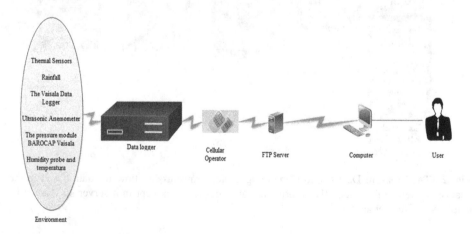

Fig. 3.   Current infrastructure of the AWS.

the GPRS transceiver is not working. If this happened the data are queued to be transmitted as soon as the GPRS signal is available.

Additionally, the station has a third option which consists in a 2 GB external memory that keeps all the data registered by the sensors; this is useful because at the moment to do a maintenance in the AWS, the data could be downloaded to a local computer by a proprietary software of the equipment provider to manage the configuration of equipment and to download data in a direct way. It should be mentioned that the time interval when the data are collected is configurable by the technician that manages the AWS.

3   Transmission Model, Storage and Processing Through Cloud Computing

As regards cloud computing, this study suggests the storage and information processing in the cloud. We resort to previous studies [14] in which the use of the cloud is emphasized to control different processes. One of these processes consists of delivering computer efficiency products in order to improve the monitoring of different atmospheric variables, meteorological forecast, and climate analysis national wide. Integrated management of the cloud resources [15] automatizes and reduces process execution time. Taking into consideration other similar studies [16], for the implementation of this proposal cloud services will be used namely virtual servers and storage.

We have also analyzed that cloud computing can play an important role integrating environmental information, offering processing and storage possibilities on demand. Example [17] -which is based on urban management- helps to identify a generic set of technical skills in information intelligence, and it proposes a SIAA layer architecture by using different cloud-based scenarios. Figure 4 shows the data transfer process of inclusion.

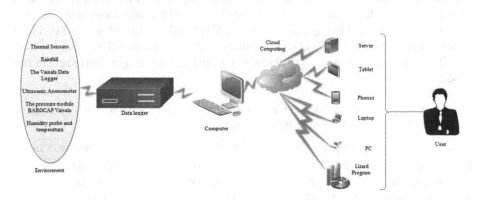

Fig. 4. Automatic Weather Station Infrastructure. It represents the data transfer process from automatic station by data logger toward a server in the cloud that will be used to keep and process whole data; once information is processed the products could be observed and analyzed from different types of devices by external or internal users.

Research on cloud [14] for the meteorological information integration shows that this technology allows better surveillance of the environment to decrease environmental issues such as climate change. On the other hand, we have analyzed how cloud computing can be the key to attain the integration of environment information, delivering processing and storage on demand. Example [17] is based on urban management and helps to identify a generic set of technical capacities for information intelligence. It also proposes a SIAA layer architecture by using different application cloud- based scenarios. Figure 4 shows the cloud inclusion within data transmission.

It was taken as reference the research done in "Cloud-based Remote Environmental Monitoring System with Distributed WSN Weather Stations" to affirm that a server in the cloud allows users to access to geo referenced data in real time [18]. It clearly shows how the information coming from the stations, in this cloud server, can use a public or private cloud according with the available resources in an institution. Nevertheless research affirms that a private cloud should be used [19].

The advantage of consolidating a solid and web access database for the analysis of meteorological patterns has been previously analyzed [20]. Thus, once meteorological information is available, different types of products can be implemented, namely maps, season statistics of variables, as well as climate observation and social conditions [21]. The direct benefits of the cloud model are detailed in Sect. 5.

4   Comparative Cost Benefits Analysis of the Proposed Model

The following analysis allows us to compare the implementation costs of a meteorological station in the proposed modalities, as well as the cost to get final data to use them for prediction in different fields previously specified.

Table 2 shows the purchase and installation costs of a meteorological station, where data equipment and registers are compared according to what has been explained in Sect. 2. Details such as workforce use for installation make a radical difference in costs among alternatives, concluding that the cost of a CWS and the costs of an AWS included in the cloud are equal, but in the latter (Automatic and cloud) we would have uncountable benefits in computer infrastructure reduction, among other advantages that are explained in Sect. 5.

Table 2. Operative costs comparison for a Conventional Weather Stations (CWS), Automatic Weather Stations (AWS), and the automate process in the cloud.

Detail	CWS	AWS	Automatic and cloud
Equipment	23,013.63	10,437.00	10,437.00
Cost of installation	6,759.89	600.00	600.00
Total equipment cost	29,773.52	11,037.00	11,037.00

Table 3 compares monthly costs associated with tabulated and processed data and processing, which are useful to final users from different sectors related to the weather.

Table 3. Comparison of storage and data processing costs for a CWS, AWS, and automated processing in cloud.

Detail	CWS	AWS	Automatic and cloud
Computational infrastructure	$543.38	$543.38	$1,437.00
Storage and data processing	$2,384.33	$1,935.59	$515.76
Total cost	$2,927.71	$2,478.97	$1,952.76

For the conventional model it has been considered that each station must have a person to take daily data, who must live nearby the station. Considering this, data are consolidated in a monthly report that is sent through post office to the regulatory office for further analysis and publishing by a specialized technician in the area, which is explained in detail in Sect. 2.1. In this process special computer equipment is used in order to get useful information of which cost is observed in Table 3. This model has the disadvantage of not allowing the users to obtain up-to-date information in real time (see Sect. 2.1.

As explained in Sect. 2.2 the Automatic model is based on a technical scheme that has GPRS data transmission to get up-to-date information. However, the disadvantage is that historical or real time information cannot be seen by final users; it depends on the processing made by specialists with special software tools.

The benefit of using this transmission, storage and information processing model through Cloud Computing detailed in Sect. 3 is not just economic (as shown in Fig. 5) but also favorable in the way reliable information is handled within a web environment

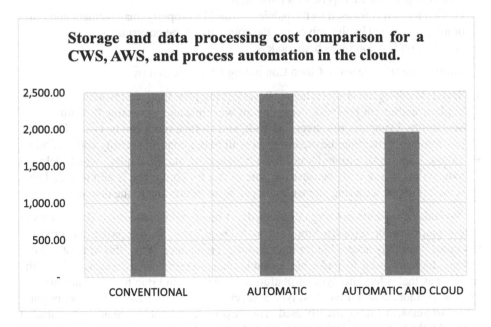

Fig. 5. Cost (dollars) of obtaining meteorological data, including storage and processing with a cloud server. Costs are represented monthly comparing the three models of transfer explained in this study.

without restrictions, allowing any user to get useful forecasts for their economic activities. The costs mentioned in this study for the cloud service are borne by the NewAccess Enterprise in Ecuador [22].

5 Transmission Model Benefits

Cloud computing tendency has shaken up the concepts of information storage, processing and monitoring [23]. It is gaining interest especially among big and medium-size companies. It represents an alternative for the traditional installed software model, considerably reducing the costs as there is no need of purchase, installation, maintenance or upgrade for hardware or software [24].

There are three service categories to which the users can access from its devices: Software as service (SaaS), platform as service [15, 16] (PaaS), and infrastructure as service (IaaS) [25]. PaaS and SaaS include applications, data, functioning time, middleware, operating system, virtualization, servers, storage, and network. These resources are managed by the provider. As for IaaS, the data, functioning time, middleware, and operating system are managed by the user, whereas virtualization, servers, storage and network are managed by the provider.

Cloud computing offers three implementation models:

- Private cloud: Resources are specifically used by the organization and there exists fast provisioning in business services. The property, management, and functioning is in charge of the Enterprise or a third party.
- Public cloud: It is focused on the public use, and its property, management and functioning is covered by the university, the company or the government.
- Hybrid cloud: It combines both models.

Among the advantages of Cloud Computing [26] we can have:

- Speed: Working under this scheme allows getting new applications without a risk of implementation for business, deceasing answer time and increasing flexibility.
- Scalability: Computer resources, network, and storage room can be created in just a few minutes, providing the organization with better control, security and flexibility
- Saving: The organization doesn't have expenses in startup capital, which helps to reduce operational costs because the time of use for equipment is eliminated. There is the option of acquiring storage room per hours according to the demand.

Nowadays, medium-size organizations don't need many technological resources to access platforms or infrastructure such as a DataCenter. In the past these types of resources were only accessible for multinational companies. Now, this kind of organizations does not need to make big technological investments to access and get the advantages that offers this type of platform. Therefore, and due to lower investment, they can be more competitive. This type of service have become more and more popular in the last years, and it is currently used in many private and public organizations around the world; the National Telecommunications Corporation (Public enterprise) in Ecuador is also offering the data storage and disaster recovery service with which they can show its customers that this kind of technology could be applicable to different sectors.

In different studies some methodologies have been analyzed for the management of big volumes of data in the cloud and its performance [27]. It is demonstrated that this kind of technology perfectly works in different areas and it is easily oriented to meteorology. [18], if we take into consideration previous research [28] that shows cost reduction due to a reduction in infrastructure and staff.

6 Conclusions and Further Research

We can conclude that it is much economic and sustainable to maintain an AWS and to get its data than a CWS, due to the fact that the hired staff has to take daily observations, causing high costs as well as different types of the employer's obligations. At the same time, the benefits of the use of cloud computing in the management and storage of information are remarked in Sect. 5.

Additionally, it makes it easy the access and it also improves the process to get meteorological information that exists at present, avoiding issues such as those mentioned in the study [9] "Meteorological data acquisition in Ecuador, South America: problems and solutions". Therefore, problems as unwillingness to communicate the data to the public as well as the lack of interest in the daily task to collect data will disappear; thereby users will be able to obtain complete access to the information, complying with the "Organic Law of Transparency and Access to Public Information" [29], established in Ecuador.

In the future it is possible to carry out a research project that includes the development of a web platform to manage meteorological data, taking as a reference the web platform developed by The International Research Institute for Climate and Society [22], which gives relevant and processed information using meteorological data. This platform can offer relevant products simulating different meteorological scenarios based on the information stored in the cloud service.

Nowadays, the concept "intelligent city" is gaining momentum. We adopt this concept as a reference [30] to indicate that the information processed and saved in the cloud storage will be available to citizens. Thus, they could access to data in real time, that is, to weather information, forecasts and climate indices. It will directly benefit to different economic sectors, for instance, tourism, transport or agricultural industry. The model here exposed will bring economic benefits to the government and private institutions. That is why future projects are necessary to evaluate in detail its implementation, functioning and scope.

Acknowledgments. The authors thank the INAMHI institution, which has served as a reference for this study. In addition, we express our gratitude to the companies "New Access" and "Technological systems" which are the official representatives of the trademark Vaisala.

References

1. Bojinski, S., Verstraete, M., Peterson, T.C., Richter, C., Simmons, A., Zemp, M.: The concept of essential climate variables in support of climate research, applications, and policy. Bull. Am. Meteorol. Soc. **95**, 1431–1443 (2014). doi:10.1175/BAMS-D-13-00047.1
2. Hydrological Services. Valuing Weather and Climate: Economic Assessment of Meteorological and Hydrological Services, WMO-No. 11. Switzerland (2015)
3. Munoz, A.G., Lopez, P., Velasquez, R., Monterrey, L., Leon, G., Ruiz, F., Recalde, C., Cadena, J., Mejia, R., Paredes, M., Bazo, J., Reyes, C., Carrasco, G., Castellon, Y., Villarroel, C., Quintana, J., Urdaneta, A.: An environmental watch system for the Andean Countries: El Observatorio Andino. Bull. Am. Meteorol. Soc. **91**, 1645–1652 (2010). doi: 10.1175/2010BAMS2958.1
4. Ciifen. Programa Regional Andino para el fortalecimiento de los Servicios Meteorológicos, Hidrológicos, Climáticos y el Desarrollo (2014). http://www.ciifen.org/index.php? option=com_content&view=category&layout=blog&id=116&Itemid=167&lang=es. Accessed 20 Jun 2016
5. Handel, A.S., Ayala, E.B., Borbor-Cordova, M.J., Fessler, A.G., Finkelstein, J.L., Espinoza, R.X.R., Ryan, S.J., Stewart-Ibarra, A.M.: Knowledge, attitudes, and practices regarding dengue infection among public sector healthcare providers in Machala, Ecuador. Trop. Dis. Travel Med. Vaccin. **2**, 8 (2016). doi:10.1186/s40794-016-0024-y
6. Stewart-Ibarra, A.M., Muñoz, Á.G., Ryan, S.J., Ayala, E.B., Borbor-Cordova, M.J., Finkelstein, J.L., Mejía, R., Ordoñez, T., Recalde-Coronel, G.C., Rivero, K.: Spatiotemporal clustering, climate periodicity, and social-ecological risk factors for dengue during an outbreak in Machala, Ecuador, in 2010. BMC Infect. Dis. **14**, 1–16 (2014). doi:10.1186/ s12879-014-0610-4
7. Nagarajan, R.: Meteorology. Drought Assessment, pp. 28–76. Springer, Netherlands (2010)
8. Truong, H.-L., Dustdar, S.: Cloud computing for small research groups in computational science and engineering: current status and outlook. Computing **91**, 75–91 (2011). doi: 10.1007/s00607-010-0120-1
9. Trapasso, L.M.: Meteorological data acquisition in Ecuador, South America: problems and solutions. GeoJournal **12**, 89–94 (1986). doi:10.1007/BF00213025
10. Jácome, H: Introducción a la Meteorología. Quininde (2014)
11. Instituto Nacional de Meteorología e Hidrologia Anuario meteorológico 1990 № 30. Quito (2013)
12. United Kingdom. M. H. W Patent Application Publication, vol. 1, pp. 73–91 (2012)
13. Sun, S.-H.: The application of the GPRS network on the design of real-time monitor system for water pollution resource. In: Gong, Z., Luo, X., Chen, J., Lei, J., Wang, F.L. (eds.) WISM 2011. LNCS, vol. 6988, pp. 65–71. Springer, Heidelberg (2011). doi:10.1007/978-3-642-23982-3_9
14. Fu, J., Wang, J., Jing, L., Zhenghong, C., He, M.: Research on meteorology indices forecasting framework based on hybrid cloud computing platforms. In: Han, Y.-H., Park, D.-S., Jia, W., Yeo, S.-S. (eds.) Ubiquitous Information Technologies and Applications: CUTE 2012. LNEE, vol. 214, pp. 727–735. Springer, Netherlands (2013)
15. Chen, X., Zhang, Y., Huang, G., Zheng, X., Guo, W., Rong, C.: Architecture-based integrated management of diverse cloud resources. J. Cloud Comput. Adv. Syst. Appl. **3**, 11 (2014). doi: 10.1186/s13677-014-0011-7
16. Munteanu, V., Şandru, C., Petcu, D.: Multi-cloud resource management: cloud service interfacing. J. Cloud Comput. Adv. Syst. Appli. **3**, 3 (2014). doi:10.1186/2192-113X-3-3

17. Khan, Z., Ludlow, D., McClatchey, R., Anjum, A.: An architecture for integrated intelligence in urban management using cloud computing. J. Cloud Comput. Adv. Syst. Appl. **1**, 1 (2012). doi:10.1186/2192-113X-1-1

18. Kanagaraj, E., Kamarudin, L.M., Zakaria, A., Gunasagaran, R., Shakaff, A.Y.M.: Cloud-based remote environmental monitoring system with distributed WSN weather stations. In: 2015 IEEE SENSORS, pp 1–4. IEEE (2015)

19. Saini, R., Sharma, B.: IT obstacles using cloud computer facility that serves European users referring to access shared computing resources using cloud computing using shared computing resources. Int. J. Adv. Sci. Res. **2**, 1–3 (2016). doi:10.7439/ijasr.v2i1.2749ijasr

20. Luengo, F., Cofiño, A.S., Gutiérrez, J.M.: GRID oriented implementation of self-organizing maps for data mining in meteorology. In: Fernández Rivera, F., Bubak, M., Gómez Tato, A., Doallo, R. (eds.) Grid Computing: First European Across Grids Conference, Santiago de Compostela, Spain, February 13–14, 2004. LNCS, vol. 2970, pp. 163–170. Springer, Heidelberg (2004)

21. IRI Climate: Analysis, Monitoring and Forecasts (2014). http://iridl.ldeo.columbia.edu/maproom/?bbox=bb%3A-90%3A-60%3A-30%3A15%3Abb. Accessed 2 Apr 2016

22. Newaccess. Newaccess-Connectivity solutions (2015). http://www.new-access.net/#. Accessed 5 May 2016

23. Ward, J.S., Barker, A.: Observing the clouds: a survey and taxonomy of cloud monitoring. J. Cloud Comput. **3**, 24 (2014). doi:10.1186/s13677-014-0024-2

24. Tchana, A., De Palma, N., Safieddine, I., Hagimont, D., Diot, B., Vuillerme, N.: Software consolidation as an efficient energy and cost saving solution for a SaaS/PaaS cloud model. In: Träff, L.J., Hunold, S., Versaci, F. (eds.) Euro-Par 2015. LNCS, vol. 9233, pp. 305–316. Springer, Heidelberg (2015)

25. TaheriMonfared, A., Jaatun, M.G.: Handling compromised components in an IaaS cloud installation. J. Cloud Comput. Adv. Syst. Appl. **1**, 16 (2012). doi:10.1186/2192-113X-1-16

26. Sandholm, T., Lee, D.: Notes on cloud computing principles. J. Cloud Comput. **3**, 21 (2015). doi:10.1186/s13677-014-0021-5

27. Bautista Villalpando, L., April, A., Abran, A.: Performance analysis model for big data applications in cloud computing. J. Cloud Comput. Adv. Syst. Appl. **3**, 19–38 (2014). doi:10.1186/s13677-014-0019-z

28. Saha, S., Sarkar, J., Dwivedi, A., Dwivedi, N., Narasimhamurthy, A.M., Roy, R.: A novel revenue optimization model to address the operation and maintenance cost of a data center. J. Cloud Comput. **5**, 1 (2016). doi:10.1186/s13677-015-0050-8

29. Ecuador CN del. Ley Orgánica de Transparencia y Acceso a la Información Pública, pp. 1–10 (2004)

30. Khan, Z., Kiani, S., Soomro, K.: A framework for cloud-based context-aware information services for citizens in smart cities. J. Cloud Comput. Adv. Syst. Appl. **3**, 14 (2014). doi:10.1186/s13677-014-0014-4

An M-Learning Open-Source Tool Comparation for Easy Creation of Educational Apps

Antonio Ortega-García, Antonio Ruiz-Martínez[✉], and Rafael Valencia-García

Faculty of Computer Science, University of Murcia, Murcia, Spain
arm@um.es

Abstract. Since the use of smartphones among students is usual, the introduction of mobile technologies in teaching and learning processes (m-learning) is becoming more and more frequent. Indeed, there are an important number of m-learning experiences using general purpose apps such as Dropbox, Facebook, apps provided by the mobile OS, etc. However, there are situations where it could be convenient to develop a customized app. The aim of this paper is making an analysis of the different open-source tools for creating m-learning apps that do not require prior knowledge of programming and choose the most mature for this purpose. Thus, the creation of these apps could be made by any teacher. We evaluate the usefulness of this tool, its accessibility for teachers without previous knowledge in programming apps, and the utility for students. Our choice was App Inventor.

Keywords: Educative app · Mobile learning · Ubiquitous learning · Virtual classroom · Creation tool

1 Introduction

Mobile learning (m-learning) approaches the use of Information and Communications Technologies (ICT) for delivering the benefits of mobile technologies in the field of teaching in a familiar way for students. Namely, its main benefit is that it facilitates the learning process anywhere, anytime. Furthermore, as stated by UNESCO [1], m-learning has a set of unique features such as: expanding the reach and equity in education, facilitating personalized learning, providing immediate feedback and assessment, etc.

Being a powerful technology of widespread use, its integration in the field of teaching is only a matter of time. Mobile technologies are not the future, they are already fully implemented in many aspects of society. According to the report published by UNESCO about the future of m-learning [1] the next decade and beyond could radically transform the incorporation of mobile technologies to formal and informal education in order to meet the needs of students and teachers from all over the world. Indeed, more and more companies engaged in development of educational content for mobile devices and worldwide market

© Springer International Publishing AG 2016
R. Valencia-García et al. (Eds.): CITI 2016, CCIS 658, pp. 102–113, 2016.
DOI: 10.1007/978-3-319-48024-4_9

for m-learning products and services is expected to grow in the next years[1]. Furthermore, as the use of mobile devices is extended among students, some organizations are adopting BYOD (Bring Your Own Device) policies allowing students to connect to institution's network to learn by means of technology in the classroom [3].

Developing useful m-learning resources for students is difficult and the success of this kind of learning largely depends on the ability of teachers to take advantage of mobile devices as stated by Mouza [3], since not all teachers have the necessary skills for the appropriate development of educational mobile applications. Therefore, it is necessary to find a way to unify and simplify the development of all types of m-learning resources and take advantage of the use of different m-learning technologies available, in order to facilitate this work to teachers.

Currently, most of m-learning experiences are based on the use of general purpose apps such as Dropbox, Facebook [4] or apps provided by the mobile OS [3, 5–7]. However, these apps limit the kind of experiences teachers can perform. Thus, it would be desirable that a teacher could develop its own m-learning app customizing contents, resources, including tests, using mobile features such as GPS, etc.

Our research work aims at studying different tools for creating educational resources on mobile devices to save these obstacles, assess whether it is powerful enough to generate resources of interest for students, and simple enough to offer teachers the generation of these resources, whether or not teachers have advanced computer programming skills. We aim to select the most suitable tool for the development of m-learning apps for non-programmers or beginners to easily generate apps that can be useful in the learning/teaching process. Hence, in this work we have analysed the available tools and, then, we selected App Inventor.

The paper is organized as follows: first, the general and specific objectives of the study are presented in Sect. 2. In Sect. 3 an overview of the theoretical framework necessary to identify the most important features of m-learning education is explained. In this section the criteria for identifying the most appropriate tool are presented. In Sect. 4, we present our main findings and a discussion of the results obtained. Finally, conclusions and issues to address in future work are obtained in Sect. 5.

2   Objectives

The aim of this paper is to make an analysis of the different open-source tools for creating apps that do not require prior knowledge of computer programming languages so as to choose the most mature and easiest tool for this purpose. Thus, the development of these apps could be made by any teacher and not only by a computer programmer, that is, for beginners or non-programmers.

---

[1] http://elearningindustry.com/elearning-statistics-and-facts-for-2015.

As these tools are open source, they could be used by any teacher although its teaching center (school, high school, university, etc.) has limitations in the budget (e.g. urban teachers in low-income underserved schools), and some professional development program could be developed easily in order to help teachers to incorporate mobile devices in teaching and learning, which is an issue that has not been deeply addressed, as Mouza sets forth [3]. Some examples of development programs can be found in the studies provided by Ekanayake and Wishart [10] and Saudelli and Ciampa [9].

2.1 Related Work

Nowadays, most m-learning studies [11] of m-learning are focused on effectiveness and m-learning system design, being mobile devices and PDA the most commonly used devices. Most of the experiences are based on the use of social networks or apps that are included in the mobile OS [3–7]. However, the purpose of our study was to find a tool that allows non-programmer teachers to develop m-learning app adapted to their teaching needs.

As a tool we have chosen App Inventor. There are a number of m-learning experiences developed with this tool (a list of them can be found on its Web page[2]). Among these experiences we highlight the experiences performed by Robertson [12] and Soares [13].

There are other works similar to the already mentioned that are also based on App Inventor, but, as the ones already mentioned, they are focused on the same point of view: how to use App Inventor so that their students create apps to learn to program or some issues related to programming. Namely, Turbak et al. [14] used it to teach the event-based model and Morelli et al. [15], Wagner et al. [16], Karakus et al. [17] and Gestwicki and Ahmad [18] use it to teach Computer Science principles and introduce them into the programming of computer applications.

Scherer et al. [19] performed an interesting study about the current teacher's acceptance and use of information and communication technology (ICT) signifying different facets of ICT-related teaching goals in classrooms. Teacher's perceived usefulness of ICT for teaching and learning is proven to be a very important factor that will be taken into account in our study, since it is positively related to self-efficacy and ICT use.

3 Theoretical Framework

In this section we present the theoretical framework needed for the understanding of our study. Thus, we analyse what m-learning is and its main features. Finally, we present a summary of the main existing tools for creating m-apps without previous knowledge in computer programming languages.

---

[2] http://appinventor.mit.edu/explore/research.html.

3.1 M-Learning

M-learning could be defined as teaching and learning taking advantage of the use of mobile technologies in such a way that they will allow the learner to perform the learning process without being in a predetermined or fixed location [11,20,21].

Nowadays, this kind of learning is possible thanks to the technological advances made in communications, wireless technologies and mobile devices. In recent years, m-learning has been significantly expanded according to Jim, Chen, Lin and Huang [11] and, as mentioned in the UNESCO report [1], in a close future, it will be more integrated and widespread in formal and informal education.

The use of these technologies has broadly shown its positive outcomes in different education context such as formal education, non-formal education and informal education [11]. However, as Chu [22] explains, we must consider the negative aspects of these technologies. A non-appropriate application of these may subject students to a high cognitive load, hurting their learning process, distracting and overloading them.

In order to understand why m-learning will be so important in the education system, we studied and classified below the various educational features that these tools are able to offer. This classification will be useful in establishing the criteria for comparing the existing tools and selecting the most appropriate.

3.2 M-Learning Educational Features

The obvious educational potential that mobile technologies have (geolocation, mobility, connectivity, apps, conferences, access to information, sharing, etc.) arises various educational features applicable in various areas of teaching.

The most immediate and obvious quality of m-learning is to learn *anywhere and anytime*. This feature enables continuous learning throughout life, without time frames, mixing education with everyday activities. A mobile device is a teacher/student who follows you at all times.

One advantage is the freedom to capture ideas when inspiration strikes, and getting knowledge when doubts appear. If in a visit to a museum curiosity and the urge to know more about a subject or author comes to us, we only have to surf on the Internet at the same time.

The functionalities of mobile devices have a large number of direct applications in education: synchronization, creation of joint tasks, information sharing, content creation by the student (graphics, images, videos, presentations, podcasts, etc.), generation of learning communities, live broadcast recordings and interviews, measurement of gravitational forces and magnetic signals, etc.

These tools have the ability to be motivating and attractive to the student. The proper use of these devices is motivating itself. Furthermore, being a lower-cost tool than others allows great access to all kinds of students and teachers. All this favours a more active role in their education for the student.

Mobile devices allow a much more personalized education. By the connection you get with mobile applications and the use of the Internet, a person can choose between their centers of interest and learn continuously and immediately, either the date of a historical event or how to repair the appliance that has failed. The flexibility these devices provide allows an education suited to the needs of each individual.

The m-learning feature of *learn anywhere and anytime* also allows the expansion of experiential learning based on location, which refers to a specific location, and the knowledge gained by the experience made at this location, through tours, museum visits, cultural sites, etc. For example, Walker [23] suggests methods for sharing information among museum visitors through m-learning activities.

The ability to provide a connection between students and teachers anywhere and anytime allows continuous monitoring of the learning process. This means that the teacher receives much more information about the difficulties of her students when assimilating specific knowledge, and the student is more aware of this learning process, being able to construct their own knowledge.

Another important feature of m-learning is the social interaction. The ease to connect educational projects among classrooms around the world, and monitoring of these projects anywhere and anytime, allows students to participate in educational activities correlating with all kinds of students, from classmates, to even people of other cultures, without barriers of space or time.

3.3   Tools for Generating Apps for Non-programmers

Currently, there are available many dedicated tools for creating mobile applications. In this section we provide an overview of the main available tools. Then, from this analysis, we present the tool we have selected as the more powerful and easy to use. Below we establish criteria on which to compare and choose the most suitable one.

The main available tools are: Claro, Appulse, Impatica, Learncast, Adrenna, H5P, SmartBuilder, Blackboard and App Inventor. Next, we provide a brief description on each one.

Claro[3] is a tool of electronic learning (e-learning) Web-based collaborative environment. This tool lets you create and share courses, adapting the content for mobile devices, hosting them in the cloud. It provides an environment for online/offline full development without the use of accessories, to create responsive HTML5 content. It uses design templates for the preparation of the contents. Its target audience is primarily the private sector and collaborative environments, but it can also adapt their applications to m-learning.

Appulse[4] is a multi-platform application that offers an easy-to-use solution. It focuses on entrepreneurial business environment, but it also provides e-learning functions. It has an attractive visual presentation, focusing on the use of images and videos with little text. It provides document sharing and synchronization

---

[3] http://www.dominknow.com/.
[4] http://www.jdb-smartlearning.com/en/content/downloads.html.

between all devices. The mobile application is synchronized with Moodle natively and offers shared storage in the cloud, these are attractive qualities for an application of m-learning.

Impatica[5] is a conversion and content creation software which enables the transformation of various types of documents, such as PowerPoint or Word, in presentations to mobile applications. It also allows the integration of content embedded on Web pages. Its aim is to create presentations quickly and easily, and make them immediately available to users. However, its range of functions and applications for teaching is rather limited, focusing almost exclusively on the creation of multimedia content.

Learncast[6] is a tool dedicated to the creation that allows the integration of surveys and provides feedback information easily. It provides real-time measurement of results and allows the discussion of these through forums. It introduces a concept of rewards by medals, which rewards the user for completing certain tasks, and uses a system of alerts and notifications for urgent content.

Adrenna[7] is an e-learning platform that records the work done by the teacher to compare educational standards and learning objectives. Its aim is to provide learning environments tailored to the user. It allows the migration of content from other platforms. It is developed by Drupal and its code is accessible, so that it can be easily updated with applications made by the community.

H5P[8] is an application for creating HTML5 content in the browser. The development platform allows you to add and update content at any time, and share it through HTML5-compatible devices. However, rather than focusing on the development of a learning environment, it focuses on the development of multimedia content, offering a few features of coordinated learning and progress tracking. It has good documentation with presentations and examples of use.

SmartBuilder[9] is very similar to H5P tool, virtually identical. It also focuses on the elaboration of multimedia content for environments that support HTML5, using a system based on the click and drag objects environment. Like H5P, it allows a few features of learning. It focuses on the use by groups of collaborative work. It also allows the use and sharing of templates for processing applications.

Blackboard[10] is a virtual learning platform compatible with mobile devices, which provides a simple user interface, online assessment and surveys, designed to encourage active collaboration throughout the course and creating project groups. It is based on the use of 5 different platforms interrelated, learning, collaboration, connection, mobility and analysis. It offers a different product depending on whether the studies are primary, secondary, complementary or superior.

---

[5] http://www.impatica.com/.

[6] http://www.learncast.com/.

[7] http://www.adrenna.com/.

[8] https://h5p.org/.

[9] http://www.smartbuilder.com/.

[10] http://es.blackboard.com/.

App Inventor[11] is an online free development environment for mobile applications, developed by the Research Institute of Massachusetts, primarily aimed at the use for education and research. It offers many educational applications and is synchronized with the mobile device so that all changes are instantly reflected. It has a very broad user community that actively generates features and documentation. To use it, it only requires a Gmail account. It does not offer cloud services. However, projects created with this tool are stored on the server.

As part of our research work we have made a detailed comparison on these tools that we present in Sect. 3.4.

3.4   Comparing Tools and Selection

In this section, on the one hand, we establish the set of criteria that we used to compare the different tools (see Sect. 3.3) that can be used to develop apps with previous knowledge in computer programming languages. On the other hand, based on these criteria, we compare the different tools and select the most interesting one.

To meet the desired objectives, the finally selected tool must meet the previously studied educational features, which must meet the following requirements:

- No programming skills required: it must enable teachers that are beginners and non-programmers to create apps.
- User-friendly: it should not take long time to learn how to use the tool, and should enable rapid content creation.
- Documentation and support: It is important for the tool to have a good documentation. Even more, it is positively assessed that the tool is widely used, and, even more so that there is an active community of users who currently develop documentation and content, with some help from forums, examples and similar applications that can support the development of applications.
- Multi-language support so that it can be adapted to the local language.
- Reuse: the tool must allow prolonging the validity of the developed applications.
- Cost of the tool: it is assessed whether the tool is free or paid, and if the contents developed are freely distributed to students or if they need some type of payment or account to access them. It is better considered that the tool is free and/or open-source since, thus, the educational center or the teacher does not have to make investment. Hence, it can be used by any educational center independently of their economical resources. Furthermore, the use of open source tools maximizes the range of students with access to the tool, which could lead to perform a meaningful experience.
- Analytical results: the provision of analytical results is interesting, for both teacher in controlling the process of teaching and students in the self-evaluation process.
- Feedback on the user experience: it offers analysis about the use of the application by the students, allowing comments about the issues occurred.

---

[11] http://appinventor.mit.edu/.

Table 1. Comparison of tools for the generation of apps

	Claro	Appulse	Impatica	Learncast	Adrenna	H5P	Smartbuilder	Blackboard	App Inventor
No programming skills required	Yes	Yes	Yes	Yes	No	No	No	Yes	Yes
User-friendly	Yes	Yes	Yes	Yes	Yes	Yes	Yes	Yes	Yes
Documentation and support	Yes	Yes	Yes	Yes	Yes	Yes	Yes	Yes	Yes
MultiLanguage	Yes	Yes	No	No	No	No	No	Yes	No
Reusable	Yes	Yes	Yes	Yes	Yes	Yes	Yes	Yes	Yes
Cost	97/month	Payment*	Payment*	Payment*	Payment*	0	0	2.00	0
Analytical results	Yes	Yes	No	Yes	Yes	Yes	Yes	Yes	Yes
Feedback	Yes	Yes	No	Yes	Yes	No	Yes	Yes	Yes
Content sharing	Yes	Yes	Powerpoints	Yes	Yes	Yes	Yes	Dropbox	Yes
Information processing	Yes	Yes	Yes	Yes	Yes	Yes	Yes	Yes	Yes
Cloud server	Yes	Yes	Yes	Yes	Yes	Yes	Unknown	Yes	Yes
Integration services	No	No	No	No	Yes	Yes	No	Unknown	Yes
Multiplatform support	Yes	Yes	Yes	Yes	Yes	Yes	Yes	Yes	Android

- Content sharing: all the information related to the courses can be presented and immediately updated online at any time.
- Information processing: it should allow the presentation of information to students and teachers in order to gather data and process the information in many formats, such as tables and forms.
- Cloud service: it should allow the use of cloud servers so courses, materials and information can be always updated and students can access information anytime and anywhere.
- Services integration: it should support the use of online services such as social networking, mail, cloud storage, etc.
- Multiplatform support: it should allow the development of applications for various mobile platforms (Android, iOS and Windows Phone). Thus, we could reach all students independently of their device.

Next, we make a detailed analysis of the tools presented in Sect. 3. The assessment of the various aspects of each tool, based on the criteria presented, is reflected in Table 1.

In Table 1 we can see that most of these tools provide powerful solutions without programming knowledge. Indeed, except H5P, Smartbuilder and Adrenna, the rest of them allow us to develop m-learning apps without previous knowledge. Smartbuilder is a powerful tool, but more complex than what we need, which restricts the use for many teachers. H5P and Adrenna require a previous installed setup in a platform like Joomla, Drupal or Wordpress for integration of the tool. These are not the conditions we are looking for.

All the tools analysed are easy to use and have good documentation and support, AppInventor being the one that provides more examples, tutorials and applications, with the wider community of users and specific forums for many subjects, as teaching. The support of the multilanguage feature is not available in all the tools. Only Claro, Appulse and Blackboard have been taken into account. The fact that a tool has not this property is not significant because we can create different versions of the same application in the different languages, which involves more development time. Regarding reusability, we can mention that these tools facilitate that the development made can be re-used to create other projects.

As for the cost of the tool, these solutions are, in most cases, very expensive. During the realization of this study, it was observed that most existing development tools offer proprietary software solutions that requires payment for its use (those marked with Payment*). Many of these tools even require registration process and a preliminary study for the realization of a budget. The cost of these tools varies depending on various factors like the educational services contracted, the number of users, modules, etc. As we defined in the previous list of requirements, we discard any tool that supposes a payment since we want to maximize the range of teachers and students with access to the use of the tool. Then, according to this criteria the best options are: H5P, Smartbuilder and App Inventor.

Except Impatica, all of them allow analytical results in one way or another. Most of them just provide the methods to manually send the student's results to teachers and to create tables with the desired information for the student's feedback, which is sufficient. However, Learncast provides automatic test and tracking student's progress with instant result and feedback. Since the specific nature of Impatica is being a tool dedicated to conversion of content and sharing, it does not allow feedback neither for students nor for teachers. H5P is dedicated to course presentations and interactive multimedia content sharing, so it does not provide feedback neither.

All the tools allow to share content and information, which is essential for a teaching tool. However, Impatica is restricted to the use of powerpoints, which is very limited for our objectives. Blackboard seems not to provide file management in their learning core pack, however, we can still share files with our students through free platforms like dropbox, even though this is privative software and requires registration of every user.

Regarding information processing, all of them allow to collect and present information and results. AppInventor does not provide a direct way of processing the information since it only allows to create lists, but nevertheless you can still manually create tables, graphs and forms to collect results with the tools provided. As for cloud service usage, App Inventor allows cloud services to save courses and update them, however, this is very limited, and for further cloud usage such as files sharing online the user should find a way to integrate cloud services on their own. Cloud functionalities are rarely provided by free tools, this being an expensive service. Most of the payment tools provide some kind of cloud service.

The integration with other services, such as online videos or mailing, is not explicitly indicated by the features of most tools. However, even if they do not provide specific tools to integrate this services, this is a minor issue, as we can always include links to dropbox, youtube, gmail, etc. However, it is appreciated that Adrenna and App Inventor provide automatic ways of services integration. Adrenna provides a feeds service integration, while App Inventor includes all kinds of automatic services integration tools such as twitter, phone calls, texting, mailing and translation. All the tools provide solutions compatible with at least Android and Apple devices, except for AppInventor, which is only compatible with Android technology.

From the tools analysed the most interesting are Learncast, Appulse, Smartbuilder, Adrenna, and App Inventor. Smartbuilder seems the most powerful and customizable solution, but it is excessively complex for the purposes of this study, since we prefer a simple and easy solution that allows access to more teachers instead of a more complex and powerful solution. Adrenna is a very complete solution, however is more an e-learning than a m-learning tool, and it does not provide as many specific services that take advantage of mobile devices as other tools do. Learncast and Appulse would be the most interesting options if we were aiming for a payment tool, since they provide all kinds of m-learning services, they are simple, easy and attractive, and compatible with most mobile devices. Among the free tools, H5P is discarded for requiring a previous setup and configuration. Only App Inventor provides an interesting solution for this study, and is the most powerful of the free tools, being very competent even comparing it with the payment ones. It is intuitive and potent, providing an easy and fast way to create mobile apps for free distribution, and it counts with the wider community of active users, providing the creators access to active forums dedicated to teachers and developers, help, examples and tutorials. This tool is very accessible and user friendly for all kinds of teachers, and this is the most important aspect to cover in this study.

Therefore, once we have analysed all the options available, from our point of view, the tool App Inventor is the most interesting one for the development of m-learning apps.

4   Result and Discussion

App Inventor is a cloud service that does not require the installation of any software. The mobile application is developed through a user interface via web. In addition, a feature that is very interesting is that the tool is synchronized with the user's mobile device. Thus, all changes made to the application can be tested at the same time it is developed. This tool use is widespread and gradually increasing, with an asset base of over 250,000 users, and more than 3 million registered.

Another great attraction that has made us opt for this solution is the large active community of existing developers. On its website we can find an exclusive forum for teachers. The number of examples, tutorials and support is broad enough so any teacher can rapidly get started in content development.

This tool requires the use of a Gmail account, but it is open code and the content created is owned by its author, in our case, the teacher. This means that the content created can be freely distributed without any restriction or hindrance among students, who do not even have to create an account to access them.

Applications and content created are completely reusable from a course to another. Applications are generated in .apk format, so they will work on Android phones as usual. The contents and projects are saved and associated with our Gmail account, so at any time you can access, update a new course, or even download and save them on your computer. However, the generated applications only work on Android platform, which restricts the number of students who can access the content generated for not being compatible with iOS or Windows Phone.

The application does not require any programming knowledge. Everything is done visually by means of blocks. After finishing the application, the tool generates an APK that you can download on your computer. Then, you only have to make it available for students to download it into their mobile devices.

5 Conclusions and Future Work

Nowadays, both teachers and students has a mobile device, which has favoured the widespread of using them in learning/teaching processes. So far, most of the experiences are based on the use of apps that are specifically designed for m-learning processes such as iBooks, Facebook, etc. However, a teacher, with no knowledge in computer programming, might want to develop apps that are adapted to her teaching needs. For this purpose, we studied the tools that are available for non-programmers and, after analyzing them, we conclude that the most suitable was App Inventor.

The fact that the tool is easy to use for non-programmers and it provides functionality to manage the different elements of a smartphone, we have identified some shortcomings: lack of sync with cloud services, not processing the information easily within the application with generated graphs and its dependence on Android technology. In the future these deficiencies could be addressed to improve the features that m-learning apps could offer. Even so, this tool has the important limitation that it is only valid for Android smartphones and there are other mobile OS that have an important penetration as iOS or Windows Phone. Currently, there are some application that support the generation of the app for multiple mobile platform. However, in most cases they are expensive or require knowledge in programming. Therefore, it is needed a simple and powerful tool to extend the development of these m-learning applications to all available devices which makes it easy for teachers to create these apps that allow them to customize the learning process of their students. From our point of view, this is the key to boost the m-learning.

As future work, we aim to develop a teaching experience to evaluate the acceptance of this tool (App Inventor) among teachers and students, and the difficulties they could find in the development and use of m-learning apps, as well as its usefulnes in education.

References

1. Shuler, C., Winters, N., West, M.: The future of Mobile Learning. Implications for policy makers and planners. United Nations Educational, Scientific and Cultural Organization (UNESCO) (2013)
2. MacKellar, B.: App. inventor for Android in a healthcare IT course. ACM (2012)
3. Mouza, C., Barrett-Greenly, T.: Bridging the app. gap: an examination of a professional development initiative on mobile learning in urban schools. Elsevier (2015)
4. Pimmer, C., Linxen, S., Grhbiel, U.: Facebook as a learning tool? A case study on the appropriation of social network sites from mobile phones in developing countries. Br. J. Educ. Technol. **43**, 726–738 (2012)
5. Engin, M., Donanci, S.: Dialogic teaching and iPads in the EAP classroom. Elsevier (2015)
6. Jahnke, I., Kumar, S.: Digital Didactical designs: teachers integration of iPads for learning-centered processes. J. Digit. Learn. Teach. Educ. **30**(3), 81–88 (2014)
7. Zhang, L.: Mobile Phone Technology Engagement in EFL Classroom. Atlantis Press (2013)
8. Wolber, D., Abelson, H., Friedman, M.: Democratizing Computing with App. Inventor. GetMobile **18**(4), 53–58 (2015)
9. Saudelli, M.G., Katia, C.: Exploring the role of TPACK and teacher self-efficacy: an ethnographic case study of three iPad language arts classes. Technology, Pedagogy and Education (2014)
10. Ekanayake, M., Sakunthala, Y., Wishart, J.: Integrating mobile phones into teaching and learning: a case study of teacher training through professional development workshops. Br. J. Educ. Technol. **46**(1), 173–189 (2015)
11. Wu, W.-H., Wu, Y.C.J., Chen, C.-Y., Kao, H.-Y., Lin, C.-H., Huang, S.-H.: Review of trends from mobile learning studies: a meta-analysis. Comput. Educ. **59**(2), 817–827 (2012)
12. Robertson, J.: Reflections on Using AppInventor to Teach Programming (2014)
13. Soares, A.: Reflections on teaching App. Inventor for non-beginner programmers: issues, challenges and opportunities. Inf. Syst. Educ. **12**(4), 56–65 (2014)
14. Turbak, F., Sherman, M., Martin, F., Wolber, D., Pokress, S.C.: Events-first Programming in App. Inventor. Elsevier (2014)
15. Morelli, R., Wolber, D., Pokress, S., Turbak, F., Martin, F.: Teaching the CS Principles Curriculum with App. Inventor. ACM (2013)
16. Wagner, A., Gray, J., Corley, J., Wolber, D.: Using App. Inventor in a K-12 Summer Camp. Elsevier (2013)
17. Karakus, M., Uludag, S., Guler, E., Turner, S.W., Ugur, A.: Teaching computing and programming fundamentals via App. Inventor for Android. ITHET (2012)
18. Gestwicki, P., Ahmad, K: App. Inventor for Android with Studio-based Learning (2011)
19. Scherer, R., Siddiq, F., Teo, T.: Becoming more specific: measuring and modeling teachers' perceived usefulness of ICT in the context of teaching and learning. Elsevier (2015)
20. Kukulska-Hulme, A.: Mobile usability and user experience. Routledge (2005)
21. Hashemi, M., Azizinezhad, M., Najafi, V., Nesari, A.J.: What is Mobile Learning? Challenges and Capabilities. Elsevier (2011)
22. Chu, H.: Potential negative effects of mobile learning on students learning achievement and cognitive load format assessment perspective. JSTOR **17**(1), 332–344 (2014)
23. Walker, K.: A method for creating collaborative mobile learning trails. Les cahiers du laboratoire Leibniz (2006)

Study of Use, Privacy and Dependence on Social Networks by Students in the Ecuadorian Universities

Marcos Antonio Espinoza-Mina[1,2(✉)]
and Patricia Leonor Suárez-Riofrío[3]

[1] Carrera de Computación e Informática, Universidad Agraria del Ecuador,
Guayaquil, Ecuador
mespinoza@uagraria.edu.ec
[2] Facultad de Ingeniería en Sistemas y Telecomunicaciones, Universidad Ecotec,
Samborondón, Ecuador
mespinoza@ecotec.edu.ec
[3] Facultad de Ingeniería en Electricidad y Computación,
Escuela Superior Politécnica del Litoral, Guayaquil, Ecuador
plsuarez@espol.edu.ec

Abstract. Universities have raised concern about the increasing use of social networks by their students, because they spend more and more time on them, than on their own college. The purpose of this paper is to present the results of the analysis done on the increased use of social networks, and specifically in relation to the experience with security and privacy. This allows us to determine the level of extreme dependence on its use. To do this research, we have designed a series of surveys, which were used with students of two Ecuadorian universities. The data were tabulated and statistically calculated, allowing us to identify which the main uses in social networks are, and gives some recommendations within the scope of these results, providing guidance for the use of these services in a more efficient and safe way.

Keywords: Social networks · Guide · University students · Internet · Privacy · Addiction

1 Introduction

In recent years, most of Latin American governments have undertaken an arduous effort to increase Internet connectivity and the use of social networks in homes, in order to create new opportunities for reducing the social gap. For example, the Colombia's National Statistics Department (DANE) has announced that in 2015, 67.7 % of Colombians of 5 or more years have used the Internet to access social networks [1]. Social networks allow people to be notified and informed; it gives people the opportunity to express ideas and feelings, especially meeting people from other cities or even different countries. They are considered a powerful tool that can even topple entire political systems, through decentralized coordination of protests [2].

© Springer International Publishing AG 2016
R. Valencia-García et al. (Eds.): CITI 2016, CCIS 658, pp. 114–128, 2016.
DOI: 10.1007/978-3-319-48024-4_10

Introvert students use social networks as an aid to socialize with different people, and express their emotions and they reveal their thoughts, ideas and tastes. With an appropriate approach, social networks also contribute to different fields of education, for example, language learning [3]. A particular case is the social network Twitter, which encourages students to engage in learning and practicing new languages, creating a beneficial effect for participants by increasing their knowledge of new languages [4].

According to the ONTSI (National Observatory for Telecommunication and Information Society) in Spain, the most common activities undertaken by social network users are: communicating with friends, family, coworkers; sharing information (photos, videos, etc.), looking up information on various topics, organizing events/meetings, following acquaintances updates, membership in groups and meeting new people [5]. Social networks may have a positive and negative impact on students' life. It is presumed that most of them know the risks involved in the use of social networks but they assume risks naturally, because they believe that the benefits obtained outweigh the existing dangers.

The platform of services that provide social networking is the Internet and its importance lies not only in the benefit of having families available online, but it is also a source of knowledge, consulting, support, training and development. It is also advantageous for those who can access it. Therefore, it constitutes part of the structural equity, equal opportunity, democracy in general and production [6].

It is the obligation of computer experts to certify to the users that their critical and personal information is well protected, so that they can feel safe sharing it with an outsourcer, just ensuring that their conversations are well protected; however, we should not confuse security and privacy on the networks.

Computer security provides information protection, such as personal information that it is used to protect privacy; but security is useless if the authorization to use or access is given to anyone unknown, due to a lack of knowledge of the program rules that regulate social networks. In the same line, that happens with all kinds of conversation such as voice by telephone (fixed/mobile) with analog (fixed) and digital (GSM, UMTS, ISDN, VoIP) technology and video conferencing; electronic short messaging (SMS, Skype, WhatsApp) or full (e-electronic, burofax); digital data line (ADSL, fiber, HFC) or wireless (wifi, UMTS, LTE); remote access networks of enterprises so that they can work their employees (telecommuting VPN) clients (web access). They use shared networks with other users and they are managed by other companies.

Telecommunication operators may qualify using secure protocols; but there are risks for companies (they are also corruptible and "vulnerable") and therefore it applies encryption in all communications (including internal networks, which can have "traitors" employees). Private users should also apply encryption because of their critical privacy (personal calls, emails exchanged with your contacts, bank statements, etc.) [7].

Computer engineers face many complex challenges to certify trust, security and privacy on each platform through which you access or when a social network is implemented; for example, one of the critical and development fields concerns security in mobile social networks [8]. Security specialists provide encryption mechanisms for user information and ensure secure access to the infrastructure used, but the level of privacy is under complete control of the user; today the use of Internet services and access to information seems free, but it has a cost, since through navigation and interaction on websites, users are providing personal information on their needs and interests. Another point to consider is that very few people read the privacy policies of the websites they use before accepting the "terms and conditions". Social networking and messaging systems are attractive to university students, because they provide quick response, high interactivity and immediate rewards.

The use, in principle, is positive, provided they are not put aside the rest of the characteristics of a normal life (studying, playing sports, hanging out with friends or family time) activities. Another aspect to consider regards overuse of social networking, which causes isolation from real life, generates anxiety, impaired self-esteem, until university students have no self-control [9]. The results obtained from the collection of usage, privacy, and incidents information that university students have with social networks are presented, as well as determine the level of excess in the use of these tools. In this way, we achieve the better recommendations to follow, which avoids any excessive use of social networks that may generate negative effects over the students' academic performance and their social life.

2 Materials and Methods

The study uses the technique of quantitative data acquisition survey, particularly a closed type. They involved a total of four hundred thirty eight (438) volunteer university students from two universities. The survey consists of twenty-four (24) points, of which twenty-one (21) were required to be answered.

The questions are geared toward understanding three aspects of social networks: use, privacy and addiction. It has been made using the application "Google Forms"; the short link to access the survey is: http://goo.gl/forms/5XfgHe0dSDytDerk2. The data have been collected over a period of five (5) months from December 2015 to April 2016. All the information has been exported to a spreadsheet in Excel 2010; for descriptive and inferential statistical analysis SPSS version 19 tool was used.

3 Results Analysis

3.1 Use

Table 1 shows the results of the survey that involve use of social networks. It is observed that the reason of being in contact with friends is the one who gets the highest score.

Considering the above, the analysis of the following hypothesis is proposed: "University students consider useful to use social networks because they are educational". It is used as the dependent variable whereas age is used as independent variable. The following questions are: Is the use of social networks useful? And Do you think social networks are educational? the value in Table 2 shows, a 0.001 significance which is less than 0.05, then the hypothesis of equal means is accepted.

Table 1. Social networks use

Frequency of use

		Responses		Percentage of cases
		N°	Percentage	
What do you use social networks?[a]	To stay in touch with friends	366	23.8 %	83.6 %
	To meet new people	54	3.5 %	12.3 %
	To contact distant friends	137	8.9 %	31.3 %
	To stay informed of national and international news	220	14.3 %	50.2 %
	For Business	94	6.1 %	21.5 %
	For Job Opportunities	91	5.9 %	20.8 %
	To obtain information	234	15.2 %	53.4 %
	To freely expose reviews	88	5.7 %	20.1 %
	To upload photos or videos	191	12.4 %	43.6 %
	Others	63	4.1 %	14.4 %
Total		1538	100.0 %	351.1 %

[a]Dichotomy group tabulated at value 1.

Table 2. Result of the hypothesis: Young university students consider the use of social networks useful because they are educational

ANOVA[b]

Model		Sum of Squares	Gl	Mean Square	F	Sig.
1	Regression	8,799	2	4,400	7,242	.001[a]
	Residual	264,262	435	.607		
	Total	273,062	437			

[a]Predictors: (Constant), Do you think social networks are educational? Do you consider useful to use social networks?
[b]Dependent Variable: Current age

After analyzing the relation of the age of the surveyed with the answers to the question: Do you think social networks are educational? It can be identified the average scale where the answer is more concentrated (Table 3).

Table 4 shows a high percentage of students visiting inappropriate content in social networks.

3.2 Privacy

For the analysis of privacy, another hypothesis is proposed: "Young University students publish relevant data on social networking sites and they accept all friend requests". It is defined as the dependent variable Gender of surveyed and as an independent variables the following questions: Do you have relevant personal information about you posted on a social network? and Do you accept all friend requests that you

Table 3. Using social networks

Current Age*Do you think social networks are educational? Crosstabulation

			Do you think social networks are educational?					Total
			1	2	3	4	5	
Current Age	Between 15 to 19 years	Counter	17	41	57	35	15	165
		% Within current Age	10.3 %	24.8 %	34.5 %	21.2 %	9.1 %	100.0 %
	Between 20 to 24 years	Counter	14	25	61	33	26	159
		% Within current Age	8.8 %	15.7 %	38.4 %	20.8 %	16.4 %	100.0 %
	Higher to 25 years	Counter	17	19	42	20	16	114
		% Within current Age	14.9 %	16.7 %	36.8 %	17.5 %	14.0 %	100.0 %
Total		Counter	48	85	160	88	57	438
		% Within current Age	11.0 %	19.4 %	36.5 %	20.1 %	13.0 %	100.0 %

Table 4. Inappropriate content in social networks

Gender* Have you ever seen inappropriate social media content? Cross tabulation

			Have you ever seen inappropriate content in social networks?				Total
			Yes, many times	Yes, once	No, hardly ever	No, never	
Gender	Male	Counter	70	85	25	38	218
		% Within Gender	32.1 %	39.0 %	11.5 %	17.4 %	100.0 %
	Female	Counter	72	108	26	14	220
		% Within Gender	32.7 %	49.1 %	11.8 %	6.4 %	100.0 %
Total		Counter	142	193	51	52	438
		% Within Gender	32.4 %	44.1 %	11.6 %	11.9 %	100.0 %

receive? The ANOVA Table 5 shows a significance value of 0.06, which means that the hypothesis of equal means is rejected.

Table 6 presents the answer given to the question: Do you think you can take risks with social networks? which resulted in a significant positive value.

Analyzing the answers to the question: Have you had any personal problem within social networks? It shows that most of surveyed do report that they have not experienced such problems. As shown in Table 7.

University students largely know that the privacy policies of social networks can be harmful, as reflected in Table 8.

3.3   Addiction

The results in Table 9 show the number of accounts of social networks that university students usually have.

Table 5. Result of the hypothesis: Are young university publishing relevant personal data on social networks? and Are young university accepting all friend requests?

ANOVA[b]

Modelo		Sum of Squares	Gl	Mean Square	F	Sig.
1	Regression	2,587	2	1,294	5,264	.006[a]
	Residual	106,910	435	.246		
	Total	109,498	437			

[a]Predictors: (Constant), Do you accept all friend requests you receive, Do you have any relevant personal information about you posted on a social network?
[b]Dependent Variable: Gender

Table 6. Risk in social networks

Current age *Do you think that you can take risks with social networks? Cross tabulation

			Do you think that you can take risks with social networks?			Total
			No	Yes	Not sure(a)	
Currentage	Between 15 to 19 years	Counter	14	136	15	165
		% within Currentage	8.5 %	82.4 %	9.1 %	100.0 %
	Between 20 to 24 years	Counter	6	133	20	159
		% within Currentage	3.8 %	83.6 %	12.6 %	100.0 %
	Higher to 25 years	Counter	6	96	12	114
		% within Currentage	5.3 %	84.2 %	10.5 %	100.0 %
Total		Counter	26	365	47	438
		% within Currentage	5.9 %	83.3 %	10.7 %	100.0 %

Table 7. Having personal problems in social networks

Gender*Have you had personal problems in social networks? Cross tabulation

			Have you had personal problems in social networks?		Total
			Yes	No	
Gender	Male	Counter	42	176	218
		% Within Gender	19.3 %	80.7 %	100.0 %
	Female	Counter	70	150	220
		% Within Gender	31.8 %	68.2 %	100.0 %
Total		Counter	112	326	438
		% Within Gender	25.6 %	74.4 %	100.0 %

Table 8. Knowledge of the privacy policies

Current Age * Did you know that the privacy policies of some social networks may be harmful because of the personal information that is considered public? Crosstabulation

| | | | Did you know that the privacy policies of some social networks may be harmful because of the personal information that is considered public? | | Total |
			Yes	No	
Current Age	Between 15 to 19 years	Counter	120	45	165
		% within Current age	72.7 %	27.3 %	100.0 %
	Between 20 to 24 years	Counter	114	45	159
		% within Current age	71.7 %	28.3 %	100.0 %
	Higher to 25 years	Counter	75	39	114
		% within Current age	65.8 %	34.2 %	100.0 %
Total		Counter	309	129	438
		% within Current age	70.5 %	29.5 %	100.0 %

Table 9. Social networks accounts

Accounts Frequencies

| | | Answers | | Percentage of Cases |
		N°	Percentage	
In which social networks you have an account?[a]	Facebook	414	30.9 %	94.5 %
	Twitter	256	19.1 %	58.4 %
	Instagram	278	20.7 %	63.5 %
	Whatsapp	387	28.9 %	88.4 %
	Otras	5	.4 %	1.1 %
Total		1340	100.0 %	305.9 %

[a]Dichotomy group tabulated at value 1.

The results of the statistics of social networks most used by university students are found in Table 10.

The statistical results for "Which is the place that you frequently use to connect to social networks?" are shown in Table 11.

Table 10. Social networks most used

Social Networks Frequencies

		Answers		Percentage of Case
		N°	Percentage	
Which social network do you use most?[a]	Facebook	312	35.9 %	71.2 %
	Twitter	56	6.5 %	12.8 %
	Instagram	146	16.8 %	33.3 %
	Whatsapp	346	39.9 %	79.0 %
	Otras	8	.9 %	1.8 %
Total		868	100.0 %	198.2 %

[a]Dichotomy group tabulated at value 1.

Table 11. Places that you frequently use to connect to social networks

Places Frequent Connections

		Answers		Percentage of cases
		N°	Percentage	
Which is the place that you have frequently use to connect to social networks?	Home	398	48.2 %	90.9 %
	Work	97	11.7 %	22.1 %
	Library,	164	19.9 %	37.4 %
	Public places (shopping center, park, restaurant, street, square, etc.)	167	20.2 %	38.1 %
Total		826	100.0 %	188.6 %

[a]Dichotomy group tabulated at value 1.

Table 12. Results of the hypothesis: You have neglected other activities by the frequent use of social networks

ANOVA[b]

Model		Square Sum	gl	Mean square	F	Sig.
1	Regression	4,595	2	2,298	3,723	.025[a]
	Residual	268,466	435	.617		
	Total	273,062	437			

[a]Predictors: (Constant), How often do you use social networks? and Have you neglected other activities for the time spent on social networks?
[b]Dependent Variable: Current age

Another hypothesis is formulated: "Have you neglected other activities by the frequent use of social networks?" Age is the dependent variable and the answers of the questions act as independent variables, namely defined; for the questions "How often do you use social networks?" and "Have you neglected other activities for the time

Table 13. Frequency of use by ages of social networks

Current age * How often do you use social networks? Crosstabulation

			How often do you use social networks?					Total
			Every day, more than two hours a day	Every day, between one hour and two hours a day	Every day, less than an hour a	Some days a week	Once a week	
Current age	Between 15 to 19 years	Counter	86	40	16	19	4	165
		% within Current age	52.1 %	24.2 %	9.7 %	11.5 %	2.4 %	100.0 %
	Between 20 to 24 years	Counter	96	34	16	11	2	159
		% within Current age	60.4 %	21.4 %	10.1 %	6.9 %	1.3 %	100.0 %
	Higher to 25 years	Counter	63	17	17	14	3	114
		% within Current age	55.3 %	14.9 %	14.9 %	12.3 %	2.6 %	100.0 %
Total		Counter		91	49	44	9	438
		% within Current age		20.8 %	11.2 %	10.0 %	2.1 %	100.0 %

Table 14. Problems with family, university representatives or work dueto the misuse of the social networks.

Current age * Have you ever had problems with your family, representatives from a place of study or work, due the misuse of social networks? Cross tabulation

			Have you ever had problems with your family, representatives from a place of study or work, due to misuse of social networks?		Total
			Yes	No	
Current age	Between 15 to 19 years	Counter	37	128	165
		% within Current age	22.4 %	77.6 %	100.0 %
	Between 20 to 24 years	Counter	36	123	159
		% within Current age	22.6 %	77.4 %	100.0 %
	Higher to 25 years	Counter	8	106	114
		% within Current age	7.0 %	93.0 %	100.0 %
Total		Counter	81	357	438
		% within Current age	18.5 %	81.5 %	100.0 %

spent on social networks?", the statistical results show a significance value of 0.025 in ANOVA box, which leads to the hypothesis of equal means (see Table 12).

The statistical results of evaluating the frequency of use of social networks, (see Table 13).

The statistical results determine that most of the times university students who have used social networks have not had family problems. See Table 14.

4 Discussion

Evaluating the results of the present study, it can be inferred that the main use that university students give to social networks has to do with keeping touch with friends in the first place, and obtaining information in the second place. These uses coincide with the first most common activities performed by users of social networks in Spain, based on ONTSI. The third use is concerned with local, national and international events, and as a fourth prominent use we find the activity of uploading pictures or videos.

At the university level, social networks have been used to support courses or informal learning spaces. They are also used to exchange knowledge, as resources that offer the ability to share and generate information in discussion groups for projects or courses [10]. One of the assumptions made in the study is that social networks are useful because they are educational. However, to independently assess this, a high percentage (36.5 %) of responses is obtained in a neutral point.

Additionally acceptance of this hypothesis contrasts with the fact that the 76.5 % has been "often" or "sometimes" inappropriate content. According to our results, the success of social networking is based on the functionality to keep in touch with people and information from networks; for college students, it should serve to be in direct contact with teachers and classmates, with which you exchange experiences and information. According to the Internet Rights & Principles Coalition, everyone has the right to privacy online. This includes the fact of not being monitored, the right to have encrypted information and the right to anonymity. Everyone has the right to data protection, including control over the collection, retention, processing, disposal and disclosure of personal data [11].

In the analysis of privacy, the hypothesis that young students have relevant data on social networking sites and accept all friend requests is rejected. This is expected, because of the students' age and educational maturity about the problem that can be generated. These results differ from the points made by the Ministry of Education of Argentina who publicly states that when teenagers build their blog or profile on a social network, they often think that only their friends can see them, or those who are interested in what they say.

They do not believe that anyone surfing the web, known or unknown, can see what they have written [12]. Another conclusion obtained from the study conducted is that almost all respondents believe that many risks are taken with social networks. Most male university students have had a problem of a personal nature within social networks and, similarly, more than half female students.

Nonetheless, 7,0 % of respondents know that the privacy policies of some social networks may be harmful. Users of social networks know the difficulties they may have if they belong to a social network.

Despite this, most of them have had a personal problem, and that is why the user should be recommended to be aware of continuous suggestions to protect your security and privacy, made by computer specialist area, ranging from knowing the detail of privacy settings, to the assessment of attitudes of contacts within the network. While these infrastructures are constantly evolving to improve safety, at the same time new problems are also emerging.

The analysis of dependency and excessive use of the services provided by the "network of networks". For example in 1996 a brief diagnosis was proposed to evaluate Internet addiction [13]:

1. Do you feel preoccupied with the Internet (think about previous online activities or next online sessions)?
2. Do you feel the need to use the Internet with increasing amounts of time in order to achieve satisfaction?
3. Have you made repeated unsuccessful efforts to control, cut down or stop Internet use?
4. Do you feel restless, moody, depressed, or irritable when attempting to cut or stop Internet use?
5. Do you stay online longer than originally planned?
6. Have you jeopardized or risk losing a significant relationship, job, educational or career opportunity because of the Internet?
7. Have you lied to family members, therapist or others to conceal the extent of involvement in the Internet?
8. Do you use the Internet as a way to escape problems or to relieve an unpleasant mood (e.g., feelings of helplessness, guilt, anxiety, depression)?

The study determined that most Ecuadorian students have three or four different social networking accounts, Whatsapp and Facebook being the most used. Despite being defined as an instant messaging software, the former is considered as a social network by some experts. Almost half of the surveyed university students regularly connect at home, whereas the rest are divided between public places, study and work.

Given the hypothesis about neglecting other activities by the frequent use of social networks, the results leads to its acceptance.

By generating information resulting from the age and frequency of use of social networks, it is determined that more than half of respondents use it every day for more than two hours a day. Students also expressed overwhelmingly that social networks have not led to problems with family members or representatives in their field of study or work.

There are many warnings about the need to make good use of social networks because in one way or another it can lead to addiction of both university students and their families, thus society in general. Other studies conducted in different countries have determined that the negative effects outweigh the positive ones and are the result of the addictive nature of social networks, which generates waste of time instead of being used for studies or academic papers [14].

Furthermore, they indicate that the use of social networks in adolescents and children can ruin their lives as well as having a negative impact on their education [15]. Beyond the definition of a maximum time of connection to social networks is the assessment of what is left to do for them and intervene in productive use for the person and how society should benefit from that.

The study shows that although students said they know the dangers of privacy and security, it does not mean that they are aware of what it really means things like the misuse of data or the danger of posting personal information, eating habits, tours, activities or communicating with people who really do not know, and share with them information that could come lead to becoming a victim of sexual harassment, blackmail, robbery, kidnapping, bank account hacking or impersonation, among many other dangers that may arise. Social networks should have a positive service.

However, if college students do not have a clear guide, and if in the worst case have not been properly trained in the use of social networks, they will be more likely to become victims of social networks and most likely not have sufficient mastery of their use, converting them into an uncontrolled addiction. That is why universities should ensure specialized programs that not only take care of training students to good use and configuration of the rules of privacy and security, but must also ensure an ongoing basis through periodic follow through interviews, review of logs access and navigation of students in the various programs more used as WhatsApp, Facebook, Twitter, Instagram, etc. Therefore, you can get some statistics on the use of social networks and take measures to monitor and custom control to students who show clear signs that they have become victims of uncontrolled addiction in the use of social networks. This fact leads to negative consequences in the use of the studies, so that the academic performance of students is seriously committed to not having self-control and a pattern of normal behavior, which can even lead the student to self-isolation from classmates, teachers and family. Consequently, students become fully devoted to addiction and misuse of social networks that seriously compromise their social, family and educational life. They become a burden to society and they cannot contribute to their own development as an individual and a professional.

People are social beings and current technologies are a quick tool to meet the need of socializing and being informed of facts related to friends and family or collective interest news. Additionally, the feel the need of sharing undertaken activities or special situations at the same time they are being made.

Social networks are a means through which you can consume positive or negative things. As a means of rapid dissemination of information, it is quite clear that alert messages make users aware of the dangers and risks of exposing sensitive data on the network.

It is difficult for people who have an addiction to recognize their problem, especially when continuous use feels good. The indiscriminate use can reverse the positive aspects. The use of social networks like any other activity can become addictive, depending on the vulnerability of the person, caused by environmental or biological factors.

5 Conclusions and Recommendations

Universities go through significant changes in the interaction with students because emerging technological tools provide a wide variety of attractive and active services. Social networks are used globally, and relevant use is a challenge for those that guide and get profit from them. Experts should develop appropriate strategies to take advantage of the speed of communication between people who give us these infrastructures. Teachers must generate and continuously publish clear and concise information of value to contribute to the individual's formation, and accompany these strategies with the motivation for participants to create new knowledge.

As with any new activity you want to start, regarding social networks, students must first have knowledge of their, including the risks that may occur, and the minimum security and privacy settings that must be implemented. It is not enough to just create a profile and start interacting with it, not even having prior knowledge of it. It is necessary to maintain the need to be attentive to the evolution of social networks.

Privacy policies and security are present in all environments and are known to be there, but it depends on the users to adopt them and regulate the level of privacy and thus increase or decrease the risks involved in publishing personal or sensitive content. It is recommended to keep updated studies on best practices in social networks regularization. A new way of dependence on technology is increasing and specifically with continuous communication and virtual interaction with another user or group of users, generating a significant human toll, causing potential problems of physical and mental kind.

It is discarding personal interaction, in exchange for the use of technological tools of socialization, leading to the isolation of the human being. If signs of addiction as a disease is present, this should be addressed as such, and therefore should go to a specialist in the field to find the solution to this problem of dependency.

The use of social networks extends rapidly, and it is important to be aware of the behavior of young students, especially because they do not necessarily know the real implications of sharing personal data on this kind of networks.

The government should be concerned with developing specialized training programs in the use of social networks that train students at schools and colleges to get to know the pitfalls in social networks, so that they are not innocent victims of network corruption or pornography. It is very important to have it clear that technology should be a supporting tool, and not become an uncontrolled addiction that does not generate anything positive in their lives. At the same time, education plans must start in schools and colleges so that young students can be better prepared to meet these challenges and to get the most out of these social networks without compromising their personal security and their families'.

Thus, when they get at the college level, they will have extensive knowledge of the rules posed by social networks and have clear concepts of privacy and security, so that they can configure without any kind of problem in these programs without a misuse of personal data.

Universities must also ensure that their students, especially those at their first course, know, manage and master social networks and their use in their personal, educational, family benefit, to ensure the promotion of good intercommunication with its university environment. They should also avoid an uncontrolled addiction that only generates problems. In this sense, universities must have departments of psychology and social services to guide students. At the same time, they should offer courses or workshops that teach students the pros and cons of these online programs of socializing, so it could reduce the rate of misuse of personal data and the risk of such data being misused by people of dubious origin.

Universities can launch special programs on campus using social networks so that you can balance the educational activities along with those of interaction with such social networking programs. This is especially to develop among young people, combining their academic commitments with recreation in social networks. Students are encouraged to develop a professional profile, having enough self-control of the use of programs or social networking sites. Bad attitudes like the ones presented here can have bad impact on society, as generations of young professionals become unproductive because they devote too many hours to the use of social networks, becoming incompetent, which will greatly harm the development of society. These future professionals will not be able to advance in their position, rather they will become the future scourges of society. They will survive on social assistance and will always occupy lower hierarchical positions in companies, this situation affecting their social and family life. Therefore, it is important to know how to guide, train and empower college students to be the ones who dominate social networks and not the opposite.

University teachers recommend further research on this topic, and encourage the creation of new knowledge through these infrastructures. Those who actively participate in social networks should know the appropriate form of action and risks that this activity has. They should make use of the best practices of intervention in social networks made by experts, being aware of the need for personal interaction beyond network interaction. They also recognize that the continued use of social networks is an addiction and if detected, we should seek professional alternative solutions.

The results of this study have provided a basis for generating new research and action plans that incorporate strategies to lead to a better use of social networks by university students, as well as evaluating the terms and conditions of use that refer to privacy carrying out periodical assessment of the levels of addiction to social networks.

References

1. Administrative Department of the Presidency of the Republic of Colombia. http://es.presidencia.gov.co/noticia/160407-Colombia-duplica-acceso-a-internet-y-avanza-en-uso-de-redes-sociales-gracias-a-las-politicas-del-Gobierno
2. Steinert-Threlkeld, Z.C., Mocanu, D., Vespignani, A., Fowler, J.: Online social networks and offline protest. EPJ Data Sci. **4**, 1–9 (2015). doi:10.1140/epjds/s13688-015-0056-y
3. Lin, S.-H., Warschauer, M., Blake, R.: Language learning through social networks: perceptions and Reality. Lang. Learn. Technol. **20**(1), 124–147 (2016)
4. Mompean, J., Fouz-González, J.: Twitter-based EFL pronunciation instruction. Lang. Learn. Technol. **20**(1), 166–190 (2016)

5. National Observatory of Telecommunications and Information Society: ONTSI. http://www. ontsi.red.es/ontsi/sites/default/files/redes_sociales-documento_0.pdf
6. Ministry of Telecommunication and Information Society: ICT Observatory Ecuador. http:// www.observatoriotic.mintel.gob.ec/biblioteca/download-info/analisis-del-porcentaje-de-hogares-con-acceso-a-internet/
7. Roa Buendía, J.: Seguridad Informática; Segunda edn. McGraw-Hill/Interamericana de España, S. L., Madrid, España (2013)
8. Najaflou, Y., Jedari, B., Xia, F., Yang, L., Obaidat, M.: Safety challenges and solutions in mobile social networks. IEEE Syst. J. **9**(3), 834–854 (2015)
9. Echeburúa, E.: Catholic University of Valencia. http://online.ucv.es/resolucion/como-prevenir-la-adiccion-a-las-redes-sociales-en-jovenes-y-adolescentes-por-enrique-echeburua/
10. Peñalosa Castro, E.: Estrategias docentes con tecnologías: guía práctica. Pearson Educación de México, S.A.de C.V, Naucalpan de Juárez, México (2013)
11. Internet Rights & Principles Coalition: Internet Rights & Principles Coalition. http://inter netrightsandprinciples.org/site/wp-content/upoads/2014/06/IRPC_10RightsandPrinciples_ 28May2014-11.pdf
12. Ministry of Education and Sports of the Nation, Argentina: Ministry of Education and Sports of the Nation. http://www.me.gov.ar/escuelaymedios/material/redes.pdf
13. Young, K.: The Center for Internet Addiction. http://www.netaddiction.com/articles/ newdisorder.pdf
14. NdegeMuhingi, W., Mutavi, T., Kokonya, D., NekesaSimiyu, V., Ben, M., Obondo, A., WangariKuria, M.: Social networks and students' performance in secondary schools: lessons from an open learning centre, Kenya. J. Educ. Pract. **6**(21), 171–177 (2015)
15. Alwagait, E., Shahzad, B., Alim, S.: Impact of social media usage on student academic performance in Saudi Arabia. Comput. Hum. Behav. **51**(B), 1092–1097 (2015)

Software Engineering

Analysis of Risk Factors of ERP (Enterprise Resource Planning) Systems Information Technologies

William Bazán[✉], Teresa Samaniego, Abel Alarcón, and Ana Rodríguez

School of Computer and Information Science, Agrarian University of Ecuador,
Guayaquil, Ecuador
{wbazan,tsamaniego,jalarcon,arodriguez}@uagraria.edu.ec

Abstract. The present paper is about collected information on software development and the implementation of the ERP system. It aims to get to know the perception on the given and installed system as well as the factors that were introduced after the system implementation.

The study explores the critical factors that were found in the implementation of ERP systems, which invites to delve into the review of these systems. The last part of the study presents conclusions and recommendations to take into consideration by enterprises about the elements which make the ERP system become successful. They allow us to classify it into each of the main aspects. The reason is that they have a positive impact on the project. In other words, they offer a series of parameters for software development of commercial organizations such as industry, which should think about the implementation of an ERP system.

Keywords: Critical factors · ERP system · Impact · Integrated systems

1 Introduction

Systems enterprise resource planning (ERP) software systems are considered software systems of a general kind, which contain modules that aid in the differentiation of areas such as production, sales, distribution, finance, human resources, and maintenance amongst others.

ERP systems are currently used to help us in order to manage any company more successfully. Within the study of ERP systems, we must not forget the existing critical risk factors of this software system, since it does not allow us to change decisions so we should try to ensure that the decisions we make are the most appropriate ones.

First of all, we face the arduous and expensive task of approving and implementing it, which requires much effort, commitment and a fully designed, planned study.

We can mention the following critical factors found:

- Transition to the new system
- Work overload
- Difficulty of estimating costs
- Rotation of key personnel
- Adjustment legislation

© Springer International Publishing AG 2016
R. Valencia-García et al. (Eds.): CITI 2016, CCIS 658, pp. 131–142, 2016.
DOI: 10.1007/978-3-319-48024-4_11

- Lack of technically trained personnel
- Lack of written procedures
- Adaptation of hardware and telecommunications

It is noteworthy that these can be improved with the aid of reengineering business processes, which will proceed to address the points of failure through continued application of feedback, which could be found before in other cases of application of ERP systems, allowing us to find the maximum benefits of these systems. It should also be taken into account that in the process of implementation of ERP systems, the provider should become the implementation consultant with possible solutions.

ERP systems are an evolution of systems Production Resource Planning, MRP (Manufacturing Resources Planning), which focus on the planning of activities of manufacturing companies. Before 1960, the main focus of the systems inventory control was based on the basics of inventory [1].

During the 1960s, the first computers and the first MRP first appeared. Planning Material Requirements (MRP-I) was one of the first applications for these businesses [2].

The MRP software supported the creation and maintenance of material master data and bills of materials across all products and parts, in one or more manufacturing plants [1].

During the 1970s some of the major software vendors such as SAP, J.D. Edwards and Oracle with its renowned Structured Query Language (SQL) appeared.

After a general overview of the article, presented in the introduction, we present a brief description of the literature review divided into three main points. Later, the article presents the methodology used. Finally, the main conclusions reached are presented.

2 Quality Software Metrics, Measurement and Indicators

We begin by defining the different concepts presented in the introduction, facilitating the understanding of the subject by the reader.

Tejerina, [3] states that Quality Software is the fulfillment of the requirements of functionality and performance explicitly established, explicitly documented development standards and implicit characteristics expected of all professionally developed software. Software quality is a complex mix of factors that may vary across different applications and according to customers who request them.

The success of the software depends on a set of qualities, which are designed to give a high degree of customer satisfaction: to the revisions of comprehensive techniques before testing, to quantitatively determine what is important for a product before starting the tests, to provide assurance and reliability to have a test plan and to list the objectives of the test concisely. To produce quality software is the major goal for engineers.

Pressman, (2010) in [4] mentions that Software Quality should be added in all product life-cycle management. The various tasks for inserting a quality control in software development in this analysis are:

1. Use of methodologies and development methods.
2. Reuse formal review procedure.
3. Constant testing of software development.
4. Adjustments to set standards for software development.
5. Verification of changes, measurable calculations and accumulation of information.
6. Managing reports about development in software quality.

There are dozens of metrics or measures exclusively oriented towards product development, as it is the case with this quality software, the life cycle from its design, coding, testing and maintenance is related to the need to control different attributes, structure, accuracy, coupling and complexity of it being difficult to have a single quality value [4]. Different types of metrics allow for the quantification and qualification needed to improve the final software, with different criteria according to the appearance, technologies, and functionalities depending on user requirements, this allows for the quality to be valued from the moment we plan to develop any software.

A measure provides a quantitative indication of the amount, full, extension, size, capacity or size of some attribute of a product or process [4]. A measure is an indication of amount and size of a product, applying it in its development.

A metric is an assessment of the degree to which a system, component or process has a specific tribute (extension, quantity, dimensions, capacity or size). A software engineer collects measures and develops metrics in order to obtain indicators [4].

The metric is more directed to the evaluation factors of the system, component or procedure for a given attribute, where a group of measures exist, and they become metrics that provide us with indicators.

An indicator is a metric, or a metric combination that provides us with unknown information. This knowledge will allow the project manager or software engineers to prepare the process, project or product for it to work better [4, 5].

All these products are based on several parameters which lead software development. These parameters are required by organizations so that their applications can be efficient. They are all related: software quality, metrics, indicators.

2.1 Quality Management Software

The objective of managing software quality is to understand what the customer expectations for quality are, and to implement and plan in order to meet these expectations. After all, as we know the customer defines quality. Therefore, it is necessary to evaluate each individual quality of the software, in order to be able to determine one or more metrics that can be obtained to reflect these properties. One example of this could be the creation of a quality characteristic that guarantees that lesser amounts of errors occur. It can be measured by counting errors which are defects of a solution [6].

2.2 Risk Management Errors

"For a long time, the software projects have been considered high-risk projects prone to failure" as stated [7], and "recognizes that risk management is one of the best practices in the software industry to reduce the surprise factor" according to [8].

2.3 Errors Management

A key aspect, important in developing reliable software, is the phase analysis of error distribution as proposed in fault types defined in IEEE (1998) [9].

This analysis reveals the existence of procedures for data acquisition and technical checks, regular checks of a software product made by a team or qualified personnel, which determines its ability to use, try and recognized specifications and standards, that can be classified in requirements for reviews, analysis, design and documentation to be established at the time of the proposal with the client [8].

2.4 Measures for Error Handling

There are many techniques for the revision of a software product from its development stage, in addition to this, they give us a future vision of the results of a product.

Verification and validation can be defined as the process of ensuring that each phase of the life cycle development correctly implements the specifications of the previous phase, and that the software obtained meets its requirements. The tests imply the controlled execution of the code program looking for errors. Formal reviews are planned and periodic reviews of the products obtained carried out by developers, customers, users and managers to assess progress. Inspections and walk-throughs are systematic reviews of software products obtained by the pairs made with the purpose of finding errors [10].

2.5 Systemic Quality Model

Systemic Model of Quality in software development allows us to measure the Systemic Quality of a developer of software, which starts off with the quality of the product at the time it occurs and the quality of the process of its production. The model provides verification of a level of quality that will change between None, Basic, Intermediate and Advanced [11].

Systemic Quality Models indicate which processes need to be improved in the company and properties that have not been fulfilled in the software product developed [11].

3   Model for Defining Stages in Metric

The proposed model for defining stages in metric is shown in Fig. 1. This model is based on the work presented in [12]. As it can be seen the process consists of five different steps that are described below:

1. Identification - Stage in which the scope is defined when creating metrics, as well as asking hypothesis to carry out measurement software during its development. Obtaining information about the main requirements to be met by the metric.
2. Creation - Stage in which the metric is defined according to the requirements preset in the previous stage. You need to perform a theoretical validation based on statistical mathematical methods, among others, that ensure that the metric used meets the objective. An empirical validation through surveys, experiments and case studies validated metrics are also performed.
3. Acceptance - After obtaining a valid metric it is usually necessary to go through a stage of acceptance of the metric, testing in real environments whether the measure meets the desired objectives.
4. Application - The metric is accepted and used for the field of application for which it was created.
5. Accreditation - This stage runs in parallel with the implementation phase and aims at maintaining the metric, as a result of this stage a metric can be withdrawn, as it is no longer useful or reused to start a new process.

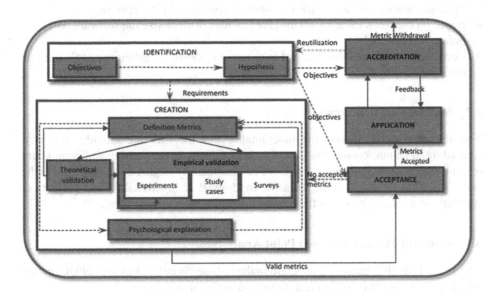

Fig. 1. Stages definition method metric.

One of the primary concerns among quality metrics is located in the measures of usability of the product produced. If the product is user friendly, it can be measured through the characteristics of how we see the end user use the system, considering the time employed in its use, the benefits provided, and how users value subjectively the system produced as mentioned [13].

Therefore, it is noteworthy that a product developed following the above steps will allow us to determine whether the software has been adequately developed, if the metric used was appropriate for the development of the product, or to identify why problems appeared. Below you can see a table of the stages of the metric model described.

3.1 Characteristics of a Functional Metric

According to Duran Rubio (2003, p. 48) "The size of the software could be measured in terms of bytes occupied on the disk, the number of programs, the number of lines of code, functionality it provides, or simply the number of screens or reports you have". The characteristics of a functional metric are as follows:

- Technological independence. - Once we have established the required functionality we must choose technology needed to achieve this functionality.
- Simplicity. - The metric should not require great efforts to achieve a measure. A disadvantage of this feature would be that the software would not be as detailed for noticeable results, such as mathematical operations.
- Focus on the functionality provided. - This refers to the advantages to be acquired by implementing the new software, when making a technical review.
- Based on user requirements. - This gives an idea of what size the software will have before it is finished.
- Consistency. - The results obtained in different systems and different people must be consistent.

3.2 Metrics Function Points

This metric tries to measure the functionality that the software provides the user. According to Duran Rubio (2003, p. 49), "It is a metric to set the size and complexity of computer systems based on the amount of functionality required and delivered to the users" or, "The Function Points measure the logical or functional size of projects or software applications based on the functional requirements of the user".

3.3 Standard Method Function Point Analysis

The method which is becoming standard in the industry is defined by the IFPUG, called Function Point Analysis (FPA) and its authors define it as follows:

"Standard Method for measuring software development from the point of view of the user" [14].

The selection of indicators includes efforts measurement (person-hours) and costs (in money), both real and planned ones, number of deliverables accepted by the user and deviations, reused effort from other projects or inactivity in human resources, number of modifications in the product and information on its evaluation (solicited, rejected and accepted), dedicated effort to error detection and correction, number of completed reviews, and information on error detection to evaluate product quality (i.e. errors detected before and after delivery). Many of the indicators also include broken down by phase measures (i.e. breakdown in requirements, design, coding and documentation) measurements.

3.4 Steps to Determine a Function Points Metric

In this section we describe the steps to determine a function points metric, where the method identifies the components of S.I. assigning a number of points based on the complexity function, and the sum of this gives us the unadjusted function points. The final adjustment is done at the end, taking into account the general characteristics of any computer system [15]. The different stages are shown in Fig. 2 and they are explained next in detail.

- Step 1. To determine the type of count. In this step we determine the target count, defined if it counts in the development, maintenance or if a software is already installed.
- Step 2. To identify the scope of measurement and limits of the application.
- Step 3. To count Data functions. Here we determine the data storage capacity. Both, internal logical file and the external interface are analyzed. A value of this complexity is assigned, considering the data. This value can be high, medium or low.
- Step 4. To count the Transactional functions. This step measures the ability to perform operations; each component is assigned a value of complexity (high, medium or low), considering the available data.

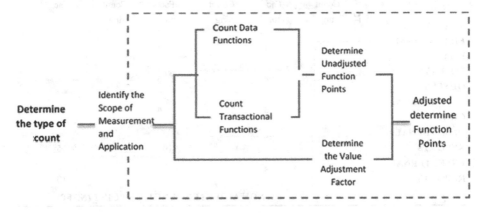

Fig. 2. Steps to determine a function points metric [14].

Function points are calculated by using information parameters and the level of complexity of the software. The information parameters are five:

- Number of external input (EI). This input is the information originated about the user or the information that is transferred from other software. The input is frequently used for the updating of logic reports.
- Number of external output (EO). This output consists of data which are generated within the application and are transformed into information for the user.

- Number of external consults or reports (ECR). They are online information based on a user's requirement.
- Number of internal reports (IR). They are the data found in the database and which are updated with external input.
- Number of external reports (ER). They are data which come from storage out of the application.

Table 1 shows how these information parameters are related to the level of complexity.

- Step 5. To determine the unadjusted function points. In this phase the total is obtained by adding up the number of components according to the assigned complexity.
- Step 6. To determine the value adjustment factor. The adjustment value is obtained by adding 0.65 to the total sum of the degrees of influence of the 14 general system characteristics multiplied by 0.01.

Table 1. Calculation of the function point

											Total
CALCULATION OF THE FUNCTION POINT											
INFORMATION PARAMETERS	**TOTAL COUNTING**	LEVEL OF COMPLEXITY									
		LOW				MEDIUM			HIGH		
		Counting	X	Factor	+	Counting	X	Factor	+	Counting	X	Factor
EI: EXTERNAL INPUT		3				4				6	
EO: EXTERNAL OUTPUT		4				5				7	
EC: EXTERNAL CONSULTS		3				4				6	
IR: INTERNAL REPORTS		7				10				15	
ER: EXTERNAL REPORTS		5				7				10	
NON ADJUSTED FUNCTION POINT (NAFP):											

In order to calculate the FP, we use the following formula:

FP = NAFPT[0,65 + 0,01 × SUMAF]

Where SUMAF (sum of the adjusted factor Table 2) are software technical parameters which are determined as it is shown in the following table. They range from 0–5, where this value is based on certain technical conditions for the development of the software.

- Step 7. To determine the adjusted function points. In this phase we considered the unadjusted function points by the adjustment factor.

Table 2. Adjust factor of technical complexity

ADJUST FACTOR OF TECHNICAL COMPLEXITY

FEATURE	VALUE
1 Data communication	
2 Distributed functions	
3 Benefits	
4 High use of configuration	
5 Transfer speed	
6 Online data input	
7 Efficiency design by the end user	
8 Online data updating	
9 Complexity of the internal logic process of the application	
10 Code reusability	
11 Ease of installation	
12 Ease of operation	
13 Multiple localizations	
14 Ease of change	
SUM OF ADJUSTED FACTOR (SUMAF)	

3.5 Software Project Risks

PMI (2013) mentions a temporary effort needed for the project to create a product complying with certain objectives [16]. Similarly, we understand risk as the event which, should it occur, produces an effect either positive or negative in any of the objectives for creating a product. For risk management software projects, we should take into account that for its definition and study we should identify, study, analyze and eliminate each and every one of the possible threats before starting the project, in order to encounter less elements of risk by the end of the project, which may impede achieving the proposed objectives.

Spector and Gifford, (2010) indicate that risks can be caused by various reasons or situations [17]. In order to improve the risk management in software projects, several guides have been published: PRINCE2, ISO standards 10006: 2003, and PMI. These guidelines provide methods and procedures focused on information systems, which help in risk management software projects.

Alba, (2008) [18] presents the stages for risk management in software projects, each of which focuses on the treatment of the risks mentioned below:

- Identify risks: It is about recognizing the potential risks which may cause problems or failures in the project.

- Analyze risks: Each of the risks is analyzed and classified by groups according to their priority.
- Assess risks: At this stage the chances of occurrence and potential grievances that may affect the project are evaluated.
- Risk treatment: we identify methods, procedures, implementations, modifications which may be needed to solve the potential risks in a project.
- Risk monitoring: This has to do with all the processes which are performed to address the risks which must be monitored, in order to ensure that controls are effective and provide valuable information to detect possible changes affecting the draft.

4   International Standard ISO

The evaluation and calculation of the functionality that a computer system has is regarded as the anguish that the whole industry dedicates to the development of the software. It is important to bear in mind that having a metric is not enough today, nonetheless, this metric should be standard so that it can be used in different companies, allowing developers to have access to, and to share indicators among the industries of software engineering products that are easy to manage and understand [19]. To compare the productivity (Function Points per person month) of a company with the industry data is critical in improvement plans [14].

5   Methodology

This research was eminently descriptive; we provided a detailed analysis of all results obtained in the exploratory study carried out, where in some organizations, ERP systems were fully settled satisfactorily. This study was supported in the review of the relevant resources available between 2013 and 2016. We examined seven implementation methodologies: Total Solution, FastTrack, ASAP, AIM, SureStep, OpenERP and Openbravo. Each of these methods was analyzed according to the proposed unified methodology of [20], which raises the following essential elements:

1. Project Management, which holds the project planning and scheduling, monitoring and feedback and risk management
2. Managing change as there seems to be a lack of focus on issues such as: activities, processes, methodologies associated with the understanding of this process, which in some cases have led to the failure of such projects.
3. Training, the complexity of these applications requires rigorous training, which if not carried out can lead to drastic consequences and is considered one of the main reasons for failure of ERP implementations.
4. Implementation level: Strategic, evaluation of current legacy systems; Tactical; Operating.

The critical factors found are studied in depth in the review of these systems, which are made including some questions about how efficient the systems are with senior management, which is the selection process for the system, composition when choosing the team, training and user participation, and the different problems facing their organizations during the implementation process and after.

This study ends by giving recommendations to companies about the issues that must be taken into account in order to implement ERP systems successfully.

6 Conclusions

Critical risk factors are presented as part of an ERP system. This research has been developed after a thorough exploratory study which does not transcend beyond the issue of the ERP. The type of solution that the author provides is reasonable in terms of representation and information shared.

Surveys, interviews and questionnaires let us know about the shortcomings of the proposed system, and after experimentation, in some companies we were able to observe some critical aspects of these systems. Thus, after a very detailed study, the author proposes feedback in order to provide solutions, where the provider must go beyond the questions raised.

Total Solutions methodologies and Fast Track, used by consulting houses, do not endorse any particular software, thus, they are more general in its recommendations and include considerations oriented more towards project management and change management. Nonetheless, it should be mentioned that Deloitte Fast Track offers on its website, its methodology focused on versions of both products SAP and Oracle.

A fully documented system with a comprehensive literature allows companies to incorporate an ERP system and thus, providing technical information regarding the proper use of this resource, which must be based on the implementation of the system for its later adjustment to an existing system.

The final conclusion of this study eradicates in the importance given to the selection process of an ERP system, taking into consideration the fact that critical risk factors can affect my current system, which measures prevent chaos in case of replacement of the current system, with one that provides more comfort to our company, and how reliable this system is if we do not have the necessary data, as mentioned is an exploratory study where the main shortcomings of these systems were found, in cases where there was not information about problems that the use of ERP presents. Good planning and integration with the systems fosters the necessary change in working procedures, and proper selection of the supplier, to deliver the fully integrated system to our company, provides us with information about the process of implementation of the system with all its resources, together with the necessary support for our organization.

References

1. Metaxiotis, K.S., Psarras, J.E., Ergazakis, K.A.: Production scheduling in ERP systems: an AI based approach to face the gap. Bus. Process Manag. J. **9**(2), 221–247 (2003)
2. Orlicky, J.A.: Material Requirements Planning—The New Way of Life in Production and Inventory Management. McGraw-Hill, New York (1975)

3. Tejerina, W.C.: Product dimensions for the software. Jujuy National University of Jujuy (2014)
4. Pressman, R.: Software Engineering, 5th edn. McGraw Hill, New York (2010)
5. Pressman, R.: Good Practices. McGraw Hill, New York (1998)
6. Scalone, F.: Estudio Comparativo de los Modelos y Estándares de Calidad de Software. Buenos Aires, pp. 22–23 (2006)
7. Bannerman, P.: Risk and risk management in software projects: a reassessment. J. Syst. Softw. **81**, 2118–2133 (2008)
8. Dolado, J.J., Aguirregoitta, A., Presedo, C.: Study metrics for project control software. In: Proceedings of the Conference on Software Engineering and Database, SISTEDES, Barcelona pp. 65–72 (2010)
9. IEEE: Standard Dictionary of Measures to produce reliable software. IEEE (1998)
10. Thayer, R.H.: Software engineering project management, 2nd edn. Wiley - IEEE Computer Society Press, New York (2001)
11. Mendoza, L., Perez, M., Griman, A.: Prototype systemic quality model (MOSCA) software. Comput. Syst. **8**, 198–199 (2005)
12. Serrano, M., Piattini, M., Calero, C., Genero, M., Miranda, D.: A method for defining software metrics. ALARCOS Group, University of Castilla (2010)
13. Gorga, G., Madoz, M., Heavy, P.: Towards a proposal of metrics for evaluating educational software. Laboratory Research and Development in Informatics, pp. 16–18
14. Duran Rubio, S.E.: Points for function. Metric standard to set the size of the software. Comput. Policy Bull. **6**, 50–63 (2003)
15. Duran Rubio, S.E.: Puntos por función. Métricas estándar para establecer el tamaño del software. Boletín de Política Informática, No. 6, pp. 50–63 (2003)
16. PMI: A Guide to the Project Management of Body (2013)
17. Spector, A., Gifford, D.: A computer science perspective of bridge design (2010)
18. Alba, C.: Prediction and classification of the risk level in systems projects. Oviedo University (2008)
19. Fairley, R.: Managing and Leading Software Projects. Wiley - IEEE Computer Society Press, New York (2009)
20. Al-Mudimigh, A., Zairi, M., Al-Mashari, M.: ERP software implementation: an integrative framework. Eur. J. Inf. Syst. **10**(4), 216–226 (2001)
21. Tomala, C., Jazmin, S.: Quality metrics information systems, application quality certification of a company in the oil and gas sector. Guayaquil-ESPOL (2009)
22. Garzás, J., Irrazabal, E.: Basic metrics and analysis of open source tools to measure maintainability. REICIS Rev. Esp. Innovación **6**(3), 55–65 (2010)
23. Scalone, F.: Comparative study of models and software quality standards (2006)
24. Kendall, K., Kendall, J.: Analysis and Design of Systems. Ed. Pearson Education, Essex (2005)
25. Lafuente, G. J.: Conceptual framework for the definition and exploitation of quality metrics. Malaga University, Malaga (2014)

Analyzing HTML5-Based Frameworks for Developing Educational and Serious Games

Humberto Marín-Vega[1(✉)], Giner Alor-Hernandez[1],
Ramón Zatarain-Cabada[2], and M. Lucía Barrón-Estrada[2]

[1] Division of Research and Postgraduate Studies,
Instituto Tecnológico de Orizaba, Orizaba, Mexico
humbert_marin@outlook.com, galor@itorizaba.edu.mx
[2] Division of Research and Postgraduate Studies, Instituto Tecnológico de
Culiacán, Culiacán, Mexico
{rzatarain,lbarron}@itculiacan.edu.mx

Abstract. The gamification of learning is an educational approach to motivate students to learn by using video game design and game elements in learning environments. Nowadays different knowledge fields, such as medicine, entertainment, education, among others, are using this approach. HTML5-based frameworks have emerged as information technologies for developing serious games and educational games. This paper presents an analysis of the most used HTML5-based frameworks in order to identify games and learning attributes supported for developing educational and serious games.

Keywords: Gamification · Games categories · HTML5-based framework · Serious games

1 Introduction

In education, game-based learning is a motivating factor, games in learning are often attractive for their rules, their rewards systems and their environments [1]. Gamification is the use of game mechanics and experience design to digitally engage and motivate people to achieve their goals [2]. Through gamification we can not only create a mindset that encourages students to try new things, to not be afraid of failing [3], but also can enable students to engage in enjoyable experiences for the purpose of learning. From this perspective, Gamification appears as the use of game mechanics in environments and applications are not playfulness, to generate and transfer knowledge, enabling the development of competencies in human talent and is related to decision-making activities [4–6]. At the same time, games have become a very useful tool to bring in knowledge management from the practice of simulated environments in the context of various knowledge fields [7–10].

An innovative implementation for learning is the use of serious games (Serious Games, SG) commonly motivated by the need to educate, report or shape about a specific topic [11]. A serious game is a game in which education (in its various forms) is the primary goal, rather than entertainment. The advantage of serious games as a tool for learning is mainly based on the ability to balance entertainment, interactivity and

R. Valencia-García et al. (Eds.): CITI 2016, CCIS 658, pp. 143–154, 2016.
DOI: 10.1007/978-3-319-48024-4_12

replay ability of the typical games with the learning objectives of a specific educational goal. Serious games offer to developers ways to reduce, cross-collaterize, to other wise mitigate some of the cost of developing technology and content for games. Serious games can also help developers keep their teams busy between larger, retail-oriented projects, In addition, serious games can allow the developer chances to experiment with new styler of gameplay and even new types of distribution. Some knowledge fields where these games are used are education, medicine, corporate and military [12].

HTML5-based framework allow developing Web applications, native mobile and hybrid applications by using game strategies and techniques [13], There are several HTML5-based frameworks and the selection process is a very difficult task, therefore the objective of this work is to provide support on the selection processes of HTML5-based framework depending on the activities to be considered in the development of an educational application. This paper presents an analysis of the HTML5-based framework considering learning activities in order to provide a reference for choosing the most suitable games engine for the development of educational applications, serious games or both.

This paper is organized as follows: Sect. 2 presents recent advances in state-of-the-art of use of gamification techniques on educational applications and the use of Serious Games on educational applications. Section 3 describes the HTML5-based frameworks for developing educational and serious games. Section 4 presents the Learning activities on educational and serious games. Section 5 presents an analysis of HTML5-based frameworks for developing educational and serious games, as well as shows the results of the analysis. Section 6 describes the conclusions and future directions to be taken.

2   State of the Art

In recent years, several studies have been proposed with the aim of improving the development of educational games. Most of these research works have been focused on the use of gamification in a variety of contexts. In this section, we present a set of related works focused on the use of educational games, serious games and both. These works have been organized according to the kind of application to be developed: (1) gamification applications, (2) serious games.

2.1   Use of Gamification Techniques on Educational Applications

Simões et al. [14] aimed to assist educators and schools with a set of powerful and engaging educational tools to improve students' motivation and learning outcomes. The research intends to develop a framework for the use of these tools to be integrated and tested in an existent social learning environment called schoooools.com. Armstrong [15] defined the concept of gamification as a way of tapping into motivational forces to increase individual investment in a system, process, or resource. A way of applying gamification is through extrinsic motivation where it is involved in external factors unrelated to the nature of the activity itself. Lubin [16] described that

Gamification offers a way to minimize disengagement while actually enhancing learning. Gamification, if correctly applied, could revolutionize an organization's approach to training, development and instructing individuals. Kapp [17] proposed that gamification offers instructional design an opportunity to re-engage these individuals and make the relevancy of the instructional situation more apparent through the implementation of gamification in training and educational settings. Kapp defined gamification as the use of game based mechanics, aesthetics and game thinking to engage people, motivate action, promote learning and solve problems. Robson et al. [18] introduced and demarcated the principles of gamification; gamification was defined as the application of game-design principles in order to change behaviors in non-game situations. Fui-Hoon Nah et al. [19] identified several game design elements that were used in education. These game design elements include points, levels/stages, badges, leaderboards, prizes, progress bars, storyline, and feedback. They provided examples from the literature to illustrate the application of gamification in the educational context. De-Marcos et al. [20] presented the results of testing both social networking and gamification in an undergraduate course, comparing them in terms their effect on students' academic achievement, participation and attitude. The effects of a gamification plugin deployed in a learning management system were compared to those of a social networking site in the same educational setting. Arias Aranda et al. [21] analyzed the entrepreneurial attitude of high school students on the basis of the EAO (Entrepreneurship Attitude Orientation) scale through the participation of students on a gamified business simulation.

2.2   Use of Serious Games on Educational Applications

Obikwelu and Read [22] showed adoption of basic tenets of constructivism in the design of learning environments. The work aims at ascertaining the extent to which serious games have adopted this pedagogical principle in its approach to facilitating learning. Pereiraa et al. [23] established a shared vocabulary with the creation of a detailed taxonomy based in Personal and Social Learning & Ethics. The presented taxonomy for the field of interest Personal and Social Learning & Ethics worked well for survey purposes. The representative games selected are an example of the type of complete categorization that can be achieved with it. Carrozzinoa et al. [24] presented the concept and the work-in-progress of SONNA, a research project aiming to analyze the impact of social networks, Web 2.0 and interactive multimedia as tools for learning. Raybourn [25] introduced a new paradigm for more effective and scalable training and education called transmedia learning. Transmedia learning is defined as the scalable system of messages representing a narrative or core experience that unfolds from the use of multiple media, emotionally engaging learners by involving them personally in the story. Barbosa and Silva [26] discussed the importance of Serious Games and development phases of a Serious Game developed for the Web by using WebGL technology. With this technology, developers can create compelling 3D environments and 3D video games that can be accessed by nearly every person that has an Internet connection. Donovan [27] intended to provide the industry partners with the research evidence for the effectiveness of serious games in learning; provided examples of serious games usage in the corporate sector; identifying the types of learning content suited to a games-based learning approach; and outline key considerations when designing games for learning. Provelengios and Georgios [28] referred to the utilization of serious games for educational purposes. A case study on the use of Food Force serious game as a learning tool in elementary education is reported.

3 HTML5-Based Frameworks for Developing Educational and Serious Games

A game engine is a software framework designed for the creation and development of video games. Developers use them to create games for consoles, mobile devices and personal computers. Typically, a game engine includes support programs, libraries and an interpreted language among others to help develop and unite the different components of a project [29]. Currently, there are different HTML5-based frameworks that allow the development of games able to be applied in a wide range of browsers and platforms from a single development in some cases [13]. The most commons HTML5-based frameworks engines are:

- **Construct 2** is an HTML5-based framework editor that uses drag-and-drop functionality to allow users creating complex and engaging games with no programming experience. It is one of the most accessible 2D game development tools available [30].
- **ImpactJS** is JavaScript game engine that allows developing stunning HTML5 Games for desktop and mobile browsers [13].
- **Quintus** is an HTML5-based framework designed to be modular and lightweight, with a concise JavaScript-friendly syntax. The engine is easy, HTML5 and JavaScript can be used to develop video games that runs in a browser on many different devices [31].
- **WADE** is a Web-based visual editor. Wade takes care of different resolutions, low-level optimizations and different input devices enabling making multiplatform games easy and quick [32].
- **pixi.js** is a graphics-rendering engine for making websites, games and mobile applications. By using pixi.js, interactive graphics can be created and displayed, scenes and animated transitions can be built, cross-platform, responsive games and applications for multiple screen resolutions by using WebGL can be developed [33].
- **EaselJS** provides a display list to allow working with display elements on a canvas as nested objects. It also provides a simple framework for providing shape based mouse interactions on elements in the display list [13].
- **melonJS** is a free, light-weight HTML5-based framework. The engine integrates the tiled map format making level design easier [34].
- **Three.js** is a library that provides a very easy-to-use JavaScript API based on the features of WebGL. 3D graphics can be created without having to learn WebGL details [35].

- **Phaser** is a free open source HTML5-based framework that allows building fully fledged 2D games in a browser with little prior knowledge about either game development or JavaScript for designing for a browser in general [36].
- **PlayCanvas** is a cloud-based HTMl5-based framework and editor for 3D games, with a focus on real-time collaboration [37].

4   Learning Activities on Educational and Serious Games

Gamification is the use of game mechanics and experience design to digitally engage and motivate people to achieve their goals. The application of gamification to real life tasks to influence behavior, improve motivation and enhance engagement [38]. From the innovation perspective, concepts such as serious gaming and gamification are the most interesting and valuable in this domain. If the first repurposes a game via different methods, in order to offer activities that go beyond mere entertainment, the second uses game design to enhance individual's willingness to participate to originally non-playful experiences. Nowadays different knowledge fields, such as medicine, entertainment, education, among others, are using this approach.

Lameras [39] proposed a serious games classification based on the design features and learning properties learning of the game. Learning attributes are proposed as collaborative learning, individual transmission of information and discussion and argument. The study also proposes various attributes of the games which are taken as a basis for the following categories: rules, goals and choices, tasks/challenges, collaboration and competition, and feedback/assessment. Learning activities, in educational games, drive the learning outcomes set out by the teacher. The output of some activities is used as inputs to others resulting in game flows that can be adapted while the student is executing the learning activity. A game-based learning activity is introduced as distinct from game content, is the central concern of work within the game-based learning design, which has historical roots in the wider field of instructional design [40].

Lameras [39] perceived that in-game learning activities to be a situated action – that is influenced by the beliefs and values held by teachers as game designers in specific contexts of practice – as an emergent iterative process that occurs during as well prior to the orchestration of the learning activity in the game. The scoping study suggests therefore, from teacher's perspective, there may be two main advantages associated with the concept of designing in-game learning activities: Firstly, it may provide a framework for linking learning with play for more creative educational practice; and secondly it offers a framework for participation in sharing and reuse/repurposing of practice with professional communities (see Table 1).

Beetham [41] defines learning activity as a "specific interaction of students with others using specific tools and resources, orientated towards specific outcomes". Therefore, the importance of designing learning activities for developing serious games and gamification applications to meet the purpose for which a game was developed. Cook [43] interpreted game attributes from an educational perspective giving emphasis to feedback properties while acknowledging the relations between player's rules and attributes The game attributes must be considered in the game design to ensure a balance between the challenges and the necessary skills to achieve the objectives.

Table 1. Types and sub-types of learning activities used in games.

Type of learning activity	Learning activities
Information Transmission – Activities that allow reflect information on learning player [29][30].	– Lecture / lecture notes / slides – Memorizing concepts – Labelling diagrams and concepts – Exampling – Incomplete statements – Lecture summary – Listening
Individual (constructivist) activities – These activities suggest that learning is more effective when a student is actively engaged in the learning process rather than attempting to receive knowledge passively [27].	– Web-quest (information search) – Exercise solving – Carrying out scientific experiments – Reflection – Simulations – Modeling – Role playing – Inquiry (pose questions) – Determining evidence – Analyzing evidence – Formulating evidence – Connect explanations to knowledge
Collaborative (constructivist) activities – Activities that allow interaction mediated and structured to acquire knowledge [27]. .	– Brainstorming – Group projects – Group web-quest – Rank and report – Group of students posing questions to each other – Group simulations – Pair-problem solving – Group data gathering – Group data analysis – Group reflection
Discussion and argumentation activities – Activities that attempts to lead the student through discussions and questions to discover, discuss, appreciate and verbalize the new knowledge [27].	– Guided discussions (discussion topic provided by teacher) – Open discussions (discussion topic provided by students) – Choices: data on events and several choices for students to make comments – Debates (justifying explanations)

Based on the game attributes, Lameras [39] classified the games depending on their relevant attributes. Lameras realized an attempt to assign games categories understanding game attributes in the game that are used for creating instances of games attributes in the educational practice; for example, rules are made by scoring. Lameras proposed this classification because there was not a taxonomy to classify the attributes of the game in specific categories, the classification was done with the aim of helping game designers and instruction. The category, presented by Lameras, is described in the Table 2, which is based according to the identification of the attributes of each kind of game:

Table 2. Game categories and associated game attributes

Game category	Game Attribute	
– Rules	– Scoring – Moving – Timers levels – Progress bars	– Game instructions including victory conditions
– Goals and Choices	– Game journal – Missions – Objective cards – Storytelling	– Nested dialogues – Puzzles – NPCs / avatars

– Tasks / challenges	– NPC-based task
	  description
	– Progress bars
	– Multiple choices to
	  select
	– Major tasks
		– Puzzles
		– Research points
		– Study
		– Requirements
		– Branch tasks

– Collaboration and competition	– Role-playing – Community collaboration – Epic meaning – Bonuses – Contest	– Timers – Coins – Inventories – Leader boards – Communal discovery – Scoring
– Feedback / assessment	– Game hints, NPCs – Game levels – Gaining/loosing lives – Progress bars – Dashboards	– Lives/virtual currencies to be used for buying game items from an online inventory – Progress dtrees

Table 2 classifies the games categories with relevant attributes. An attempt [39] is made to map overarching gaming categories discerned to game attributes that can be used to afford the instantiation of game attributes with focus on educational practice. This work would pave the way on helping game and instructional designers to select particular types of games that afford distinct mechanisms for supporting certain game categories and thereby aligning specific types of game-play with congruent practices.

5 Analysis of HTML5-Based Frameworks for Developing Educational and Serious Games

In this section, an analysis of HTML5-based frameworks for game development is presented. In order to validate the aforementioned analysis, we have selected ten HTML5-based frameworks. HTML5-based frameworks selected allow developing Web application, mobile applications and hybrid applications in some cases. The HTML5-based frameworks selected were: Construct 2, ImpactJS, Quintus, WADE, pixi.js, EaselJS, melonJS, three.js, phaser and playCanvas.

Table 3. Analysis of HTML5-based frameworks

Game engines	Game Attribute				
	Rules	Goals and Choices	Task / Challenges	Collaboration and competition	Feedback / Assessment
Construct 2	-Scoring -Moving -Timers Levels -Progress bars	-Missions -Avatars -Nested dialogues	-Progress bars -Major tasks -Multiple choices to select -Branch tasks	-Role-playing -Community collaboration -Bonuses -Timers Levels -Communal discovery -Coins -Scoring -Inventories -Leader boards	-Game hints -NPCs -Game levels -Gaining / loosing lives -Progress bars -Dashboards
ImpactJS	-Scoring -Timers Levels -Progress bars	-Puzzles -Storytelling -Missions -Avatars	-Progress bars -Major tasks -Multiple choices to select	-Role-playing -Bonuses -Timers Levels -Coins -Scoring -Inventories -Leader boards	-Game hints -NPCs -Game levels -Gaining / loosing lives -Progress bars -Dashboards
Quintus	-Scoring -Moving	-Puzzles -Missions -Avatars	-Progress bars -Major tasks	-Role-playing -Timers Levels -Scoring	-Game hints -Gaining / loosing lives -Progress bars
WADE	-Scoring -Moving -Timers Levels -Progress bars -Instructions	-Missions -Game journal -Storytelling -Nested dialogues -Puzzles -Avatars	-Progress bars -Major tasks -Puzzles	-Role-playing -Bonuses -Timers Levels -Coins -Scoring -Inventories -Leader boards	-Game hints -NPCs -Game levels -Gaining / loosing lives -Progress bars -Dashboards
pixi.js	-Scoring -Moving -Timers Levels -Progress bars	-Missions -Objective cards -Storytelling -Puzzles -Avatars	-Progress bars -Multiple choices to select -Major tasks -Branch tasks -Puzzles -Research points -Requirements	-Role-playing -Bonuses -Timers Levels -Coins -Scoring -Inventories -Leader boards	-Game hints -NPCs -Game levels -Gaining / loosing lives -Progress bars -Dashboards
EaselJS	-Scoring -Moving -Timers Levels -Progress bars	-Missions -Objective cards -Storytelling -Nested dialogues -Puzzles -Avatars	-Progress bars -Multiple choices to select -Major tasks -Branch tasks -Puzzles -Requirements	-Role-playing -Bonuses -Timers Levels -Coins -Scoring -Inventories -Leader boards	-Game hints -NPCs -Game levels -Gaining / loosing lives -Progress bars -Dashboards
melonJS	-Scoring -Moving -Timers	-Missions -Objective cards	-Progress bars -Multiple choices to	-Role-playing -Bonuses -Timers Levels	-NPCs -Game levels -Gaining /

(Continued)

Table 3. (*Continued*)

Game engines	Game Attribute				
	Rules	Goals and Choices	Task / Challenges	Collaboration and competition	Feedback / Assessment
	Levels -Progress bars -Instructions	-Storytelling -Puzzles -Avatars	select -Major tasks -Branch tasks -Puzzles -Requirements	-Coins -Scoring -Inventories -Leader boards	loosing lives -Progress bars -Dashboards
Three.js	-Scoring -Moving -Timers Levels -Progress bars	-Missions -Objective cards -Storytelling -Puzzles -Avatars	-Progress bars -Multiple choices to select -Major tasks -Branch tasks -Puzzles -Requirements	-Role-playing -Bonuses -Timers Levels -Coins -Scoring -Inventories -Leader boards	-NPCs -Game levels -Gaining / loosing lives -Progress bars -Dashboards
Phaser	-Scoring -Moving -Timers Levels -Progress bars -Instructions including victory conditions	-Game journal -Missions -Objective cards -Storytelling -Nested dialogues -Puzzles -Avatars	-Progress bars -Multiple choices to select -Major tasks -Branch tasks -Puzzles -Research points -Requirements	-Role-playing -Community collaboration -Bonuses -Timers Levels -Coins -Scoring -Inventories -Leader boards	-Game hints -NPCs -Game levels -Gaining / loosing lives -Progress bars −Dashboards
PlayCanvas	-Scoring -Moving -Timers Levels -Progress bars	-Game journal -Missions -Storytelling -Nested dialogues -Puzzles -Avatars	-Progress bars -Multiple choices to select -Major tasks -Branch tasks -Puzzles -Research points -Requirements	-Role-playing -Community collaboration -Bonuses -Timers Levels -Communal discovery -Coins -Scoring -Inventories -Leader boards	-Game hints -NPCs -Gaining / loosing lives -Progress bars

At the end of the analysis process, we have determined that importance of the game attributes for the educational context and the availability of each game attributes on a game categories according to the selected HTML5-based frameworks. Nonetheless, it is possible that, according to the type of educational game and the academic level to which this educational game is aimed, some other attributes can be required that they may have been omitted in this evaluation.

Table 2 shows the set of games attributes available for each HTML5-based framework. It is important to mention that some of the attributes are repeated in two or more classifications because they reinforced objectives of each classification. Table 2 shows the available games attributes and game category established by Lameras of each game engines.

The objective of this analysis was to obtain a reference to choose a HTML5-based framework for the development of educational applications, serious games or both.

Table 3 shows each one of the attributes supported in each framework and serves as a reference based on what type of application can be developed to choose a framework that meets the game attributes stablished by a developer.

6   Conclusions and Future Directions

Gamification is a new technology that incorporates elements of game play in nongame situations. It is used to engage customers, students, and users in the accomplishment of quotidian tasks with rewards and other motivators. On the other side, serious games are games that do not have entertainment as the main objective. The use of serious games and gamification for training and knowledge is promising. If users have a positive and meaningful game-based experience that is well-connected to the underlying non-game setting, then the knowledge will benefit in the long term.

As future direction, the inclusion of additional framework such as Panda.js, Kiwi.js, voxel.js, enchant.js, to mention but a few, will be considered.

Acknowledgments. This work was supported by the Tecnológico Nacional de México (TecNM). Additionally, this work was sponsored by the National Council of Science and Technology (CONACYT) and the Public Education Secretary (SEP) through PROMEP.

References

1. Prensky, M.: Digital Game-Based Learning. Paragon House Ed edition, Minnesota (2005)
2. Burke, B.: Gartner Redefines Gamification. 4 de Abril de (2014). http://blogs.gartner.com/ brian_burke/2014/04/04/gartner-redefines-gamification/. (último acceso: 31 de Marzo de 2016)
3. Chung-Ho, S., Ching-Hsue, C.: A mobile game-based insect learning system for improving the learning achievements. Procedia – Soc. Behav. Sci. **103**, 42–50 (2013)
4. Deterding, S., Dixon, D., Khaled, R., Nacke, L.: From game design elements to gamefulness. In: Proceedings of the 15th International Academic MindTrek Conference on Envisioning Future Media Environments - MindTrek 2011, p. 9. ACM Press, New York (2011)
5. Deterding, S., Sicart, M., Nacke, L., O'Hara, K., Dixon, D.: Gamification using game-design elements in non-gaming contexts. In: Proceedings of the 2011 Annual Conference Extended Abstracts on Human Factors in Computing Systems - CHI EA 2011, p. 2425. ACM Press, New York (2011). http://doi.org/10.1145/1979742.1979575
6. Morford, Z.H., Witts, B.N., Killingsworth, K.J., Alavosius, M.P.: Gamification: the intersection between behavior analysis and game design technologies. Behav. Anal. **37**(1), 25–40 (2014)
7. Hamari, J., Koivisto, J., Sarsa, H.: Does gamification work? – A literature review of empirical studies on gamification. In: 2014 47th Hawaii International Conference on System Sciences, pp. 3025–3034. IEEE (2014)
8. Rojas, D., Kapralos, B., Dubrowski, A.: The missing piece in the gamification puzzle. In: Proceedings of the First International Conference on Gameful Design, Research, and Applications - Gamification 2013, pp. 135–138. ACM Press, New York (2013)

9. Thom, J., Millen, D., DiMicco, J.: Removing gamification from an enterprise SNS. In: Proceedings of the ACM 2012 Conference on Computer Supported Cooperative Work - CSCW 2012, p. 1067. ACM Press, New York (2012)
10. Yamabe, T., Nakajima, T.: Playful training with augmented reality games: case studies towards reality-oriented system design. Multimedia Tools Appl. **62**(1), 259–286 (2012)
11. Michael, D., Chen, S.: Serious Games: Games that Educate, Train and Inform. Cengage Learning PTR, Mason (2005)
12. Susi, T., Johannesson, M., Backlund, P.: Skövde: Institutionen för kommunikation och information. 28 (2007)
13. Nagle, D.: HTML5 Game Engines: App Development and Distribution, pp. 41–43 (2014)
14. Simões, J., Díaz-Redondo, R., Fernandez-Villas, A.: A social gamification framework for a K-6 learning platform. Comput. Hum. Behav. **29**, 245–253 (2013)
15. Armstrong, D.: The new engagement game: the role of gamification in scholarly publishing. Learn. Publish. **26**(4), 253–256 (2013)
16. Lubin, L.: The gamification of learning and instruction field book. New Horiz. Adult Educ. Hum. Resour. Dev. **28**(1), 58–60
17. Kapp, K.: Gadgets, Games, and Gizmos for Learning, 1st edn. Wiley, San Francisco (2007)
18. Robson, K., Plangger, K., Kietzmann, J.H., McCarthy, I., Pitt, L.: Game on: engaging customers and employees through gamification. Bus. Horiz. **59**, 29–36 (2016). (Elsevier)
19. Fui-Hoon Nah, F., Zeng, Q., Rajasekhar-Telaprolu, V., Padmanabhuni-Ayyappa, A., Eschenbrenner, B.: Gamification of education: a review of literature. HCI Bus. **8527**, 401–409 (2014)
20. De-Marcos, L., Domínguez, A., Saenz-de-Navarrete, J., Pagés, C.: An empirical study comparing gamification and social networking on e-learning. Comput. Educ. **75**, 82–91 (2014)
21. Arias Aranda, D., Bustinza Sánchez, O., Djundubaev, R.: Efectos de los juegos de simulación de empresas y Gamification en la actitud emprendedora en enseñanzas medias. Revista de educación, pp. 134–155 (2016)
22. Obikwelu, C., Read, J.: The serious game constructivist framework for children's learning. Procedia Comput. Sci. **15**, 32–37 (2012)
23. Pereiraa, G., Brisson, A., Prada, R., Paiva, A., Bellotti, F., Kravcik, M., Klamma, R.: Serious games for personal and social learning & ethics: status and trends. Procedia Comput. Sci. **15**, 53–65 (2012)
24. Carrozzinoa, M., Evangelistaa, C., Brondia, R., Loren, C.: Social networks and web-based serious games as novel educational tools. Procedia Comput. Sci. **15**, 303–306 (2012)
25. Raybourn, E.M.: A new paradigm for serious games: transmedia learning for more effective training and education. J. Comput. Sci. **5**, 471–481 (2014)
26. Barbosa, A.F.S., Silva, F.G.M.: Serious games - design and development of OxyBlood. In: Proceedings of the 8th International Conference on Advances in Computer Entertainment Technology, ACE 2011 (2010)
27. Donovan, L.: The Use of Serious Games in the Corporate Sector, pp. 4–38. Learnovate Centre, Dublin (2012)
28. Provelengios, P., Fesakis, G.: Educational applications of serious games: the case of the game "Food Force" in primary education students. In: Proceedings of the 5th European Conference on Games Based Learning (ECGBL 2011), Athens, Greece, 20–21 October 2011, pp. 476–485 (2011)
29. Viveros, M.C., García, D.: Elaboración de una guía para el desarrollo de aplicaciones en extjs. Instituto Tecnológico de Orizaba (2009)
30. Bura, J.: Construct 2 Game Development by Example. Packt, Birmingham (2014)

31. Sonmez, J.: Beginning HTML 5 Game Development With Quintus. Recuperado el Junio de 2016 (2016). de Plural Sight: https://www.pluralsight.com/courses/beginning-html5-game-development-quintus?utm_medium=affiliate&utm_source=1058191
32. Chilli, C.: WADE. Recuperado el Junio de 2016 (s.f.). de Clockwork Chilli: http://www.clockworkchilli.com/index.php/main/tech
33. Van der Spuy, R.: Learn Pixi.js. Apress, New York (2015)
34. melonJS.: Melon JS. Recuperado el Junio de 2016, de melonJS: A lightweight HTML5 game engine (2016). http://melonjs.org/
35. Dirksen, J.: Learning Three.js: The JavaScript 3D Library for WebGL. Packt, Mumbai (2014)
36. Palef, T.: Discover phaser (2014)
37. Eastcott, W.: Building WebGL games on ARM devices with playcanvas. The Architecture for the Digital World (2015)
38. Burke, B.: Gartner Redefines Gamification. 4 de Abril de (2014). http://blogs.gartner.com/brian_burke/2014/04/04/gartner-redefines-gamification/ (último acceso: 31 de Marzo de 2016)
39. Lameras, P.: Essential features of serious games design in higher education. Soc. Res. High. Educ., 3–22 (2015)
40. McLean, P., Scott, B.: Competencies for learning design: a review of the literature and a proposed framework. Br. J. Educ. Technol. **42**(4), 557–572 (2011)
41. Beetham, H.: Review: design for learning programme phase 2. Review of Learning Design as Part of the JISC's Design for Learning Programme (2008). http://www.jisc.ac.uk/whatwedo/programmes/elearningpedagogy/designlearn.aspx. Accessed 28 Apr 2011
42. Lundgren, S., Bjork, S.: Game mechanics: describing computer-augmented games in terms of interaction. Paper presented at the TIDSE (2003). http://www.itu.dk/stud/speciale/worlddomination/files/rikke/rh/speciale/staffan_docs/mechanics.pdf. Accessed 23 Feb 2015
43. Cook, D.: Lostgarden (2006). What are game mechanics available at: http://www.lostgarden.com/2006/10/what-are-game-mechanics.html. Accessed 23 Feb 2015

A Dynamic Recognition Approach
of Emotional States for Car Drivers

Jose Aguilar[1,2,3(✉)], Danilo Chavez[2], and Jorge Cordero[3]

[1] CEMISID, Universidad de Los Andes, Mérida, Mérida, Venezuela
aguilar@ula.ve
[2] Escuela Politécnica Nacional, Quito, Pichincha, Ecuador
danilo.chavez@epn.edu.ec
[3] DCCE, Universidad Técnica Particular de Loja, Loja, Loja, Ecuador
jmcordero@utpl.edu.ec

Abstract. In this paper, we propose a recognition model of emotional state using multi-modal perception, a temporal logic paradigm (in particular, we use chronicles), and dynamical patterns. In this way, our recognition approach is based on chronicles to model the patterns, a definition of the emotions as dynamic patterns, and the idea that they are perceived in a multi-modal way (sound, vision, etc.). In this paper, we present these elements of our approach, and give one example of an application for the recognition of the emotions of the driver of a vehicle.

Keywords: Recognition of emotions · Chronicles · Dynamic patterns recognition

1 Introduction

The problem addressed here is linked to Affective Computing (AC). The AC aims the recognition and generation of emotions in the computer [1, 2]. Particularly, in this paper, we study the problem of emotion recognition, using a different approach from the classical approaches, which normally recognize the emotions based on the analysis of the facial expressions, sound, or body language [3–5].

In our case, we are interested in the detection of the following set of emotions: happiness, sadness, anger, fear, and surprise. We define a set of patterns for each emotion, which are composed of a set of events, from different sources of perception. The set of emotion patterns, the temporal interval between the events in each pattern, introduces some type of dynamism in the definition of the emotions: there are not only a type of emotion pattern, they are defined by different sources of perception, the relationship between events of an emotional pattern is defined by an interval of time, among other aspects.

We test our approach to recognize the emotions in the driver of a vehicle. For that, the vehicle has an equipment to detect/perceive different components: a camera for the facial expressions, a pressure sensor on the steering wheel, a Smart-phone application that obtains the heart rate of the driver, the On Board Diagnostics system (OBD) is used to obtain the status of the various vehicle subsystems, and specific data as its speed.

© Springer International Publishing AG 2016
R. Valencia-García et al. (Eds.): CITI 2016, CCIS 658, pp. 155–168, 2016.
DOI: 10.1007/978-3-319-48024-4_13

This case study is interesting because one of the current research domains in automobile development is dominated by the driver assistance. The capability of a car to provide a human-like driver assistance system is a decisive factor for the automatic driving systems. Emotional factors and affective states are crucial for these systems.

There are several works in AC in different domains: human computer interface, for virtual world, robotics, etc. For example, [9] describes an agent with fuzzy emotions to help him to make decisions. They apply this model in robots, using three negative emotions: anger, pain and fear. A work based on the recognition of facial expressions is presented in [10]. In this work, they propose the recognition of six basic emotions using patterns based on facial expressions. Other works propose patterns of emotions in humans based on physiological signals, as the sound of the voice [11, 12].

Previous work in the emotion recognition for vehicles are: [13] presents an affective intelligent car interface, to map certain physiological signals (heart beat, temperature and galvanic skin response) to certain driving-related emotions (Frustration, Sleepiness, and Panic). [14] shows the emotions elicited from the driving task. Driving behavior is analyzed relying on the traffic situations and the driver tolerance. The work is focused on the alerting mechanism and the driver state recognition, as the driver's stress and fatigue. [15] proposes a generalized framework to estimate emotions from the speech using an emotion space concept. They test the system in the acoustically demanding environment of vehicular noise while driving. The system provides information about the driver's perception of the traffic situation and thus reveals his/her level of stress. They describe emotions as points in a 3D emotion space consisting of three basic primitives (attributes): valence (negative positive), activation (calmexcited), and dominance (weak strong). All primitives are continuous and normalized to a range of [−1, +1]. Such a real-valued concept is helpful to distinguish the emotions. [16] analyses intrusive and non-intrusive techniques to monitor car driver's emotions using thermal cameras. The paper presents face detection techniques in each thermogram, prior to emotion recognition. In [17] they propose a technique for speech emotion recognition for drivers, considering the changing environment while driving. They utilize contextual information about the environment outside the car as well as the user information which is inside the car, in order to improve the emotional recognition accuracy. They use a noise cancellation technique to suppress the noise adaptively based on the driving context, and analyse the gender-based context information to develop a classifier of the driver emotions. [18] offers an extensive overview related to influence of emotions on driving safety and comfort, and improvement of in-car interfaces. Various uses-case applications for emotion-oriented technology in the vehicle are presented. They evaluate the possible acceptance of such future technology by drivers, and the feasibility of automatically recognizing various driver states. Finally, in [19] they propose an Emotion Recognition System based on classical neural networks and neuro-fuzzy classifiers. Emotion recognition is performed in real time starting from a video stream acquired by a common webcam monitoring the users' face. Particularly, they develop a device capable to analyze in real time the ability to drive of a given person, in order to discourage him to drive when he is not considered eligible to drive safely.

These methods have their complexities and specific problems [4, 5]. One of the main problems with the previous works is that they are based on unimodal approach, where they consider a type of descriptor, normally, based on the face, physiological signals, or speech recognition. It implies that the recognition process depends on the quality of the information of the sensors for these descriptors, and that only the emotions which are well identified/discriminated by these descriptors can be recognized.

In this paper, we try to solve this problem, proposing a multimodal approach, which considers several types of descriptors in order to have a rich emotional model, based on different sources of information. We propose a multi-modal approach in order to exploit the advantage of each one. To integrate each one, we suggest the use of the temporal logical paradigm, called chronicles [6–8]. This approach allows the integration of events, with temporal relationships between them, in order to define complex patterns.

The paper is organized as follows: Sect. 2 defines the main concepts used in this paper. Our recognition architecture is presented in Sect. 3. Section 4 proposes an example of application in the context of recognition of emotions of drivers of vehicles. Finally, Sect. 5 presents concluding remarks.

2 Theoretical Aspects

2.1 Chronicles

A chronicle is defined as a set of events, linked by a set of temporal constraints. Each chronicle is an event pattern with temporal relationships between them, with a context specified by hold statements. A set of chronicles characterizes the dynamical behaviour (a possible evolution) of a given system (for example, an abnormal operation) [6–8, 20].

The temporal constraints can be quantitative (for example: 100 s before) or qualitative (for example: after). In general, the temporal relationships can be the sequence (ordered events) and the absence of events between two events (for example, event C should not occur between A and B), extended by logical operators, as the conjunction (A and B) or disjunction (A or B).

To define a chronicle mainly two predicates are used: events and hold. An event expresses a change in an attribute, for example: *Event(state(light): (on, off), t2)*. A hold specifies that an attribute holds a value during a time interval, for example: *Hold (position(robot, home), (t2, t4))*. An example of a chronicle taken from [21] is:

```
Chronicle RobotLoadMachine {
event (Robot1: (outroom, inroom), e1);
event (Robot1: (introom, outroom), e4);
event(MachineInput: (unloaded, loaded), e2);
event(Machine: (Stopped, Running), e3);
e1 ≤ e2;
1 ≤ e3-e2 ≤ 6;
3 ≤ e4-e2 ≤ 5;
hold (Machine: Running, (e2, e3));
hold (SafetyConditions: true, (e2, e3));
when recognized { report successful load; }}
```

A chronicle can be modelled by a time constraint graph labelled by predicates. The predicates are [20]:

- *event(A: (v1, v2), t):* it describes a change of value (from v1 to v2) of an attribute A at time t.
- *hold(A:v, (t1, t2)):* it defines the persistence of the value v of an attribute A between two instants t1 and t2.
- *noevent(b, [t1,t2]):* it specifies the absence of event b in the interval [t1, t2].
- *occurs ((2,5), c, [t1, t2]):* it defines that event c occurs between twice and five times during the interval [t1,t2].

Figure 1 shows a chronicle, which contains three events: event C must occur between 4 and 8 units of time after the instantiation of A, and between 1 and 4 units of time after B.

In general, a chronicle model C is defined as a pair (S, T), where S is the set of events (for example, alarms) and T the constraints graph of the instants when the events occur. A chronicle instance c of a chronicle model C is a set of event occurrences, which is consistent with the time constraints of C. For example, (A, 1) (B, 3) (C, 7) is an instance of the chronicle of Fig. 1.

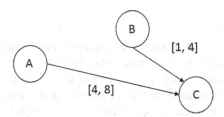

Fig. 1. Example of a chronicle

2.2   Dynamic Patterns

In general, a pattern is an abstraction of an object, defined by a set of descriptors (normally, they define its characteristics). A dynamic pattern is a pattern with changes in its characteristics or in its perception, in a time interval Δt (its negation is a static pattern).

The change in the pattern shows the dynamics of the pattern, reflected by physical changes in it (in its properties, for example, the diameter of the pupil of the face pattern), and/or changes in as perceived (e.g., views of a moving vehicle). Dynamic patterns can be classified into two types: dynamic patterns oriented by features, and dynamic patterns oriented by the perception.

- *Dynamic patterns oriented by features:* A dynamic pattern is oriented by characteristics when some of its features change over time. A feature is a physical property of the pattern, represented by a descriptor (a variable defined in a universe of values). One example is the facial expression and the tone of voice in a pattern of emotion.

- *Dynamic patterns oriented by perception:* A dynamic pattern is oriented by perception when the perception about it changes along time. An example of this pattern is a plane flying, through its views that are observed in flight.

This classification is not exclusive, i.e., a dynamic pattern can be recognized by both.

2.3 Emotions

Affective computing (CA) is the science that studies the recognition and generation of emotions by computers [2]. Rosalind Picard argues that CA is a tool that improves the relationship between man and computer, to include affective or emotional aspects of processing performed by computers, and thus it meets the needs of users [1]. As the importance of recognizing emotions has increased in recent years, researchers have proposed several methods of recognition of emotions, mainly based on the analysis of facial expressions [4, 5] as well as those based on acoustic aspects and the body language [3].

Facial expressions play a fundamental role in human communication. Most work in this area has focused on analyzing faces to recognize emotions, or characterizing attributes to identify to recognize an emotion reflected on a face [4, 5, 22]. An important factor in the development of systems to recognize emotions out of voice is to efficiently identify the traits that characterize different emotions [23]. The voice is the primary way of communication between people. It also contains extra-linguistic emotional information on physical characteristics and physiological states. Finally, body language plays an important role in the transmission of intrapersonal information; similarly, some studies have shown that body expressions are as useful as facial expressions to express emotions and feelings [5, 24].

There are different proposals to recognize emotions in people. Some of these proposals are based on biological signals, others on facial expressions and voice [25, 26].

3 Our Recognition Model

Although there are jobs that perform this process using a unimodal approach [4, 5], we will use a multimodal approach. Our multimodal approach allows considering more details in the model of the driver emotions, regarding recognition systems based on unimodal approaches.

To recognize the emotions of the driver of a vehicle using a multimodal model, we consider events that describe aspects of different nature: facial, acoustic, body language, among others. Variables such as the pressure on the steering wheel, the speed or the acceleration, are also considered for better recognition.

In this paper, we are going to use two ways to build the emotional patterns as a multimodal model. The first one, the emotional patterns are based on complex events that describe states of the driver; and the second one, the emotional patterns are defined as the flow for events for each type of sensor (e.g., pressure sensor on the steering wheel, sensor of the heart rate of the driver, sensor of the speed of the car).

3.1   Emotional Patterns Based on Complex Events

We need to define the different states of a driver (tired, concentrated, static, boring, quiet, etc.) as events. We use information from the different sensors in the car to characterize these states. The state of a driver is determined by the combination of the values of the sensors, so the emotion of a driver is defined as a combination of states.

Let's suppose we have the set of sensors in the car as listed in Table 1. The states of the individuals, are defined according to the value determined for each variable. Table 2 contains some examples of states, using the variables. The value of "any" means that the value of the attribute can be any. We add a large number of states (calm, impatient, passive, etc.) in order to define the different situations in a driver.

Table 1. Input data from the sensors.

Device	Variable	Values
Camera	Facial expressions	Smile, seriousness, etc.
OBD2 system	Speed of the car	(0, 200) km/s
Microphone	Sound of the voice	High, low, etc.
Sensor on the steering wheel	Pressure on the steering wheel	Strong, light, etc.
Sensor on individual	Heart rate of the driver	Fast, slow, etc.

With these states, now we can define the chronicles. Each emotion is defined by a chronicle, and an emotion can have different patterns. For example, anxiety can be defined by:

Table 2. States of the drivers.

Id event	State of the driver	Facial expression	Speed	Sound of the voice	Pressure	Heart rate
1	Fatigue	Exhausted	Any	Low	Light	Slow
2	Relaxed	Smile	Normal	Normal	Normal	Normal
3	Exuberant	Smile	High	High	Normal	Normal
4	Concentrated	Seriousness	Any	Silence	Normal	Normal
5	Falling asleep	Exhausted	Any	Slow	Very light	Very slow
6	Stressed	Seriousness	High	High	Strong	Fast

According to the pattern in Table 3, the anxiety pattern is recognized when the "Concentrated" event (1) arrives at time t4, and the "Fatigue" event (4) arrives at time t1, and finally, the "Stressed" event (6) arrives at time t6 and this event holds between t6 and t10, and the following temporal constraints are accomplished: event 1 occurs between 1 to 4 units of time before the event 4, and event 1 occurs between 6 to 8 units of time before event 6.

Table 3. Chronicle to recognize the anxiety

Chronicle Anxiety {
event (4, t4);
event (1, t1);
event(6, t6);
Hold(6, (t6, t10)
$1 \leq t1\text{-}t4 \leq 4$;
$6 \leq t6\text{-}t1 \leq 8$;
$2 \leq t10\text{-}t6 \leq 4$;
when recognized { report driver anxiety; } }

In our case, Happiness is defined by two chronicles (see Tables 4 and 5):

Table 4. First chronicle to recognize Happiness

Chronicle Happiness 1 {
Hold(3, (t3, t10)
$5 \leq t10\text{-}t3 \leq 10$;
when recognized { report driver happiness; } }

---

or

Table 5. Second chronicle to recognize Happiness

Chronicle Happiness 2 {
event (4, t4);
event (2, t2);
$1 \leq t2\text{-}t4 \leq 4$;
Occurs ((2,4), (4, 2), [t5, t6])
$1 \leq t6\text{-}t5 \leq 20$;
when recognized { report driver happiness; } }
}

According to the patterns in Tables 4 and 5, the Happiness pattern can be recognized when the "Exuberant" event (3) arrives at time t3 and holds among 5 and 10 unit of times; or when the "Fatigue" event (4) arrives at time t4 and the "Relaxed" event (2) arrives at time t2, and they occur between twice and four times during the interval of time [t5, t6].

In this way, we can define the set of chronicles for the rest of emotions (anger, sadness, fear, surprise, etc.).

3.2 Emotional Patterns Based on Flow of Events from Each Sensor

In this case, we use the information extracted directly from the sensors as the source of events. For example, for the speed of the car we can define this set of events (see Table 6):

Table 6. Events of the speed of the car.

Id event	Description	Speed up
S1	High speed	≤ 150 km/s
S2	Low speed	≤ 40 km/s and 150 km/s
S3	Normal speed	≤ 40 km/s

In the case of the heart rate, we define the events of the Table 7:

Table 7. Events of the heart rate.

Id event	Description	Heart rate
H1	Fast heart rate	200–100 beats/min
H2	Slow heart rate	40–60 beats/min
H3	Normal heart rate	60–100 beats/min

For the sound of the voice we can use these characteristics, based on [22]: Tone (bass, treble) in Hertz, intensity - volume (high, medium, low) in decibels, speaking rate (fast, slow). Thus, we define a set of events (they are the combination of these characteristics) in Table 8. In the case of facial expression, we use the same characteristics defined in [22] to describe them: eyes (open, with tears, hard look, etc.), eyebrows (raised, curved), lips (open, tight, tense, etc.) and face (wrinkles in the center, extended, horizontal wrinkles, etc.). Similar to the previous descriptor, the combination of these characteristics defines the events of this descriptor (see Table 9).

Finally, the events of the pressure of the steering wheel can be defined as the events of the speed of the car (see Table 10):

Now, with this set of events, we can redefine the chronicles for each emotion. For example, the chronicles for the happiness can be defined by Tables 11 and 12.

Table 8. Events of the sound of the voice

Id Event	Description
V1	Tone treble and volume high and speaking rate fast
V2	Tone treble and volume medium and speaking rate fast
V3	Tone bass and volume medium and speaking rate fast
Vn	...

Table 9. Events of the facial expression.

Id event	Description
F1	Eyes open and eyebrows raised and lips open and face extended
F2	Eyes with tears and eyebrows raised and lips open and face extended
F3	Eyes open and eyebrows with curves and lips tight and face wrinkles in the center
Fn	...

Table 10. Events of the speed of the car.

Id event	Description
P1	Strong pressure
P2	Light pressure
P3	Normal pressure

Table 11. First chronicle to recognize Happiness with our multimodal approach

Chronicle Happiness1 {
event (V3, t1);
event (F1, t2);
event(H3, t3);
Hold(H3, (t4, t5)
$0 \leq t1-t2 \leq 5$;
$-2 \leq t1-t3 \leq 8$;
$8 \leq t4-t5 \leq 12$;
when recognized {report driver happiness }}

Table 12. Second chronicle to recognize Happiness with multimodal approach

Chronicle Happiness2 {
event (S3, t1);
event (H3, t2);
event(P3, t3);
Hold(H3, (t4, t5)
Hold(P3, (t4, t5)
$0 \leq t3-t1 \leq 5$;
$-1 \leq t2-t1 \leq 6$;
$10 \leq t4-t5 \leq 20$;
when recognized { report driver happiness; }}

According to the pattern in Table 11, now the Happiness pattern can be recognized when the V3 arrives at time t1, F1 arrives at time t2, H3 arrives at time t3 and it holds between t4 and t5 unit of time, and the following temporal constraints are accomplished: V3 occurs between 0 to 5 units of time before F1, and V3 occurs between −2 to 8 units of time before H3.

According to the pattern in Table 12, the happiness pattern can be recognized when S3 arrives at time t1, H3 arrives at time t2 and it holds between 10 and 20 unit of times, P3 arrives at time t3 and it holds between 10 and 20 unit of times, and the next temporal constraints are accomplished: S3 occurs between 0 to 5 units of time before H3, and S3 occurs between −1 to 6 units of time before P3.

In this way, we can define the rest of emotions using chronicles.

4 Example of Application: Emotions in the Drivers of Vehicles

A Man-machine system is defined as the system in which at least one of the components involved in the operation is a human operator [21]. Human intervention is essential for a man-machine system and the ability of the operator greatly affects the performance of the target of control. Therefore, many efforts have been made to perform control based in humans that could exploit the recognition of the information to perform a task [21, 23]. Within this field, great efforts have been made to detect human factors that affect system performance, and know how to mitigate possible effects.

In order to design a human-machine system for cars more naturally and intuitively, we propose the incorporation of a pattern recognition system based on our chronicles. Particularly, in this section we analyze how we can use a pattern recognition system based on the chronicles presented in this paper, in the context of a human-machine system based on the concept of human-oriented compensators, called "collaborator" [27] (see Fig. 2). This compensation mechanism in the human–machine system requires a human dynamic model which can be modeled with the chronicles presented in this paper. This mechanism improves the control performance of the human–machine system with some equipment that compensates the shortage of operation.

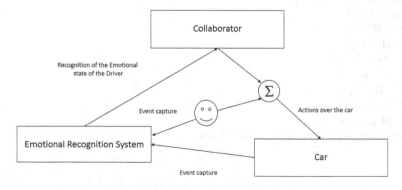

Fig. 2. Structure of the collaborator.

The collaborator can be regarded as a new control element that cooperates with the human and the machine.

An example of this can be found when a person is driving a vehicle. A skillful person can drive a vehicle satisfactorily, whereas an unskilled person cannot do so. The difference between the two is based on whether or not they have the knowledge about vehicle dynamics. In a driving school, a learner handles a vehicle, according to the instructor's advice. When its driving is not suitable, the instructor compensates the driver's action. The task of a collaborator is given an adequate feedback in different contexts. In this scenario, we include our recognition system.

In this system, we define three safety-related states that must be recognized: countersteering strategies, adaptation strategies, and communicating the driver's emotional state (e.g., anger/rage, fatigue, and high workload, stress, or uncertainty) to other vehicles.

- The Countersteering Strategies category contains negative affective states, defined by specific emotions (anger, fatigue, stress, confusion, nervousness, sadness, etc.), to be detected by our system, in order to guide the driver into a happy or neutral state which is known to be best suited for safe driving
- The Adaptation Strategies category adapts the personality of an automated in-car assistant to the driver. For that, our recognition system defines the parameters of the assistant for the different emotions of the driver. In this case, there is a learning process of the driver's patterns (chronicles) of emotions.
- The Communicating the Driver's Emotional State category consists of describing how a driver's state can be communicated to others. Locating potentially dangerous drivers can aid the driver assistance systems in other vehicles to warn their drivers. In this case, we need a distributed recognition system of chronicles for a car-to-car communication system warning other drivers.

There are other situations where our recognition system can be used in order to improve the safety of drivers: Driving Pleasure, etc. We have proposed two ways to describe the emotions based on chronicles. In the first case, the emotional patterns based on complex events; and in the second based on the flow of events from each type of variable to sense. Each one can be used in the case previously described.

In the first case, it is an interesting approach because it is based on the state of a driver. We can define these states relying on the psychological theory, and determine the information to be sensed from the car, in order to determine these states. A lot of states can be defined to determine the emotions in an accurate way. This approach can exploit the theories about the human mind to define the states of a driver, and define the descriptors to be sensed from the car to determine these states. With this information, we must redefine the emotion model, based on the theories about the mind and psychology which can be sensed from a car.

In the second approach, we analyze each descriptor which has been obtained from the car in order to determine the emotions. In this case we can use a dual approach: we define the emotions with the specific values of the descriptors, or we determine the combinations of descriptors for each emotion. The problem in the second case is that there are a lot of possible combinations, and it can be a NP-complete problem.

In general, the detection of safety-related or Driving Pleasure states using our model can exploit the different sensors in a car, and can be extended very easily. What is more, the addition of more sensors might improve the description of the emotions.

5 Conclusion

Emotions affect many cognitive processes - highly relevant to driving - such as decision-making, communication, performance, attention, and learning. There is a need for detecting and diagnosing the driver's emotional state. This can ensure a safer and more pleasant driving experience.

As basic strategies, we have proposed a pattern model of emotions for the drivers, which must be linked to complex patterns of situations that will be studied in other works. Some of these states can be categorized in groups, as safety-related states or Driving Pleasure states.

The construction of complex patterns with the chronicle is one interesting aspect, but it must be adapted to the car functionalities (like sensors). The in-car driver interfaces can influence the definition of the patterns in several ways. The future "car assistants" must exploit these aspects, in order to avoid confusing situations. Additionally, the growing complexity of in-car electronics demands new interfaces to be exploited in the patterns.

In this paper, we present the basis for a driver state recognition system, which can be automated for the detection of different situations (driver distraction, etc.) and could be implemented in a car with the technology available today. This system could be extended with a more complex architecture, which considers the analysis of the data from the car, the driver, or other cars, based on the internet of things [28, 29], in order to discover knowledge to be exploited by the "car assistants".

Additionally, we have explained how our recognition approach can be used in a collaborator system in the context of a car. At this moment, we have developed the first versions of the recognition system. Future works will include our system in a collaborator for cars, and will simulate real driving scenarios. In fact, we will extend our patterns in order to consider other aspects like the analysis of the data from the car or other cars. Some disadvantages of our model are that the recognition system needs real time processing, which can be complex, and requires the capture of different source of information that may require preprocessing.

Acknowledgments. Dr Aguilar has been partially supported by the Prometeo Project of the Ministry of Higher Education, Science, Technology and Innovation of the Republic of Ecuador.

References

1. Picard, R.W.: Affective computing: challenges. Int. J. Hum Comput Stud. **59**, 55–64 (2003)
2. Picard, R.W.: Affective computing for HCI. In: 8th HCI International on Human-Computer Interaction: Ergonomics and User Interfaces, pp. 829–833 (1999)

3. Majumder, A., Behera, L., Subramanian, V.K.: Emotion recognition from geometric facial features using self-organizing map. Pattern Recogn. **47**(3), 1282–1293 (2014)
4. Singh, M., Majumder, A., Behera, L.: Facial expressions recognition system using Bayesian inference. In: International Joint Conference on Neural Networks (IJCNN), pp. 1502–1509 (2014)
5. Zhang, L., Hossain, A., Jiang, M.: Intelligent facial action and emotion recognition for humanoid robots. In: International Joint Conference on Neural Networks (IJCNN), pp. 739–746 (2014)
6. Aguilar, J.: Temporal Logic from the Chronicles Paradigm: Learning and Reasoning Problems, and Its Applications in Distributed Systems. LAP Lambert Academic Publishing, Germany (2011)
7. Dousson, C., Duong, V.: Discovering chronicles with numerical time constraints from alarm logs for monitoring dynamic systems. In: 16th International Joint Conference on Artificial Intelligence, pp. 620–626 (1999)
8. Dousson, C.: Extending and unifying chronicle representation with event counters. In: 15th European Conference on Artificial Intelligence, pp. 257–261 (2002)
9. El-Nasr, M.S., Skubic, M.: A fuzzy emotional agent for decision-making in a mobile robot. In: The IEEE World Congress on Computational Intelligence, vol. 1, pp. 135–140 (1998)
10. Robinson, P., Baltrusaitis, T., Davies, I., Pfister, T., Rick, L., Hull, K.: The emotional computer. In: International Conference on Pervasive Computing (2011)
11. Cowie, R., Douglas-Cowie, E., Tsapatsoulis, N., Votsis, G., Kollias, S., Fellenz, W., Taylor, J.G.: Emotion recognition in human-computer interaction. IEEE Sig. Process. Mag. **18**(1), 32–80 (2011)
12. Kwon, I.K., Lee, S.Y.: An emotional space modeling for the adaptive emotional model design based on sugeno fuzzy inference. Int. J. Softw. Eng. Appl. **8**(6), 109–120 (2014)
13. Lisetti, C.L., Nasoz, F.: Affective intelligent car interfaces with emotion recognition. In: 11th International Conference on Human Computer Interaction (2005)
14. Katsis, C., Rigas, G., Goletsis, Y., Fotiadis, D.: Emotion Recognition in Car Industry, pp. 515–544. Wiley, Hoboken (2015)
15. Grimm, M., Kroschel, K., Schuller, B., Rigoll, G., Moosmayr, T.: Acoustic emotion recognition in car environment using a 3D emotion space approach. In: 33rd German Annual Conference on Acoustics (2007)
16. Kolli, A., Fasih, A., Al Machot, F., Kyamakya, K.: Non-intrusive car driver's emotion recognition using thermal camera. In: Sixteenth International Symposium on Theoretical Electrical Engineering, pp. 1–5 (2011)
17. Tawari, A., Trivedi, M.: Speech based emotion classification framework for driver assistance system. In: IEEE Intelligent Vehicles Symposium, pp. 174–178 (2010)
18. Eyben, F., Wöllmer, M., Poitschke, T., Schuller, B., Blaschke, C., Färber, B., Nguyen-Thien, N.: Emotion on the road—necessity, acceptance, and feasibility of affective computing in the car. Adv. Hum.-Comput. Interact. **2010**, 17 (2010). http://dx.doi.org/10.1155/2010/263593
19. Paschero, M., Del Vescovo, G., Benucci, L., Rizzi, A., Santello, M., Fabbri, G., Mascioli, F.F.: A real time classifier for emotion and stress recognition in a vehicle driver. In: IEEE International Symposium on Industrial Electronics (ISIE), pp. 1690–1695 (2012)
20. Dousson, C., Le Maigat, P.: Chronicle recognition improvement using temporal focusing and hierarchization. In: International Joint Conference on Artificial Intelligence, vol. 7, pp. 324–329 (2007)
21. Ghallab, M.: Past and future chronicles for supervision and planning. In: 14th International Conference on Artificial Intelligence, pp. 23–34 (1994)
22. Cordero, J., Aguilar, J.: Reconocimiento multimodal de emociones en un entorno inteligente basado en crónicas, pp. 525–541. Gráficas El Portatítulo (2016)

23. El Ayadi, M., Kamel, M.S., Karray, F.: Survey on speech emotion recognition: Features, classification schemes, and databases. Pattern Recogn. **44**(3), 572–587 (2011)
24. Kleinsmith, A., Bianchi-Berthouze, N.: Affective body expression perception and recognition: a survey. IEEE Trans. Affect. Comput. **4**(1), 15–33 (2013)
25. Kessous, L., Castellano, G., Caridakis, G.: Multimodal emotion recognition in speech-based interaction using facial expression, body gesture and acoustic analysis. J. Multimodal User Interfaces **3**(1–2), 33–48 (2010)
26. Zeng, Z., Pantic, M., Roisman, G.I., Huang, T.S.: A survey of affect recognition methods: Audio, visual, and spontaneous expressions. IEEE Trans. Pattern Anal. Mach. Intell. **31**(1), 39–58 (2009)
27. Ohtsuka, H., Shibasato, K., Kawaji, S.: Experimental study of collaborater in human–machine system. Mechatronics **19**(4), 450–456 (2009)
28. Suresh, P., Daniel, J., Parthasarathy, V., Aswathy, R.: A state of the art review on the Internet of Things (IoT) history, technology and fields of deployment. In: International Conference on Science Engineering and Management Research, pp. 1–8 (2014)
29. Díaz, M., Martín, C., Rubio, B.: State-of-the-art, challenges, and open issues in the integration of Internet of things and cloud computing. J. Netw. Comput. Appl. **67**, 99–117 (2016)

Towards Supporting International Standard-Based Software Engineering Approaches Using Semantic Web Technologies: A Systematic Literature Review

Ricardo Colomo-Palacios[1]([⊠]), Luis Omar Colombo-Mendoza[2],
and Rafael Valencia-García[2]

[1] Computer Science Department, Østfold University College, Halden, Norway
ricardo.colomo-palacios@hiof.no
[2] Faculty of Informatics, University of Murcia, Murcia, Spain
{luisomar.colombo,valencia}@um.es

Abstract. Motivated by the assumption that Semantic Web technologies are not sufficiently leveraged in the Software Engineering discipline (SE) to provide support regarding the standardization of software development processes by means of international software standards, we investigate the existence of systematic literature reviews in this regard. We concluded that none of the available reviews is specifically focused on analysing international standard-based SE approaches, but on investigating SE approaches in a general way. In this paper, we present the details about all the stages in the conducting of a systematic literature review on the Semantic Web technologies-based support for the standardization of the SE discipline regarding software development processes; one of the major findings of the presented review is that nowadays there is a shortage of approaches providing support for the standardization of software development processes for small and very small software companies.

Keywords: Systematic literature review · Semantic Web · Software Engineering · Software standards · Ontologies

1 Background

Semantic Web technologies are gaining momentum in the development of software systems among different domains because of their ability to enable computer systems to integrate, share, process and interpret the information formerly readable by humans – the Web of documents. The term "Semantic Web" refers to the W3C's vision of the Web of linked data that is made up of technologies for publishing and linking data, building vocabularies to enrich data with additional meaning, querying data and reasoning over data through rules. In this context, Resource Description Framework(RDF) provides the foundation for publishing and sharing data, Web Ontology Language (OWL) is the language used to build vocabularies in the form of ontologies, and SPARQL Protocol and RDF Query Language (SPARQL) is the language for querying linked data. In this work, the term ontology is used to refer to a formal and explicit

© Springer International Publishing AG 2016
R. Valencia-García et al. (Eds.): CITI 2016, CCIS 658, pp. 169–183, 2016.
DOI: 10.1007/978-3-319-48024-4_14

specification of a shared conceptualization. Knowledge in ontologies is mainly formalized by defining classes, properties, axioms and instances. Semantic Web technologies, as one of the major components of the Semantic Web stack, can be leveraged with mainly two purposes: knowledge representation and reasoning.

Motivated by the assumption that Semantic Web technologies are not sufficiently leveraged in the Software Engineering discipline to provide support regarding the standardization of software development processes by means of international software standards, we investigate the existence of systematic literature reviews in this regard.

We found that there are some systematic literature reviews analysing the state-of-the-art on the application of Semantic Web technologies to the improvement of specific activities in Software Engineering (SE), or more precisely, to the enhancement of certain phases of the software lifecycle. These studies are more commonly focused on phases such as requirements engineering and maintenance [1, 2]. There are also other reviews investigating the state-of-the-art on Knowledge Management in SE [3, 4]. These studies rely on the assumption that activities in SE are by nature knowledge-intensive and include not only approaches aimed at the semantic level but also approaches aimed at the syntactic level. Nonetheless, the wide range of application areas of the Semantic Web technologies go beyond Knowledge Management and embrace areas such as data integration and resource discovery and classification, to name but a few. Furthermore, all these reviews are not specifically focused on analysing international standard-based SE approaches but on investigating SE approaches in a general way, which can result in discarding information which is relevant to professionals and academicians interested in implementing international software standards.

Thus, we actually identified the need for a systematic literature review on the Semantic Web technologies-based support for the standardization of the SE discipline regarding software development processes. In this paper, we present the details about all the stages in the conducting of a systematic literature review on this regard. The paper is structured as follows: in Sect. 2, the details about the planning phase of the proposed review are described; in Sect. 3, we present the details related to the execution of the review; in Sect. 4, the details about the review's evaluation phase are described; finally, in Sect. 5, conclusions and future directions of this work are presented.

2   Review Planning: Review Protocol

The systematic review that will be reported throughout this paper will be performed mainly by following the guidelines proposed by Kitchenham in the technical report entitled "Procedures for Performing Systematic Reviews" [5]. These guidelines are specifically designed to be used by Software Engineering community and cover the three major phases of systematic reviews: planning, execution and evaluation. In addition, we have followed the review protocol template proposed by Biolchini et al. in the technical report entitled "Systematic Review in Software Engineering" [6]. This template is aimed at facilitating the planning and execution of systematic reviews, and it is in fact based on the work by Kitchenham.

Every systematic review in any domain is expected to be started by defining a review protocol, i.e., the set of research questions to be addressed and the research method to be employed to answer these questions. The planning of the systematic review to be conducted are presented below in the form of the main parts of the review protocol related to both the research questions and the research method.

2.1   Research Questions

The research questions that are expected to be answered by executing the systematic review are the following:

- Q1. Which Software Engineering activities have been typically supported?
- Q2. Which standards have been primarily used as frameworks for conducting these activities?
- Q3. Which Semantic Web technologies have been primarily employed to support the activities identified?
- Q3.2. What are the specific approaches that have been proposed for this purpose?
- Q3.1. What are the main motivations for the usage of the Semantic Web technologies in these approaches?

In the context of the research questions outlined above, the population to be observed in this systematic review corresponds to those publications proposing Semantic Web technologies-empowered SE approaches based on international standards, including both software process and quality standards; the intervention, i.e., what is going to be observed, corresponds to the details of how and why the Semantic Web technologies are used to empower the standard-compliant SE approaches. The keywords and synonyms that can be extracted from the research questions and will be used to perform the systematic review are the following: Software Engineering, Software Engineering Process, CMM, CMMi, 15504, SPICE, 12207, TSP, PSP, Semantics, Ontology and Ontologies. As it can be inferred from these terms, the effect that is expected as a result of the systematic review corresponds to the identification of the proposals on the integration of Semantic Web technologies and international standard-compliant SE approaches. Finally, the outcome measure, i.e., the metric that will be used to measure the effect, corresponds to the number of proposals identified.

2.2   Research Method

In this systematic review, the research method is considered to be formed by a data source selection strategy and a study selection strategy, which are described below.

Data Source Selection Strategy. The aim of this strategy is to identify the data sources from which primary studies will be retrieved as a result of the execution of the systematic review. For this purpose, the selection criteria which we have defined is the possibility of searching for digital versions of research papers (including both conference papers and journal and magazine papers) on Computer Science topics, namely Software Engineering topics, through the Internet using keyword-based searches. In addition, we will discard those data sources having studies written in languages other than English since we have planned to review studies written only in English.

According to the selection criterion stated above, the search for primary studies will be primarily carried out by using Web search engines provided by digital research libraries on the Internet. The specific search string that we have initially planned to use for this purpose is the following:

("Software Process" OR "Software Engineering Process" OR "CMM" OR "CMMI" OR "15504" OR SPICE OR 12207 OR "TSP" OR "PSP") AND ("Semantics" OR "Ontologies" OR "Ontology")

The initial list of data sources we have proposed for this systematic review is composed of the following data sources: (1) ScienceDirect, (2) IEEE Xplore Digital Library and (3) SpringerLink.

After evaluating these data sources against the selection criteria defined, it was concluded that all of them fit the criteria, so that the final list of data sources in this systematic review is finally considered to be composed of all the data sources in the initial list. Furthermore, it is worth to mention that the validity of the data sources in the final list was assessed by a group of two experts working on both Software Engineering and Semantic Web research areas (full-time professors from University of Murcia and Orizaba Institute of Technology). They concluded the resulting final list of data sources is sufficient and complete. The same group of experts was commissioned to validate the review protocol to ensure its quality before its execution. The group concluded the evaluated version of the review protocol is able to lead to the expected results and encouraged its execution.

Study Selection Strategy. This strategy is mainly aimed at identifying the criteria to use to select primary studies resulting from running the search string over the data sources in the final list that correctly answers the research questions posed. In this context, the inclusion and exclusion criteria in this systematic review corresponds to the following criteria: (1) only the studies published in the last five years (2011 to 2015) will be finally selected since the systematic review is aimed at compiling the most recent proposals and (2) only those proposals clearly depicting the integration of the technologies of the Semantic Web stack and Software Engineering approaches based on international software standards will be finally considered, so that the proposals concerning semantics modelling as addressed by conceptual data models such as the Entity-Relationship Model (ERM) and the Unified Modelling Language (UML) will be discarded.

Once the search string is run over each selected data source, each one of the primary studies in the resulting lists shall be evaluated against the inclusion and exclusion criteria by means of the procedure that is described below.

First, the title, abstract and keywords associated to the publication (which are commonly shown as part of the result lists by most digital libraries' search engines) will be read by a human agent to ensure the publication fit the criteria related to the topic of the paper (the second inclusion and exclusion criteria). Second, in the case there is no certainty of the topic which the publication is about at first glance, the full-text paper shall be accessed and other sections of the publication such as the introduction and conclusions section shall be read. Ultimately, a further keyword-based search shall be performed on the full text by taking advantage of the capabilities of the Web browser employed; thus, the human agent will need to search for keywords other than the keywords including in the search string, for example, terms describing Semantic Web technologies other than ontologies, or terms describing international software standards other than CMM, CMMI, ISO 15504 (or SPICE), ISO 12207, TSP and PSP.

Regarding the criteria related to how recent the publications are (the first inclusion and exclusion criteria), a refinement will be simply added to the search string by means of the filters provided by the digital libraries' search engines, so that the resulting lists will be retrieved as refined lists containing only those publications whose publication year is 2011 or later. Among the filters that are typically provided by the digital libraries' search engines there are filters related to the type and discipline of the publications; these filters will be leveraged in this systematic review to ensure that primary studies to be retrieved are in accordance with the criteria stated for selecting data sources (i.e., selection criteria).

3 Review Execution

As a result of running the search string over each one of the three selected data sources, three different lists of primary studies were retrieved. It is worth to mention that this task was executed manually by a human agent; the search string was run once for each data source, so that three different searches were asynchronously run. In detail, from ScienceDirect, 530 search results were obtained; from IEEE Xplore Digital Library (IEEE Xplore), 1069 results were obtained; and from SpringerLink, 802 results were obtained (a total of 2401 results). One point to take into account here is that, unlike ScienceDirect and IEEE Xplore, SpringerLink allows refining search results by sub-discipline; therefore, it was possible for SpringerLink to select Software Engineering (SE) as the sub-discipline of interest within Computer Science.

As a result of evaluating each one of the primary studies in the three resulting lists against the criteria stated for including and excluding studies from the review (i.e., the study inclusion and exclusion criteria), a total of 28 studies were finally selected: 9 primary studies were selected from the list resulting from ScienceDirect, 10 primary studies were selected from the list resulting from IEEE Xplore, and 9 primary studies were selected from the list resulting from SpringerLink. The usage of the study inclusion and exclusion criteria allowed us to ensure that, from the 2401 candidate studies, the 28 studies eventually selected were the studies in which we were really interested, i.e., the studies that were truly relevant for the research questions posed at the planning stage of the systematic review. Nonetheless, it is always possible to reduce the number of studies to be evaluated against the study inclusion and exclusion criteria, i.e., the number of candidate studies, by customizing the original search string, i.e., by adding/removing keywords from the original search string. It is worth to mention that any new keyword must fit the research questions initially posed. In order to ease the information extraction procedure, the selected studies were finally downloaded and locally managed using the Zotero reference management software tool.

3.1 Information Extraction Strategy

The aim of this strategy is to define the kind of information that must be obtained from selected primary studies and to define the criteria by which this information will be evaluated to present as findings of the systematic review.

Regarding the first point, only the following kind of objective information will be extracted from studies: (1) identification information (namely the publication title and authors), (2) information related to methodologies (namely, the kind of approach, its purpose, the software standards supported and the semantic Web technologies used) and (3) results (namely, the domain of the case study proposed, if any, and the effect of the proposal in SE support). It is worth mentioning that information concerning limitations of studies will be discussed in Sect. 4 of this paper, as part of the systematic review result analysis. Regarding the second point, the information inclusion and exclusion criteria which we have stated is applicable only to the kind of information related to the methodologies and results of the primary studies, and it is simply defined as the possibility of obtaining a clear, complete and sufficient conception about either the methodology or the results (as applicable).

For the gathering and presentation of the aforementioned information, one single data extraction form was designed (see Tables 1 and 2). It is intended at summarizing and contrasting the different kinds of information in an integrated way. For practical purposes, we have defined the following nomenclature related to the kinds of approaches found in the primary studies analysed: (1) O = Ontology, (2) S = Software System or architecture/Computable model, (3) F = Conceptual Framework, (4) M = Method/Methodology/Process.

3.2 Results

The list of primary studies finally selected in this systematic review, as well as the information gathered from them is presented in Tables 1 and 2, which depict the data extraction form defined as part of the information extraction strategy. It is worth noting that the way in which the studies are listed in these tables is completely random; however, there are partially ordered by the data source from which they come.

It is important to notice that a few considered studies do not actually rely on Semantic Web technologies; therefore, they do not completely fit study inclusion and exclusion criteria. These contributions make use of the concept of ontology, but they employ formalisms other than the Web Ontology Language (OWL) for its definition, for example, the Software & Systems Process Engineering Metamodel (SPEM) or the first-order logic formalism. The concepts of ontology and meta-model, although different, are closely related; both are often used in the description of relations between concepts. In fact, meta-models, as well as ontologies based on the first-order logic formalism, both have the potential to be moved into the OWL technical spice. That is why these studies were not left out from this systematic review.

Semantic Web technologies are primarily used in international standard-compliant SE approaches to formally and unambiguously represent the concepts in the domain of the standards (as domain ontologies) or as the basis to construct conceptual models of

Table 1. List of primary studies finally selected and summary of relevant information- part 1.

Paper	Data source[a]	Kind of app.[b]	Purpose
[7]	SD	M	Knowledge integration of various software-related bodies of knowledge to deploy safety critical software development processes
[8]		S, M	Support the development of Software Engineering Environments (SEEs)
[9]		M	Extend the traditional business process life-cycle for the improvement of business processes.
[10]		O	Construct a clear, unambiguous and comprehensive definition of all SC7 terminology (existing and future)
[11]		O	Apply the approach in [11] in a proof of concept development project
[12]		O, S	Support and leading the implementation of improvement projects where multiple reference models are harmonized by providing a consistent terminology and an accompanying tool
[13]		F, M	Support the work of harmonization of multiple models in harmonization projects by means of a conceptual and methodological framework
[14]		S	Automate the analysis of architectural patterns descriptions in natural language with respect to software quality models
[15]		F, M	Support process improvement in small and medium-sized software companies using a multi-model approach
[16]	IEEEX	F	Support software process improvement in small and medium sized software enterprises by means of Bayesian analysis of process models
[17]		O	Enable knowledge management in software testing processes starting from a common understanding of the concepts in the software testing domain
[18]		S	Support accessibility requirements engineering and promote requirements traceability to coding phase of software life-cycle processes
[19]		O, S	Support quality assessment inspections processes by means of a common understanding of the concepts in the software inspection domain
[20]		F, M	Improve the analysis and evaluation of business/Information Technology (IT) alignment at collaborative environments in small and medium sized IT companies using a conceptual model of the processes in the environment
[21]		F, M	Support the assessment of Service Oriented Architecture (SOA) security maturity at organizations by mapping conceptual models of information security best practices and the SOA paradigm

(Continued)

Table 1. (*Continued*)

Paper	Data source[a]	Kind of app.[b]	Purpose
[22]		F, M	Enable companies to predict the complexity of introducing Semantic Web technologies into development projects starting from a set of conceptual models about companies and projects
[23]		S, F, M	Support companies' survival strategy processes by deploying environments for processes management and improvement based on an agent-based approach
[24]		O, S	Support student practicing software development process by providing an e-learning platform using a common understanding of the events in teaching and software development
[25]		S, F, M	Enhancing semantic-aware software process support tools by integrating conceptual models of processes in IT service management and conceptual models of SE processes
[26]	SL	F	Enable software companies to prepare themselves regarding statistical process control in software measurement by means of common understanding of the concepts in the measurement domain
[27]		F, M	Promote consistency and repeatability for management and evaluation discipline by extending the GOCAME's conceptual and methodological framework
[28]		F, M	Enable the transformation of process assessment results between different process reference models providing an intermediate transitional process model based on a formal and shareable conceptualization
[29]		F, M	Support and guide organizations in introducing/improving quality management and software development practices by means of a multi-reference model harmonization approach.
[30]		F, M	Support organizations in identifying improvement findings for their actual organizational processes starting from a formal and shareable conceptualization of the CMMI standard
[31]		M	Support the customization of software capability/maturity models to specific environments by integrating previous experiences using a Knowledge Engineering approach
[32]		F, M	Enable the learning and evaluation of ISO/IEC 15504-compliant software processes by means of a graph-based Knowledge Representation approach
[33]		S	Support software organizations in transforming process assessment results between different process models by providing a support tool for [29]

(*Continued*)

Table 1. (*Continued*)

Paper	Data source[a]	Kind of app.[b]	Purpose
[34]		F	Directly align conceptual models of open source software development processes for open source e-learning systems with the outcomes of the ISO/IEC 12207 standard

[a]SD = ScienceDirect, IEEEX = IEEEXplore, SL = SpringerLink
[b]For the nomenclature related to the kinds of approaches see previous section of this paper.

Table 2. List of primary studies finally selected and summary of relevant information- part 2.

Paper	Supported standards	Sem. web tech. in use	Application domain	Effect in SE support
[7]	CMMI, ISO/IEC 25010	OWL (Ontologies)	Development of safety critical software	Software life-cycle processes
[8]	ISO/IEC 12207	OWL (Ontologies)	Development of SEEs for testing activities	Software life-cycle processes
[9]	CMM, CMMI	OWL (Ontologies)	Healthcare	Business processes improvement
[10]	ISO/IEC JTC1's SC7 standards	OWL (Ontologies)	No validation method is provided	Harmonization of ISO standards (e.g. software life-cycle processes)
[11]	ISO/IEC JTC1's SC7 standards	OWL (Ontologies)	Software endeavour	Harmonization of ISO standards (e.g. software life-cycle processes)
[12, 13]	Process-focused standards (e.g. CMMi and ISO 9001)	OWL (Ontologies)	Software endeavour (viz., consultancy and certification support), IT governance	Harmonization of standards for process improvement
[14]	ISO/IEC 9126	OWL (Ontologies)	Software endeavour	Software quality evaluation
[15]	CMMI, TSP, ISO/IEC 12207, ISO/IEC 15504, ISO 9001	OWL (Ontologies)	Development of multi-model SEEs for project management	Harmonization of standards for process improvement
[16]	CMM (others like ISO 26550)	OWL (Ontologies)	Telecommunications consultancy	Process improvement
[17]	ISO/IEC 12207	OWL (Ontologies)	No validation method is provided	Software testing processes

(*Continued*)

Table 2. (*Continued*)

Paper	Supported standards	Sem. web tech. in use	Application domain	Effect in SE support
[18]	ISO/IEC 12207	OWL (Ontologies), RDF	Development of Web search engines	Requirements engineering processes
[19]	CMMI	OWL (Ontologies), RDF and SPARQL	Software endeavour (development and management consultancy)	Process and product quality assurance
[20]	CMMI	OWL (Ontologies)	Customer-supplier relationship management	Business process improvement
[21]	CMM (SSE-CMM) (others like ISO 27002)	OWL (Ontologies)	No validation method is provided	Software process assessment
[22]	CMMI	OWL (Ontologies)	Development of an Information Extraction and Integration (IEI) system	Process improvement
[23]	PSP (other like 6-Sigm)	Not specified (Ontologies)	Customer-supplier relationship management	Business process management and improvement
[24]	TSP	OWL (Ontologies)	Graduation projects practicing	Software life-cycle processes
[25]	Others like SPEM	OWL (Ontologies), SWRL (rules)	IT consultancy	Software life-cycle processes
[26]	CMMI (others like ISO/IEC 15959 and IEEE Std. 1061)	OWL (Ontologies)	No details about application domain are provided	Software measurement processes
[27]	CMMI, ISO 12207 (others like SPEM)	OWL (Ontologies)	No validation method is provided	Software quality evaluation, software measurement processes
[28]	CMMI, ISO/IEC 15504	Not specified (Ontologies)	No validation method is provided	Software process improvement
[29]	CMMI, ISO 9001	SPEM (Meta-model)	ICT consultancy	Software process improvement
[30]	CMMI	OWL (Ontologies)	Academics research and development	Software process improvement

(*Continued*)

Table 2. (*Continued*)

Paper	Supported standards	Sem. web tech. in use	Application domain	Effect in SE support
[31]	Software process capability/maturity standards, ISO/IEC 15504	OWL (Ontologies)	Cloud computing (viz., SaaS model), development of embedded medical software	Software process improvement and assessment
[32]	ISO/IEC 15504	RDF (Graph database)	SE course practicing	Software process improvement and assessment
[33]	CMMI, ISO/IEC 15504, Enterprise SPICE	Not specified (Ontologies)	No validation method is provided	Software process improvement
[34]	ISO/IEC 12207	DEMO notation (Ontologies)	E-learning	Software life-cycle processes

different elements in software companies (e.g., software processes and projects, stakeholders, activities). These approaches are typically aimed at dealing with one single reference model (i.e., only one standard), and they are given either in the form of an ontology or in the form of a software system (viz., a SE support tool). On the other hand, there are multi-reference model approaches, in which Semantic Web technologies are used to enable the harmonization of the different models in a single shareable conceptual base; these approaches are mainly given in the form of conceptual and methodological frameworks. There is one last kind of contribution, the one that relies in Knowledge Engineering approaches to promote the management of the knowledge inherent to software development across the different elements in software companies; this kind of contribution is commonly given in the form of a framework also. It is worth mentioning that a few approaches use Semantic Web technologies also to enable the storage and retrieval of semantic data as knowledge bases.

4 Result Analysis: Discussion

As it can be inferred from the results obtained from the execution of this systematic literature review, nowadays, there is little Semantic Web technologies-based support for the standardization of the Software Engineering discipline, much less than it would be expected taking into account that SE is considered to be a mature discipline and that Semantic Web technologies have been widely used in many domains and applications as a means to enable computer systems to integrate, share, process and interpret the information formerly readable by humans.

In fact, as it can be observed from the information contrasted in Tables 1 and 2, OWL-based ontologies are the Semantic Web stack's building block most widely used among international standard-compliant Software Engineering (SE) approaches. Nonetheless, ontologies are primarily leveraged for knowledge representation purposes, and the reasoning of an inference capability that is enabled with OWL is not yet sufficiently exploited. Needless to mention the case of other technologies like rule languages (e.g. RIF and other not standardized proposals like SWRL), which can be used to enable advanced reasoning capabilities, but they are not nearly as exploited as OWL is. Further research on the use of RDF and SPARQL as a means to enable the storage and retrieval of the semantic data that is represented using ontologies is also required.

As it was previously outlined in this paper, the major motivations for the usage of the Semantic Web technologies to support standardization in SE can be summarized as follows: (1) to clearly, formally and unambiguously represent the concepts in a domain (e.g., a reference standard, a company, a software/business process), and to construct conceptual models about the domain, (2) to enable the unification of the different concepts in multiple domains; a typical application in this case is the harmonization of the concepts in multiple reference standards (for a complete state-of-the-art analysis on the different techniques for the harmonization of multiple reference models using Semantic Web technologies, refer to the work by Pardo et al. [13]) and (3) to enable the management of the knowledge inherent to SE across a domain. Not surprisingly, these motivations mainly refer to the usage of OWL and ontologies.

Regarding the expected effect of the contributions selected as a result of the execution of this systematic literature review, it was found that the SE standardization areas which academicians and practitioners are putting more effort in are Software Process Improvement (SPI) (and by inclusion software process assessment) and life-cycle processes, whereas the less favoured areas are software quality evaluation, software measurement and process/product quality assurance. In this context, it was found that SPI is being empowered mainly by the adoption of CMMI, and minimally by the adoption of ISO/IEC 15504 (SPICE). In the case of life-cycle processes support area, we can observe a trend in proposals in addressing full life-cycle processes standardization instead of standardization of particular life-cycle process phases. In any case, this area is being empowered mainly by the adoption of ISO/IEC 1220.

Furthermore, it is worth mentioning that, although some contributions focused in SPI claim to be aimed at small and medium-sized software organizations, it is well known from the SE literature (both industrial and academic research) that this kind of software companies often experience several challenges in the adoption of standards like CMMI and ISO/IEC 15504 (SPICE). In this context, we have to highlight that, there is an evident gap in the Semantic Web technologies-based support for the standardization of software development processes for small software organizations, not to mention the case of very small software companies. This contradicts the fact that small and very small software organizations are becoming increasingly popular, and that SPI is gaining momentum among them [17]. Thus, we encourage academicians and practitioners to put more effort into filling this gap by relying on international software standards aimed at this kind of companies, namely the ISO/IEC 29110 standard.

5 Conclusions and Future Work

Starting from the identification of the lack of systematic literature reviews on the Semantic Web technologies-based support for the standardization of the Software Engineering (SE) discipline regarding software development processes, in this paper we presented the details about the planning, execution and evaluation of results of a systematic literature review performed within that context. Judging by the results we obtained, we have successfully answered the research questions that we posed at the early stages of this review (i.e., at planning stage) to lead the entire process.

In fact, the results obtained shed light on the necessity of further Semantic Web technologies-based support for the standardization of software development processes for small and very small software organizations, especially in the specific area of software process improvement.

We expect this systematic review to contribute to the field of standardization in the SE discipline and to be especially valuable for researchers as a preliminary step towards filling this gap. For instance, from the results obtained it can be concluded that, the need to exploit the wide range of technologies offered by the Semantic Web stack, beyond OWL and ontologies, as well as the need to fully exploit the capabilities enabled by OWL and ontologies by themselves, beyond knowledge representation, are two areas of opportunity for further research in this line.

We hope this systematic review could serve also as a complementary guideline for software companies (i.e., practitioners) interested in the implementation of international standards for the support of both novel and already deployed software processes, especially for medium-sized Semantic Web-enabled software companies.

We have planned to extend this review by considering data sources (i.e., digital research libraries) other than the ones used in the designed review protocol (e.g., ACM Digital Library and Taylor & Francis Online), and to investigate the use of graphics and other visualization techniques to contrast the results of the systematic review in amore adequate way. We expect this future work will result on more findings on the current integration of Semantic Web technologies and international standard-compliant SE approaches. In addition, we have planned to construct an ontology for representing the concepts involved in the domain of the systematic literature reviews for SE, and to create a model for the specific case of the review conducted in this research from the instantiation of that ontology. We believe this further research would be very interesting taking into consideration the domain of the intended review.

References

1. Mellado, D., Blanco, C., Sánchez, L.E., Fernández-Medina, E.: A systematic review of security requirements engineering. Comput. Stand. Interfaces **32**, 153–165 (2010)
2. Dermeval, D., Vilela, J., Bittencourt, I.I., Castro, J., Isotani, S., Brito, P., Silva, A.: Applications of ontologies in requirements engineering: a systematic review of the literature. Requirements Eng. **21**(4), 405–437 (2016)
3. Vasanthapriyan, S., Tian, J., Xiang, J.: A survey on knowledge management in software engineering. In: 2015 IEEE International Conference on Software Quality, Reliability and Security - Companion (QRS-C), pp. 237–244 (2015)

4. Sánchez Guinea, A., Nain, G., Le Traon, Y.: A systematic review on the engineering of software for ubiquitous systems. J. Syst. Softw. **118**, 251–276 (2016)
5. Kitchenham, B.: Procedures for performing systematic reviews. Keele UK Keele Univ. **33**, 1–26 (2004)
6. Biolchini, J., Gomes-Mian, P., Cruz-Natali, A.C., Horta-Travassos, G.: Systematic Review in Software Engineering: Relevance and Utility. PESC - COPPE/UFRJ, Rio de Janeiro (2005)
7. Jędrzejowicz, P., Czarnowski, I., Howlett, R.J., Jain, L.C., Yamamoto, S.: Knowledge-Based and Intelligent Information and Engineering Systems: 18th Annual Conference, KES-2014 Gdynia, Poland, September 2014. In: Proceedings of Knowledge Integration Approach of Safety-Critical Software Development and Operation Based on the Method Architecture (2014). Procedia Comput. Sci. **35**, 1718–1727
8. Nakagawa, E.Y., Ferrari, F.C., Sasaki, M.M.F., Maldonado, J.C.: An aspect-oriented reference architecture for Software Engineering Environments. J. Syst. Softw. **84**, 1670–1684 (2011)
9. Delgado, A., Weber, B., Ruiz, F., Garcia-Rodríguez de Guzmán, I., Piattini, M.: An integrated approach based on execution measures for the continuous improvement of business processes realized by services. Inf. Soft. Technol. **56**, 134–162 (2014)
10. Henderson-Sellers, B., Gonzalez-Perez, C., McBride, T., Low, G.: An ontology for ISO software engineering standards: 1) creating the infrastructure. Comput. Stand. Interfaces **36**, 563–576 (2014)
11. Gonzalez-Perez, C., Henderson-Sellers, B., McBride, T., Low, G.C., Larrucea, X.: An ontology for ISO software engineering standards: 2) proof of concept and application. Comput. Stand. Interfaces **48**, 112–123 (2016)
12. Pardo, C., Pino, F.J., García, F., Piattini, M., Baldassarre, M.T.: An ontology for the harmonization of multiple standards and models. Comput. Stand. Interfaces **34**, 48–59 (2012)
13. Pardo, C., Pino, F.J., Garcia, F., Baldassarre, M.T., Piattini, M.: From chaos to the systematic harmonization of multiple reference models: a harmonization framework applied in two case studies. J. Syst. Softw. **86**, 125–143 (2013)
14. Velasco-Elizondo, P., Marín-Piña, R., Vazquez-Reyes, S., Mora-Soto, A., Mejia, J.: Knowledge representation and information extraction for analysing architectural patterns. Sci. Comput. Program. **121**, 176–189 (2016)
15. Mejia, J., Muñoz, E., Muñoz, M.: Reinforcing the applicability of multi-model environments for software process improvement using knowledge management. Sci. Comput. Program. **121**, 3–15 (2016)
16. Bibi, S., Gerogiannis, V.C., Kakarontzas, G., Stamelos, I.: Ontology based Bayesian software process improvement. In: 2014 9th International Conference on Software Engineering and Applications (ICSOFT-EA), pp. 568–575 (2014)
17. Souza, E.F., Falbo, R.A., Vijaykumar, N.L.: Using ontology patterns for building a reference software testing ontology. In: 2013 17th IEEE International Enterprise Distributed Object Computing Conference Workshops, pp. 21–30 (2013)
18. Branco, R.G.D., Cagnin, M.I., Paiva, D.M.B.: AccTrace: accessibility in phases of requirements engineering, design, and coding software. In: 2014 14th International Conference on Computational Science and Its Applications (ICCSA), pp. 225–228 (2014)
19. Silva, J.P.S.D., DallOglio, P., Pinto, S.C.C.D.S., Bittencourt, I.I., Mergen, S.L.S.: OntoQAI: an ontology to support quality assurance inspections. In: 2015 29th Brazilian Symposium on Software Engineering (SBES), pp. 11–20 (2015)

20. Hachicha, M., Moalla, N., Ouzrout, Y.: An analysis and assessment approach for collaborative process in service-oriented architectures. In: 2014 IEEE/ACS 11th International Conference on Computer Systems and Applications (AICCSA), pp. 707–714 (2014)
21. Kassou, M., Kjiri, L.: SOASMM: a novel service oriented architecture security maturity model. In: 2012 International Conference on Multimedia Computing and Systems (ICMCS), pp. 912–918 (2012)
22. Santillán, L.I.B., de Mon y Rego, I.Á.: Towards measuring the complexity of introducing semantics into a company. In: 2013 IEEE Systems and Information Engineering Design Symposium (SIEDS), pp. 86–91 (2013)
23. Choi, S.: Semantic process management environment. In: 2011 International Conference on Ubiquitous Computing and Multimedia Applications (UCMA), pp. 106–110 (2011)
24. Liu, W., Wang, D., Wu, Y., Liu, Y., Zheng, Y.: A software engineering practice platform based on event ontology. In: 2012 7th International Conference on Computer Science Education (ICCSE), pp. 1474–1479 (2012)
25. Valiente, M.C., García-Barriocanal, E., Sicilia, M.Á.: Applying ontology-based models for supporting integrated software development and IT service management processes. IEEE Trans. Syst. Man Cybern. Part C (Appl. Rev.) **42**, 61–74 (2012)
26. Barcellos, M.P., de Almeida Falbo, R., Rocha, A.R.: A strategy for preparing software organizations for statistical process control. J. Braz. Comput. Soc. **19**, 445–473 (2013)
27. Becker, P., Papa, F., Olsina, L.: Enhancing the conceptual framework capability for a measurement and evaluation strategy. In: Sheng, Q.Z., Kjeldskov, J. (eds.) Current Trends in Web Engineering, pp. 104–116. Springer, Cham (2013)
28. Peldzius, S., Ragaisis, S.: Framework for usage of multiple software process models. In: Mas, A., Mesquida, A., Rout, T., O'Connor, R.V., Dorling, A. (eds.) Software Process Improvement and Capability Determination, pp. 210–221. Springer, Berlin (2012)
29. Baldassarre, M.T., Caivano, D., Pino, F.J., Piattini, M., Visaggio, G.: Harmonization of ISO/IEC 9001:2000 and CMMI-DEV: from a theoretical comparison to a real case application. Softw. Qual. J. **20**, 309–335 (2012)
30. Miranda, J.M., Muñoz, M., Uribe, G., Uribe, E., Márquez, J., Valtierra, C.: Identifying improvement findings in IT SMEs through an ontological model for CMMI-DEV v1.3. In: Rocha, Á., Correia, A.M., Tan, F.B., Stroetmann, K.A. (eds.) New Perspectives in Information Systems and Technologies, Volume 1. AISC, vol. 275, pp. 421–429. Springer, Cham (2014)
31. Hauck, J.C.R., von Wangenheim, C.G.: Proposing an ISO/IEC 15504-2 compliant method for process capability/maturity models customization. In: Caivano, D., Oivo, M., Baldassarre, M.T., Visaggio, G. (eds.) Product-Focused Software Process Improvement, pp. 44–58. Springer, Berlin (2011)
32. Carpio, A.F., Angarita, L.B.: Towards the development of a framework for encouraging the learning of SPICE model by using knowledge graphs. In: Clarke, P.M., O'Connor, R.V., Rout, T., Dorling, A. (eds.) SPICE 2016. CCIS, vol. 609, pp. 203–216. Springer, Heidelberg (2015). doi:10.1007/978-3-319-19860-6_16
33. Peldzius, S., Ragaisis, S.: Usage of multiple process assessment models. In: Woronowicz, T., Rout, T., O'Connor, R.V., Dorling, A. (eds.) Software Process Improvement and Capability Determination, pp. 223–234. Springer, Berlin (2013)
34. Krishnamurthy, A., O'Connor, R.V.: Using ISO/IEC 12207 to analyze open source software development processes: an E-learning case study. In: Woronowicz, T., Rout, T., O'Connor, R.V., Dorling, A. (eds.) Software Process Improvement and Capability Determination, pp. 107–119. Springer, Berlin (2013)

Expert Systems and Soft Computing

Autonomous Cycle of Data Analysis Tasks for Learning Processes

Jose Aguilar[1,2]([envelope]), Omar Buendia[1], Karla Moreno[1], and Diego Mosquera[3]

[1] Universidad de Los Andes, Mérida 5101, Venezuela
aguilar@ula.ve
[2] Escuela Politécnica Nacional, Universidad Técnica Particular de Loja,
Loja, Ecuador
[3] Universidad Nacional Experimental de Guayana, Puerto Ordaz 8050, Venezuela
http://www.ing.ula.ve/~aguilar/

Abstract. The data analysis has become a fundamental area for knowledge discovery from data extracted from different sources. In that sense, to develop mechanisms, strategies, methodologies that facilitate their use in different contexts, it has become an important need. In this paper, we propose an "Autonomic Cycle Of Data Analysis Tasks" for learning analytic (ACODAT) in the context of online learning environments, which defines a set of tasks of data analysis, whose objective is to improve the learning processes. Each data analysis task interacts with each other, and has different roles: observe the process, analyze and interpret what happens in it, or make decisions in order to improve the learning process. In this paper, we study the application of the autonomic cycle into the contexts of a smart classroom and a virtual learning platform.

Keywords: Data analysis task · Learning analytic · Smart classroom · Virtual learning environments

1 Introduction

In this paper, we propose an autonomous cycle of data analysis tasks (ACODAT), and its application in learning processes. ACODAT is composed by a set of tasks of data analysis to reach a goal for a given problem, where each task has a different role: observes the system to study, analyses it, makes decisions to improve it. In this way, there is an interaction and synergy between the tasks of data analysis, in order to generate the knowledge required, with the goal of improving the process under study. In our proposition, the autonomous cycle defines a closed loop of tasks of data analysis, which supervises constantly the process under study.

Learning Analytics (LA) is a discipline to optimize and adapt online learning environments to the needs of students; where strategies, resources and tools for teaching must be adapted to the learning styles and abilities of students. The utilization of the learning analytic in the context of learning environments is very

© Springer International Publishing AG 2016
R. Valencia-García et al. (Eds.): CITI 2016, CCIS 658, pp. 187–202, 2016.
DOI: 10.1007/978-3-319-48024-4_15

useful, due to the large quantity of information about the learning processes generated in them, because it allows discovering knowledge to be used during the learning process, in order to improve it. In this paper, we propose an autonomous cycle of Learning Analytic, to organize the different types of tasks of Learning Analysis applied to these environments, in order to improve their learning processes. To do this, the different elements of an autonomous cycle in two different online learning environments will be analyzed, in a smart classroom and in an virtual learning environment (VLE). The obtained results are: the specification of the "autonomous cycle of data analysis tasks", which includes the analysis of the online platform to define the objective of the integration of an autonomous cycle in it, and the specification of the roles and types of tasks of data analysis.

2   State of the Art

In this section, we explain some recent works in LA. Buckingham et al. [7] have defined social learning analytics for the analysis of social aspects like tags, ratings and metadata, supplied by learners. These include content analytics, recommender systems and automated methods for examining, indexing and filtering online media assets in order to guide learners through the available resources. In general, social learning analytics allow building up a holistic picture of student progress. Baylon University is one of the university pioneers in higher educational analytics, and has created an Enrolment Predictive Model as a supportive tool for the student admissions [14]. They use a predictive model that analyzes various factors about the students. Most of these factors are about student's motivation, extracurricular activities, among others. Scores generated by the predictive model are considered by the admissions staff to identify those students most likely to be admitted. Purdue University has developed a prediction model which extracts data from the Course Management System (CMS) and predicts which students may be at a risk in academic work [6]. Using factor analysis and logistic regression mechanisms, the model predicts the student success in a given course.

Ferguson presents the challenges and opportunities of LA for both research and educational organizations, in three important respects [9]. The first is the challenge of implementing analytics that has pedagogical and ethical integrity, in a context where power and control over data is now of primary importance. The second challenge is that the educational landscape is extraordinarily turbulent at present. The last challenge is about the diversity of learning contexts, each of which has specific technical and pedagogical challenges.

In the Computers in Human Behavior Journal, Vol. 47 of 2015, it is presented a special issue about the current state of the art on LA. There is a predominance of research focused on course level analysis and visualization of student behaviors. Some of the papers in this issue explore how to gather data in educational virtual worlds. These data are later used to identify students and teachers behaviors, usage patterns, etc. Cruz-Benito et al. explore ways to define and configure student workgroups in Computer-Supported Collaborative Learning (CSCL) [8]. The authors propose a method for configuration of groups of learners based on the analysis of indicators from previous activities. Gomez-Aguilar et al. show how student interactions with their resources and peers may have an impact on their academic performance [10]. The empirical study unveils recurrent patterns in student behaviors, in terms of frequency of use and performance, which are consistent across different courses. In [11], it is defined the relation between social network analysis parameters and student outcomes, as well as between network parameters and global course performance. Their study also shows how the visualizations of social learning networks can help observing the visible and invisible interactions occurring in online distance education. [12] analyses the interactions in Virtual Learning Environments (VLE) to determine the potential relationship between learning platform interactions and two cross-curricular competences: teamwork and commitment. Munoz-Merino et al. propose a methodology for defining metrics that enable the calculation of the effectiveness of students when interacting with educational resources and activities in MOOCs [13]. They conclude that effectiveness is negatively correlated with the students behavioral patterns. In [17], they address the problem of how to define a predictive model of students performance that is both practical and understandable for users. The authors summarize different approaches used in LA, educational data mining and human-computer interaction, to explore the development of usable prediction models.

The goal of [15] is to evaluate the use of LA in Higher Education. In particular, that paper tries to reach the following objectives: to identify factors that influence the decision of an distance learning student to abandon their studies, and get the profile of susceptible students to abandon their university studies. Anupamar et al. predict the student overall performance based on decision tree approaches. They used internal assessments in the VLE and concluded that classification techniques can be applied on educational data for predicting the student outcome [5]. Finally, they argue that data mining brings a lot of advantages in learning institutions, so that these techniques can be applied to optimize the resource allocations according to the student learning capacity.

The previous works give an idea of the variety of research in LA. They show how the knowledge generated can be used to solve educational problems, support educational decision making, but at the same time, they pose new research questions. One of them is the goal of this work, How can be organized the LA tasks in order to reach strategic goals in educational institutions?

3   Eco-Connectivism as the Base of the Learning Process in the Online Learning Platform

The eco-connectivism is a framework to address and optimize Connectivist Learning Environments (CLE) assisted for computer technologies. For the eco connectivism, the system to manage/optimize is seen as an ecology of knowledge, whose constituent elements are Personal Learning Environments (PLE).

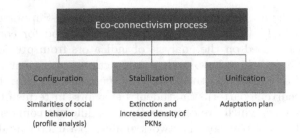

Fig. 1. Eco-connectivism phase in learning environment

The pedagogical model to manage/optimize is based on a process of ecological transformation that occurs in three phases. Figure 1 shows these phases. In the configuration phase it is established what is known as ecological survival threshold, a parameter set by an external entity (e.g. supervisor/teacher of the learning process), to specify the degree of diversity required in ecology. In previous work [1] we have defined this threshold of survival and its role within the optimization model. Also, in the configuration phase, a set of tasks is executed to establish the preliminary ecological distribution. In particular, a method of Web usage mining is executed, using records of the user navigation. Web usage mining allows for each learner, capture the fundamental elements of its PLE (consultation resources, resources reflection/production and Personal Knowledge Network (PKN)). Similarly, the Web usage mining provides the grouping necessary through interpretation of social learning patterns. Finally, the subsequent phases (stabilization and unification), are carried out according to the PKN information provided.

In the stabilization phase is established the stabilize parameters of the ecology. The ecological stability is achieved through a mechanism of migration of entities (PLEs) from non-apt ecosystem to apt ecosystems. An ecosystem is apt if it can survive. In [1], it is explained this phase.

In the unification phase, the parameterized information in the stabilization phase is used to propose an adaptive plan of the entities that have migrated, based on the information about the elements of the ecosystem where it has migrated. As explained in [1], the adaptive plan uses a model of collaborative filtering. Finally, the ecological unification is achieved when there are no entities in non-apt ecosystems.

This configuration, stabilization and unification processes, are performed cyclically and continuously throughout the learning process. An ecology of knowledge reaches the "climax" (interactivity, autonomy, interactivity and openness), once the fitness function (configuration phase) provides an ecology, in which the ability of all knowledge ecosystems equalize or exceed the threshold of ecological survival.

4   SaCI

SaCI (Salon de Clase Inteligente, for its acronym in Spanish) is a smart student-centered classroom, which supports the learning process, through of devices and applications, working together to form an intelligent environment in the context of educational learning (for more details of SaCI, see [16, 18]). SaCI proposes two types of separate agent frameworks, one to represent the software components of SaCI and other to represent its hardware components [16]. SaCI generates a lot of information, this information has to be exploited to improve the performances of SaCI. ACODAT is used in this context, to exploit this large quantity of information generated in SaCI.

SaCI has several conversations, for example, the Online Tutoring Process (OTP), the Setting of the Environmental Variables, the Feedback Process, etc. In this work, we will focus on the Online Tutoring Process (OTP) conversation. The OTP uses hardware and software, necessary during a learning session. In the OTP conversation there are a lot of tasks, in the next Figure we can appreciate the process model of the OTP conversation in SaCI.

4.1   Model of Activities of Online Tutoring Process (OTP)

Figure 2 represents the process model of the OTP conversation, where we can see how the first activity is the initialization of the session by the students.

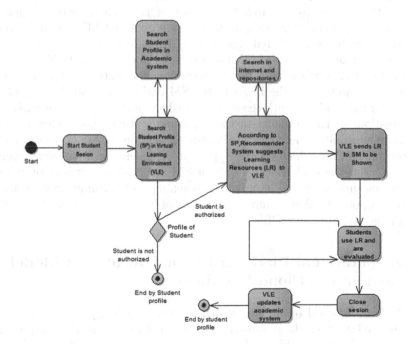

Fig. 2. OTP process model in SaCI

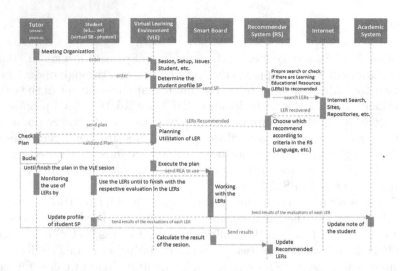

Fig. 3. OTP Conversation in SaCI (source [18])

That session is verified by the VLE, the VLE maintains communication with academic system, to obtain the Student Profile (SP). This SP is passed through a filter to decide if the SP is valid or not; if it is not valid then the process ends, otherwise it sends the profile to the recommender system (RS). The RS based on the SP makes a search in Internet of learning objects adequate to the SP of the student. This information is sent to the VLE (the information about the Learning Educational Resources (LERs) recommended sent is: title, website, etc.). The Smart Board (SM) executes the plan sent by the VLE, to work with the LERs that where sent by the recommender system to the VLE (The VLE sends the website of the LERs to the SM), where the learning objects are deployed for the students until the session finishes. In that point, the VLE sends the evaluations of the students to the academic system, the academic system updates its information, and the VLE closes the session. In Fig. 3, we can see the conversation OTP, in which we can appreciate the iteration with every agent of SaCI (the tutor, the student, the VLE, the SM, etc.). This conversation requires a continuous supervision to improve the teaching and learning process. In this work, we propose creating an autonomic cycle of learning analytical tasks, using data mining, to improve SaCI.

5   Computational Platform for an Educational Model Based on the Cloud Paradigm

This platform is based on an educational model, which exploits the new tools offered in the Internet. The proposed educational model focuses on the paradigm of learning by doing [3]. This model is based on a metaphor of clouds, which has been explained in detail in [3]. In general, this metaphor introduces the idea of "clouds effect", which makes their internal dynamics move with the wind (with the global and national events, industry, etc.), in order to allow the emergence of activities, generating a powerful educational synergy. This educational model is composed by three clouds.

5.1 Learning Cloud Paradigm

This cloud is related to the paradigms, strategies, forms of assessment and learning tools. Its aim is to provide the learning mechanisms necessary for the process of self-formation. It will guide the dynamics of self-training, establish ways of accrediting courses, collaborative work, among other things. The learning process provided to the students is adapted permanently, based on the characteristics of each student (learning profile of the student). Some characteristics are:

1. It is inspired on the paradigm of "learning by doing", which seeking the active participation of the students in a work, which can be artistic, technological, scientific, etc.
2. All forms of learning that promote learning by doing (active learning, agile learning, blended learning, etc.) are possible to use.
3. The collaborative work, sharing knowledge, multidisciplinary work, are issues that enrich the teaching process. The different strategies, tools, etc. must promote those aspects.
4. It requires many tools and applications from the Internet, to manage shared spaces and groups, to assign responsibilities, to monitor works/projects.

5.2 Knowledge Sources Cloud

This cloud is composed of connections to repositories in the Internet, which contain LERs and other educational digital materials. Its purpose is to enable greater access to knowledge available worldwide. Learning objects, online courses, e-books, etc., become fundamental sources of knowledge. The methodologies, tools and techniques of this cloud, must allow an access critical to the knowledge [3]. So, we are not talking about a passive, neutral, access to knowledge, but critical, seen from the process of self-formation according to the curriculum established, and the learning process dictated by the Learning Paradigm Cloud.

5.3 Self-formation Cloud

This cloud is composed of everything related to the student's education. The student self-formation consists of the building of the curriculum, which is composed of modules which are self-contained. In the curriculum, there is the option to various degrees, these depend on the number of credits reached and profile chosen by the student. The possible profiles of the students are inspired in the curriculum defined by the IEEE/ACM. Paths for these profiles initially are proposed, but as the student is autonomous, he/she guides his/her own process of self-education.

5.4   Architecture

The design of the web platform is based on SOA [4]. The system functionality is described in Fig. 4, which is composed of three layers; each one manages one of the cloud concepts (the details of this architecture are given in [4]). The first layer manages everything regarding the student, teacher and curriculum. This layer has the different services they need, both the student and the teacher, to manage the process of self-education, such as student registration services, queries to the curriculum, etc. The second layer manages the search of virtual objects, both learning objects and digital contents, and offering the student the proper learning resources to their needs, according to their educational profile and position in the curriculum. The last layer manages the learning paradigms, in order to specify the tools, types of evaluations and educational activities appropriate for the student's learning style. The implementation of each layer is made as web services, and clients to these services. Each layer is composed with an ontology that works with the web services to manage information in order to discover knowledge and use this information to interact with the other layers. Each layer has its own ontologies, whose instances represent the stored and inferred information. That is called in Fig. 4 Extended Data Base, which also has the ability to support processes of reasoning.

This platform involves three important aspects: digital resources, the learning style, and the curriculum graph. The main objective is to give customized resources to the user for a better experience. Figure 5 shows the learning process. The first step is the student login, where the user can select the module to attend, which belongs to an initial study profile related to the curriculum graph; once the user choose the module, each topic for each module has resources customized for

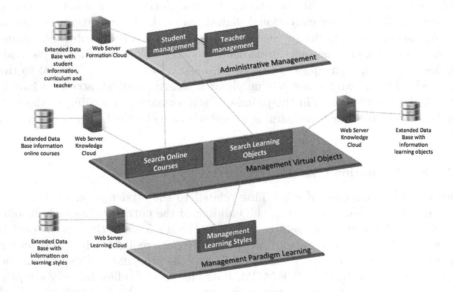

Fig. 4. General architecture (source [4])

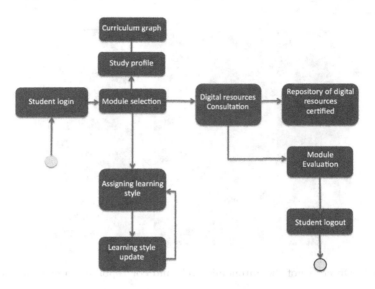

Fig. 5. Learning process

the student, as a result of a learning paradigm that is in continuous assessment. The digital resources are ready to be consulted, for this, the connections are established with them (with the repositories where they are stored). The evaluation process is the way to validate the learning process, and if necessary, to update the learning style. This method of allocating a specific paradigm related to student characteristics, ensures optimization of the learning process on the web platform.

6   Autonomic Cycles in Each Context

We can build an autonomic cycle to improve some specific aspects of the learning process, with the main objectives of customizing the learning process to the student. This will result in adaptations of the platforms.

In order to make an autonomic cycle to optimize the learning process, we will divide the tasks of analysis of data in three types, which are observation, analysis and decision-making.

6.1   Autonomic Cycles for SaCI

Figure 6 shows a general autonomic cycle of tasks of learning analytical, with the objective to update the learning process for the students in SaCI.

This autonomic cycle of tasks of learning analytical can be instanced to reach the specific objective of: Avoid school dropouts. The specific tasks of this autonomous cycle are defined as follows (see Tables 1, 2 and 3):

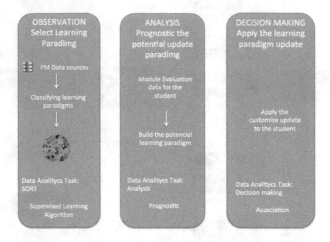

Fig. 6. Objective of the autonomic cycle and corresponding tasks for SaCI

Table 1. Classify the students as deserters or not

Task number	1
Task name	Classify the students in deserters and not deserters
Description	Classifies the general population in groups, according to whether or not deserters
Data source	Databases of SaCI
Task type of data analytics	Classification
Tasks that is related	Classify the students in deserters and no deserters → Elaborate a desertor profile
Task type in the cycle	Monitoring

Table 2. Prognostic the potential group of deserters

Task number	2
Task name	Prognostic the potential group of deserters
Description	Prognostic the potential group of deserters according with the performance of the students
Data source	Databases of SaCI
Task type of data analytics	Prognostic
Tasks that is related	Prognostic the potential group of deserters → Build a motivacional pattern
Task type in the cycle	Analysis

Table 3. Build a motivational pattern

Task number	3
Task name	Build a motivational pattern
Description	Apply motivational techniques for every student according with the student profile
Data source	Databases of SaCI
Task type of data analytics	Association
Tasks that is related	Build a motivational pattern → End of Cycle
Task type in the cycle	Execution

6.2 Autonomic Cycles for the Educational Model Based on the Cloud Paradigm

As part of the automation process it is been determined work flows in each layer of platform of educational processes. One of the processes that are involved directly with the student lies in the selection of educational profile that the user makes initially at the moment to do the register on the platform. Selecting this profile may not be successful for the student; it is for this reason that the student tasks suggest the more tailored to their needs and according to a study of their profile information, is proposed. This objective is shown in the Fig. 7.

In order to specify the tasks related to the autonomic cycle, a division in three important aspects is made (see Tables 4, 5 and 6).

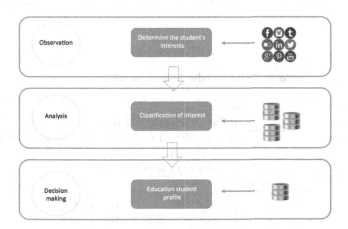

Fig. 7. Autonomic cycle for selection of educational profile

Table 4. Classify the students interest, needs and information

Task number	1
Task name	Classify the students interest
Description	Classifies the general population in groups, according to the needs and interest
Data source	Databases of web platform
Task type of data analytics	Classification
Tasks that is related	
Task type in the cycle	Monitoring

Table 5. Prognostic the potential educational profile

Task number	2
Task name	Prognostic the potential educational profile
Description	Prognostic the potential educational profile according with the performance of the student
Data source	Databases of web platform
Task type of data analytics	Prognostic
Tasks that is related	
Task type in the cycle	Analysis

Table 6. Build an educational profile suggestion

Task number	3
Task name	Build an educational profile suggestion
Description	Apply inferred techniques for the information of every student
Data source	Databases of web platform
Task type of data analytics	Association
Tasks that is related	
Task type in the cycle	Execution

6.3 Autonomic Cycles Based on Eco-Connectivism Paradigm for Each Platform

In a previous work we have specified ARMAGAeco-c [1], a reflective middleware that provides a model of autonomic computing to manage and optimize a learning process using the eco-connectivism paradigm. ARMAGAeco-c describes two levels of reflection, each with an autonomic loop task. The first makes introspection over the PLE of apprentices. The second makes introspection over the knowledge ecology distribution emerging from the process. The intersection of the first level of reflection is carried out through eco- connectivist plan adaptation. The intersection of the second level of reflection is performed with analytical learning procedures and analytical social learning.

Additionally, we have defined an Independent Reflection Model (IRM), based on a dynamic Multi-Agent System (MAS). IRM can generate instances of agents adapted to the level of reflection of ARMAGAeco-c. Figure 8 shows the architecture of IRM. Figure 9 shows the distribution of the agents in the middleware, whose agents allow the implementation of the loop MAPE+K proposed in [1].

Through the autonomic loop of ARMAGAeco-c, it is possible to enrich a process of conventional learning (e.g. constructivist model, social constructive or immersive), in which qualitative and quantitative knowledge is generated, combined with the connective knowledge paradigm. The latter allows exploring and exploiting the social dynamics of the learning environment, with the aim of establishing and evaluating knowledge networks (networks learning) that emerge during the process.

ARMAGAeco-c can be integrated into learning environments according to the methodological aspects proposed in [1]. The intent of this article is to show how ARMAGAeco-c can be used for two purposes:

1. Enrich other autonomous systems with the paradigm of connective knowledge. This includes the incorporation of the social learning analytics tasks.
2. Guide and optimize the learning processes in environments that incorporate the use of social networking and collaboration tools.

In particular, we consider the implementation of the autonomic loops for SaCI and for the Computational Platform for the Educational Model based on the

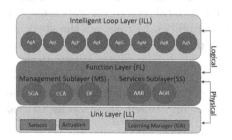

Fig. 8. IRM-architecture

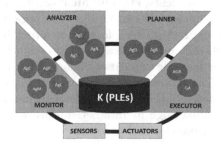

Fig. 9. IRM-ARMAGA relationship

Cloud Paradigm, in order to influence the decisions made by the agents (in the case of SaCI) and ontologies (in the other case) during the learning process. In the particular case of SaCI, a new restriction must be satisfied: to achieve an ecology of knowledge based on four fundamental criteria: interactivity, autonomy, diversity and openness.

In both platforms, MRI-ARGAMAeco-c parameterizes the connective knowledge. For SaCI, it comes from an external source which extends the conceptual minable view, with performance parameters related to collaborative learning. It also provides a strategy for organizing working groups, which optimizes student performance in the learning process. This latter is related to the appearance of diversity, and is controlled by the threshold ecological survival.

In the other case, it will extend the management learning paradigms layer. On the one hand, with the connective knowledge, MRI-ARGAMAeco-c updates the student's learning style. This indirectly influences the other layers (management of virtual objects and administrative management), for the proper selection of digital resources during the learning process. Finally, as for the SaCI, ARMA-GAeco allows communities to establish a model to characterize and optimize the social relationships of learning.

7   Conclusion

In recent years has grown the idea of using large-scale educational data, to transform practice in education. LA has appeared as a domain which tries to define useful applications with these data, in order to improve the learning processes. In this paper, we propose an autonomous cycle of LA. The utilization of this knowledge in real time is an enormous challenge for learning platforms.

We have proposed a LA autonomic closed loop, which allows an effective use of the results of the LA tasks. We test our approach in two contexts: SaCI, and a Computational Platform for the Educational Model based on the Cloud Paradigm. LA tasks allow an autonomic behavior, in order to manage a diversity of situations, educational materials, students styles, etc. In this way, the educational platform can carry out a correct adaptation of its components. The introduction of ACODAT improves the learning process, utilizing a large amount of knowledge effectively, based on the understanding and covering the actual needs of the students, etc. Our architecture can use data mining and semantic mining techniques, and can be based on organizational databases (data warehouse) or big data. ACODAT focuses on providing capabilities to discover the students with difficulties of learning, to define the guidance to the students to improve their learning capacities, among other things.

The eco-connectivism paradigm introduces the social learning process. Particularly, this paradigm allows including social learning analysis tasks, to use the knowledge in Internet. Future works must implement these cycles in real situations, for real problems.

Acknowledgement. Dr. Aguilar has been partially supported by the Prometeo Project of the Ministry of Higher Education, Science, Technology and Innovation (SENESCYT) of the Republic of Ecuador.

References

1. Aguilar, J., Mosquera, D.: Middleware reflexivo para la gestión de aprendizajes conectivistas en ecologias del conocimiento (eco-conectivismo). Lat.-Am. J. Comput. **2**(2), 25–31 (2015)
2. Aguilar, J., Valdivieso, P., Cordero, J., Riofrio, G., Encalada, E.: A general framework for learning analytic in a smart classroom. In: Valencia-García, R., et al. (eds.) CITI 2016. CCIS, vol. 658, pp. 214–225. Springer, Heidelberg (2016)
3. Aguilar, J., Moreno, K., Hernandez, D., Altamiranda, J., Viloria, M.: Propuesta de un Modelo Educativo Utilizando el Paradigma de la Nube. ReVeCom **1**, 1–11 (2014)
4. Aguilar, J., Fuentes, J., Moreno, K., Dos Santos, O., Portilla, O., Altamiranda, J., Hernandez, D.: Computational platform for the educational model based on the cloud paradigm. In: Proceeding of the 45th Annual Frontiers in Education, pp. 2399–2407 (2015)
5. Anupamar, S., Vijayalakshmi, M.: Efficiency of data mining techniques in edifying sector. Int. J. Adv. Found. Res. Comput. **1**(8), 56–62 (2014)
6. Ari, J., White, B.: Learning Analytics From Research to Practice. Springer, New York (2014)
7. Buckingham, S., Ferguson, R.: Social learning analytics. Educ. Technol. Soc. **15**(3), 3–26 (2012)
8. Cruz-Benito, J., Theron, R., Garcia-Penalvo, F., Pizarro, E.: Discovering usage behaviors and engagement in an educational virtual world. Comput. Hum. Behav. **47**, 18–25 (2015)
9. Ferguson, R.: Learning analytics: drivers, developments and challenges. Int. J. Technol. Enhanc. Learn. **4**(5/6), 304–317 (2012)
10. Gomez-Aguilar, D., Hernandez-Garcia, A., Garcia-Penalvo, F., Garcia-Penalvo, J., Theron, R.: Tap into visual analysis of customization of grouping of activities in eLearning. Comput. Hum. Behav. **47**, 60–67 (2015)
11. Hernandez-Garcia, A., Gonzalez-Gonzalez, I., Jimenez-Zarco, A., Chaparro-Pelaez, J.: Applying social learning analytics to message boards in online distance learning: a case study. Comput. Hum. Behav. **47**, 68–80 (2015)
12. Iglesias-Pradas, S., Ruiz-de-Azcarate, C., Agudo-Peregrina, A.: Assessing the suitability of student interactions from Moodle data logs as predictors of cross-curricular competencies. Comput. Hum. Behav. **47**, 81–89 (2015)
13. Munoz-Merino, P., Ruiperez-Valiente, J., Alario-Hoyos, C., Perez-Sanagustin, M., Delgado, C.: Precise effectiveness strategy for analyzing the effectiveness of students with educational resources and activities in MOOCs. Comput. Hum. Behav. **47**, 108–118 (2015)
14. Ranbaduge, T.: Use of data mining methodologies in evaluating educational data. Int. J. Sci. Res. Publ. **3**(11), 25–39 (2013)
15. Riofrio, G., Encalada, E., Guamn, D., Aguilar, J.: Aplicacin de un general learning analytics framework para analizar la desercin estudiantil en carreras a distancia. In: Proceeding XLI Conferencia Latinoamericana en Informtica, pp. 567–576 (2015)
16. Sanchez, M., Aguilar, J., Cordero, J., Valdiviezo, P.: A smart learning environment based on cloud learning. Int. J. Adv. Inf. Sci. Technol. **39**(39), 39–52 (2015)

17. Xing, W., Guo, R., Petakovic, E., Goggins, S.: Participation-based student grade prediction model through interpretable Genetic Programming: integrating learning analytics, educational data mining and theory. Comput. Hum. Behav. **47**, 168–181 (2015)
18. Valdiviezo, P., Cordero, J., Aguilar, J., Snchez, M.: Conceptual design of a smart classroom based on multiagent systems. In: International Conference Artificial Intelligence (ICAI 2015), pp. 471–477 (2015)

The Present World of the Expert System and its Competitive Contribution in Medicine

William Bazán[✉], Valeria Bazán, Abel Alarcón, Teresa Samaniego,
Oscar Bermeo, and Ana Rodríguez

School of Computer and Information, Agrarian University of Ecuador, Guayaquil, Ecuador
{wbazan,jalarcon,tsamaniego,obermeo,arodriguez}@uagraria.edu.ec,
v-bazan90@hotmail.com

Abstract. In the world of computer application, one of the latest concepts that has been generated is that of the "Expert Systems", which has been reviewed from the mid-60s to the present time. Expert Systems have become fundamental elements mainly in the area of medicine, since users have favorably valued the results obtained. This article presents/displays a literature review, identifying how the accomplishment or development of the Expert Systems is carried out within the field of medicine. In this way, we try to analyze the importance of Expert Systems that have on different aspects of our lives, stating that there is a high percentage of satisfaction with the analyzed information in scientific articles.

Keywords: Expert system · Fuzzy logic · Artificial intelligence · Medicine

1 Introduction

Artificial Intelligence (AI) has become one the fundamental branches of study nowadays. Despite the fact that it has been evolving, not maybe as many optimistic people of last century had wanted o wished it. Perhaps, it was due to this optimism that AI was neglected for a while, given that some of those optimistic people who financed research in the area withdrew the financial support faced with the lack of imminent results. Nonetheless, in the last few years AI has experienced a growth that is expected to continue in the foreseeable future.

As we know AI has many branches, amongst which we may find: increased reality, neuronal networks, intelligent robotics, agents, etc., being one of its main branches Expert Systems (ES) [1, 2], considered a previous stage in the creation of knowledge, programs or applications that try to simulate a specialist in certain areas (medicine, engineering, science, etc.), that is to say, these systems have a certain degree of reasoning that aids or allows them to solve certain kind of problems. These systems can be used by non-experts to improve their abilities in problem solving [1]. We are almost certain that people can learn from these systems, since they contain a great amount of data provided by the knowledge and experience of experts. Nevertheless, it is important to emphasize that from its beginnings in the decade of the 80s [3], Expert Systems need to comply with the following objectives:

© Springer International Publishing AG 2016
R. Valencia-García et al. (Eds.): CITI 2016, CCIS 658, pp. 203–213, 2016.
DOI: 10.1007/978-3-319-48024-4_16

- Identify the precise information that we want to store in the database of the Expert System.
- Evaluate efficiently the methods to use to codify the information.

The objective of this article is to identify, through the literature review mentioned above, the importance of using Expert Systems and its competitive contribution in the field of medicine. The following section shows a brief definition of the main concepts. Later, the article presents the methodology used, followed by the discussion and results. Finally, the main conclusions reached are presented.

2 Literature Review

2.1 Beginning of the Expert Systems

Expert Systems appeared last century, in the mid-60s to be more precise, with the appearance of the well-known GPS (General Problem Solver) [4], nevertheless, this was not like the systems we know nowadays, given that it could only solve a limited number of problems, such as the Hanói tower, which is made up of a kind of mental game, that consists of three bars, on one of these the disc sets are introduced, the one at the base being the wider, being the ones on top a little narrower each time, the result being a pyramid-like shape. However, the objective is to move the last one to another bar, considering rules such as: moving one piece at a time (only the one at the top), and a big disk cannot be placed on top of a smaller one. It is for these reasons that it could not deal with daily situations.

The Expert System is linked with AI, the different technologies associated with it and its application to medicine and industry. Also it is to be found in technologies and frameworks available at present to design and to implement these systems in other areas and markets [1].

An Expert System (ES) is basically a computer program based on knowledge and argument that carries out tasks that usually only takes a mind-human expert; that is to say, it is a program that imitates human behavior in the sense that, it uses the information that is provided in order to give an option about a specific subject. Other authors define it as follows: An Expert System (ES) is an interactive computer program that contains the experience, own knowledge and ability of a person or group of people, so that it is capable of solving specific problems of that area, in an intelligent and satisfactory way [5].

2.2 Expert Systems in Medicine

Due to the significant advances experienced in technology throughout history, it has been possible to make great improvements within the fields of medicine and humanity in general. Robotic surgery is an indispensable tool in the field of medicine. Thanks to these tool human beings have been able to explore the human body without the need of resorting to incisions, it has been possible to perform surgery at long distances, reaching objectives which would have been impossible to attain in the past, allowing established systems to evolve and develop.

This evolution has allowed Expert Systems to evolve, an example of this is the DENDRAL, which was developed in 1967, and that allowed for the identification of chemical structures (having great acceptance for several years between scientists of this branch) [1]. We can also mention MYCIN, the first Expert System [6] able to diagnose diseases by means of a blood analysis; it could also prescribe the necessary medicines, being based on the characteristics or state of each patient (height, weight, etc.). Another example is CADUCEUS, which was created in 1980, and was programmed to make diagnoses in medicine.

In their article, [7] comment on the advances experienced within the field of medicine thanks to the influence of AI.

We will look at the example of Mycin, which deals with issues related to robotics and its application in surgery and in diagnosis, thanks to neuronal networks and Expert Systems. We will analyze advantages and disadvantages of these methods, which will in turn lead us to our conclusions.

The first major revolution within the field of surgery took place in the XIX century, when the efforts joined of: Bilrothwithhis new techniques and instruments, Lister with the antisepsis, Virchow withhis pathology and Moore with the anesthesia. Since then, only small improvements were experienced, mainly dealing with the improvement or variation of instruments in laparoscopic surgery, which are almost the same that were used thirty years ago.

The World Health Organization is searching for ways of integrating new systems that allow for a greater efficiency and quality for our professionals in the fields and for patients too [8]. Thanks to Expert Systems no information is loss of the data base, thus there is access to all medical histories and diagnostics of each patient treated, this way doctors save time and energy, providing a good service lowering costs and maximizing the use of resources.

2.3   Characteristics of the Expert Systems

We could define Expert Systems as a unit composed of two main parts: one which is mainly an environment that allows us to add, modify or alter the information contained in the Expert System, and the second would be the environment that is provided the final user for him/her to work with the program, in order for the user to be able to solve or obtain the answer from a specific problem.

Amongst the main characteristics to be found in an Expert System we find: the knowledge database, the same one it contains for problem solving, it is important to emphasize that this information is gathered by the 'engineer of knowledge' (she/he interviews specialists of different areas in order to obtain precise and useful information). Another element we find here is a fact database and a motor of interference, the latter being the one that allows for deducing a solution automatically, which will be used to solve a problem. And finally, we find the justification system, which helps the user to understand the result that the Expert System comes up with [6].

– It is possible to understand an ES as an intermediary between the user and the specialist, justifying it as follows:
– There are few experts and many users.
– Decisions must be taken very quickly, and the system cannot stop working at any time.

Berbel's study (1989) summarizes it in the following way that it is shown in Fig. 1:

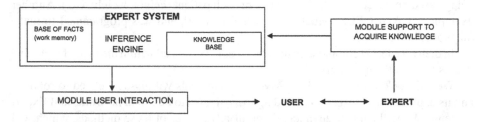

Fig. 1. SE as an intermediary between a user and expert Berbel [6].

3 Materials and Methods

This article is based on a literature review of scientific empirical studies which focus on how Expert Systems are an integrated tool in our society. For this, we have studied the methodology presented in these scientific articles in order to evaluate their efficiency. We have also identified the development methods applied in order to get to the different Expert Systems, together with this, we have studied the technological tools (programming language, database managers, etc.) on which the Expert Systems are based. This way, we can know how these Expert Systems are developed and implemented, in different studies and in research carried out in different parts of the world.

3.1 Studies of Expert Systems

The articles studied here are related with the use of Expert Systems applied within the field of medicine, shows us the advantages of using an Expert System in this field, whether it is to carry out surgery, or to establish a quality control at the hospital, in order to be able to help patient and doctors in their job. The sources used in order to find said articles were the ones available at university: springer, ebrary, cengage learning, e-libro, as well as Google Scholar. Thanks to these we carried out careful investigation of the Expert Systems and their use in medicine, the search was done through fields of knowledge related to title and key words.

Next, the main scientific articles studied are explained. Once we have analyzed these we have observed how the technique of Fuzzy Logic is very much used in the projects that have been carried out. One of the most remarkable studies being one where an Expert System is used to help with the heating in a building, benefiting managers [9], given that one of the objectives was to save on electricity, for this a set of incoming elements were identified (percentage of occupation, and whether the user is satisfied with the temperature). Afterwards, according to the feedback offered they established a set of categories, in order to facilitate understanding, to then write up the rules (including operators and conclusions), the same ones which were determined by the final results [9]; the following compilation of articles has been very relevant for this literature review, given that they offer material for us to be able to compare and study the influence of Expert Systems within the field of medicine.

Paper 1. Type-1 Fuzzy Logic-Based Expert System Model for Preeclampsia Risk Assessment [10]. The main objective of this work is to present an Expert System based on fuzzy logic TYPE I identifying the risk level of undergoing preeclampsia making it possible to come up with an early diagnosis and strict monitoring of the pregnant woman.

A bibliographical review is realized to know the risk factors that generate the disease, establishing factors that are due to be considered, and the rules, which are the main components of the ES. Later the implementation of software with the MySql used as database and Java as the programming language.

The relative error or margin of error between risk levels given by the expert and the application is 5.83 %, a result which does not vary much from reality, giving reliability to future tests to be performed to benefit patients with this application.

The ES has become increasingly popular and it is an important point of reference in decision making, remarkable at the time of implementing systems that support tasks in medical diagnoses.

Paper 2. Expert System for Diagnosis Neurodegenerative Diseases [11]. The primary target is to design an Expert System for the diagnosis of cerebral diseases.

The methodology applied in this study improves the previous methodologies in the field of computer science, by means of the engineering and software engineering of knowledge that will allow for the integration of these engineering disciplines in the Expert Systems.

The Expert System used in in hospitals health management presents as one of the best applications to derive the significant diagnosis of the challenges for the human health.

The applied Expert Systems used in hospitals for the health management presents a great variety of advantages when using these systems.

Paper 3. Dental Expert System [12]. The main objective of this work is to emphasize the use of the Expert System to diagnose dental problems.

The study and application of the methodologies used in dental medical applications to develop Expert Systems are based on:

- Analysis of Expert Systems in medical applications.
- Verification of the theory and application in a dental clinic.
- Creating an expert system prototype called erectile dysfunction.

It was possible to understand the study of the application of the Expert Systems in dental medicine and by means of the development of systems of erectility's function. That is thanks to the combination made of two techniques that are artificial intelligence and fuzzy logic.

This article exposes the relevance of the use of Expert Systems in dental medicine, after concluding that Expert Systems based on the use of a database can be used to save time and costs, making the practice more effective in relation with the patient.

Paper 4. "La Informática Médica y los Sistemas de Información" [13]. The main objective of this work is to implement new computerized programs to all the medical doctor's offices of the country, to consequently be able to offer a better service to patients, to then be able to have a greater number of customers and to earn much more.

In this sense we will say that an Information System, within the field of health or of any other type, is an instrument that allows us to know the distance, and the alternatives where upon we counted to obtain a goal, which must be previously defined (the information is for the action).

It raises an interesting aspect, that is, to consider that a failure or deficiency of a part of the information system, does not have to influence in a significant way the rest of the system.

Any health institution handles a great amount of information, both of its users, and its workings, which in many cases are not available to be interpreted at the time they are needed, and where methodology for the recollection and processing is very varied.

Paper 5. A Laboratory Test Expert System for Clinical Diagnosis Support in Primary Health Care [8]. The main objective of this work is to help the medical personnel of primary attention of health in the diagnosis process, with the purpose of improving quality, precision and agility of the service offered. Reducing costs and avoiding wasting resources.

To avoid losing information thanks to the Expert Systems, enabling having access to any clinical file very quickly, saving time and preventing professionals from over tiring.

To provide information for doctors, becoming an aid to increase the experience of the personnel, as well as to provide consistent results and permanent availability to information.

It contributes to strengthening service in primary healthcare. A significant amount of the diagnoses is based on the interpretation of the clinical report (which is based on blood and urine tests, together with body samples). Thus, our system offers a set of possible diagnoses based on rules that take into consideration these reports.

Paper 6. Expert Systems: Fundamentals, Methodologies and Applications [1]. The main objective of this work is to present the technique to identify the supposed diseases in order to help investigation within the field of medicine.

A methodology to save time at the time of observing a disease.

Diagnoses are carried out with the Expert System CADUCEUS. The technique is shown and applied to different simulations.

Systematics offers information that surrenders the necessary decision making. It allows a great reserve when it comes to execution in the diagnosis of a disease.

Paper 7. Review: Use of Expert System in Medical Science [14]. The main objective of this work is to provide incoming information by means of the selection of one or several options of the list or by means of the introduction of data. It is based on a knowledge database, a verification of the program, to then simulate the data and finally take a decision.

Their purpose is to help to arrive to the probable diagnoses, on the basis of the data of the patient. They criticize the therapy and the planning: The systems can either look for inconsistencies, errors and omissions in a plan of existing treatment, or it can be used to formula teatreatment based on the specific condition of a patient and the accepted guidelines of treatment.

The main results that it analyzes and processes the rules, it looks for the next part within the base of rules and reaches some solution or conclusion. These three parts together form an Expert System. The knowledge base can be a specific diagnosis. The knowledge compiled by a consultancy company.

The main conclusion is to provide a set of clinical cases that serve as examples, a machine learning system can produce a systematic description of the clinical features that uniquely characterize the clinical conditions.

Paper 8. Medical Informatics and Information Systems [15]. The main aim of this work is to implement new computerized programs to GP offices all over the country so that better service is offered to the patient, thus increasing the number clients.

In this sense we will say that an Information System, whether of health type or of another type, is an instrument that allows us to know the distance and alternatives to reach a goal, which must be previously defined (information for the action).

The aim is to obtain a realistic degree of interaction. It also shows an interesting aspect, that is, considering that a failure or lack in any part of the information system does not necessarily have to affect the rest of the system.

A health institution manages a great volume of information on users and working. These data are not always available for interpretation when needed, and the collection method and processing highly differ.

Paper 9. "Sistema Experto para el diagnóstico de enfermedades" [16]. The authors has the aim of accepting the right diagnosis – made by the expert system - out of the patient's síndrome, manifesting some diseases such as dengue AHIN1 flu, meningitis and ordinary flu.

One of the CLIPS applications was released. It uses a specific number of examples, which allowed us to understand a small number of activities.

They were carried out in order to show random data. It was confirmed that diagnosis was right for each of the cases. When symptoms do not point to any disease in the system, the patient is informed.

The aim of the expert system is remarked in this document, accepting the right diagnosis based on the patient's syndrome and manifesting diseases such as dengue, AHIN1 flu, meningitis and ordinary flu.

Another Expert System (in Colombia) had the possibility to detect preeclampsia disease (it occurs during pregnancy and it is an illness that can cause death to the mother or the child). In this study, system input variables and specialist of a field were determined: body mass index (it defines the nutritional degree, overweight, it indicates the existing risk to have this disease; it can take values between 0 to 50, from ideal thinness, to overweight to obesity), blood pressure (considering systolic which can take values from 35 to 135, and according to its values can be optimum, normal or normal high), age (it may be between 10 to 45 years of age, coming into the set of young, adult or older. It is also important to bear in mind that the system presents as outward information the level of risk (values from 0 to 10, varying from low, medium or high levels). Finally, specialists created a set of rules, which show the risk level, according to the different values that the above-mentioned variables can take. Besides, when it comes to its development, they used MySQL y JAVA. And once it was tested, taking 30 clinical reports from the Health Department of Caquetá (using sample patients), where a 94.17 % of effectiveness was obtained [17].

Fernandez-Millan et al. (2015) declares that an Expert System is very useful within the field of medicine, given that it helps expert doctors in each area to take correct decisions in a very precise way, when it comes to diagnosing a patient's disease. All these, taking into account the tasks to be performed, predictions and diagnosis of the possible diseases amongst others.

These studies have been selected because of similarities between them, such as exploration, analysis, application and creation of expert systems for Medicine through combining artificial intelligence and fuzzy logic. Each of these works help understanding and knowing the importance of expert systems in the provision of methodologies and techniques in the area of Medicine.

4   Discussion

According to the analyzed information in scientific articles it is possible to state that there exists a high degree of satisfaction (more than 90 %) from those who have used these systems, because they have obtained a greater efficiency and effectiveness in their operations, as compared to doing it in the traditional way.

In addition it is also remarkable the way in which the studies presented here, the method used (we could say that almost in 100 % of the cases) has been fussy logic, given that it is simple and easy to use (it is only necessary to identify some variables to begin with, the same ones that need to be managed adequately in order to come up with rules, being the latter the ones that need to provide a solution for a specific problem); another positive aspect is the fact that it can be applied to different situations or problems.

After having evaluated and analyzed in a precise and meticulous way in which way Expert Systems have been used in different areas, we can say that these systems will become more relevant and important as time goes by. Moreover, as an additional piece of information, we can say that students at the UTE and PUCE University have already carried out assessment projects using Expert Systems. We also believe that for this reason companies will gradually come to realize how important and useful these systems are, and they will in turn start using them, which will in turn allow them to be more competitive. For this reason, in a not too distant future, we will be able to find them and use them considerably more, given that we will most probably come across some of these Expert Systems.

One of the issues we discussed was the one related to the use of fuzzy logic, which we now believe was the correct choice, given that it is easy to use at the time, and it is also very efficient. We believe that it is necessary that those Expert Systems, which have been developed on private platforms, migrate to free software platforms, given that it is a way to save economic resources, whereby the money saved can be invested in other things (to invest in recruiting experts in the field).

Finally, we would like to mention, that out of all the Expert Systems developed, only one was carried out only using one expert, which is not very adequate, given that, as we know, the Expert System should create its data base thanks to the input offered by several specialists and experts, in order to be more efficient when providing the results.

The World Health Organization is searching for the way of integrating new systems which facilitate efficiency and quality for both our professionals and patients. These systems avoid information loss from the database where the patients' medical histories are found. They show the doctor all necessary information so that there is a reduction in time, effort and cost [18].

The work presented in [7] shows the evolution in the field of Medicine thanks to the intervention of artificial intelligence. It will deal with robotics and its application to surgery; and disease diagnosis thanks to the neuronal networks and expert systems, for instance Mycin. Advantages and drawbacks of these methods will be analysed and thanks to these results conclusions will be reached.

The first revolution in surgery happens at the end of the 19th century, with the combination of Bilroth's new techniques and instruments, Lister's antisepsis, Virchow's pathology and Moore's anesthesia. Since then, only small variations in techniques and instruments of laparoscopic surgery had been achieved. They have been used for thirty years for the management of toxic and radioactive materials.

It could be said that thanks to technology, the human being can make great progress in Medicine. Robotic surgery is an essential tool within this field. This type of surgery allows us to explore the body without aggressive techniques and do remote interventions. Thus, it has helped us to reach aims which had been considered impossible in the past. Nevertheless, robotic surgery has several drawbacks to be overcome by the human being. The challenge of engineers is to create new technology which improves the established systems.

5   Conclusions

When we talk about Expert Systems we are really talking about applied artificial intelligence, which was developed by mid 1960s. Thanks to these systems we can transfer all the information needed from a human being to a computer, which will allow for its later use in medical practice, allowing for the saving of time and resources [14]. In this way, the Expert Systems can help us guarantee better health for citizens in a specific area, city or country, where there are not enough human resources to provide an efficient service.

The Expert Systems must be seen as tools that help any company to be more competitive and efficient. It is necessary to make use of free software in all developments.

These systems offer a considerable amount of advantages given that they provide the necessary information for specialists in medicine, given that these tools aim to be user friendly, saving time and resources. Let us remember that the main objective for the World Health Organization is to provide quality service to patients.

Technological evolution [19] has been found within Medicine as regards instruments and equipment in order to offer the patient better medical care, helping doctors to know the patient's disease and avoiding unnecessary surgery. What is more, surgeons do not necessarily to be present in the operation room.

The first steps in artificial intelligence were taken by Alan Turing in the 50s. Later it was Edaward F. and others who decided to study artificial intelligence in relation to Chemistry. Along the following years many procedures have been developed, and many systems have been planned in different fields. These systems can reproduce the thought of a human expert.

In this work we present expert procedures with which different diseases can be diagnosed – dengue, AHIN1 flu, meningitis, ordinary flu. Diagnosis can be achieved and a series of questions can be asked to the patient on the basis of the answers about symptoms offered by the patient.

An expert system can help reach potencial diagnosis based on the patient's data. Systems can look for inconsistencies, errors and omissions in an existing treatment plan. They can also be used to formulate some treatment based on a patient's specific condition. The accepted treatment pattern sindicate that the structure of the expert system consists of three parts: (1) Knowledge database (Rule database), (2) work memory and (3) inference engine. These systems can offer a systematic description of the clinical features that characterize the clinical conditions.

References

1. Badaró, S., Ibañez, L.J., Aguero, M.J.: Expert systems: fundamentals, methodologies and applications. J. Sci. Technol. **13**, 349–363 (2013)
2. Rossini, P.: Using expert systems and artificial intelligence for real estate fore-casting. In: Sixth Annual Pacific-Rim Real Estate Society Conference (2000)
3. Waltz, D.L.: Artificial intelligence: realizing the ultimate promises of computing. AI Mag. **18**(3), 49–52 (1997)
4. Turban, E.: Decision Support and Expert Systems, 4th edn. Prentice-Hall, Upper Saddle River (1995)
5. León Quintanar, T.: Sistemas Expertos y sus Aplicaciones (2007)
6. Berbel Vecino, J.: Artificial intelligence in agriculture: perspectives experts sisthemes. Agro-Social Studies, 149 (1989)
7. Hermoso Sánchez, M.J., Crespillo Mirón, C.: Aplicaciones de la Inteligencia (2015)
8. Fernandez-Millan, R., Medina-Merodio, J.A., Barchino Plata, R., Martinez-Herraiz, J.-J., Gutierrez-Martinez, J.-M.: A laboratory test expert system for clinical diagnosis support in primary health care. Appl. Sci. **5**, 222–240 (2015)
9. Aparicio-Ruiz, P., Fernández Valverde, J.R., Onieva Giménez, L.: Sistema experto basado en lá lógica difusa para la detección de configuraciones climáticas asociadas al confort, Sevilla (2010)

10. Núñez Ramírez, M.A.: Autoestima y habilidades emprendedoras en estudiantes de Nivel Medio Superior. Revista Electrónica de Psicología Iztacala, vol. 18, no. 1 (2015)
11. Ibrahim, A.J., Oluwafemi, J.A.: Expert system for diagnosis neurodegenerative diseases. Int. J. Comput. Inf. Technol. 4(4), 694–698 (2015)
12. Tinuke, O.O., Yetunde, S.: Dental expert system. Int. J. Appl. Inf. Syst. (IJAIS) 8(2), 1–15 (2015)
13. González Salamea, C.G.: La Informática Médica y los Sistemas de Información (2003)
14. Kumar, Meena A., Kumar, S.: Review: use of expert system in medical science. Int. J. Adv. Res. Comput. Sci. Softw. Eng. 5(10), 371–373 (2015)
15. González Salamea, C.: Medical Informatics and Information Systems (2014)
16. Gazón-Alfonso, W.: Sistema Experto para el diagnóstico de enfermedades. Sistema Experto para el diagnóstico de enfermedades
17. Núñez Flórez, E.R., Vergara Ortiz, R., Bocanegra García, J.J.: A type-1 fuzzy logic-based expert system model for preclampsia risk assessment. *INGE CUC*, 10(1), 43–50 (2014)
18. Fernandez-Millan, R., Medina-Merodio, J.A., Plata, R.B., Martinez-Herraiz, J.J., Gutierrez-Martinez, J.M.: A laboratory test expert system for clinical diagnosis support in primary health care. Appl. Sci. 5(3), 222–240 (2015)
19. Hermoso, M.J., Crespillo, C.: Aplicaciones de la Inteligencia. Universidad Carlos III, Madrid (2014)
20. Parraga Chamorro, R.: Expert System development testing to qualify in students of the Continental University (2014)
21. Sánchez Vila, E., Lama Penín, M.: Monograph: techniques artificial intelligence applied to education. RevistaIberoamericana Artificial Intell. 11(33), 7–12 (2007)
22. Sosa, M.D.C., Carmen, D.: Artificial intelligence in corporate financial management. Pensamiento Gestión 23, 153–189 (2011). ISSN 1657-6276
23. Tabares-Ospina, H., Monsalve-Llano, D., Diez-Gomez, D.: Expert System Model for Selection of University Teachers (2012)
24. Navarro Torres, C., Córdova Neira, J.: Design Expert System for decision making purchasing materials (2014)
25. Luchau, V.: Sistemas expertos educativos en medicina. Boletín de Informática Educativa, 2(2) (1989)
26. Errasti, A., Chackelson, C., Santos, J.: Expert System to improve inventory management supported demand forecasting methods: study (2010)

A General Framework for Learning Analytic in a Smart Classroom

Jose Aguilar[1,2(✉)], Priscila Valdiviezo[2], Jorge Cordero[2],
Guido Riofrio[2], and Eduardo Encalada[2]

[1] CEMISID, Universidad de Los Andes, Mérida, Mérida, Venezuela
aguilar@ula.ve
[2] DCCE, Universidad Técnica Particular de Loja, Loja, Ecuador
{pmvaldiviezo,jmcordero,geriofrio,aeencalada}@utpl.edu.ec

Abstract. In this paper, we propose the utilization of the "Learning Analytics" paradigm in a Smart Classroom, a classroom that integrates artificial intelligence technology on the educational process. Learning Analytics can extract knowledge from the Smart Classroom platform, to better understand students and his/her learning processes. In this way, a Smart Classroom can understand and optimize the learning process and the teaching environments proposed. The smart classroom can adapt its components to improve students' performance, among other aspects. Particularly, this paper proposes a framework about how the Learning Analytics paradigm can be used in a Smart Classroom, in order to provide knowledge about the activities taking place within it. The framework is defined like a closed cycle of Learning Analytics tasks, which generate metrics used like feedback to optimize the pedagogical model proposed by the smart Classroom. The metrics evaluate the learning process and pedagogical practice provided by the smart Classroom. So, our main contribution is about how the Learning Analytics paradigm can be used in a Smart Classroom in order to improve the students' performance.

Keywords: Learning analytics · Smart classroom · Ambient intelligence · Data mining

1 Introduction

Ambient Intelligence (AmI) is an environment where the advances in information technology, mainly in ubiquitous and pervasive computing, allow the interaction with all computation devices as a whole. This idea is being used in the educational domain, and it is used in spaces where ubiquitous technology helps the learning process in an unobtrusive manner. A smart classroom is an expression of this, where a traditional classroom is redefined, with the integration of sensor technology, communication technology, artificial intelligence, among others, into the classroom. But, a smart classroom can generate enormous volumes of data about the educational process, which must be exploited by it, in order to improve the educational experiences of its users (students, teachers, etc.).

© Springer International Publishing AG 2016
R. Valencia-García et al. (Eds.): CITI 2016, CCIS 658, pp. 214–225, 2016.
DOI: 10.1007/978-3-319-48024-4_17

In previous works has been defined a smart classroom based on the multiagents paradigm, called SaCI (Salón de Clase Inteligente, for its acronym in Spanish) [1]. Particularly, the components of SaCI generate a lot of information about the learning processes. This information must be exploited in order to reach its main challenge: to cover the actual needs of the learners. Due to different learning patterns of students, it is vital for SaCI, to understand each student. For that, SaCI can obtain a proper understanding of a student based on the information that he or she has generated through its platform. To exploit this information, SaCI must use the "Learning Analytics" (LA) paradigm to identify the different learning capacities of the students, in order to provide them the necessary guidance to improve their capabilities. In this way, to improve the learning capabilities of the students, SaCI should be capable of monitoring the overall performance of each student, separately, and dynamically adjust their teaching methodologies and to take decisions about the learning resources to use, among other things, in order to improve learning of students.

Similar researches about this job are the generic framework for Learning Analytics proposed by [2], which act as a useful guide for setting up Learning Analytics. In the same way, the Framework of Quality Indicators for Learning Analytics that aims to standardize the evaluation of learning analytics tools, was proposed in [3]. Unlike these frameworks, our approach can be used in a Smart Classroom, in order to provide knowledge about the activities taking place within it and improving the students' performance on educational practices.

LA extracts knowledge from the SaCI platform to better understand students and the way they learn. The utilization of LA paradigm allows the knowledge discovering, from the data generated by the SaCI components. This knowledge allows response to questions like: How can SaCI adapt its components to improve students' performance? How can SaCI exploit the information in its different components? among others. Thus, in this paper, we propose a framework about how LA paradigm can be used in SaCI in order to improve its performance. Particularly, the framework defines the cycle of LA tasks to be implemented, in order to generate useful information for the learning process provided by SaCI. This framework combines different LA tasks with a global goal, improve the learning experiences inside SaCI, where each task provides an essential knowledge that can be used individually or globally.

The aim of the utilization of LA in SaCI is to generate knowledge about learners and their learning contexts, for the purpose of understanding and optimizing the learning process and the teaching environments proposed by SaCI. LA leverages data from SaCI to provide insight into the activities taking place within it. The metrics derived are used like feedback to optimize the pedagogical model proposed by SaCI. In particular, the application of LA in SaCI allows the evaluation of the learning process and pedagogical practice provided by it, in order to improve them. This paper mainly focuses on the presentation of the framework.

2   Learning Analytics

At the present, Learning Analytics emerges as a fundamental discipline to the challenge of optimizing and adapting learning environments to the needs of modern society; where strategies, resources and tools for teaching must be adapted to the learning styles and abilities of students. In [4] conceptualizes LA as "an emerging field in which sophisticated analytic tools are used to improve learning and education", [5] defines LA as "the use of intelligent data, learner-produced data, and analysis models to discover information and social connections, and to predict and advise on learning", whilst LAK'11 (https://tekri.athabascau.ca/analytics/) in its most widespread definition establishes that LA "is the measurement, collection, analysis and reporting of data about learners and their contexts, for purposes of understanding and optimizing learning and the environments in which it occurs". In all cases, clearly it states the importance of having detailed and historical data, educational, on student interaction with their learning environment and the results obtained in different scenarios; data which in turn are a source of learning for the generation of new knowledge that support the evolution and innovation of current education systems, ensuring a personalized approach adapted to the characteristics of each individual.

LA encompasses a range of cutting-edge educational technologies, algorithms, models, techniques, methods, and best practices, to analyze the trajectory of a student's learning. LA is an emerging and promising field and defines an IT-supported learning process. Particularly, LA proposes tools for the optimization of learning processes based on the retrieval of useful information and knowledge about learning dynamics, and on the transformation of the data gathered in knowledge for making educational decisions. The virtual learning environments (VLEs) (also known as learning management systems, LMSs, such as Moodle), the academic systems, among others, are the main educational data sources that educational institutions must deal with. These systems amass amounts of academic information, interaction data, personal data, among others. In addition, significant amounts of learner activities take place externally, and so records are distributed across a variety of different websites. LA searches extract value from these big sets of learning-related data. In this way, LA tries the collection and analysis of data about learners and their context in order to understand and optimize the learning, for example, optimizing educational contents based on the knowledge about learner and his necessities.

Pardo suggests five phases of design and execution of a LA solution [7]: The first stage, "capture," corresponds to the earliest collection of student data. The second stage, "report," delivers that data to a specifically defined set of stakeholders. The third stage, "prediction," deploys any of a number of techniques to provide non-intuitive answers to educational questions, such as general LA specified by us more below. The "act" stage offers the possibility of issuing automated solutions or implementing manual ones that have the potential to reverse the consequences of the earlier prediction. In the final stage, "refinement," the efficacy of the resulting actions is assessed anew so that the long-term viability of the analysis can itself be modified as needed. On the other hand, in [8] defines a business intelligence (BI) methodology to implement LA tasks, which is composed by the following steps: (a) Defining target situations, (b) Data Model of the BI project, (c) The knowledge extraction (indicators).

In general, there are a lot of propositions of LA for different type of problems in the domain of educational environment. A set of problems which are solved by LA are: to predict the student overall performance, to discover the relationship of tutors with their students, to discover the different learning patterns of each student, to help tutors to identify the students who need more attention among a larger set of students, to prevent student dropouts in distance education university, to provide the instructors with appropriate advising, to analyze collaboration and interaction in learning environment, To analyze the effectiveness of students with educational resources, to investigate student motivation in the context of a learning process.

Some future challenges in LA defined in [6] are: (i) Establish a bridge between LA and the learning sciences (cognition, metacognition and pedagogy); (ii) Exploit a wide range of data around learning environments, including not only the VLE or LMS data, but also from informal or blended learning environment, the behavior of the students in Internet, academic information, among others. (iii) Focus on the perspectives of learners, in order to analyses the necessities of the students rather than to the needs of institutions. (iv) Must be transparent, enabling learners to respond with feedback naturally that can be used to refine the analytics, and see how their data are being used, (v) Must provide knowledge with pedagogical and ethical integrity, (vi) Must revalue the role of teachers/ mentors, who have unique skills, which will never be replicated by machine intelligence.

3   SaCI

SaCI is a smart classroom proposed in [1], where its deployment environment (middleware), called AmICL, was proposed in [9, 10]. SaCI proposes a student-centered smart classroom, which supports the learning process, through collaborative devices and applications that facilitate self-training. To do this, the smart classroom have different types of components: hardware (e.g., smart boards, cameras, etc.) and software (e.g., Intelligent Tutoring Systems (ITS), VLE, repositories of learning objects, recommender system of educational resources, among others), which adapt and integrate to the course according to the necessities of the students. This adaptation of the different components of SaCI is possible due to its autonomic and reflective capacities. They have proposed the SaCI model that characterizes a smart classroom, using the paradigm of Multiagent Systems (MAS) [10, 11], specifying a smart classroom based on agent communities. AmICL is shown in Fig. 1.

Specifically, the last two layers proposed in AmICL are those that define SaCI. In these layers are where the devices (sensors, smart cameras, among others) and software (VLE, etc.) of SaCI are deployed. Particularly, the layer "IE Logical Layer Management" (ILL) specifics all applications (software) and individuals present at SaCI as agents, which contain metadata that defines them.

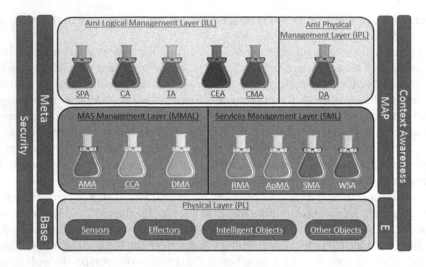

Fig. 1. Middleware AmICL

4   Our General Proposition of LA on SaCI

4.1   LA on SaCI

The works in LA give an idea of the variety of researches in this domain. In [7, 12] they show how the knowledge generated can be used to solve educational problems, support educational decision making as it is usual in business intelligence, but at the same time they pose new research questions. One of them is the goal of this work, how can be used LA in the context of SaCI?

Currently, learning and teaching in a virtual classroom environment depend on the way in which the information is used by the users of the system. In modern e-learning environments, teachers and students depend on the course outline, and how these activities are arranged using the functionalities available in LMS. The online environments allow the generation of large amounts of data related to learning/teaching processes, which offers the possibility of extracting valuable information that may be employed to improve students' performance [13, 14]. Due to the different learning capabilities of the students, these course activities are performed in a dissimilar fashion by the students. Nevertheless, SaCI can overcome this problem, by applying LA tasks to define the teaching principles or the teaching methodologies on the students in SaCI in different manners. For that, SaCI requires a proper understanding of the students overall performance, using the information that SaCI has gathered, in order to identify the different learning capacities of the students, and to provide the necessary guidance to the students to improve their capabilities.

Using LA in SaCI to understand the student behavior becomes a new relative area of practice and research. The tasks of collection of data, of preparation of this data for LA tasks, the utilization of the knowledge generated (to discover patterns and trends) by the LA tasks by the different component of SaCI (e.g., intelligent tutoring systems), the actions derived from the LA tasks (like games and simulation programs), open a very large domain of research. In our case, we need to understand how to use LA tasks in SaCI.

LA in SaCI must attempt to leverage all data present in SaCI to provide insight into the activities taking place within the classroom. Particularly, the metrics derived are a vital feedback into SaCI, in specific, to define the pedagogical model to apply in the classroom. LA must evaluate all the aspects of the learning process in SaCI. LA seeks to understand entire systems and to support SaCI in the decision making.

Thus, in the case of SaCI must be analyzed its components in order to determine the source of data, how exploit the metrics generated by the LA tasks, among others things. Particularly, like the idea is to improve the learning process, we must determine the components with more influence on it.

Particularly, the knowledge generated by the LA tasks must be exploited by SaCI. We need to give it information to help it. In special, one of the main goals of SaCI is "to understand the student behavior and how students can be motivated on learning in order to self-adapt". To reach that, there are SaCI aspects which must be analyzed by the LA tasks (see Fig. 2):

- To observe the learning process: in this case, LA must generate indicators to understand the current learning process (paradigm, methods, tools, etc.).
- To observe the student behavior: in this case, the LA tasks must generate indicators about the performance of each student.

Fig. 2. Goals of the LA task in SaCI

With the data provided by SaCI, we can produce large amount of knowledge which is distributed around SaCI. Sharing and manipulation this knowledge in real time, is an enormous achievement of SaCI, in order to improve its behavior. It can be used to define the learning methodologies in an accurate manner. This problem has not been solved in the current e-learning systems. Virtual LMSs enable the teachers and tutors to manage diverse educational materials manually. The LMSs provide mechanisms that can be used by teachers to view the outline performance of each student and see the final marks that the student has gained in the given activity on the course, but manually. But the differences among the students, the large quantity of different data about the learning process, is very bad used to define the learning resources, study materials, among others. Additionally, the utilization of the performance of each student to parameterize SaCI in accordance with the behavior of the student has not been studied.

Our approach attacks two of the main reasons for student's dropping out the school [8]: Lack of educational support, or student with special needs (they require specific attention to a certain need). The lack of educational support and the special needs can be easily managed using LA tasks, like a predictive analysis approach, since student who are at risk of failing, can be identified at an early stage, by analyzing their historical data of learning behavior. The utilization of LA, as an early warning system, is a useful and effective tool. Particularly, LA in our SACI must:

- Accurately define and uncover students' problems and needs
- Successfully identify interventions and improvement strategies
- Effectively target and initiate programs and reforms
- Monitor the ongoing efforts and progress of the 'at-risk' students

We can exploit the knowledge hidden in SaCI for three different interest groups: governments, educational institutions and teachers/learners. Each one requires LA on different scales and at different granularities. In this work, we choice as target audience teachers/learners, but in future works we will analyze the rest of the groups. Depending on the groups, the conceptualization of the problem is different, and equally, the capture of data, the reports, the models, etc. In this case, the goal is 'turning learners into effective better learners'. The research focused on LA task techniques that could be used by SaCI to better understand the learning process. In this way, SaCI can use this information to improve teaching, learning and success of the students, and to customize learning paths or provide personalized instruction to specific learning needs.

4.2 General Architecture

If we want to apply LA in SaCI, then it is imperative that we define the architecture to support the LA tools like services in SaCI (see Fig. 3). Such an infrastructure needs to consider the different components to be used in order to develop LA task. In this way, we propose a general architecture composed of three levels: a first question that answers the architecture is how to model the relevant data. According to our early work about BI methodology, requires the definition of the Conceptual data (CAM) [8] that means, a model with the data that need the LA tasks. This is the data storage level, and is the classical data warehouse generated from the transactional databases of the educational institutions. But in our case, it is extended with semantic information generated by the LA tasks. For this reason, all this level is called *semantic knowledge level*, because it describes additionally the knowledge generated for the LA tasks. This level guarantees that the information follows standards to describe the different aspects of SaCI, like in the case of learning resources to use the Learning Object Metadata (LOM). The next level defines the different tasks to prepare the data. This level, called *data preparation level*, has the different mechanisms to prepare the data, according to the techniques used by the LA tasks. For example, if the LA tasks are based on data mining mechanisms, in this level, there are three steps, the ETL (Extract, Transform and Load) operations; otherwise, if the LA tasks are based on big data and semantic mining, the main tasks are collection and curation of data (CCA). Finally, the last level, called *service bus level*, has a set of services linked to the LA tasks. Additionally, in this level, there are other services linked to tools and applications of machine learning, data visualization, etc. In this way, our architecture can exploit the data from the organizational database, and data outside of the organization (using big data paradigm).

In resume, the data preparation level, extracts and prepares the data from SaCI, in order to extract the knowledge hidden in them, using LA tasks; the semantic knowledge level defines the different forms to store the data, the information, and the knowledge generated; and the service bus level, is a bus to access the different services available,

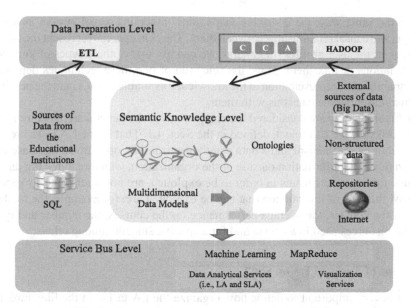

Fig. 3. Our general architecture for LA tasks in SaCI

maybe in the cloud, in order to be used by the LA tasks of SaCI (services linked to big data, machine learning, etc.).

Our architecture, by collecting data about learning process, can be mined for different tasks: recommendations of resources, activities or people, turn the abundance of learning resources into an asset, among others. We can remark that the different components of SaCI participate in the LA tasks, like sources of data and information (like the students, the institutional LMS, the VLE, etc.) or like users of the knowledge generated, like the students, tutor agents, recommender systems, among others.

In particular, the recommender system recommends learning resources in the smart classroom based on specific knowledge about how the item features meet the user needs and preferences. Also, this system uses the rating of the items like a collaborative approach, it discovers the aspects, interests, properties that the user would like about the items (criticality system), infers the rating of the items, etc. The service provides high-quality recommendations of educational resources, to students in the smart classroom, to assist the learning process. Our LA framework proposes to exploit this knowledge of the recommender system, and additionally, help to improve its quality with the knowledge generated.

Other important remarks are that our architecture can execute data and semantic mining tasks, it can store information from SaCI (its different components), but additionally, can include other information outside of SaCI (for example, from internet), and can use different type of knowledge representations: ontologies, cognitive maps, among others. Additionally, it is transparent to the techniques of data processing.

The mix of the different knowledge representations is a strength of our middleware. For example, considering that an ontology is a form of conceptualization of the knowledge of a domain, we can use an ontology to represent user profiles and to reason about that. In the same way, the cognitive maps allow modeling a real system as a set of concepts and causal relationships between them. The concepts can represent the different attributes of the user profiles. In general, we can use one of these types of knowledge representations or mix them. Thus, the selection of one these techniques depends on their capabilities of representation of the knowledge available in SaCi, and the possibility to define reasoning mechanisms with them.

In this study only are considered the components of the general architecture to carry out LA tasks for the BI project, defined in the Sect. 4.1. That is, the LA tasks are based on data mining mechanism and a data warehouse from the operational database of the organization. The information outside of the organization, which requires big data and semantic mining mechanisms in order to be exploited, are not studied in this paper. In this way, the type of information that can be exploited are, for example, the total time spent on the courses, the average performance on the courses, the number and type of learning resources used in a course and for a specific student, among others.

4.3 Type of Tasks of LA on SaCI

Now, it is very important to define how organize the LA tasks. In the literature, there are a lot of LA tasks (see Sect. 3). We propose to use for SaCI a closed loop of LA tasks, in order to guarantee an autonomic behavior for SaCI. That is, the knowledge generated by each LA task is chained with the input to the next one, in order to allow an adaptive process in SaCI. Particularly, because the goal of SaCI is to adapt it to the needs of the students, the LA tasks must allow observe the learning process and student behavior. In this way, the LA must be (see Fig. 4):

- Focused on the learning process: some of the LA tasks that requires SaCI to analysis the learning process are: (a) Monitor efforts and progress of the students: in this case is necessary to generate knowledge about the behavior and performance of the students. (b) Analyze the evaluation process: in this case are studied the aspects evaluated, the average performance of the student, among other things. There are two types of evaluation to consider: diagnostic and formative evaluation. A main element here is the pattern generate of the evaluation. The patterns allow determine weaknesses, approval rates, if the student has appropriated the issue, the types of questions that the student cannot answer, among other aspects. (c) Search resources and activities to recommend: in this case, based on the knowledge about the student profile, about the performance of the students in previous activities or resources, the recommender system can exploit that to recommend new items.
- Focused on the students: some of the LA tasks that requires SaCI to analysis the behavior of the students are: (a) Discover learning styles: in this case the idea is to discover the learning styles of a student, of a group of students (for example, during a course). The idea is (re)build the student profiles based on what the student does. (b) Determine how the performance of each student varies according to the learning patterns of the courses. For that, the LA tasks must analysis the student's participation against the learning style of the course. (c) Identify uncover students' problems and needs: in this case are used the LA tasks in order to discover the subjects not covered

in assessments, identify topics that students need more attention, which questions students fail more, among other things.

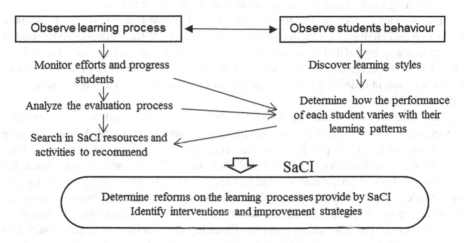

Fig. 4. The autonomic control loop based on LA tasks for SaCI

But these set of tasks that observes the learning process and student behavior must reach the following goals of the control loop (defined again like LA tasks, which use the knowledge generate for the previous tasks): (a) Determine reforms on the learning processes: in this case, the LA task must determine the changes of methods of teaching, proposing learning paradigm shifts, etc. (b) Identify interventions and improvement strategies in a given moment: in order to be introduced in the dynamics of activities to be proposed inside of SaCI during a learning process. In this way, it is defined as a feedback loop in order to optimize the learning process provide by SaCI. Figure 4 shows the LA control loop for SaCI. It is important to remark that these LA tasks can be exploited individually by SaCI, in order to adapt specific aspects of it.

5   Conclusions

In this paper, we propose a LA architecture for SaCI, in order to exploit the large amount of knowledge which is diverse and distributed around SaCI. LA tasks allow an autonomic behavior of SaCI in order to manage a diversity of situations, educational materials, student styles, in a much easier manner. In this way, SaCI can carry out a correct adaptation of its components.

The learning process in SaCI, using this feedback loop, depends on the way in which the knowledge flowing through the different agents of SaCI, in order to adapt their behaviors. SaCI does not depend on the course module or professor, it has an autonomic behavior based on the knowledge generated by the LA tasks. They can determine the activities to be used in VLE, the functionalities to be available in LMS, etc., considering the different learning styles of the students, the knowledge level which they have gathered in each activity, among other aspects. That mean, SaCI proposes an ecosystem of learning where different students with different learning style can share a same learning environment, the difference with the classical learning environment where is used the same teaching methodologies on all the students in the same manner.

The autonomic loop is the framework of the LA tasks in SaCI. The systematic collection and analysis of data that identifies the patterns of the students can be used in envisioned way by SaCI. The manner in which this can affect and alter SaCI is undeniable, for that is necessary an autonomic loop where SaCI determines the best way to self-adaptation in order to guide the students. It facilitates the services and resources to offer to students.

In this paper, we have only studied LA in the context of SaCI, not SLA. Particularly, the architecture that we have proposed in this paper, can be used for SLA. The following works need to test these possibilities. This is a significant advances because the integration of Social Network Analysis (SNA) within SaCI will consider the knowledge constructed through social negotiation. In the context of learning, SNA can be used to investigate and promote collaborative and cooperative connections between learners, tutors and resources, helping them to extend and develop their capabilities. Particularly, that allows to research about the process of learning through individual participation in social interactions, in order to generate a collaborative knowledge construction. We need to test all the feedback loop in order to prove the adaptive capabilities that define this loop for SaCI.

Acknowledgment. Dr. Aguilar has been partially supported by the Prometeo Project of the Ministry of Higher Education, Science, Technology and Innovation (SENESCYT) of the Republic of Ecuador.

References

1. Aguilar, J., Valdiviezo, P., Cordero, J., Sánchez, M.: Conceptual design of a smart classroom based on multiagent systems. In: Proceedings on the International Conference on Artificial Intelligence (ICAI), pp. 471–477 (2015)
2. Greller, W., Drachsler, H.: Translating learning into numbers: a generic framework for learning analytics. Educ. Technol. Soc. **15**(3), 42–57 (2012)
3. Scheffel, M., Drachsler, H., Stoyanov, S., Specht, M.: Quality indicators for learning analytics. Educ. Technol. Soc. **17**(4), 117–132 (2014)
4. Lias, T.E., Elias, T.: Learning analytics: The definitions, the processes, and the potential (Report). http://learninganalytics.net/LearningAnalyticsDefinitionsProcessesPotential.pdf
5. Siemens, G.: What are learning analytics? vol. *10*. Accessed March 2010
6. Ferguson, R.: Learning analytics: drivers, developments and challenges. Int. J. Technol. Enhanced Learn. **4**(5–6), 304–317 (2012)
7. Pardo, A.: Designing learning analytics experiences. Learning Analytics, pp. 15–38. Springer, New York (2014)
8. Riofrio, G., Encalada, E., Guamán, D., Aguilar, J.: Business intelligence applied to learning analytics in student-centered learning processes. In: Computing Conference (CLEI), pp. 567–576. IEEE Latin American (2015)
9. Sánchez, M., Aguilar, J., Cordero, J., Valdiviezo, P.: A smart learning environment based on cloud learning. Int. J. Adv. Inf. Sci. Technol., 39–52 (2015a)

10. Sánchez, M., Aguilar, J., Cordero, J., Valdiviezo, P.: Basic features of a reflective middleware for intelligent learning environment in the cloud (IECL). In: Asia-Pacific Conference on Computer Aided System Engineering (APCASE), pp. 1–6. IEEE (2015)
11. Aguilar, J., Chamba-Eras, L., Cordero, J.: Specification of a smart classroom based on agent communities. In: Rocha, Á., Correia, A.M., Adeli, H., Reis, L.P., Teixiera, M.M. (eds.) New Advances in Information Systems and Technologies, vol. 444, pp. 1003–1012. Springer International Publishing, Heidelberg (2016)
12. Brooks, C., Greer, J., Gutwin, C.: The data-assisted approach to building intelligent technology-enhanced learning environments. Learning Analytics, pp. 123–156. Springer, New York (2014)
13. Krumm, A.E., Waddington, R.J., Teasley, S.D., Lonn, S.: A learning management system-based early warning system for academic advising in undergraduate engineering. Learning Analytics, pp. 103–119. Springer, New York (2014)
14. Siemens, G.: Learning analytics: envisioning a research discipline and a domain of practice. In: Proceedings of the 2nd International Conference on Learning Analytics and Knowledge, pp. 4–8. ACM (2012)

Platform for Project Evaluation Based on Soft-Computing Techniques

Gilberto Fernando Castro[1](✉), Iliana Pérez[2], Pedro Piñero[2], Surayne Torres[2],
Mitchell Vásquez[3], Jorge Hidalgo[3], and Néstor Vera-Lucio[3]

[1] Facultad de Ingeniería, Carrera de Sistemas Computacionales,
Universidad Católica de Santiago de Guayaquil, Av. Carlos Julio Arosemena Km. 1½ Vía Daule,
Guayaquil, Ecuador
gilberto.castro@cu.ucsg.edu.ec
[2] Universidad de las Ciencias Informáticas, Carretera San Antonio km 2½. Municipio La Lisa,
19370 La Habana, Cuba
{iperez,ppp,storres}@uci.cu
[3] Escuela de Ingeniería en Computación e Informática, Facultad de Ciencias Agrarias,
Universidad Agraria del Ecuador, Av. 25 de Julio y Pio Jaramillo, P.O. BOX 09-04-100
Guayaquil, Ecuador
{mvasquez,jhidalgo,nvera}@uagraria.edu.ec

Abstract. Project management tools require a high added value. However, most standards do not refer to the use of techniques that treat uncertain information.

This paper presents experiences in project evaluation process by using soft computing techniques. We present a project management tool based on LABPRO Software Ecosystem, which combines R functionalities with postgres database system. LABPRO is a Software Ecosystem which contains tools for making decisions in project management organizations, and implements processes of PMBOOK standard. We present the results of applied different soft computing algorithms, published in FRBS package, and included in LABPRO platform. We compare algorithms Anfis, Hyfis, FS.HGD based on neural networks with the algorithms GFS LS RS, GFS THRIFT based on genetic algorithm techniques. The algorithms selected learn from a database that contains projects already evaluated, and after that, they classify other projects. We applied cross validation techniques combined with Friedman test and Wilcoxon test. Finally, we present the comparison results and the conclusions.

Keywords: Project management · Soft-computing · Decisions making

1 Introduction

There is a growing demand for tools with high added value for the management of project-oriented organizations. This is particularly important in the stages of development of new technologies of information where numerous efforts for the development of methodologies and tools that help generalize good practices and success in projects have been conducted. However, results are still disappointing considering the large number of projects that are cancelled or renegotiated due to difficulties in its

© Springer International Publishing AG 2016
R. Valencia-García et al. (Eds.): CITI 2016, CCIS 658, pp. 226–240, 2016.
DOI: 10.1007/978-3-319-48024-4_18

implementation. A study in 2014 by The Standish Group International, Incorporated threw as a result that projects delivered successfully, or failed and closed or renegotiated move around 35 %, 18 % and 43 % respectively [1]. Among the fundamental causes of the failed projects we can find:

- Shortcomings in the processes of planning and logistics management [2, 3].
- Difficulties in the scope of projects management and management of the associated risks [4, 5].
- Difficulties in objectivity and the agility of the control and monitoring processes, specifically in the management of indicators and tools to achieve it [6, 7].
- Inadequacies in the treatment of such factors as the inaccuracy of the information, the ambiguity in the criteria of measurement and the uncertainty; elements common in real-world scenarios [8].

Some of them are schools that have developed standards for the introduction of good practices among which the Project Management Institute (PMI), the Software Engineering Institute (SEI) and the organization of international standards (ISO) are found. However, most of these rules do not make reference to the use of techniques to deal with the uncertainty of the information or the ambiguity, which are frequent causes of subjectivity in the development of the projects. To better understand these concepts in the context of the management of the projects some examples are explained below.

- Imprecision is evident at the time that users insert numeric values in fields as the real percentage of execution, estimated time, or dedicated real-time tasks, taking into consideration subjective elements.
- Vagueness manifests during the allocation or use of linguistic terms to identify features such as priority or complexity of the tasks.
- Uncertainty, on the other hand, appears in the type of assessment assigned to tasks, which logically depend on human perception and the experience of the evaluator.

In this context not only do standards influence the success or failure of the projects, but it is also very important to have appropriate tools and techniques. The development of computer tools for the management of projects is currently concentrating on achieving greater agility in decision-making processes [9, 10]. But most of the efforts are concentrated on applying traditional models and do not usually develop high value-added applications that significantly improve agility in process control and monitoring.

In this work we present the experiences in the development of the software ecosystem that combines soft-computing techniques with traditional techniques for the evaluation of projects in a court. The main idea is to experiment with different algorithms to identify those who will allow us to:

- Evaluate the status of a project considering indicators proposed in the literature.
- Handle the uncertainty, the vagueness and imprecision of the data entered during the calculation of the indicators.
- Achieve automatic evaluation of projects imitating human experts' action.

We thus enter these algorithms in a tool that will help reduce time associated with the management and control of projects. We want to enhance the objectivity in decision-making and agility beyond meetings of comprehensive control and monitoring which affect the implementation of the timetable.

Section 2 presents a brief review of the State of the art related to various schools in the management of projects and practices suggested for the control and monitoring. Then, Sect. 3 is a proposal for ecosystem management of projects combining facilities of R packages based on soft-computing with the PostgreSQL and other techniques for the evaluation of projects during failure of control and monitoring. Experiments, statistical tests applied and the results obtained are presented in subsection 4. Finally, in Sect. 5 we discuss the conclusions.

2 A Brief Analysis of Different Schools of Project Management and the Practices Suggested for the Control and Follow-up

The Project Management Institute develops the PMBOOK standard that explains 47 processes for the management of projects organized in five groups of processes and 10 areas of knowledge [11–13]. This is a standard consolidated with a high level of generalization to global sphere. The PMBOOK suggests the use of indicators but mainly associated with the areas of cost management and management of time. However, there is a group of elements that constitute opportunities for improvement:

- It does not present a system of indicators that cover all areas of knowledge or strategies for the evaluation of the projects considering the level of maturity of the organization that develops it.
- Despite including indicators of costs, it does not propose specific mechanisms for the management of the uncertainty in the calculation these.

Another school which offers good practices for the management of projects is the SEI. It produces the standard CMMI for certification of organizations developers of software projects [14]. The SEI presents in its design 25 areas of process related to 4 categories. This standard is targeted at organizations and proposes two approaches for improvement. A phased approach with 5 levels of maturity to classify organizations, and a continuous focus that has 6 levels of capacity and analyzes the capacity of each process separately. Despite their good aspects and the model of CMMI, there are some characteristics that may be improved for their application in different contexts, namely:

- It addresses information systems as a tool to accelerate and share learning, and it makes organizations responsible for implementing them, without referring to the treatment of imprecision, vagueness and uncertainty contained in the information that is managed.
- Like PMBOOK, CMMI raises the importance of continuous improvement and the use of indicators associated with time and cost. But it is inadequate in the proposal of indicators covering all the areas of processes.

The ISO [15] is an organization responsible for promoting the development of international standards of manufacture (both of products as of services). It should be noted that, for project management, ISO sets the standard 21500. This rule has as main background the PMBOOK in its 4th Edition [16], although it also takes aspects from other models as the ICB IPMA Competence Baseline of 2006, sponsored by the International Project Management Association (IPMA) model [17]. The ISO 21500 has 39 processes organized into 5 groups and 10 areas of knowledge, similar to the PMBOK. As it happens with schools analyzed up to this point, it does not propose specific mechanisms that ensure adaptation to the implementation monitoring. Moreover, it does address the treatment of imprecision, vagueness or uncertainty contained in the information, which negatively affects support for decision-making.

We must point out that around 125 solutions [18] associated with project management have been reported in the bibliography. Regarding tools, we should note that:

- Only 44 % include facilities for the management of indicators in data analysis.
- Among the most deployed indicators, we can find those generally associated to costs and which are described in the PMBOOK, such as: the value livestock (EV), the rate of yield of the costs (ICC - Cost Performance Index), the rate of yield of the planning (SPI - Schedule Performance Index), the cost variation (CV - Cost Variance), the cost planned (PV) and the actual cost (AC).
- They do not report tools using algorithms that allow the treatment of the imprecision, vagueness or uncertainty contained in the information.

From the discussed above, and considering that all schools pose as necessary the use of electronic tools for the management of projects, we identify the need that the tools used allow the calculation of indicators and the treatment of phenomena such as uncertainty, vagueness and the inaccuracy of information.

The scope of this work includes the identification of the best algorithms of soft-computing that allow learning from historical data associated to the assessment of projects and that can use this knowledge in the semi-automatic assessment of new projects.

3 Proposal of Ecosystem for the Project Evaluation Based on Skills of Soft Computing

In this section and considering the elements discussed in the previous sections, the ecosystem of software LABPRO appears in this section for the project management. Emphasis is also done in its ease for the project evaluation. It includes numerous functionalities grouped in different modules among which we can find, see Fig. 1:

- Project planning module: it makes the integrated project briefcase direction possible. It allows the management of scope and time, as well as semiautomatic timetables construction.
- Module of control and pursuit: it includes several methods for the project evaluation from pre-studied basic indicators. It is on this module where the main results of this investigation concentrate.

- Module of management of risks: it makes it possible the identification, analysis and answer of the risks.
- Module of management costs and invoicing: it allows the management of the budgets and the costs of the projects.
- Module of management of interested parties that includes facility for the management of competitors, clients and providers as well as the contracts with the two last ones.
- Module of documentary management, among others.

Fig. 1. Ecosystem modules LabPro

3.1 Module of Control and Pursuit

In this investigation we will concentrate on explaining some details of the module of control and pursuit, which is the main module that intervenes in the processes of evaluation of the state of the projects. We will show next a simplified view of this module and of the algorithms that it involves.

The fundamental steps for the control and pursuit of the projects implemented in this module are the following ones:

1. Step 1. Data-based calculation of indicators.
2. Step 2. Review of the quality of the product.
3. Step 3. Automatic evaluation of the project based on indicators.
4. Step 4. Detection of the fundamental difficulties of the project and the areas of the knowledge with difficulties.
5. Step 5. Checking of no problems to finish checkup and to congratulate
6. Step 6. In case of difficulties, going down in the indicators cascade and analyzing the causes.
7. Step 7. Identification of the causes to proceed to decision making and final evaluation of the project.

In the previous algorithm steps 1 to 4 are those who take longer.
In step 1 the indicators proposed in Table 1 are applied.

Table 1. Indicators for the decision making

Analysis area	Indicators
Integration management	Comprehensive assessment IAP (implementation of agreements of the cuts) project
Management of the client and the commitments	IE (performance index) IRE (performance execution index)
Time management	SPI (planning performance index)
Costs management	CPI (cost performance index) PV (planned cost), AC (real cost), EV (explained above)
Logistics management	IRL (the logistics performance index)
Human resource management	IRRH (Performance Index of human resources)
Management of scope and quality	IREF (Index performance effectiveness)
Consistency of the information	ICD (Index data quality)

To comply with our main objective of decreasing the time of control and monitoring while maintaining a high efficiency in the evaluation of the projects, we focus on the identification of those algorithms that efficiently and effectively allow project evaluation together with an explanation of its implication for results. Thus, we included in our platform the following algorithms:

- Algorithm based on ANFIS, it being a hybrid neuro-fuzzy system of Sugeno type [19]. With this algorithm, we intend to leverage the potential of neural networks and the interpretability of fuzzy inference systems. The proposed ANFIS uses a multi-layer node-oriented network architecture.
- Algorithm FIR. DM proposed by [20]. This algorithm uses a method based on the descending gradient to build and optimize a system of inference fuzzy in the line of Sugeno degree zero.
- Algorithm FS. HGD proposed by [21]. It is based on the combination of heuristic search and descending gradient.
- GFS.LT algorithm. RS proposed in [22] for the generation of fuzzy rules in the evaluation of projects. This technique implements evolutionary side adjustment of the membership functions with the aim of obtaining linguistic models with higher levels of precision. It uses a model representation of rules based on the linguistic representation of 2-tuples which allows the lateral displacement of the labels (light transfers to the left/ right of the original membership function).
- Algorithm GFS. THRIFT proposed in [23]. This algorithm generates fuzzy rules and it then optimizes them using a basic genetic algorithm (AG).
- Algorithm HyFIS proposed by [24] is a neuro-fuzzy model of hybrid type used to build and optimize fuzzy systems. It also combines the prediction of capabilities of neural networks with the systems of fuzzy inference generating rules of Mamdani type.

- Algorithm based on WM: proposed by Wang and Mendel [25]. In our particular case it generates a set of fuzzy rules which are candidates for the evaluation of projects, which are refined in a second phase. The generated rules are of Mandani type. In the exploitation stage it employs a system of fuzzy inference Mandani type and it is capable of displaying the rules that influence the final decision.

As can be seen, all of the algorithms proposed for this module comply with the following requirements:

To learn from the experience, which is an essential element, because the idea is to support the expert decision-making. That is to say, the proposed algorithms should be based on the experts' experiences and learn from them.

All are based in soft computing allowing the treatment of phenomena such as imprecision, ambiguity and uncertainty.

All generate fuzzy rules, which are important elements because they help with the interpretability of the results once the project is evaluated.

In addition, we chose a set of algorithms that cover different techniques, among which we find neural networks, downward gradient or evolutionary algorithms. In this way we intend to cover a broad spectrum of possible techniques, identifying those which can really help to effectively evaluate the projects.

The fundamental way out of the control module and monitoring is a control board as shown in Figs. 2 and 3.

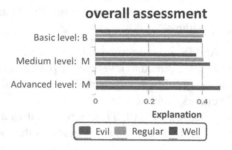

Fig. 2. Image of the automatic evaluation of a project by the system, considering maturity levels.

Figure 2 shows some of the potential in the use of soft-computing techniques. You can first assess the same project according to different levels of maturity of the Organization. In this case three levels are used: basic, intermediate and advanced. This is achieved because the classification systems were trained using the same set of training but considering more or less indicators depending on the level. In addition, for each level the implemented system allows the simultaneous assessment of the project in three tags (good, regular and bad) but with different degrees of certainty in its inference leaving the final decision for the human expert.

Figure 3 shows the use of colors in the control panel to assess each indicator independently. We use linguistic labels R (Regular), M (Bad) or B (good) that were obtained from evaluating each indicator in its respective fuzzy linguistic variable sets. The principle of maximum membership applies to offer the evaluation of each indicator.

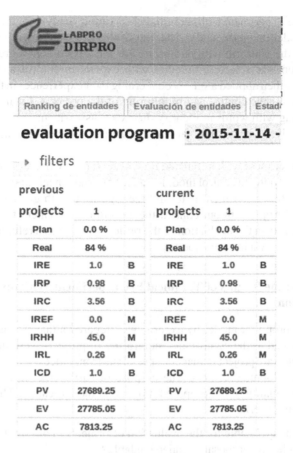

Fig. 3. Indicators, some of them included in the PMBOOK standard, which are used for automatic assessment

In general, it can be seen that the use of soft computing techniques helps with the interpretability of results in the evaluation process, as well as with the treatment of the ambiguity and imprecision of the information.

The platform is being applied in various real-world scenarios. The algorithms proposed for monitoring and follow-up were validated from experimenting with the behavior in a database of completed projects. The design of experiments and the results thereof are related below.

4   Analysis of Results

In this section we present the design of experiments for the validation of this investigation and the results obtained. Listed below there are the three techniques that were used for the validation of the results.

Technical pre-experiment without initial observation: analysis of the results of application of the model in a case study. The aim of this pre-experiment is to evaluate the potentialities of the platform with end users. For this experiment a group of end users of the application was selected, together with experts in control and monitoring of projects. They are then applied a survey concerning their experiences in the use of system and the facilities for the control and monitoring of the projects. Finally technique was applied computing with words to identify the expert assessment.

Technical analysis of normality: applied techniques for the normality analysis of the data.

Technical experiment with initial and final observation: Comparison of the different algorithms proposed in the control module and monitoring on an experimental database. The objective of this experiment is to find the algorithm with greater effectiveness in the evaluation of projects. In our context the algorithm of greater efficiency is the one who has fewer errors in the evaluation of the projects, taking as a reference the previous classification made by a human expert.

4.1   Analysis of the Results of Technical Pre-experiment Without Initial Observation

To evaluate the proposed model by experts, we prepared a questionnaire in which 53 specialists dedicated to the control and monitoring of projects were involved. Among the specialists there are project managers, specialists from offices of project management and heads of development centers. The purpose of survey was to know the existing criteria about the quality of the proposed model and the indicators. This questionnaire was based on four criteria:

- Is the proposal applicable for the evaluation of projects in different scenarios?
- Do you consider the proposal is understandable?
- Is the proposed model usable, comfortable to apply?
- Do the proposed indicators cover the areas of knowledge of the management of projects?

The survey was validated by 14 experts. We also used the tool SPSS with which the test Cronbach's alpha coefficient test was run. This type of test is applicable to surveys with answers of Likert-type, where each item or question is answered according to numbers that represent degrees of agreement or disagreement (The Highest, Very High, High, Medium, Low, Very Low, None).

The coefficient Cronbach's alpha was equal to 0.873. According to the literature it is considered that values of alpha greater than 0.7 are valid to ensure the reliability of the scale. Given the positive results obtained in this test it is considered valid to apply the survey mentioned above. Once the questionnaire has been distributed, word computing techniques are applied to consolidate the criteria obtained. The following steps were taken:

1. A basic set of linguistic terms (LBTL) for the assessment of the criteria are defined. LBTL = {nothing, very low, Low, Medium, High, Very High, perfect}.

2. The specialists evaluated each criterion by using one of the linguistic terms.
3. The experts' preference is transformed into fuzzy sets based on the linguistic variable of Fig. 4.

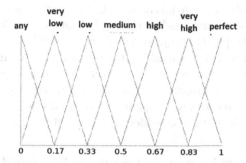

Fig. 4. Linguistic Variables used by experts to evaluate a proposal.

4. Following the model 2-tuples [26] of computing with words the experts' evaluations are added by consolidating them for each criterion to assess. See Eq. 1.

$$x^e(x) = \left(\frac{1}{n} \sum_{i=1}^{n} {}^{-1}\left((s_i, \alpha_i) \right) \right) = \left(\frac{1}{n} \sum_{i=1}^{n} \beta_i \right) \tag{1}$$

5. Analyze the results, see Table 2.

Table 2. Results of the assessment.

Criteria	Evaluation of the experts summarized
Applicability in different scenarios	High
Understandability of the proposal	Very high
Usability of the proposal	Media
Coverage of the indicators of the knowledge areas	High
Aggregation end	High

"Usability of the proposal" obtains the lowest mark in evaluation. This is motivated by the use of non-traditional methods and the need for platforms like R that implement the proposed algorithms. The best evaluated criterion was the understandability and applicability of the proposal. This is a positive element that displays the acceptance of experts consulted for the application of the model in different scenarios. In general, the final evaluation given by experts to the proposal was high.

4.2 Analysis of the Results of Technical Analysis of Normality

It was explored using a knowledge base of finished projects from the development environment of software projects of the University of Informatics Sciences with more than 10 production centres dedicated to this activity. Each record in the database corresponds to a cut of a project where control and monitoring indicators are picked up. The retrieved performance data correspond to projects with dates of court between 2013 and 2015.

The knowledge base that was used has the following distribution: out of the 7843 projects, 40 % were evaluated as good, 14 % were considered regular and 46 % were classified as bad. Each court project was evaluated by a human expert in such a way that a pattern was obtained to compare the quality of the results of classification [9, 27].

Experts evaluated the projects considering the indicators described in Table 1.

4.3 The Assumption of Normality of the Samples Was Found Through the Shapiro-Wilk Test

This showed that for each outcome metrics at least one technique has probability (p-value) values lower than 0.05, so it refuses the idea of normal distribution with a 95 % confidence. Since not all the samples show a normal distribution, we opted for by the use of non-parametric tests to detect significant differences.

For the comparison of the algorithms the following set of metrics as criteria of measurement are mentioned:

- Percentage of correct classifications
- Number of false positives
- Number of false negatives

- MSE calculated by the equation $\dfrac{1}{n} \sum_{i=1}^{n} \left(Y_{real} - Y_{pred} \right)^2$

- SMAPE, calculated as: $100 * \dfrac{1}{n} \sum_{i=1}^{n} \dfrac{|Y_{real} - Y_{pred}|}{(Y_{real} + Y_{pred})/2}$

Where the number of cases of validation is n, real Y is the value of expected output and the output is calculated by the system. Once the algorithm learned from the training cases, metrics are calculated on the cases selected for testing.

For the comparison of the algorithms proposed in the model we applied the method of Cross-validation randomly with k = 20 iterations of test and n = 7, the end parameter representing the 7 algorithms proposed. For each iteration, the data set is randomly divided in a set of training with 70 % of the cases and another test with the remaining 30 %.

As they are related samples, the tests of Wilcoxon and Friedman are used. In both cases, significant differences when p-value < 0.05 are considered. In the case of the Wilcoxon test the Monte Carlo method is applied in a 99 % of the confidence interval. During the application of the tests, in cases where significant differences were found between the techniques, different groups of techniques were formed.

The groups meet the following property: techniques of a same group do not show significant differences between them. The groups also meet the following property: Group1 < Group2 < Group_n. The techniques in the smaller groups are those that exhibit the best results, while those located in the biggest Groups have the worst outcome.

With respect to the Metric "percent of correct classifications" the Friedman test was applied, comparing the samples obtained from the application of algorithms. In this context it is considered as the best result that technique which statistically provides greater value to the metric. As a result, there are significant differences between the techniques with p-value = "7.8547750364149E-18". The Wilcoxon test is applied, conveniently comparing pairs of techniques, and eventually obtaining the following groups:

1. Group 1: ANFIS, FS.HGD, FIR.DM
2. Group 2: GFS.THRIFT
3. Group 3: GFS.lt.RS
4. Group 4: WM
5. Group 5: HyFIS

As regards the Metric "Number of false or positives" the Friedman test was applied, comparing the obtained samples from the application of algorithms. In this context it is considered as the best that technique with statistically less value contributed to this metric. Consequently there are significant differences between the techniques with p-value = "1.57230970124996E-17". The Wilcoxon test is applied, comparing pairs of techniques, obtaining the following groups:

1. Group 1: ANFIS
2. Group 2: WM, HYFIS, FIR.DM,
3. Group 3: FS.HGD, GFS.lt.RS, GFS.THRIFT

In this case the ANFIS obtained the best results because it was the technique with the fewest false positives. Obtaining false positives (classification of Good when the project is actually evaluated of Bad) in the area of the management of projects is detrimental; a project evaluated as good, which in fact is not, can be a handicap in the decision-making giving place to unreal schedules.

With respect to the Metric "Number of false positives", in this context it is considered as the best result that technique which contributes less to the value of this metric. The Friedman test was applied to compare the samples obtained. As a result there are significant differences between the techniques with p-value = "5.19919647410999E-14". The Wilcoxon test is applied, conveniently comparing pairs of techniques, and eventually obtaining the following groups:

1. Group 1: WM
2. Group 2: ANFIS, GFS.lt.RS
3. Group 3: FS.HGD, HYFIS, GFS.THRIFT
4. Group 4: FIR.DM

It can be said that the technique WM gets significantly better results in the number of false negatives in the set of cases.

Obtaining false negatives (classification of Bad when the project is in fact evaluated as Good) in the area of the management of projects is not as harmful as the false positives, but classifying a project as Bad, when it is not, can lead to bad decisions.

As regards the Metric "MSE" in the context of this experiment, it is considered as the best that technique with statistically less value contributed to this metric. The Friedman test is applied comparing the samples obtained. It was shown that there are significant differences between the techniques with p-value = "1.45922235866844E-16". The Wilcoxon test is applied, conveniently comparing pairs of techniques, and eventually obtaining the following groups:

1. Group 1: ANFIS, FIR.DM
2. Group 2: GFS.thrift, WM
3. Group 3: GFS.lt.RS
4. Group 4: FS.HGD
5. Group 5: HyFIS

It can be said that the technique ANFIS and FIR.DM gets significantly better results with regard to the mean quadratic error in the set of cases.

5 Conclusions

Based on the analysis of the results presented above we reach the following conclusions. It is possible to integrate soft computing techniques in the evaluation of projects enabling better treatment of phenomena such as imprecision, vagueness and uncertainty contained in primary data. The proposed model makes intensive use of soft computing techniques both for the visualization of the results and the classification of projects. The use of algorithms based on soft computing, which learn from evidence and can then be used in the classification of new instances, enables the adaptation of models of evaluation of projects to changing conditions associated with the styles of management and the level of maturity achieved by the organizations that manage projects. It was found that the technique ANFIS shows the best general behavior among all the analyzed techniques with 97 % effectiveness in the correct classification.

We recommend the combination of systems to help automatic classification of projects combined with systems of recommendations that improve the usability of the models and platforms for the management of projects.

References

1. The Standish Group International: Big Bang Boom, Chaos report. The Standish Group International, Inc, New York (2014)
2. Pacelli, L.: The Project Management: 18 Major Project Screw-Ups, and How to Cut Them Off at the Pass. Prentice Hal, Upper Saddle River (2012)
3. Amoui, M., Derakhshanmanesh, M., Ebert, J., Tahvildari, J.: Achieving dynamic adaptation via management and interpretation of runtime, models. J. Syst. Softw. **85**, 2720–2737 (2012)

4. Mossalam, A., Arafa, M.: The role of project manager in benefits realization management as a project constraint/driver. HBRC J. 56–67 (2014). Housing and Building National Research Center

5. Aguiar, D., Fenner, G., Sampaio, A.: A risk management methodology proposal for information technology projects. IEEE Latin Am. Trans. **12**(4), 634–656 (2014). ISSN: 1548-0992

6. Piñero, P., Torres, S., Izquierdo, M.: GESPRO: Paquete para la gestión de proyectos. Revista Nueva Empresa, Cuba **9**(1), 45–53 (2013). ISSN: 1682-2455

7. Piñero, P.: Experiencias en el uso de PostgreSQL en el sistema GESPRO, un enfoque práctico. Revista Cubana de Ciencias Informáticas, Cuba **5**(1) ISSN: 2227-1899 (2011)

8. Torres, S.: Modelo de evaluación de competencias a partir de evidencias durante la gestión de proyectos, La Habana: Laboratorio de Investigaciones en Gestión de Proyectos, Universidad de las Ciencias Informáticas (2015)

9. Pérez, I., Piñero, P., Torres, S.: Diseño de Repositorio para el Aprendizaje y Descubrimiento de Conocimiento para la toma de decisions en Gestin de Proyectos. In: Conference Proceedings XII Congreso de la Sociedad Cubana de Matemática y Computación (COMPUMAT 2011), Universidad Central Marta Abreu de las Villas; 11/2011 (2011). doi: 10.13140/RG.2.1.3219.1443

10. Cabral, D., Ribeiro, M., Leomar, J.: Knowledge engineering: survey of methodologies, techniques and tools: IEEE Latin Am. Trans. **12**(8), ISSN: 1548-0992 (2014)

11. Project Management Institute: A Guide to the Project Management Body of Knowledge (PMBOK® Guide), 5th edn. Project Management Institute, Estados Unidos de América (2013)

12. Project Management Institute: Global Dynamics of Innovation and Project Management. Project Management Institute Inc, New York (2015)

13. Project Management Institute: IBM: Keys to Building a Successful Enterprise Project Management Office. Project Management Institute, Inc, New York (2015)

14. Software Engineering Institute. CMMI para Desarrollo, Versión 1.3. Mejora de los procesos para el desarrollo de mejores productos y servicios. Technical report, Software Engineering Institute, EE, UU (2010)

15. ISO: ISO 21500:2012 Guidance on Project Management. International Organization for Standardization (2012)

16. Verástegui, J.: ISO 21500 Directrices para la Dirección y Gestión de Proyectos. IV Congreso Internacional de Dirección de Proyectos, pp. 24–35 (2014)

17. IPMA: International Project Management Association (2015). http://ipma.ch/about/

18. Piñero, P., Pérez, I., González, M.: Sistema de información para la gestión de organizaciones orientadas a proyectos. V Congreso Iberoamericano de Ingeniería de Proyectos, Loja, Ecuador (2014). doi:10.13140/2.1.3491.1522

19. Jang, J.: ANFIS: adaptive-network-based fuzzy inference systems. IEEE Trans. Syst. Man Cybern. **23**(3), 665–685 (1993)

20. Nomura, H., Hayashi, I., Wakami, N.: A learning method of fuzzy inference rules by descent method. In: IEEE International Conference on Fuzzy Systems, San Diego, CA (1992)

21. Ishibuchi, H., Nozaki, K., Hosaka, T.H.: Empirical study on learning in fuzzy systems by rice taste analysis. Fuzzy Sets Syst. **64**(2), 129–144 (1994)

22. Alcalá, R., Alcalá, Herrera F.: A proposal for the genetic lateral tuning of linguistic fuzzy systems and its interaction with rule selection. IEEE Trans. Fuzzy Syst. **15**(4), 616–635 (2007)

23. Thrift, P.: Fuzzy logic synthesis with genetic algorithms. In: Proceedings of the Fourth International Conference on Genetic Algorithms (ICGA 1991), San Diego, United States of America (1991)

24. Kim, J., Kasabov, N.: HyFIS: Adaptive neuro-fuzzy inference systems and their application to nonlinear dynamical systems. Neural Netw. **12**(9), 1301–1319 (1999)

25. Wang, L., Mendel, J.: Generating fuzzy rule by learning from examples. IEEE Trans. Syst. Man Cybern. **22**(6), 1414–1427 (1992)

26. Herrera, F., Martınez, L.: A 2-tuple fuzzy linguistic representation model for computing with words. IEEE Trans. Fuzzy Syst. **8**(6), 746–752 (2000)

27. Torres, S., Piñero, P., Capretz, L.: Creation and evaluation of software teams - a social approach. Int. J. Manuf. Technol. Manag. **28**(4), 1–21 (2014). doi:10.1504/IJMTM.2014.066695

MiSCi: Autonomic Reflective Middleware for Smart Cities

Jose Aguilar[1,4,5(✉)], Marxjhony Jerez[1], Maribel Mendonca[2], and Manuel Sánchez[3]

[1] Universidad de los Andes, Mérida, Venezuela
{aguilar,marxjhony}@ula.ve
[2] Universidad Centroccidental Lisandro Alvarado, Lara, Venezuela
mmendonca@ucla.edu.ve
[3] Universidad Nacional Experimental del Táchira, San Cristóbal, Venezuela
mbsanchez@unet.ve
[4] Escuela Politécnica Nacional, Quito, Ecuador
[5] Universidad Técnica Particular de Loja, Loja, Ecuador

Abstract. Context analysis in intelligent environments allows making the services and information available to support the activities of individuals ubiquitously. Under this premise we define smart cities, which are intelligent large-scale environments, with large amounts of data that are used to improve the quality of life for its citizens. The smart cities support activities to improve traffic, health, government, sociability, among others. This proposal seeks to create a middleware for Smart Cities from the vision of intelligent environments modeled as intelligent agents that can be adapted to the existing dynamism in a city, using emerging ontologies that not only adapt to the context of the moment and in real time, but respond unforeseen situations (emerging). Similarly, the middleware should allow scalability of the environment, to maintain the performance both in small big towns.

Keywords: Smart city · Multiagent systems · Context awareness · Ontological emergency

1 Introduction

In smart cities and communities, the context in applications continuously changes, as well as the situation, the accessibility to (ICT-based) services, the people, their interactions, requirements and preferences. Moreover, the way that applications can react to such changing environment is at run-time, since we cannot a priori predict different situations, requirements, interactions, and availability of (ICT) services. Continuous context-aware, incremental adaptation to sudden situations (emergent contexts), become, therefore, in the key enabling property for the delivery of ICT based value added services, to manage the dynamics of the continuously changing environments and unpredictable situations [1].

One of the major problems in developing a Smart City is to describe the enormous quantity and the multiple sources of information, and the use of data from different domains using a semantic presentation. The different areas or domains of application of intelligent cities are presented in [1–3]: Government, Education, Health, Buildings,

© Springer International Publishing AG 2016
R. Valencia-García et al. (Eds.): CITI 2016, CCIS 658, pp. 241–253, 2016.
DOI: 10.1007/978-3-319-48024-4_19

Mobility, Infrastructure, Technology, Energy and Citizens. In [1], Tan et al. describe a semantic representation of the framework of unstructured data in Smart Cities. Also, they apply fuzzy ontologies for the semantic recognition of information and services. In [2] Pellicer et al. distinguish some basic technological areas in Smart cities, such as collecting, transmission, storage and processing of data. In [3], Neirotti et al. present a relevant taxonomy for the domain of Smart Cities, calling them: natural resources and energy, transport and mobility, buildings, living, government and economy, and people. They propose policies and guidelines for defining strategies and planning actions in the Smart Cities through appropriate application domains, based on these subdomains. In [4], Fujiwara et al. present an example of Smart Cities and trends, where the social public infrastructure is efficiently managed, using Information and Communications Technology. Fujiwara et al. describe trends in Smart Cities approach, like context awareness in Smart Cities [5]. In [6], Komninos et al. discuss the impact of several applications of Smart Cities. This impact depends on their ontologies and technological features. Komninos develops an Ontology for Smart Cities.

In this paper, the user interacts with a multi-agent system that represents the smart city, which is aware of context, through emergent ontologies arising from the dynamics of the moment, thanks to an autonomous middleware that is context-aware, based on the works [7–9]. In previous works like [4], some middleware implementation was described, and the definition of services for smart cities, but not the architecture [10].

We define an autonomic reflective architecture as a Multi-Agent System (MAS), which will have agents to characterize both individuals, devices and applications (which provide services to individuals) that coexist in the smart city. Its architecture will be based on web services, allowing its services to be consumed by applications (in our case, agents), aware of context or not. Agents can create temporary or permanent emerging ontologies, which allow solving a particular situation, according to the context. The intelligent agents can be adapted to the existing dynamism in a city, using emerging ontologies that not only allow adapting to the context of the moment and in real time, but they also respond to unforeseen situations (emerging).

In Sect. 2, we discuss the MiSCi Architecture divided in layers, we show the Multi-agent system (Sect. 2.1), the Context awareness layer (Sect. 2.2) and the emerging ontology layer (Sect. 2.3). In Sect. 3, we describe how MiSCi is geospatially deployed within the city, and finally, the conclusions and future works are presented in Sects. 4 and 5.

2   MiSCi Architecture

This section describes the architecture of MiSCi (Autonomic Reflective Middleware for Smart Cities) as the basis for making context-aware smart decisions in the Smart City. MiSCi is able to sense the environment, to reason, plan and execute a solution in an independent, proactive, context-aware and intelligent way. The three main components of the architecture of MiSCi are detailed as follows.

2.1 Agent Based Multi-layer Architecture of MiSCi

MiSCi is composed by a multi-layer architecture based on a multi-agent system, allowing it to have capabilities of such systems, like: sociability, proactivity, adaptability, intelligence, etc. Consequently, the agents of MiSCi may perceive the interactions of the users (monitoring the environment, using the sensors available on it), think in an appropriate solution (services to be offered to the user) according to the context, plan and deploy the solution in the environment (using the effectors), thus improving the activities carried out by the citizens of the city, always focused in improving the quality of life and the comfort of the citizens in the environment (see Fig. 1).

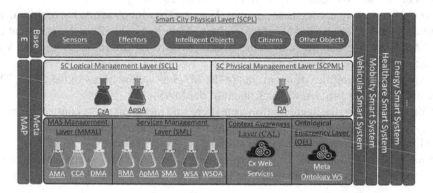

Fig. 1. Architecture of MiSCi.

The architecture of MiSCi consists of 3 levels and 7 layers; also, it contains cross layers that bring support to the operations carried out by the agents of MiSCi. The layers that make up the architecture are detailed below:

1. *MAS Management Layer (MMAL):* This layer is an adaptation of the FIPA (Foundation for International Physical Agents) standard [11, 12], which defines the rules that allow a society of agents to co-exist and be administered, encouraging the interoperability with other technologies.

2. *Service Management Layer (SML):* Like the MMAL, this layer is an adaptation of the FIPA standard [11, 12], with the exception that in this case it is not only extended to be the responsible to manage resources and applications, but it also allows the integration between MAS and SOA paradigms in a bidirectional way, enabling the use of the SaaS model of the cloud computing in MiSCi, which is fundamental in a Smart City. Thus, agents can expose their capabilities as web services, allowing other web services in the cloud to request the activation of the agents' tasks as a service. On the other hand, agents can invoke web services in the cloud in a natural way; this feature especially increases the integration capabilities of MiSCi with those based on the cloud computing paradigm.

The SML and MMAL layers provide operational services to SCLL and SCPML (described below) layers, which allow the agents of these two layers to meet the objectives for which they were designed. The MMAL and SML layers allow agents of MiSCi to:

- Know the services, agents, and applications available in the platform, grouped by levels, types, or any other classification (these tasks are performed by the AMA, RMA, APMA, DMA and SMA).
- Know the agents providing a service and where they are located (these tasks are performed by the AMA and RMA), as well as the services available in the cloud that can be invoked by agents of the MAS (task carried out by SMA).
- Know the ways to access these services: How are they invoked?, What requirements must be met to access them?, among others. Also, it should allow the agents of the MAS to invoke Web Services in the cloud. This task is carried out by the WSA for each web service registered.
- Expose the capabilities of the agents of the MAS as web services in the cloud. This work is done by WSOA, for each agent of the MAS.
- Control mobility, the agent platform must provide mechanisms to control the mobility and migration processes of the agents (task performed by the AMA).
- Allow the communication between the agents (task performed by the CCA).
- Enable or disable the possibility to be invoked, etc. that is, the overall management of them (task performed by the AMA).

Some of these features are based on [11], but others are derived from the extension of the SML to support the SaaS model of cloud computing, enabling the MAS-SOA integration (particularly with the introduction of the SMA, WSOA and WSA agents). More details can be found in [7, 13, 14].

1. *Context Awareness Layer (CAL):* It provides the components of MiSCi with context awareness services, so that the decisions of the agents are nurtured with contextual information at every moment. This layer is specified in more detail in Sect. 2.2.
2. *Ontological Emergence Layer (OEL):* In this layer is where the services of semantic mining are deployed. These services are required to create contextual ontologies that allow to deal with each situation in the Smart City. It is detailed in Sect. 2.3
3. *Smart City Logical Management Layer (SCLML):* It is responsible for providing the Smart City with intelligence. This layer is where all the applications (software, objects) and people present in the Smart City are characterized. Basically, each application/person is characterized by an agent (is an abstraction of it) that contains metadata that define its properties. This layer contains agents like, CzA (characterizes each citizen of the Smart City) and AppA (characterizes useful applications in the Smart City, such as the Vehicular Smart System, the Healthcare Smart System, etc.). Those agents are aware context agents that coordinate and cooperate with each other, to take decisions that are needed at a particular time, to help real people to perform their tasks in the Smart City, encouraging comfort and improving the quality of life of the citizens.
4. *Smart City Physical Management Layer (SCPML):* It allows to manage the physical devices in the Smart City. In this layer, all the physical elements of the environment

are characterized, allowing the use and communication with each one of the other agents of MiSCi. Thus, each physical device is characterized by an agent (is an abstraction of it) that contains metadata that defines its properties. Some of these physical devices are intelligent (Smart) Objects, so that the properties of learning, autonomy, reasoning, among others, are critical to characterize in them. This layer communicates with the real physical device that is in the SCPL layer, because it's through SCPL that agents have access to the physical hardware of the devices.

5. *Smart City Physical Layer (SCPL):* This layer represents the Smart City itself. It is here where all the physical components of the Smart City are deployed, such as: (a) Sensors, to capture useful information for services and smart objects in the environment (b) effectors, to modify the physical conditions of the environment (c) Smart Objects, which are components of the Smart City that may adapt and respond to situations in the current context.

In the same way, the architecture of MiSCi includes the main sub-systems of a Smart City, which are responsible for managing the elements of the city in a global way, such as: Vehicular Smart System, responsible for controlling the traffic; Mobility Smart System, responsible for facilitating the mobility of citizens (public transport); Smart Healthcare System, responsible facilitating the access to health services, etc. An agent of MiSCi can communicate with these systems through the AppA agents, because they characterize the applications in the Smart City in the architecture. Thus, global systems can be coordinated with local systems to meet the needs of citizens in a given time (this is explained in more details in Sect. 3).

Moreover, the reflective capability of MiSCi is based on the Autonomic Computing loop known as MAPE [16], where the Device Agents, AppA and CzA perform the monitoring process, the AppA and CzA perform the processes of analysis and planning, in conjunction with the context awareness services and the meta-ontology, while that the execution of the plan is performed in the SCPL layer by using the effectors (DA). In that sense, the Meta level (reflective capacity) of the middleware occurs in the SCLL, SCPML, CAL and OEL layers, while the base level (system functionality) corresponds to the SCPL layer.

2.2 Context Awareness Layer (CAL)

The contextual awareness is an important part of the architecture of the middleware, because it allows delivering relevant information to characterize the situation of a person, place or an object, for interaction between them and devices/applications smart in Smart Cities. The purpose of this layer is to offer context services, for the information management about the context, this information goes in a cycle that is formed by: the discovering of the Context, modeling, reasoning and distribution of context. It is also important to know the quality of the information presented in the context (Quality of context). For this, we take as reference the services offered in [8], where they propose a Context-Aware Reflective Middleware based on the Cloud Computing, with a range of contextual services to manage context information.

Features and Context Services. CAL incorporates seven services for managing the context, the services can be provided internally (I) (required for the same services of the CAL) or called independently from external services (E). These services are required to manage the lifecycle of a context, which are:

CAL_1. *Context Acquisition.* Within this service activities and semantic annotation of context are discovered. Also, the pre-processing of data, outlier detection, data matching, among others, is carried out.

CAL_2. *Context Modeling.* In this service performed the knowledge modeling, and knowledge extraction, on a specific domain is. It invokes the OEL services. Another function within this service involves the storage of data, and the management tools for its exploitation, such as data mining, pattern recognition, among others. A final task is the management of the data problems (e.g., imperfect data, ambiguous data, etc.).

CAL_3. *Context Reasoning.* It is responsible for applying the techniques of reasoning, event management (analysis of patterns, trend analysis), merging data, uncertainty analysis of the context and Quality Context. In addition, it suggests possible actions to be taken in context. This service interacts with OEL to perform a fusion of contexts.

CAL_4. *Context Distribution.* It is responsible for delivery the context to users. It is responsible for implementing distribution techniques, and its features are: data formatting (including data transformation, unit conversion, data customization, etc.), accessibility (offers documentation, alternatives and multiple access options), management of the user requirements (query processing, semantic knowledge construction) and management of consumer services (logs, keeping profiles: history, preferences, etc.).

CAL_5. *Context Verification.* It is responsible for detecting inconsistencies in context and take action to solve them. The context verification will be based on the Quality of Context (QoC), and it depends on the precision, the correctness, the trustworthiness, of the context. At first instance, these variables can be calculated from the data sensed by the sensors. The context will be always verified before the context distribution.

CAL_6. *Context Security and privacy.* It is responsible for security and data privacy tasks within the entire life cycle of a context.

CAL_7. *Context Services Manager.* It is responsible for the management of services in the context; these include services that may be in the cloud. This is an orchestrator of the internal services of CAL.

Context Management Process in the Smart Cities. The context-aware services is a trend in the new Smart Cities projects, allowing services to adapt and emerge when these are required [4]. In a Smart city at every moment there exists a number of inherent contexts that could be instantiated when a set of events and variables appear. Within MiSCi, the discovering of context is performed by CAL1 through the SCPML layer, collecting data from the environment, which is then passed to OEL for processing and obtaining the ontological model of the moment, which is managed by the CAL2 service. With this information, the quality of the Context (CAL5) is verified. Finally, the CAL3 service is used to reason about the context (invoking OEL services). The CAL6 is used by CAL7 all the time, which is invoked by the SML, in order to use the context services in the smart city.

2.3   Ontological Emergence Layer (OEL)

An essential element of the Smart City in the proposed architecture is the Ontological Emergency Layer (OEL). The purpose of this layer is to provide a set of services with very specific tasks for handling ontologies. The ontologies provide an adequate conceptual model of the context of the Smart City. These services are based on [9], where the initial ideas of some semantic services are provided. Services for automatic updating of ontologies are proposed to adapt them to the dynamics and evolution of an environment.

This layer may be required at some point to perform self-management processes, which will be based on the meta-ontologies that make up a generic model in composing and update of the ontologies required by the different processes of the Smart City [15]. This layer allows monitoring the ontologies to adapt and fit them to new requirements, and allows defining the elements that must have the ontologies, making the necessary adjustments and self-managing the evolutionary process of ontological framework of the Smart City.

The Ontological Framework for Smart Cities. The ontological framework is composed of distributed ontologies that are managed by different agents and services involved in the Smart City, which are heterogeneous (different data structures, languages, data types, etc.), since each source of knowledge has its own designers, and they usually have different designs and structures. The meta-ontologies are managed on the OEL, which supplies ontological services to other agents in the system. Agents of the Smart City, use their local ontologies for their services, interact with other agents, etc. When they detect the need to update their knowledge (e.g. the coming of a new service, changes in behavior patterns of components, context change etc.), the agents request the services of the OEL.

OEL Functions and Services.
   Among the functions of OEL we find:

- Providing services for self-management of the ontological framework of the Smart City.
- Intelligently managing the semantics of the system through ontological mining services, as ontological integration mechanisms, the ontological learning, etc.
- Modeling the new signals and elements of the context of the Smart City, reflecting them in its ontological framework.
- Maintaining consistency and semantic evolution of the ontological framework of the Smart City.

The Services Offered by the OEL are:

- *Semantic Register and Exploration of Ontologies Services:* These services allow knowing, publicizing and locating semantic information in the Smart City. Through the service "Semantic Register", agents and devices participating in the Smart City, must record information about the conceptual models that handle. In this process, a "Semantic Directory" (SD) is generated with semantic annotations of the sources of knowledge (a level metadata) used in the Smart City. The SD consists of a "semantic annotations table" where the semantic system events are recorded and an "Ontological Directory" with the registration of ontologies available in the Smart City. The service "Search Ontologies" allows to explore the ontological directory.

- *Ontology Update Services:* These services allow to create new ontologies or enrich the already existing, considering the dynamic process of the Smart City, which demands an ontological framework updated. These services are: Generation of new ontologies and meta-ontologies, ontological population and ontology enrichment.
- *Ontology Integration Services:* In the process of emergent ontologies, it is required to carry out ontological mining processes (alignment, fusion, etc.), in order to enrich or generate integral and consistent conceptual models. These services are mainly fusion and alignment of ontologies.
- *Verification and Analysis Services:* This is essential to check the quality of the generated ontologies, and perform the analysis of the semantic of the ontologies to determine, for example, the ontologies in the same domain, the correspondence between them, or to discover new knowledge associated with the domain, based on semantic data mining or ontological mining. These services are: the analysis of the ontologies, and the quality verification of the ontologies. To verify the quality of an ontology, two aspects are considered:
  - *Coherence:* detect inconsistencies through reasoners, for determining whether ontologies are coherent and not contradictory.
  - *Redundancy:* measures the degree of redundancy or semantic overlap in an integrated ontology, to improve their understanding.

Ontological Emergence process in a Smart City. Ontologies involved in the Smart City must be dynamic, i.e. they must change and adapt to the needs and services in the city. The ontological framework of a Smart City should be able to represent the new signs, objects and behaviors in the city, therefore, although some elements can be predefined, others must necessarily be "emerging".

Ontologies represent the model of knowledge that is present in the Smart City. This knowledge can be dispersed in different data sources and devices: databases, documents, monitored data, wearable devices, etc., and can evolve according to the dynamics of context.

Specifically, in our approach Knowledge as a Service, the architecture can handle multiple ontologies distributed in agents of the Smart City, and core meta-ontology. This core meta-ontology is managed by the OEL that provides the multiagent system with ontological services to allow the ontological emergence.

The core Meta-Ontology is used to define the general model of the components and domains present in the Smart City. An example of this meta-ontology is shown in Fig. 2. In particular, this meta-ontology links and structures the domain and context ontologies, and organizes the semantic information from different data sources that arise in the Smart City, by the incorporation of new devices, agents, services, etc. Through the service "Population de Meta-ontologies" may be obtained the ontological model of the moment. In this ontological model are considered data on the user's profile, and activities or events that take place, considering the context in which they occur: the spatial domain (places, objects, etc.) and functional domain (health, economy, energy, etc.). In each domain can also exist meta-ontologies to generically defining its conceptual model, maintaining the integrity and consistency between the concepts, showing global information about how they should be structured and how they relate to each other.

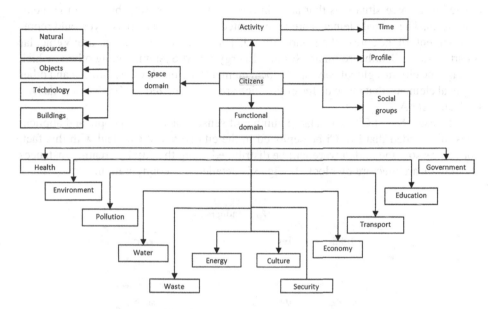

Fig. 2.   Smart city meta-ontology

In particular, in the proposed architecture the agents involved in the Smart City register information about the system events, and about the ontologies that handle, making semantic annotations of the sources of knowledge (in terms of meta-data) used in the Smart City. In this process of semantic registration must relate the concepts and ontologies with some meta-concepts, through its description or analyzing their properties, to establish a relationship. Before performing, the "Register of Semantics" can view the meta-concepts of the Meta-Ontology through the "Query of Concepts" service. These concepts come to play the role of super-classes for concepts that are handled and emerge in the Smart City. The process of emergence ontology can occur when performing ontological mining tasks, among registered ontologies and meta-ontologies, through, for example, the alignment and the population of the meta-ontologies (using update and integration services).

The generation of new meta-ontologies, or the updating of the existing ones, represent mechanisms of the semantic evolution of the ontological framework. The service "generation meta-ontologies" allows that. If there are more than two ontologies of the same domain aligned, our middleware performs a process of generating new categories or meta-concepts that can conform a meta-ontologies.

3   Geospatial Deployment of MiSCi Within a Smart City

MiSCi contains elements in the global and local level, those elements should be coordinated to resolve situations that arise in the city in the best way by using the meta-ontologies. The global elements are incorporated in MiSCi like cross layers and represent elements of the core of the Smart City as [2] proposes; those elements are: Vehicular Smart System, Healthcare Smart System, Energy Smart System, among others, which manage the city in a global way; while local elements are the devices, citizens and other physical elements that make up the city, which are characterized in MiSCi as agents DA, CzA and AppA.

Because a Smart City has a large number of sensors, actuators, people and applications, it's needed that MiSCi be deployed in the city so that it can deal with this fact. For this reason, the middleware will be distributed along the city by creating instances of MiSCi's architecture by block. In Fig. 3 is detailed this configuration.

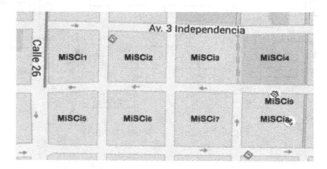

Fig. 3. Geospatial deployment of MiSCi.

In the above figure, a local instance of MiSCi was deployed on every block of the city, in which all the physical elements present in that sector were characterized; also, each block should manage its own ontologies (context, components, domain, etc.). Thus, the middleware is not affected by the number of devices available around and along the city; however, because the middleware is a distributed system, we need to have better control over the operations performed by each $MiSCi_i$; besides, each $MiSCi_i$ need to communicate with another $MiSCi_j$ to share information about devices that are on its borders. To deal with this trouble, we use the mechanisms for coordination and interaction proposed by FIPA, which allow two agents in different SMA to be able to establish a conversation; in that sense, each $MiSCi_i$ should know all the $MiSCi_j$ in its neighborhood, so they can exchange information. Accordingly, the $MiSCi_1$ know the MiSCi 2, 5 and 6, the $MiSCi_5$ know the MiSCi 1, 2 and 6 and so on. Similarly, the $MiSCi_i$ are coordinated with the global systems to resolve the situations that arise locally, for example, if a local MiSCi reports a traffic accident to the Vehicular Smart System, it must report this information to the vehicles in that route, so they can take an alternative route, avoiding traffic congestion. If an ambulance requests a route to the nearest hospital using the Vehicular Smart System, it should contact the local MiSCis (each global system has global ontologies of context and domain that contains information about the MiSCis on each block) in the same route of the ambulance, to instruct the traffic lights, vehicles, among others, to give priority to the ambulance, according to the route generated. In this way, the geospatial distribution of MiSCI in the city supports the activities of citizens towards improving their living conditions and comfort.

The number of physical elements that can be supported by each node of MiSCi depends on the resources of each node and the characteristics of the physical elements. The node will be a Platform as a Service (PaaS).

4   Conclusions

In the smart cities, there are various approaches to support the full set of information, sensors, individuals, etc., found in there [4]. Additionally, several domains of applications have been defined for the smart cities: Governance, Education, Healthcare, Building, Mobility, Infra-structure, Technology, Energy and Citizen. MiSCi is a framework that allows to manage individuals/applications, sensors and actuators, through a multi-agent systems. The information management of MiSCi can act in various application domains through of the merge of the information of the meta-ontologies, which allows to give a semantic meaning to data according to the contextual awareness that emerges from the situation presented at a given time.

The main advantages of our proposal are the ubiquity and emergent properties of the architecture, through intelligent agents that can be adapted to the dynamism in a city, and ubiquitously respond to the requirements of citizens, using emerging ontologies that not only allow to adapt to the context of the moment and in real time, but they also respond unforeseen situations. Consequently, by using the ontological emergence, we have the possibility of creating temporary ontologies that are used to solve a particular situation in the city, while permanent ontologies allow addressing repetitive situations, from which MiSCi may have learning processes, to improve the responses of the smart city in similar situations.

In particular, MiSCi is deployed as a distributed middleware, this feature allows to deal with scalability and performance troubles, besides, it is coordinated with the core systems of the Smart City, to find solutions to situations that arises in the local city. This feature allows to accomplish the main objectives of a Smart City.

5   Future Works

MiSCi is an ongoing research project, this means that the prototype is still under development and undergoing controlled tests. Currently, we are still developing some agents like AppA, and CzA, as well as some ontological emergency services. The final stage of the project will be to test MiSCi in real situations. We will test our middleware initially in small towns, to guarantee the correct performance of MiSCi, and then we will continue in big cities.

MiSCi will exploit the prototypes about the services of acquisition of context and quality of context currently in development, and we will execute tests about the trust of data from the sensors that are linked to the nodes of MiSCi.

Finally, future works must include our experiences in data analysis and ambient intelligence, for the construction of knowledge models and smart environments, useful in a smart city. Particularly, MiSCi allows the connection of two paradigms, cloud computing and multiagent systems [7], and according to the model proposed in this paper of a smart city as a multiagent system, the components of a smart system can invoke data analysis services in the cloud, in order to exploit the large amount of data in the city, to generate the knowledge required in their activities to produce smart environments in the city. The ubiquity and the emergence, again, are properties that must be exploited during these developed ones.

Acknowledgements. Dr Aguilar has been partially supported by the Prometeo Project of the Ministry of Higher Education, Science, Technology and Innovation of the Republic of Ecuador.

References

1. Tan, Y., Zhang, C., Mao, Y., Qian, G.: Semantic presentation and fusion framework of unstructured data in smart cites. In: 10th Conference Industrial Electronics and Applications (ICIEA), pp. 897–910 (2015)
2. Pellicer, S., Santa, G., Bleda, A.L., Maestre, R., Jara, A.J., Gomez, A.: A global perspective of smart cities: a survey. In: Seventh International Conference, Innovative Mobile and Internet Services in Ubiquitous Computing (IMIS), pp. 439–444 (2013)
3. Neirotti, P., De Marco, A., Cagliano, A.C., Mangano, G., Scorrano, F.: Current trends in smart city initiatives: some stylised facts. Cities **38**, 25–36 (2014)
4. Fujiwara, Y., Yamada, K., Tabata, K., Oda, M, Hashimoto, K., Suganuma, T., Georgakopoulos, A.: Context aware services: a novel trend in IoT based research in smart city project. In: IEEE 39th Annual International Computers, Software & Applications Conference, pp. 479–480 (2015)
5. An EU/Japan collaboration to deliver Intelligent Knowledge-as-a-Service. http://iKaaS.com
6. Komninos, N., Bratsas, C., Kakderi, C., Tsarchopoulos, P.: Smart city ontologies: improving the effectiveness of smart city applications. J. Smart Cities **1**, 31–46 (2015)
7. Sánchez, M., Aguilar, J., Cordero, J., Valdiviezo, P., Chamba-Eras, L.: Cloud computing in smart educational environments: application in learning analytics as service. In: Rocha, A., Correia, A., Adeli, H., Reis, L., Mendonça, M. (eds.) New Advances in Information Systems and Technologies. AISC, vol. 444, pp. 993–1002. Springer, Heidelberg (2016)
8. Aguilar, J., Jerez, M., Exposito, E., Villemur, T.: CARMiCLOC: context awareness middleware in cloud computing. In: Latin American Computing Conference (CLEI), pp. 1–10 (2015)
9. Mendonça, M., Aguilar, J., Perozo, N.: Middleware Reflexivo Semántico para Ambientes Inteligentes. In: Segunda Conferencia Nacional de Computación, Informática y Sistemas (CoNCISa), pp. 24–32 (2014)

10. Meier, R., Lee, D.: Context-aware pervasive services for smart cities. In: Ubiquitous Developments in Ambient Computing and Intelligence: Human-Centered Applications, vol. 1, pp 1–16 (2011)
11. Aguilar, J., Rios, A., Hidrobo, F., Cerrada, M.: Sistemas MultiAgentes y sus aplicaciones en Automatización Industrial, Talleres Gráficos, Universidad de Los Andes, Mérida, Venezuela (2013)
12. Poslad, S.: Specifying protocols for multi-agent systems interaction. ACM Trans. Auton. Adapt. Syst. **2**, 15 (2007)
13. Sánchez, M., Aguilar, J., Cordero, J., Valdiviezo, P.: Basic features of a reflective middleware for intelligent learning environment in the cloud (IECL). In: 2015 Asia-Pacific Conference on Computer Aided System Engineering (APCASE 2015), pp. 1–6 (2015)
14. Sánchez, M., Aguilar, J., Cordero, J., Valdiviezo, P.: A smart learning environment based on cloud learning. Int. J. Adv. Inf. Sci. Technol. **39**, 39–52 (2015)
15. Guizzardi, G.: On ontology, ontologies, conceptualizations, modeling languages, and (meta) models. Front. Artif. Intell. Appl. **155**, 18–39 (2007)
16. Vizcarrondo, J., Aguilar, J., Exposito, E., Subias, A.: ARMISCOM: autonomic reflective middleware for management service composition. In: 4th Global Information Infrastructure and Networking Symposium, pp. 1–8. IEEE Communication Society (2012)

Designing Assistive Technologies for Children with Disabilities: A Case Study of a Family Living with a Daughter with Intellectual Disability

Janio Jadán-Guerrero[1(✉)], Ileana Altamirano[1], Hugo Arias[1], and Johann Jadán[2]

[1] Universidad Tecnológica Indoamérica, Quito, Ecuador
janiojadan@uti.edu.ec, ile.28nov@gmail.com,
hugopaf@hotmail.com
[2] Universidad San Francisco de Quito, Quito, Ecuador
jijadan@usfq.edu.ec

Abstract. Children with disabilities are one of the most vulnerable groups of the population. They experience social exclusion and inequity, as do their difficulties to integrate into society. Many families raising children with disabilities try to do everything to improve their quality of life. This paper describes a case study of an Ecuadorian family who was encouraged to integrate Information and Communication Technologies (ICT) in the everyday life of their girl with intellectual and language disabilities. The experience with the most popular technologies at home -Computer, tablet, smartphone, and videogame console- motivated the whole family to adapt and design assistive technologies for their daughter. Their motivation allowed us to find people and institutions who supported the design of ICT for different disabilities: AINIDIU, HELPMI, CANDI, LUCKI, MAGIC GLASS, JADAN VERBAL, TIC@ULA and KITERACY. An interdisciplinary group of experts participated in the development of these technologies: A Computer Engineer, a Phycologist, a blind person, students and Especial Education teachers. Since 2009, about 50 children with disabilities and 20 Especial Education teachers have been involved in the evaluation of the prototypes. With the support of Universidad Indoamérica and Ecuadorian Government, 1500 children with visual impairment were benefited with the software AINIDIU in some provinces of Ecuador. The article describes the history of this great experience.

Keywords: ICT · Assistive technology · Children with disabilities · Quality of life

1 Introduction

Families raising children with disabilities experience some problems in society. Among the critical difficulties are social exclusion, health, financial Well-Being, relationships, communication and education [1]. These difficulties tend to have somewhat less sustainable daily routine and affect the quality of life of the family.

The care of children with disabilities is a difficult and draining task, and this responsibility is often taken over the mother. She is challenged to develop different activities

© Springer International Publishing AG 2016
R. Valencia-García et al. (Eds.): CITI 2016, CCIS 658, pp. 254–268, 2016.
DOI: 10.1007/978-3-319-48024-4_20

at home to strengthen the therapies that children receive from their teachers or therapists [2]. The activities of everyday family life vary in the line of the needs, interests and competencies of individual family members. For example, the daily routine that accommodates the needs of very young children will be different from the daily routine that accommodates the needs and wants of teenagers [3].

This paper describes a case study of an 11-year-old girl with language and moderate intellectual disabilities who inspired her family to adapt and design technology for children with disabilities. She belongs to an Ecuadorian Family of 4. Her father is a Computer Science teacher, her mother is a psychologist specialized in children rehabilitation, her brother is a college student in Electronic Engineer.

The paper highlights the importance to support children with disabilities through technology in their everyday life activities. Assistive technology is vital to helping children with disabilities so that they can develop the necessary skills to solve problems by themselves [4]. According to UNICEF, assistive technology is one of the key elements to advancing inclusion of children with disabilities. This technology includes products and related services that improve the functioning of children with disabilities. It can be instrumental for children's development and health, as well as for participation in various facets of their life. These include communication, mobility, self-care, household tasks, family relationships, education, and engagement in play and recreation. Assistive technology can enhance the quality of life of both children and their families [5]. Access to assistive technology for children with disabilities gives some benefits in education, for example, personal assistance, sign language interpreters, Augmentative and Alternative Communication (AAC) or kits with educational resources, not only at school, but also at home, anyway an inclusive environment for children with disabilities begins at home [3, 5].

In a middle class family, computers, tablets, smartphones, smart TVs or videogame consoles are part of their environment. Children with disabilities like other children have the ability to interact with technology in a natural way [6]. The study focused on exploring general issues related to the use of these technologies into the everyday life activities at home of a family living with a daughter with intellectual disability. The observation of different interactions contributed to understand features for designing emerging assistive Information and Communication Technologies (ICT).

The passion and commitment of the family allowed them to search support in academic and government institutions. In this process the family had the opportunity to meet a visually impaired person, an engineer expert in the use of a computer screen reader and accessible technology. In 2009, the two families came together and coordinated efforts to create assistive technologies to support other parents and caregivers in the everyday life activities of their children.

The rest of the paper is organized as follows: Sect. 2 describes the related work about integration of technology in daily life activities. Section 3 introduces the study background, motivation and experiences in everyday life activities of the family. After that, Sect. 4 details the features of the assistive technologies. Section 5 reveals the results in the design, evaluation and implementation of ICT in society, and finally, Sect. 6 summarizes the conclusions and future work.

2 Related Work

A literature review about assistive technology for Individuals with disabilities summarizes the content analysis of 68 studies (1988–2003). The results presented by the authors reveal that only 15 (22.06 %) studies mentioned family involvement. In the conclusion the authors mentioned that it is imperative that professionals who are working directly with these people and their family members be adequately trained to provide the support and accommodations necessary for people with disabilities to enjoy the full benefits of assistive technologies [18].

Another literature review summarizes the results of 42 empirical studies (1990–2005) focusing on the use of assistive technology as a self-management tool for persons with intellectual disabilities. The author identified studies the effects of technologies on: (a) independent performance of tasks (25 studies), (b) task engagement (5 studies), (c) on task behaviors (4 studies), (d) accuracy of task performance (3 studies), (e) initiation of tasks (2 studies), (f) transitioning between tasks (2 studies), (g) fluency of work performance (1 study). The experimental evaluation was carried out with different devices in daily life activities, such as picture prompt, audio cassette players, hand held computer-based systems and appliances. The conclusion of the study was that technology is an effective tool for providing better quality of live, decrease dependence on others, and promote greater inclusion in community settings and daily activities [19].

A systematic literature review about promoting the use of assistive technology devices by young children with disabilities indicates that the devices are likely to promote child engagement in typically occurring learning activities and permit children to perform functions that otherwise might prove difficult or even impossible without the use of devices. The types of devices that were the focus of investigation included: (a) Switch interface devices, (b) powered mobility devices, (c) computer devices, (d) augmentative communication devices, and (e) weighted and pressure vests [20].

An interesting article discusses a home-centered approach to the use of assistive technology. The study addressed two questions: (a) How can assistive technology interventions for children with disabilities be successfully implemented in the home environment? And (b) How can the family system be considered in the use of assistive technology in the home environment? The article provides suggestions for working with families in the process of identifying and providing assistive technologies for young children in the home environment and the authors conclude that all children, including those with intellectual disabilities, should be given opportunities to develop the attitudes, abilities, and skills to take control over their lives. One of the most important environments where this begins for the child is found in his or her own home [21].

In a systematic literature review about designing technology for developmentally diverse children the author analyzed 88 studies (2003–2014). The results revealed that the most prominent context was the school (47 %), followed by therapy centers or rehabilitation institutes (11 %), and the home (8 %) [22].

Based on the results of these studies, we can observe the importance to integrate assistive technology in daily life activities of children with disabilities. The families are a key element to promote the use of assistive technology at home. In this scenery the study aimed to explore the use of emergent technologies, such as, computer, tablet, smartphone, videogame console and sensors. The experience obtained into a family with a daughter with intellectual disability encouraged to take advance of the strengths of the members in order to adapt and design new assistive technologies.

3   Background

The goal of this section is to present a brief retrospective of two families who have a member with disabilities. The authors, as part of both families, describe their motivations and experiences about the relationship between technology and the daily routine activities at home. They focus on the interaction and emotional behavior of the member with disabilities and summarize some observational findings collected during the last 7 years (2009–2016).

3.1   Motivation

The motivation of this work is based on the experience of two families who have a member with disabilities. The first family has an 11-year-old girl with language and moderate intellectual disabilities. In the second family the parent has visual impaired disability. Both families have experienced difficulties and barriers in the society or the education system. Their members have witnessed the lack of opportunities for personal development and social inclusion, especially in Ecuador and Costa Rica where this research is carried out.

Each family has its own history and particular circumstances. The girl was born with craniosynostosis which caused her skull to fuse prematurely, leaving no room for her brain to develop. It is possible that this incident was the cause for her disability. On the other hand, the father of the second family lost his sight in a car accident. He affirmed that it was a traumatic experience and it was not easy to accept, but with the support of his family he was able to overcome some difficulties. The problems and frustrations experienced by both families encouraged them to enhance their quality of live.

The girl received different therapies since her problem was detected. Her family supported in her rehabilitation with physical, language, hippo therapy and even dolphin therapy. All these initiatives allowed her to grow up in an environment with many challenges. Like other children she developed needs and interests, among them the interaction with technology.

On the other hand, the visual impaired parent encouraged to learn the use of a computer screen reader, a software application that identifies and interprets what is being displayed on the computer screen. This assistive technology helped him to develop some daily life activities, such as, listen music, read news or explore the internet. He discovered different ways to interact with laptops, scanners, smarthphones, tablets, speaking clock and emerging apps to identify colors, bills, lights and others.

In 2009 two families joined by their circumstances and it gave them the opportunity to coordinated efforts to design assistive emerging technologies in benefit to other families in similar situation.

3.2 Exploring the Interaction with Technology in Daily Life Activities

In this section we describe an exploratory case study of the experiences of both families using technology. In Human Computer Interaction (HCI), an exploratory case study is frequently used to investigate specific situations and collect data to help understand problems and needs of new solutions [7]. Typically researchers use some methods of observation to look for patterns of activity, and general user concern [8, 9]. However, as part of the research group and families at the same time we did not design a formal case study, although we used some methods in an informal way to collect perceptions and experiences in our own daily living.

In the case of the girl with disabilities we used a video camera in some situations to capture data for later analysis, as well as non-structured interviews with the rest of members of the family. In the case of the parent with visual disability we use non-structured interviews to gather information about his experiences with technology in his work, studies and daily living with his family.

Technology has become a pervasive element of society. People use technology for communication, work, education and entertainment [10]. The case study focused to explore the experiences of both families in these contexts. First, we summarize the relevant experiences in the family of the girl with disabilities. After that, we summarize the experiences of the father with visual disability.

The interest to explore how the girl used to interact with technology began in 2007, when she was 6 years old. In that year she started to study in a regular school and complementarily she was receiving language therapies. We have observed the girl had difficulties in learning read. This fact motivated to the whole family to help her in that process. Figure 1 shows some daily life activities where the technology was present.

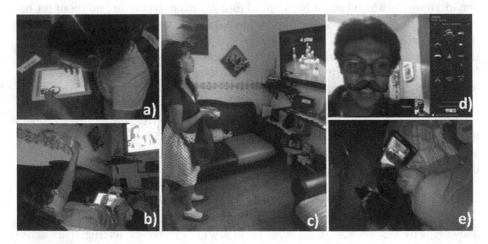

Fig. 1. (a) Learning to read with tablet apps, (b) Watching TV with her father on videoconference, (c) Playing with game console, (d) Her brother interacting with Hangouts, (e) Her father tales a story though a videoconference.

Figure 1a shows an activity designed by the mother, in which the objects at home were labeled with their name. The goal was the girl relates the objects with the word. The whole family was responsible to read and point the name wrote in the label. The brother complemented this idea with some apps downloaded in a tablet and he taught the basic interactions. Eventually we realized that she discovered several types of interaction, such as, tap, drag, double tap, long press, scale down and two-finger rotation.

Figure 1b shows the girl enjoying of her favorite TV program. When the girl wanted to watch TV, she used to request for help to any member of her family, due to the difficulties to change channels or play a movie in a DVD. We observed that she learnt to identify her favorite channel with remote control or operate another remote control for DVD player, as well to turn on/off the electronic devices.

Figure 1c shows the girl playing with a Wii console. She really enjoyed when the whole family shared entertainment activities with her. She learned to be patient and respect her turn in videogames. The entertainment activities were exploited to promote an inclusive environment with other children and relatives.

Figure 1d shows a session of a videoconference established with Google Hangouts between the parent and son. The parent motivated to know more about assistive technologies started in 2013 a Doctoral Program at University of Costa Rica. The family was separated for three years. The first six months the software Skype was used to share time in family. Usually the connection was started by father, mother or brother to the girl. After that time the girl discovered how to run Skype by herself. We observed that she learnt to identify the logo of the app in the tablet. This experience motivated her family to research other ways of interactions in order to give a sense of presence of the parent [6]. The brother discovered some interactive applications on Google Hangouts, such as, Google effects, shared blackboard or share a YouTube video. This functionality was tested by both in different activities, such as, solve math or physics problems over the shared blackboard.

Figure 1e shows a session of a Google Hangouts videoconference at bedtime between father and daughter. The functions provided by the tool made an enjoyable time for the girl. The parent used to create stories based on YouTube videos or interactive apps.

In order to know the experiences in the everyday life activities of the family with the parent with visual disability, we used a non-structured interview to explore his experiences. He related that the use of the screen reader JAWS (Job Access With Speech) was fundamental for his development in his academic and professional life. After he lost his sight he began using a computer running the Windows operating system. He learnt to use accessibility programs, as part of his daily routine. He started to study at university where throughout a business career used Microsoft Word to create documents, take notes, and complete tests. He also used Microsoft Excel spreadsheet software to organize information and perform calculations for math and science lessons. After that he continued his studies with a Master Business Administration.

Although he became a professional and overcame some barriers in the academic life, he had experienced difficulties to get a job. People not believe that he can work like anyone. He has worked in odd jobs installing and configuring software in government institution related to visual impaired disabilities. He has also given courses of the use of assistive technology, such as, JAWS and NVDA (NonVisual Desktop Access).

Respect to the emerging technologies he said "I am now able to read e-mail on my smarthphone, select messages, read books, explore the web or post something in Facebook"

The interaction with electronic devices at home is like any person. His family, wife and 5-year daughter helps that the things be in the same place. It helps him to identify the different objects or food. With some apps in his smarthphone he can identify the color of the clothes or if a light is turned on. He shares time with his daughter using accessible games. In addition, both father and daughter interact with a computer or tablet to practice vowels, colors, numbers and educational games.

These life experiences of both families made possible to understand some problems and challenges in the daily life routine. In the following section we can summarize some insight and perceptions.

3.3 Observational Findings

This section provides a brief overview of some of the insights we gained living with people with disabilities. We experienced emotions and enjoyable time using technology for entertainment, education and communication. We observed some skills developed by the girl. The videoconference software provided sense of presence of a familiar living at a distance. With the help of technology, the members of the family created an inclusive environment between them and other relatives.

We observed that the happiness of the girl was evident and her emotional behavior was contagious to the rest of the members of the family. The girl shared time with her parents and her brother watching educational TV programs, movies or playing video-games. The girl learned to use the devices by herself and it gave a feedback to think if entertainment technology can be used for caregivers as powerful learning tool, especially in free time.

In the interaction with a tablet the girls were engaged by multimedia and interactive tools. These experiences showed us that if children are in a pleasant environment, they can learn. The appropriate assistive technology can be a powerful tool to increase a child's independence and improve their participation in society. An educated child with a disability supported by assistive technology will have greater opportunities for educa-tion, resulting in less dependence on their parents [5].

At the highest level, we tried to understand the experiences of the everyday life activities related with technology including their judgments about the benefits to enhance their quality of life. This rewarding experience has developed our cooperation and our commitment to design assistive emerging technologies.

4   Designing Assistive Technologies

Designing technologies for children with disabilities is highly complex due to the diver-sity of needs, information of interest, the size of the user population involved, the research philosophy, and the experience of the researchers involved. [8]. However, we challenged to merge our knowledge in order to design assistive technology for families raising children with disabilities.

We describe eight assistive technologies developed by the member of two families and collaborators who organized an interdisciplinary group. The first four were developed in Ecuador between 2009 and 2013. Figure 2 shows a graphical representation of them. The others were developed in Costa Rica between 2013 and 2016 (see Fig. 3).

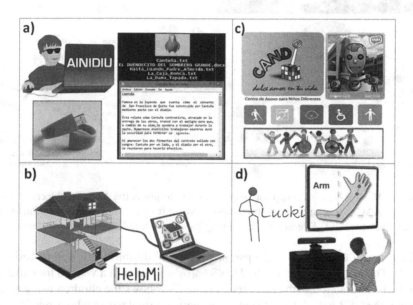

Fig. 2. (a) *AINIDIU* is a bracelet with software to assist visually impaired children, (b) *HELPMI* is an AAC to communicate and control electric devices at home, (c) *CANDI* is a framework to share educational resources and promote teleworking, (d) *LUCKI* is interactive software to teach the body parts.

4.1 AINIDIU

(AINIDIU, for its acronym in Spanish "*Agente Inteligente para NIños con DIscapcidad vIsual*") is an intelligent agent for visually impaired children. The software plays the role of computer assistant in training computer skills for blind and visually impaired children. The system uses the metaphor of a "virtual friend" with whom a visually impaired child can interact with some learning activities. Like a friend AINIDIU software can be carried on a USB bracelet everywhere. When the child inserts the USB bracelet in any computer, the software runs automatically. One character with a voice synthetized interacts with a child through playful and learning activities. The system contains a number of challenges, and gives visually impaired children opportunity to explore and identify the keyboard and basic functions of the operative system [11].

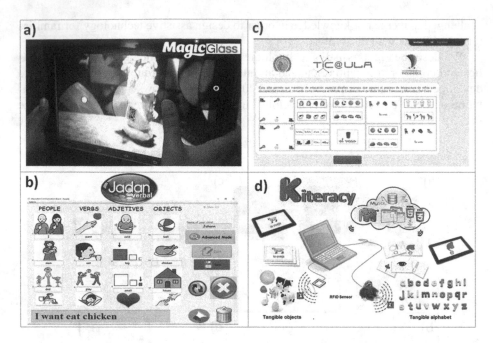

Fig. 3. (a) *Magic Glass* is an app for Android tablets to guess the name of objects, (b) *Jadan Verbal* is an AAC to communicate with synthesized voice,(c) *Tic@ula* is a web platform to design and share flash cards, (d) *Kiteracy* is a kit of tangible objects and letters to support literacy.

The personal experience of the parent with visual disability allowed to design this software. The idea was based on the JAWS software, but with a version for children to facilitate the interaction with computers. Figure 2–a shows the children using a laptop computer, the USB bracelet and the interface with a virtual parrot who is reading a tale. This virtual friend has the capacity to interact with children through "questions and answers" game.

4.2 HELPMI

(HELPMI, for its acronym in Spanish "*Herramienta que Emula Lenguaje de Palabras Mediante Imágenes*") is a communication dashboard through images. The system has both hardware and software components. The hardware is an electronic circuit connected between a USB port of computer and a power strip. The software displays a set of images in the screen of a computer, some of them customized to the child (e.g. actions and photographs of electrical devices connected to the power strip). The system was designed with the metaphor of "universal remote control" to assist children with language impairment through a synthesized voice to communicate with family members or control some electrical devices through the computer or a tablet [12]. The system integrates voice recognition to support children with physical limitations.

4.3 CANDI

(CANDI, for its acronym in Spanish *"Centro de Apoyo a Niños Diferentes"*) is a framework designed to share information, guidelines and assistive technologies for families raising children with disabilities [12]. The Framework has a user interface and configuration module to administer the information and resources. It was developed in response to needs of families with children with disabilities. The goal was to create a space where teachers, parents and caregivers can download assistive technologies or general information to support the education of their children. In addition, the idea for the framework was to promote teleworking for people with disabilities.

4.4 LUCKI

(LUCKI, for its acronym in Spanish *"Lúdica en Universos controlados por Kinect para Inclusión"*) is software designed with a Natural User Interface (NUI) to teach reading to children with intellectual disabilities. The system uses the Kinect sensor, which uses technology to track people movement and combines a depth sensing camera to recognize the parts of the body of a person. The system identifies the part of the body and the word with the name is showed in the screen. The idea was born from the observation in the case study when the girls enjoyed playing Wii Console with her family. The system is still being developed and we are planning to integrate a playful activity. The goal with the system is propitiate the integration with other children without disabilities into a classroom while they learn to read [13]. Figure 2d shows an example when a child moves his arm.

4.5 MAGIC GLASS

Magic Glass is an app for Android tablets for storytelling. The app was designed with the metaphor of the "crystal ball" that can predict the future. In the same way the software "guess the name of objects" and tell stories. The app scans QR codes previously labeled in physical objects at home, such as, furniture, toys or electronic devices. The app has two interfaces; in the administration interface the parents can generate labels with QR codes. In the configuration the parents link each label with the URL of a video or image. The user interface enables the camera of a tablet and shows the environment like a crystal. When the system identifies a QR Label it draws a green box in the screen over the label. If a child closes the tablet to the QR label the tablet vibrates and launches the video.

This app was finalist in the contest of innovative toys[1]. Figure 2a shows an example when the girl points the tablet toward a princess doll to watch a video of some story.

---

[1] 'Citi microemprendedor del año' 2015 https://www.youtube.com/watch?v=S594XR41Weo.

4.6 JADAN VERBAL

Jadan Verbal is a web Augmentative and Alternative Communication (AAC) for computers and mobile devices. This web platform shows pictograms to support the communication of children with language impairments. The system runs on a browser and can be personalized to the child needs. The child selects multiple images to build a sentence, which can be interpreted by the system through a synthesized voice. The software has two interfaces, the first is a user interface with pictograms grouped in four categories: subjects, verbs, adjectives and objects. Each pictogram has a word which can be read using text-to-speech algorithms. The second one is an administration interface in which parents or caregivers can configure the language, pictograms and words. Figure 2b shows the sentence "I want to eat chicken" built with the pictograms.

4.7 TIC@ULA

(Tic@ula, for its acronym in Spanish "Tecnologías de la Infomación y la Comunicación para las aulas de Costa Rica") is a virtual repository of Digital Learning Objects based on the IEEE LOM (Learning Object Metadata) standard. The web repository centralizes educational resources related to reading methods [14].

This web repository is the result of the lack of educational resources for teaching reading in Costa Rica. A survey was carried out to collect data in an exploratory study about literacy methods, educational resources and technological tools used in children with intellectual disabilities. Figure 2c shows the interface of Tic@ula where teachers can download cards or create an account to design their own cards and share.

4.8 KITERACY

Kiteracy (Kit for Literacy) is an educational kit designed to improve the literacy process of children with Down syndrome by enabling higher levels of interaction. The kit is based on two Spanish literacy methods: global and phonics. The kit incorporates a Tangible User Interface (TUI), which has physical objects and 3D letters with a RFID (Radio Frequency Identification) tag. These objects can be built with a 3D printer or low cost toys. A puppet bear with RFID reader can identify the code of each object and a retrieval algorithm connects to Tic@ula through a web service. The information is presented on any computer, tablet or smartphone with a user session. The system uses natural language processing techniques to play phonemes and words audio. It incorporates Text-to-Speech libraries or MP3 audio with different voices. This work was published in [15, 16]. Figure 2d shows the general schema of Kiteracy.

Table 1 shows a summary of the features of the assistive technologies developed by two families.

Table 1. Summary of assistive technologies developed by two families

ICT	Target group	Advantages
AINIDIU	Visual impairment	Children can familiarize with computers though synthesized voice
HELPMI	Language impairment	Children can communicate with other people and operate devices at home by a computer
CANDI	Teachers, parents and caregivers	Families with children with disabilities can access to educational resources
LUCKI	Physical and cognitive disabilities	Children can practice cognitive and rehabilitation activities while learn to read
MAGIC GLASS	Language impairment	Children can learn the name of the objects with a tablet and QR codes
JADAN VERBAL	Language impairment	Children can use an AAC to communicate with others
TIC@ULA	Intellectual disability	Teachers and parents can design, share or download educational resource for literacy
KITERACY	Intellectual disability	Children can learn to read with tangible objects and enhance interaction

5   Impact on Society

All of the assistive ICTs described in the last section have been the result of the needs in the daily life activities of both families. This effort was made in benefit of our families, however we experienced the involvement of many people and seems to be that together have made a positive impact on society.

In Ecuador neighbors and teachers of the school of the girl were motivated to contribute with our cause. We needed to create contents for AINIDIU, for that, we met with an Ecuadorian author of children's literature who gave the rights of his books. With the participation of 10 children and 5 parents we created the audio book "El duendecito del sombrero grande". All of them were involved in the story as actors with their voices. The audiobook was the winner in a Latin-American contest organized by Club de Reporteros 3D FATLA (Fundación para la Actualización de la Tecnología en Latino América)[2].

Afterwards, the Government of Ecuador took interest in AINIDIU software. The Vice President of the Republic, FENCE (National Federation for blind People) and Universidad Indoamérica signed a tripartite agreement to install the software in about

---

[2] Audiobook "El Duendecito del sombrero grande", September 2013 https://soundcloud.com/user126357461/el-duendecito-del-sombrero.

1500 laptop computers. This fact opened the opportunity that 1500 children with visual disability and their families have assistive technologies in their homes. At the same time students and teachers of Universidad Indoamérica were the responsible to teach in the use of the software in 22 provinces of Ecuador [11].

This rewarding experience helped that colleagues and authorities from Universidad Indoamérica develop new initiatives, among them the development of virtual web platform for people with visual disability, and the development of the software TEVI, an Augmentative and Alternative Communication (AAC) for computers. This software was designed to facilitate communication and learning for children with language problems caused by a physical disability. Teachers and students carried out an experimental evaluation with 75 children (80 % with physical and language disabilities) in two provinces of Ecuador. This work was published in a Congress of Natural Language Processing in Costa Rica [17].

In Costa Rica, with Tic@ula and Kiteracy assistive technologies we count with the participation of the author of a literacy method for children with intellectual disabilities. In addition, we count with about 10 special education teachers from Universidad de Costa Rica, INIE and PROTEA. In the evaluation there were involved 4 special education teachers, 2 boys and 4 girls also with Down syndrome in Fernando Centeno Güell School in Costa Rica.

In Spain, with Kiteracy we count with the participation of the author of a literacy method for children with Down syndrome from Down 21 in Santander. We carried out an experimental evaluation in ASINDOWN, a special education in Valencia. The participants involved 4 pedagogues, 10 boys and 2 girls with Down syndrome [15, 16].

In the world, after the publications in scientific databases an editor of the RFID Journal published the article "RFID to Bring Literacy to Down Syndrome Children". This article was referenced and translated to Germany and Chinese[3].

6   Conclusion

In this paper, we described a case study of two families with a girl and a parent with disabilities, respectively. The everyday life activities at home helped to understand how assistive ITC can contribute to enhance the quality of life. Based on our observations, we designed novel technologies for children with disabilities.

The design process allowed to know the lack of assistive ICT to support communication, learning and entertainment. The results of evaluation of some ICT conducted to identify that prototypes evaluated in a real context not only assist to children with disabilities, but also support the learning strategies of caregivers and other members of the family. However, it is important to mention that the success of assistive ICT often depends on having a good group of involved people – parents, caregivers, teachers and other children.

---

[3] RFID Journal, http://www.rfidjournal.com/articles/view?13478
Entwickler Magazins, https://entwickler.de/?p=173130 RFID World, http://3g.rfid-world.com.cn/NewsView.aspx/91312, 22-Sep-2015.

It is important to note that the change of the attitude of families raising children with disabilities, can help create an inclusive and enabling learning environment. In this case of study, a girl with disabilities gave the possibility to do a positive impact in society.

Since 2009, about 50 children with disabilities and 20 Especial Education teachers have involved in the design and evaluation process. Some of these technologies have impacted in about 1500 children with disabilities in Ecuador and there is a potential impact in other countries.

Our future work will focus on the debug of these assistive technologies, as well as the search of partners to support the transfer of technology. We wish share the ICTs with families or schools through an open source and tutorial of use.

References

1. Brown, R.I., Keumja, H., Shearer, J., Wang, M., Wang, S.: Family quality of life in several countries: results and discussion of satisfaction in families where there is a child with a disability. Soc. Indic. Res. Ser. **41**, 17–32 (2011)
2. Kober, R.: Enhancing the Quality of Life of People with Intellectual Disabilities. Social Indicators Research Series, pp. 81–87. Springer, Heidelberg (2014)
3. McConnell, D., Breitkreuz, R., Uditsky, B., Sobsey, R., Rempel, G., Savage, A., Parakkal, M.: children with disabilities and the fabric of everyday family life (2013)
4. Plowman, L.: Researching young children's everyday uses of technology in the family home. Interact. Comput. **27**, 36–46 (2015)
5. UNICEF: Assistive Technology for Children with Disabilities: Creating Opportunities for Education, Inclusion and Participation A discussion paper. World Health Organiztaion (2015)
6. Yarosh, S., Abowd, G.D.: Mediated parent-child contact in work-separated families, pp. 1185–1194 (2011)
7. Lazer, J., Fenq, J.H., Hochheiser, H.: Research Methods in Human-Computer Interaction. Wiley, New York (2010)
8. Druin, A.: The role of children in the design of new technology. Behav. Inf. Technol. **21**, 1–25 (2002)
9. Hutchinson, H., Mackay, W.E., et al.: Technology probes: inspiring design for and with families. In: Proceedings of SIGCHI Conference Human Factors in Computing Systems, CHI 2003, pp. 17–24 (2003)
10. Fails, J., Guha, M.L., Horn, M., Isola, S.: Technology for today's family. In: CHI 2012 Extended Abstract Human Factors in Computing Systems, pp. 2739–2742 (2012)
11. Jadán-Guerrero, J.: An experience of technology transfer success of software for children with disabilities. CLEI Electron. J. **17**, 1–12 (2014)
12. Guerrero, J.: AINIDIU, CANDI, HELPMI: ICTs of a personal experience. In: 2012 Workshop on Engineering Applications, WEA 2012, pp. 1–7 (2012)
13. Jadán-Guerrero, J.: LUCKI: A non-traditional user interface for SEN children. Dr. Consort. In: 7th International Conference on Ubiquitous Comput. Ambient Intelligence (UCAmI 2013) (2013)
14. Jadán-Guerrero, J., Guerrero, L.A.: A virtual repository of learning objects to support literacy of SEN children. Rev. Iberoam. Tecnol. del Aprendiz. **10**, 168–174 (2015)
15. Jadán-Guerrero, J., Jaen, J., Carpio, M.Á., Guerrero, L.A.: Kiteracy: a kit of tangible objects to strengthen literacy skills in children with down syndrome. In: Proceedings of the 14th International Conference on Interaction Design and Children (IDC '15), pp. 315–318. ACM, New York (2015). http://dx.doi.org/10.1145/2771839.2771905

16. Jadán-Guerrero, J., Guerrero, L., López, G., Cáliz, D., Bravo, J.: Creating TUIs using RFID sensors–a case study based on the literacy process of children with down syndrome. Sensors (Basel). **15**, 14845–14863 (2015)
17. Jácomne, L., Jadán-Guerrero, J.: TEVI: Teclado virtual como herramienta de asistencia en la comunicación y el aprendizaje de personas con problemas del lenguaje vinculados a la discapacidad motriz. Rev. Artes y Let. Káñina, Universida Costa Rica, pp. 1–13 (2016)
18. Alper, S., Raharinirina, S.: Assistive technology for individuals with disabilities: a review and synthesis of the literature. J. Spec. Educ. Technol. **2**(21), 47–64 (2006)
19. Mechling, L.: Assistive technology as a self-management tool for prompting students with intellectual disabilities to initiate and complete daily tasks: a literature review. Division Autism Dev. Disabil. **42**(3), 251–269 (2007)
20. Dunst, C., Trivette, C., Hamby, D., Simkus, A.: Systematic review of studies promoting the use of assistive technology devices by young children with disabilities. Res. Brief **8**(1), 1–21 (2013)
21. Brotherson, M., Cook, C., Parette, H.: A home-centered approach to assistive technology provision for young children with disabilities. Focus Autism Dev. Disabil. **11**(2), 87–95 (1996)
22. Börjesson, P., Barendregt, W., Eriksson, E., Torgersson, O.: Designing technology for and with developmentally diverse children - a systematic literature review, focus on autism and other developmental disabilities. Interact. Des. Child. IDC **2015**, 79–88 (2015)

ADL-MOOC: Adaptive Learning Through Big Data Analytics and Data Mining Algorithms for MOOCs

Juan Miguel Gómez-Berbís and Ángel Lagares-Lemos[✉]

Departamento de Informática, Universidad Carlos III de Madrid, Getafe, Spain
{juanmiguel.gomez,angel.lagares}@uc3m.es

Abstract. Massive Open Online Courses (MOOCs) have had an impact in current higher education as an online phenomenon gathering momentum over the past couple of years.

However, one of the major challenges for MOOCs is capitalizing their potential as a tremendous data source for adaptive learning, whose large datasets growing exponentially are size-wise up to what has been recently named as "Big Data".

In this paper, we present a specific proof-of-concept oriented approach for enriching adaptive learning by applying Big Data Analytics and Data Mining algorithms for MOOCs in order to facilitate subject- and context-sensitive teaching and learning experiences, which results in an innovative technology-enhanced learning solution for intuitive and personalised interactions of students and teachers with educational contents, tools and data.

Keywords: MOOCs · Ontologies · Big data · Data mining

1 Introduction

Recent changes in higher education on the Web through Massive Open Online Courses (MOOCs) are raising a number of concerns on how this type of online education could be leveraged.

As an online phenomenon gathering momentum over the past few years, a MOOC integrates the facilitation of an acknowledged expert in a field of study, and a collection of freely accessible online resources. Nevertheless, they also have been imposing a number of challenges on how to benefit from particular Big Data size datasets to enhance adaptive learning. From an Information Theory perspective, Big Data datasets are covered by a number of strategies trying to increase the quality of information retrieval, from query expansion to the collaborative filtering or multifaceted browsing [1] or relying on Semantic Technologies cornerstones, ontologies [2], whose maintenance and complexity have also been deemed as very cost-intensive and not productive, not fulfilling expectations, leading the user in many cases to frustration.

Big Data consists on large datasets that grow exponentially and become difficult to work with, i.e. Big Datasets. These Big Datasets have brought into the arena scale and computational capacity issues into senior but mature technology, such as RDBMS

© Springer International Publishing AG 2016
R. Valencia-García et al. (Eds.): CITI 2016, CCIS 658, pp. 269–280, 2016.
DOI: 10.1007/978-3-319-48024-4_21

[3]. Its proliferation has triggered new storage and data management technologies such as NoSQL databases [4].

The challenge remains then in shifting the quality of adaptive learning by collecting, analyzing and deciding on Big Datasets provided by MOOCs - since both the MOOcs and the Big Data approaches are evolving to a more mature state. The analysis of learning data is called Learning Analytics and it is one of the main techniques applied in ADL-MOOC.

Increased "on-line" learning brings an unprecedented opportunity to transform the education system into a student-centered system; ADL-MOOC wants to take a step further with the aim to provide efficient teaching and to enable it to create a differentiating value against potential competitors. This difference should be based on improved efficiency in learning and generating greater success in learning, based on this two-fold differentiation. The ADL-MOOC goal is to effectively customize educational content adapted to the different needs of students, allowing all students to learn at their own pace and in a way that is appropriate to their circumstances, thus obtaining the full potential of each student.

In this paper, we hereby propose a platform built on Big Data Analytics and Data Mining algorithms to draft a potential software-based proof-of-concept.

The remainder of the paper is organized as follows. In Sect. 2 we discuss MOOCs as the underlying data source model of our approach. In Sect. 3 we describe "Big Data" and "Big Datasets". In Sect. 4 we describe how Data Mining can be added and both approaches are coupled together as well as their breakthroughs for data organization management and efficiency. In Sect. 5 we show our ADL- MOOC proof-of-concept implementation and the first preliminary results of the evaluation of our prototype. Section 6 spans over and binds together a number of related works. Finally, Sect. 7 concludes the paper and outlines our future work.

2 Massive Open Online Course

Cornier [5] defines the Massive Open Online Course (MOOC) as an online phenomenon gathering momentum over the past few years, a MOOC integrates the connectivity of social networking, the facilitation of an acknowledged expert in a field of study, and a collection of freely accessible online resources.

The academic courses are free to take notwithstanding; learners may sometimes pay an institution to receive credit. Usually, all the work within the course is shared with everyone else: readings, discussions, videos and repurposing of material, to mention a few. One of the biggest gains from participating in a MOOC is the network of connections formed between all the elements that make up the course [6].

Furthermore, a MOOC generally carries no fees, no prerequisites other than Internet access and interest, no predefined expectations for participation, and no formal accreditation [7].

Institutions like MIT, Harvard, Stanford, Princeton, and Caltech have recently offered online courses. These are not off-curriculum pet projects but rather up-to-date degree courses offered simultaneously to a few tuition-paying students on campus and to thousands of would-be learners auditing online. (At least for now, only the tuition payers earn credits toward a degree.) Most of these courses get a few thousand online participants, although an artificial-intelligence MOOC given by Stanford in late 2011 filled a whopping 160 000 virtual seats [8].

The application of Semantic Web technologies such as RDF, SPARQL, URIs, among others, and the correct use of its architecture and standards provides an environment that allows the performing of various operations among which the query of data and obtaining inferences through vocabularies are included.

3   Learning Analytics

Learning Analytics (LA) is a significant area of technology-enhanced learning that has emerged during the last decade, aiming to address challenges related to online learning and specifically to adaptive learning. The Society for Learning Analytics Research (SoLAR[1]) defined Learning Analytics as the measurement, collection, analysis and reporting of data about learners and their contexts, for purposes of understanding and optimising learning and the environment in which it occurs.

Approaches to learning analytics include social network analytics and discourse analytics [9, 10]. Discourse analytics are a relatively recent addition to the learning analytics toolset, but they draw on extensive previous work in areas such as exploratory dialogue, latent semantic analysis [11] and computer-supported argumentation [12].

The term 'social learning analytics' includes content analytics – recommender systems and automated methods of examining, indexing and filtering online media assets in order to guide learners through the ocean of available resources [13]. These analytics take on a social aspect when they draw upon tags, ratings and metadata supplied by learners [14]. Disposition analytics focus on the experience, motivation and intelligences that influence responses to learning opportunities [15], are socialized when the emphasis is on the learner engaged in a mentoring or learning relationship.

The development of social learning analytics represents a move away from data driven investigation towards more strongly grounded research in the learning sciences and, increasingly, dealing with the complexities of lifelong learning that takes place in a variety of contexts. Building up a holistic picture of student progress and taking sentiment into account in order to enable 'computer-based systems to interact with students in emotionally supportive ways' is now seen as a real possibility [16]. New tools such as the GRAPPLE Visualisation Infrastructure Service (GVIS) do not deal with just one VLE, but can extract data from different parts of a learner's Personal Learning Environment (PLE) and employ these data to support metacognitive skills such as self-reflection [17].

Analytics tools and techniques that focus on the social pedagogical aspect of learning are required. Numerous techniques have been developed outside of the education system, often from business intelligence research. In other instances, the tools used for analysis have not scaled with the increase in data size or sophistication of analytics

---

[1] http://www.solaresearch.org/.

models. For example, discourse analysis has a long history in educational research [18]. However, dramatic increases in the size of discoursed data sets, such as those generated in large online courses, can overwhelm manual coding. In response, to automated analysis of discourse De Liddo et al. build on existing models while scaling to accommodate the analysis of larger data sets in [9].

Some analytics techniques, such as early warning systems [19], attention metadata [20], recommender systems [21], tutoring and learner models [22], and network analysis [23], are already in use in education. A few papers in LAK11 presented analytics approaches that emphasized new techniques, such as participatory learning and reputation mechanisms [14], recommender systems improvement [13], and cultural considerations in analytics [24].

4 Big Data and Big Datasets

A substantial number of business and technology trends are disrupting the traditional data management and processing landscape. "Big data" is rapidly emerging as the preferred solution, since it consists of datasets that grow so large that they become awkward to work with using on-hand database management tools. Difficulties include capture, storage, search, sharing, analytics and visualizing [25].

Enterprises should not delay implementation just because of the technical nature of big data analytics. As a number of projects matures and BI tool support improves, the complexity of implementing big data analytics will reduce. The risk of implementing this technology will be reduced by adapting existing architectural principles and patterns to the new technology and changing requirements rather than rejecting them.

Big data analytics and the Apache Hadoop open source project [26] are rapidly emerging as the preferred solution to address business and technology trends that are disrupting traditional data management and processing. Enterprises can gain a competitive advantage by being early adopters of big data analytics.

5 Data Mining

Due to the increment of data that is stored in the repositories of educative information is necessary the use of Methods for Knowledge Discovery in databases (KDD). The KDD Methods include procedures for data query and extraction; they also provide functionalities for data cleaning, data analysis, and methods of knowledge representation. Some common data mining tasks include the induction of association rules, the discovery of functional relationships (classification and regression) and the exploration of groups of similar data objects in clustering [27].

The data mining techniques can be classified according to different views, including the kinds of knowledge to be discovered, the kinds of databases to be mined, and the kinds of techniques to be adopted [28].

One of the most widely used techniques in data mining are decision trees due to its flexibility and understandability However, there are other advanced techniques that are used in data mining, both in classification and other areas of automatic data exploration, well-known methods [29], such as:

- Bayesian classifier/Naive Bayes
- Neural networks
- Support vector machines
- Association rule mining
- Rule-based classification
- k-nearest neighbor
- Rough sets
- Clustering algorithms
- Genetic algorithms

Data mining is currently used in several domains among which we include Science and Engineering.

6   Architecture and Implementation

The combination of Big Data and Map-Reduce algorithms with Data Mining techniques on our proposed prototype result provides a large set of filtered data based on search criteria.

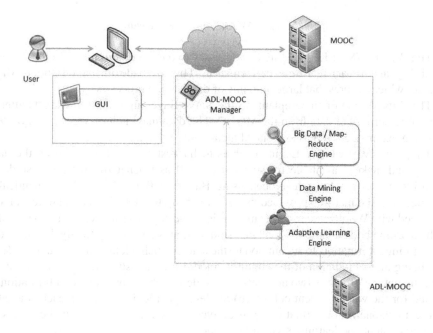

Fig. 1. ADL-MOOC software architecture subsystem distribution

Firstly, through Map-Reduce algorithms, we will filter the behavior of students and categorize them following a particular pattern. Secondly, through Data Mining techniques we will classify, cluster and analyze the behavior of the MOOC students.

The ADL-MOOC software architecture component distribution is shown in Figs. 1 and 2. As it can be seen the system is composed of the GUI and the server components. More concretely, in the server there are three main modules: Big Data/Map Reduce engine, Data Mining Engine and the Adaptive Learning Engine.

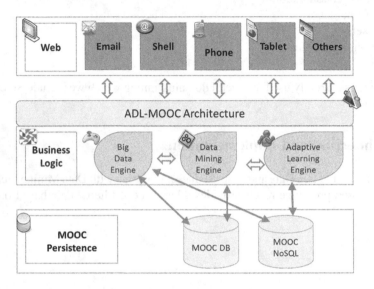

Fig. 2. ADL-MOOC - layer architecture

The Big Data/Map-Reduce Engine addresses two main requirements in the system, scalability and (near) real-time performance. This is made through Hadoop Map-Reduce, which ensures that large amounts of data can be processed.

The Data Mining Engine implements the Naïve Bayes algorithms to extract patterns from large corpora of data from the MOOC. The data may include videos, audio files, texts (e.g. exams), as well as associated meta-data.

The Adaptive Learning Engine enables to harvest the information from the data mining and make it available for students as well as teachers/instructors, a student-cognitive model has been developed using Bayesian Belief Networks, semantically enriched with the mark-up provided using Topic Map to allow for linking to resources, combined with WordNet to resolve ambiguities. The cognitive model is an initial model of the learning behaviour of a "standard" student that is adapted on the fly, based on the data-mining information, to accommodate the learning behaviour of a particular student, thus being an instantiation of the cognitive model for each student. Thus, information from the network realises two artefacts: (a) Student Cohort specific, i.e. information is created for the whole student cohort, (b) Student specific, i.e. based on each student's profile a personalised information set is derived. This allows the informed changes of learning content and learning style of the student.

This software architecture yields a new ADL-MOOC system which will be able to improve, extend and build on the Adaptive Learning Engine results. The GUI is prepared to be displayed in different ways such as web, email, shell, smartphone, tables or smartTVs.

An example of how ADL-MOOC would work is described as follows: Let us suppose that Peruvian students who live in Lima and particularly in "Los Naranjos" area could be classified through the Big Data Engine as very talented and interested in a particular Financial Engineering MOOC, like the ones found in Coursera. Through Data Mining, according to other parameters such as other higher education degrees, working areas, estimated income and gender, a number of more tailor-made MOOC courses could be offered to them, e.g. Computational Economics or Financial Planning. The enhanced ADL-MOOC would also suggest particular lectures which will be easier for them (since they already took a similar course or simply because part of the course information is redundant).

ADL-MOOC could also relate them with students of a similar profile (a simple Data Mining cluster function), or even suggest further reading, a career-service advice and tutor-supported lectures to those students who could further benefit from a more extended services offered by the MOOC platform.

7 Related Work

Since the work on improving adaptive learning on MOOCs spans over and binds together a number of research initiatives, in this section we describe related work.

Searching has been subject of intensive research but a more concrete survey on filtering search results and optimizing results also yields a remarkable amount of efforts. Following research successfully implemented in the Google search engine [30], a number of search variants related to the work presented have been explored such as using faceted search [31], including its application to multimedia faceted metadata for image search and browsing or navigating RDF data [32].

Collaborative filtering was coined by Goldberg in [33] and it has been extensively used for data-intensive recommendation systems for personalized recommendations for music albums and artists as can be found in Ringo [34]. Active Collaborative Filtering solutions such as the one discussed in [35] focus on one-to- one recommendations and a social collaborative filtering system where users have direct impact in the final process is described in [36]. A similar work has been intended in SITIO, a Social Semantic Recommendation System [37], which combines the use of semantics with socially-oriented collaborative recommendation systems for the discovery and location of Web resources. Also, Semantic Social Collaborative Filtering has been used with FOAF [38].

Researchers are already working on tools that respond to challenges related to LA. Contextualised Attention Metadata (CAM) [39] addressed the problem of collecting and combining data from different tools by providing a method of collection metadata from office tools, web browsers, multi-media players and computer-mediated communication, and bringing these together in an attention repository in order to build a rich source of information about user attention. The LOCO-Analyst [40] educational tool aims to help instructors rethink the quality of the learning content and learning design of the courses they teach. To this end, it provides instructors with feedback about the relevant aspects of the learning process taking place in the online learning environment they use. The provided feedback is based on the analyses of the context data collected in the learning environment. In particular, LOCO-Analyst informs instructors about: (1) the activities the learners performed and/or participated in during the learning process; (2) the usage of the learning content they had prepared and deployed in the online learning environment and (3) the peculiarities of the interactions among members of the online learning community. The SMILI Open Learner Modelling Framework was used to support reflection by providing a method for describing, analyzing and designing open learner models [41]. Social network analysis became increasingly influential and the Social Networks Adapting Pedagogical Practice (SNAPP) [42] tool was developed to aid analysis of interaction patterns on courses, supporting a focus on areas such as learner isolation, creativity and community formation. The Signals tool [43], developed at Purdue University, is well-known by academic analytics and has also been cited as an example of 'action analytics' that led to useful outcomes and 'nudge analytics' that prompt individuals to take action [44]. The Signals project mines large datasets and applies statistical tests in order to predict, while courses are in progress, which students are in danger of falling behind. The aim is to produce actionable intelligence, guiding students to appropriate resources and explaining how to use them. A traffic-signal status display shows students whether things are going well (green), or whether they have been classified as high risk (red) or moderate risk (amber).

Even more numerous are the initiatives related to Big Data and Big Data Mining in the learning field. Big Data Public Private Forum (BIG)[2] is an FP7 project that works on the definition and implementation of a strategy that addresses the necessary effort in research and innovation, and provides a great impetus for the adoption of technology and support actions of the European Commission in the successful implementation of the Big Data economy. As part of this strategy, the results of this project will be used as input for 2020 and remain beyond the project duration. SCAPE Project[3]: Big Data Meets Digital Preservation is a project of the EU FP7 ICT in operation since February 2011. It was initiated in order to address the challenges of preserving digital content worldwide tablets many of which are already in petabyte range through intensive computations combined with scalable monitoring and controlled. In particular, analysis of data and workflow management science play an important role. The benchmarks SCAPE very large collections examined from three different application areas: digital repositories community libraries (including nearly two petabytes of streaming audio and video files from the State Library of Denmark, which is adding more 100 terabytes per year), the contents of the web File community (including more than a petabyte of data), and research data sets of the scientific community (including millions of objects of science of the UK and the source Technology Facilities Council ISIS suite Diamond Synchrotron and neutron and Muon instruments [45] (μ)). The work of Gulisano [46]

---

2 BIG: http://www.big-project.eu/.
3 SCAPE: http://www.scape-project.eu/.

describes an initiative to deal with Big Data using continuous sequences of various events (including safety and incidents) through the MASSIF Project[4] (Management of Security information and events in Service Infrastructures) which is part of the solution SIEM (Security Information and Event Management). This initiative is important because in many emerging applications, the volume of transmitted data sequence is so large that the traditional paradigm "store-then-process" is no longer adequate or too inefficient. Four industrial domains serve as a source for the acquisition of requirements, validation and demonstration of project results.

A great number of Big Data solutions have been supported by the government, e.g. in 2012 the USA president Barack Obama administration announced the Big Data Research and Development Initiative with an investment of $200 million, which explores how Big Data could be used to address important problems (Executive Office of the President, 2012, Big Data Across the Federal Government[5]). Likewise, several companies in the private and public sector have used Big Data technologies for different purposes some of which are briefly described below: Scientists from the NASA Center for Climate Simulation[6] (NCCS) work with Big Data storing 32 petabytes of climate observations and simulations on the Discover supercomputing cluster.

In the field of education, Big Data analysis has been incorporated with the ultimate goal of improving student outcomes, using determined common metrics as the end- of-grade testing, attendance, and dropout rates. At present, the application of Big Data analysis into education sector is to create "learning analytic systems"[7].

A number of research initiatives by the authors of this work are related to combining Semantics with Web Services or to software components [47, 48].

8   Conclusions and Future Work

In this article, we have presented a novel approach to shift the quality of adaptive learning by collecting, analyzing and deciding on Big Datasets provided by MOOCs. Particularly, we have discussed how these strategies can enhance adaptive learning effectiveness in very concrete and well-defined domains. We use Map-Reduce algorithms to filter the behavior of students and categorize them following a particular pattern. Then, through Data Mining techniques we will classify, cluster and analyze the behavior of the MOOC students. The combination of Big Data and Map- Reduce algorithms with Data Mining techniques on our proposed prototype result improves adaptive learning for MOOCs.

Our future work will consist of evaluating our implementation more carefully and look for case studies or datasets where pooling out of results can determine more accurately if the effectiveness of the adaptive learning takes place and how to follow this

---

[4] MASSIF: http://www.massif-project.eu/.

[5] http://www.whitehouse.gov/sites/default/files/microsites/ostp/big_data_fact_sheet_final_1.pdf.

[6] NASA's Big Data Mission: http://www.csc.com/cscworld/publications/81769/81773-super-computing_the_climate_nasa_s_big_data_mission.

[7] Big Data in Education: http://hortonworks.com/blog/big-data-in-education-part-2-of-2/.

path, this is also vital to prove the forthcomings of the approach versus the current state of the art techniques or various similar attempts that were described in the state of the art section.

Acknowledgements. We thank our colleagues from Nimbeo Estrategia e Innovacion who provided insight and expertise that greatly assisted our research, although they may not agree with all of the interpretations/conclusions of this paper.

We thank Yuliana Gallardo for assistance with Bayesian Belief Network model, and for comments that greatly improved the manuscript.

References

1. O'Reilly, T.: What is Web 2.0 – design patterns and business models for the next generation of software (2005)
2. Fensel, D.: Ontologies: A Silver Bullet for Knowledge Management and Electronic Commerce. Springer, Heidelberg (2002)
3. Ramakrishnan, R., Johannes, G.: Database Management Systems, 2nd edn. Osborne/McGraw-Hill, New York (2000)
4. Cattell, R.: Scalable SQL and NoSQL data stores **39**(4) (2010)
5. McAuley, A., Stewart, B., Siemens, G., Cormie, D.: Massive open online courses digital ways of knowing and learning. In: The MOOC Model for Digital Practice, pp. 3–6 (2010). http://davecormier.com/edblog/wp-content/uploads/MOOC_Final.pdf
6. Chamberlin, L., Parish, T.: MOOCs: massive open online courses or massive and often obtuse courses? ELearn **8**, 1 (2011)
7. Martin, F.G.: Will massive open online courses change how we teach? Commun. ACM **55**(8), 26–28 (2012)
8. Mcfedries, P.: I'm in the mood for MOOCS. IEEE Spectr. **49**(12) (2012)
9. De Liddo, A., Shum, S.B., Quinto, I., Bachler, M., Cannavacciuolo, L.: Discourse-centric learning analytics. In: Proceedings of the 1st International Conference on Learning Analytics and Knowledge, pp. 23–33 (2011)
10. Ferguson, R., Shum, S.B.: Learning analytics to identify exploratory dialogue within synchronous text chat. In: Proceedings of the 1st International Conference on Learning Analytics and Knowledge, pp. 99–103 (2011)
11. Landauer, T.K., Foltz, P.W., Laham, D.: An introduction to latent semantic analysis. Discourse Process. **25**, 259–284 (1998)
12. Rider, Y., Thomason, N.: Cognitive and pedagogical benefits of argument mapping: LAMP guides the way to better thinking. In: Okada, A., Buckingham Shum, S., Sherborne, T. (eds.) Knowledge Cartography. Advanced Information and Knowledge Processing, pp. 113–130. Springer, Heidelberg (2008)
13. Verbert, K., Drachsler, H., Manouselis, N., Wolpers, M., Vuorikari, R., Duval, E.: Dataset-driven research for improving recommender systems for learning. In: Proceedings of the 1st International Conference on Learning Analytics and Knowledge, pp. 44–53 (2011)
14. Clow, D., Makriyannis, E.: iSpot analysed: participatory learning and reputation. In: Proceedings of the 1st International Conference on Learning Analytics and Knowledge, pp. 34–43 (2011)
15. Crick, R.D., Broadfoot, P., Claxton, G.: Developing an effective lifelong learning inventory: the ELLI project. Assess. Educ. Principles Policy Pract. **11**, 247–272 (2004)

16. Blikstein, P.: Using learning analytics to assess students' behavior in open-ended programming tasks. In: Proceedings of the 1st International Conference on Learning Analytics and Knowledge, pp. 110–116 (2011)
17. Mazzola, L., Mazza, R.: Visualizing learner models through data aggregation: a test case. In: Red-Conference, Rethinking Education in the Knowledge Society (2011)
18. Brown, G., Yule, G.: Discourse Analysis. Cambridge Textbooks in Linguistics Series. Cambridge University Press, Cambridge (1983)
19. Campbell, J.P., Finnegan, C., Collins, B.: Academic analytics: using the CMS as an early warning system. In: WebCT Impact Conference (2006)
20. Duval, E.: Attention please!: learning analytics for visualization and recommendation. In: Proceedings of the 1st International Conference on Learning Analytics and Knowledge, pp. 9–17 (2011)
21. Cho, Y.H., Kim, J.K., Kim, S.H.: A personalized recommender system based on web usage mining and decision tree induction. Expert Syst. Appl. **23**, 329–342 (2002)
22. Brusilovsky, P.: Adaptive hypermedia: from intelligent tutoring systems to web-based education. In: Gauthier, G., VanLehn, K., Frasson, C. (eds.) ITS 2000. LNCS, vol. 1839, pp. 1–7. Springer, Heidelberg (2000)
23. Newman, M.: Networks: An Introduction. OUP Oxford, Oxford (2009)
24. Vatrapu, R.: Cultural considerations in learning analytics. In: Proceedings of the 1st International Conference on Learning Analytics and Knowledge, pp. 127–133 (2011)
25. Cohen, J., Dolan, B., Dunlap, M., Hellerstein, J., Welton, C.: MAD skills: new analysis practices for big data. Proc. VLDB Endowment **2**(2), 1481–1492 (2009)
26. White, T.: Hadoop: The Definitive Guide, 1st edn. O'Reilly Media, Sebastopol (2009)
27. Hegland, M.: Data Mining Techniques, vol. 10, pp. 313–355. Cambridge University Press, Cambridge (2001)
28. Han, J.: Data mining techniques. In: Proceedings of the ACM (SIGMOD) International Conference on Management of Data, vol. 25, no. 2, p. 545 (1996). ISBN: 0-89791-794-4
29. Gorunescu, F.: Data Mining Concepts, Models and Techniques. Intelligent Systems Reference Library, vol. 12. Springer, Heidelberg (2011). ISBN 978-3-642-19721-5
30. Bring, S., Page, L.: The anatomy of large-scale hypertextual web search engine. Comput. Netw. ISDN Syst. **30**(1–7), 107–117 (1998)
31. Ranganathan, S.R.: Elements of Library Classification. Asia Publishing House, Bombay (1962)
32. Oren, E., Delbru, R., Decker, S.: Extending faceted navigation for RDF data. In: Cruz, I., Decker, S., Allemang, D., Preist, C., Schwabe, D., Mika, P., Uschold, M., Aroyo, L.M. (eds.) ISWC 2006. LNCS, vol. 4273, pp. 559–572. Springer, Heidelberg (2006). doi: 10.1007/11926078_40
33. Goldberg, D., Nichols, D., Oki, B.M., Terry, D.: Using collaborative filtering to weave an information tapestry. Commun. ACM **35**(12), 1992 (1992)
34. Shardanand, U., Maes, P.: Social information filtering: algorithms for automating "Word of Mouth". In: Proceedings of the ACM CHI 1995 (1995)
35. Maltz, D., Ehrlich, K.: Pointing the way: active collaborative filtering. In: Proceedings of the Conference on Computer Human Interaction (1995)
36. Sugiyama, K., Hatano, K., Yoshikawa, H.: Adaptive web search based on user profile constructed without any effort. In: Proceedings of the WWW 2004 (2004)
37. Gomez, J.M., Alor, G., Posada, R., Abud, A., Garcia, A.: SITIO: a social semantic recommendation platform. In: Proceedings of the 17th International Conference on Electronics, Communications and Computers (CONIELECOMP 2007) (2007)

38. Kruk, S., Decker, S.: Semantic social collaborative filtering with FOAFRealm. In: Proceedings of the Semantic Desktop Workshop, ISWC 2005 (2005)
39. Wolpers, M., Najjar, J., Verbert, K., Duval, E.: Tracking actual usage: the attention metadata approach. J. Educ. Technol. Soc. **10**, 106 (2007)
40. Jovanovic, J., Gasevic, D., Brooks, C., Devedzic, V., Hatala, M., Eap, T., Richards, G.: LOCO-analyst: semantic web technologies in learning content usage analysis. Int. J. Continuing Eng. Educ. Life Long Learn. **18**, 54–76 (2008)
41. Bull, S., Kay, J.: Student models that invite the learner. Int. J. Artif. Intell. Educ. **17**(2), 89–120 (2007). The SMILI Open Learner Modelling Framework
42. Dawson, S., Bakharia, A., Heathcote, E.: SNAPP: realising the affordances of real-time SNA within networked learning environments. In: Proceedings of the 7th International Conference on Networked Learning, pp. 125–133 (2010)
43. Arnold, K.E.: Signals: applying academic analytics. Educause Q. **33**(1) (2010)
44. Carmean, C., Mizzi, P.: The case for nudge analytics. Educause Q. **33**(4) (2010)
45. King, R., Schmidt, R., Becker, C., Schlarb, S.: SCAPE: big data meets digital preservation. ERCIN News **89**, 30–31 (2012)
46. Gulisano, V., Jimenez-Peris, R., Patiño-Martinez, M., Soriente, C., Valduriez, P.: A big data platform for large scale event processing. ERCIN News **89**, 32–33 (2012)
47. Gomez, J.M., Paniagua, F., García, A., Bussler, C.: Modelling B2B conversations with COOL for semantic web services. In: Proceedings of the International Conference on Internet and Web Applicaitons and Services (ICIW06), 19–25 February 2006, Guadaloupe, France (2006)
48. Gomez, J.M., Han, S., Toma, I., García, A.: A semantically-enhanced component-based architecture for software composition. In: Proceedings of the International Multi-Conference on Computing in the Global Information Technology (ICCGI 2006), 1–3 August 2006, Bucarest, Romania (2006)

Author Index

Aguilar, Jose   155, 187, 214, 241
Aguirre-Munizaga, Maritza   3, 14, 90
Alarcón, Abel   131, 203
Alor-Hernandez, Giner   143
Altamirano, Ileana   254
Álvarez-Sagubay, Paul Javier   63
Arias, Hugo   254
Aviles, María   14, 90

Barrón-Estrada, M. Lucía   143
Bazán, Valeria   203
Bazán, William   131, 203
Bermeo, Oscar   203
Buendia, Omar   187

Castejón-Garrido, Juan Salvador   26
Castro, Gilberto Fernando   226
Cevallos-Torres, Lorenzo   39
Chavez, Danilo   155
Colombo-Mendoza, Luis Omar   169
Colomo-Palacios, Ricardo   169
Cordero, Jorge   155, 214

Delgado-Vera, Carlota   3

Encalada, Eduardo   214
Espinoza-Mina, Marcos Antonio   114

Gomez, Raquel   90
Gómez-Berbís, Juan Miguel   269
Guijarro-Rodríguez, Alfonso   39

Hidalgo, Jorge   14, 226

Jadán, Johann   254
Jadán-Guerrero, Janio   254
Jerez, Marxjhony   241

Lagares-Lemos, Ángel   269
Lagos-Ortiz, Katty   14, 51, 63, 79
Leyva-Vázquez, Maikel   39
Luna-Aveiga, Harry   79

Marín-Vega, Humberto   143
Medina-Moreira, José   14, 63, 79
Mendonca, Maribel   241
Moreno, Karla   187
Mosquera, Diego   187
Muñoz-García, Ana   14, 51

Ortega-García, Antonio   102

Paredes, Ruth   79
Paredes-Valverde, Mario Andrés   26, 63
Peña-González, Miriam   39
Pérez, Iliana   226
Piñero, Pedro   226

Real-Aviles, Karina   51
Recalde-Coronel, G. Cristina   90
Riofrio, Guido   214
Rodríguez, Ana   131, 203
Ruiz-Martínez, Antonio   102

Salas-Zárate, María del Pilar   26, 63
Salavarria-Melo, José   51
Samaniego, Teresa   131, 203
Sánchez, Manuel   241
Santos-Baquerizo, Eduardo   39
Sinche, Andrea   3
Solis-Avíles, Evelyn   3
Suárez-Riofrío, Patricia Leonor   114

Torres, Surayne   226

Valdiviezo, Priscila   214
Valencia-García, Rafael   26, 63, 79, 102, 169
Vásquez, Mitchell   90, 226
Vera-Lucio, Néstor   3, 51, 226
Vergara, Vanessa   14
Vergara-Lozano, Vanessa   51
Vivancos-Vicente, Pedro José   26

Zatarain-Cabada, Ramón   143

Printed in the United States
By Bookmasters